Lecture Notes in Computer Science　12124

More information about this series at http://www.springer.com/series/7409

Andreas Harth · Valentina Presutti ·
Raphaël Troncy · Maribel Acosta ·
Axel Polleres · Javier D. Fernández ·
Josiane Xavier Parreira · Olaf Hartig ·
Katja Hose · Michael Cochez (Eds.)

The Semantic Web: ESWC 2020 Satellite Events

ESWC 2020 Satellite Events
Heraklion, Crete, Greece, May 31 – June 4, 2020
Revised Selected Papers

 Springer

Editors
Andreas Harth (iD)
University of Erlangen-Nuremberg
Nuremberg, Germany

Raphaël Troncy (iD)
Eurecom
Sophia Antipolis, France

Axel Polleres (iD)
Institute for Information Business
at WU Wien
Vienna, Austria

Josiane Xavier Parreira
Siemens AG Österreich
Vienna, Austria

Katja Hose (iD)
Aalborg University
Aalborg, Denmark

Valentina Presutti (iD)
National Research Council
Rome, Italy

Maribel Acosta (iD)
Karlsruhe Institute of Technology
Karlsruhe, Germany

Javier D. Fernández (iD)
Institute for Information Business
at WU Wien
Vienna, Austria

Olaf Hartig (iD)
Linköping University
Linköping, Sweden

Michael Cochez (iD)
Vrije Universiteit Amsterdam
Amsterdam, The Netherlands

ISSN 0302-9743 ISSN 1611-3349 (electronic)
Lecture Notes in Computer Science
ISBN 978-3-030-62326-5 ISBN 978-3-030-62327-2 (eBook)
https://doi.org/10.1007/978-3-030-62327-2

LNCS Sublibrary: SL3 – Information Systems and Applications, incl. Internet/Web, and HCI

This Springer imprint is published by the registered company Springer Nature Switzerland AG
The registered company address is: Gewerbestrasse 11, 6330 Cham, Switzerland

Preface

This volume contains the proceedings of the satellite events of the 17th edition of the Extended Semantic Web Conference (ESWC 2020). ESWC is a major venue for presenting and discussing the latest scientific results and technology innovations related to the semantic web, linked data, and knowledge graphs.

As in previous years and due to the schedule of the production process, the satellite proceedings are published as post-proceedings after the conference has taken place. The satellite events at ESWC were: the poster and demo session, the PhD symposium, the industry track, and the workshops and tutorials. The poster and demo session offered researchers the chance to present their latest results in direct discussions with the participants. A total of 16 posters and 20 demonstrations were accepted for the conference.

The PhD symposium provided an outlet for doctoral students to present their research to the semantic web community. Every submission was reviewed by three senior members. The symposium received 11 submissions from which 7 doctoral proposals were accepted. A mentor was assigned to each accepted submission to guide the doctoral students in the preparation for the camera-ready paper and the conference presentation. The research problems addressed in this years' doctoral proposals covered topics about constructing and querying knowledge graphs, ontology matching, natural language processing for question answering and semantic parsing, as well as semantic representations for supervised learning. Orthogonal, some of the works presented innovative solutions tailored to specific knowledge domains including biomedicine, industry, and cultural heritage. The PhD symposium chairs would like to thank the Program Committee members and the mentors for their valuable contribution to the event and to the students. We would also like to thank the authors, the keynote speaker Stefan Schlobach, and the online participants who delivered high-quality presentations and questions, respectively, that led to fruitful discussions and made it possible to have a successful virtual PhD symposium.

The industry track targeted the adoption of semantic technologies in industrial applications, conforming a session to facilitate a discussion about what current industry challenges can be addressed with semantic technologies. This year, we accepted four papers that leverage the power of knowledge graphs and semantic technologies in diverse domains, such as pharma, industry 4.0, and legal domains. This year the industry track received 6 submissions, of which 4 were accepted.

During ESWC 2020, the following six workshops took place: i) the Third Workshop on Humanities in the Semantic Web (WHiSe 2020), ii) the Second Workshop on Deep Learning for Knowledge Graphs (DL4KG 2020), iii) the First Workshop on IoT infrastructures for safety in pervasive environments (IOT4SAFE 2020), iv) the Second Workshop on Large Scale RDF Analytics (LASCAR 2020), v) the First Workshop on Semantic Digital Twins (SeDiT 2020), and vi) the First Workshop on Cross-lingual Event-centric Open Analytics (CLEOPATRA 2020). Additionally, we also had four tutorials which covered the following topics: i) "Modular Ontology Engineering with CoModIDE," ii) "Constructing Question Answering Systems over Knowledge Graphs," iii) "Example-based Exploration: Exploring Knowledge through Examples," and iv) "Entity Summarization in Knowledge Graphs: Algorithms, Evaluation, and Applications." We thank all the workshop chairs and the tutorial presenters for their efforts to organize and run their respective events.

The chairs of the satellite events would like to thank all those who were involved in making ESWC 2020 a success. In particular, our thanks go to the numerous reviewers for ensuring a rigorous review process that led to a world-class scientific program. We also thank the authors and the participants for making the conference a lively and interactive event.

May 2020

Andreas Harth
Valentina Presutti
Raphaël Troncy
Maribel Acosta
Axel Polleres
Javier D. Fernández
Josiane Xavier Parreira
Olaf Hartig
Katja Hose
Michael Cochez

Organization

General Chair

Andreas Harth

University of Erlangen-Nuremberg, Fraunhofer IIS-SCS, Germany

Research Track Program Chairs

Sabrina Kirrane   Vienna University of Economics and Business, Austria
Axel Ngonga   Paderborn University, Germany

Resource Track Program Chairs

Heiko Paulheim   University of Mannheim, Germany
Anisa Rula   University of Milano-Bicocca, Italy

In-Use Track Program Chairs

Anna Lisa Gentile   IBM, USA
Peter Haase   metaphacts GmbH, Germany

Industry Track Program Chairs

Javier D. Fernández   F. Hoffmann-La Roche AG, Switzerland
Josiane Xavier Parreira   Siemens AG, Austria

Poster and Demo Chairs

Valentina Presutti   University of Bologna, Italy
Raphaël Troncy   Institut Eurécom, France

PhD Symposium Chairs

Maribel Acosta   Karlsruhe Institute of Technology, Germany
Axel Polleres   Vienna University of Economics and Business, Austria

Workshops and Tutorials Chairs

Olaf Hartig   Linköping University, Sweden
Katja Hose   Aalborg University, Denmark

Sponsoring Chair

Victor Charpenay   University of Erlangen-Nuremberg, Germany

Project Networking Chair

Basil Ell   Bielefeld University, Germany

Publicity and Web Presence Chairs

Uldis Bojārs   University of Latvia, National Library of Latvia, Latvia
Valentina Ivanova   Research Institutes of Sweden (RISE), Sweden

Semantic Technologies Coordinator

Ruben Taelman   Ghent University, Belgium

Proceedings Chair

Michael Cochez   Vrije Universiteit Amsterdam, The Netherlands

Posters and Demos Program Committee

Maribel Acosta   KIT, Germany
Mehwish Alam   FIZ Karlsruhe - Leibniz Institute for Information
                                  Infrastructure, AIFB Institute, KIT, Germany
Grigoris Antoniou   University of Huddersfield, UK
Luigi Asprino   University of Bologna, STLab, ISTC-CNR, Italy
Pierpaolo Basile   University of Bari, Italy
Davide Buscaldi   LIPN, Université Paris 13, Université Sorbonne Paris
                                  Cité, France
Valentina Carriero   University of Bologna, Italy
Yoan Chabot   Orange Labs, France
Victor Charpenay   University of Erlangen-Nuremberg, Germany
Olivier Corby   Inria, France
Anastasia Dimou   Ghent University, Belgium
Mauro Dragoni   Fondazione Bruno Kessler, IRST, Italy
Catherine Faron Zucker   Université Nice Sophia Antipolis, France
Flavius Frasincar   Erasmus University Rotterdam, The Netherlands
Luis Galárraga   Inria, France
Daniel Garijo   Information Sciences Institute, Spain
Rafael Goncalves   Stanford University, USA
Paul Groth   University of Amsterdam, The Netherlands
Maria Hedblom   Free University of Bozen-Bolzano, Italy
Jack Hodges   Siemens, USA
Tomi Kauppinen   Aalto University School of Science, Finland

Takahiro Kawamura	National Agriculture and Food Research Organization, Japan
Mayank Kejriwal	Information Sciences Institute, USA
Tomas Kliegr	University of Economics, Prague, Czech Republic
Christoph Lange	Fraunhofer FIT, RWTH Aachen University, Germany
Pasquale Lisena	Institut Eurécom, France
Albert Meroño-Peñuela	Vrije Universiteit Amsterdam, The Netherlands
Nandana Mihindukulasooriya	Universidad Politécnica de Madrid, Spain
Diego Moussallem	Paderborn University, Germany
Andrea Giovanni Nuzzolese	University of Bologna, Italy
Francesco Osborne	The Open University, UK
Julien Plu	Leboncoin Lab, France
José Luis Redondo García	Amazon Research, UK
Giuseppe Rizzo	LINKS Foundation, Italy
Harald Sack	FIZ Karlsruhe - Leibniz Institute for Information Infrastructure, KIT, Germany
Fatiha Saïs	University of Paris-Saclay, France
Stefan Schlobach	Vrije Universiteit Amsterdam, The Netherlands
Jodi Schneider	University of Illinois at Urbana-Champaign, USA
Ruben Taelman	Ghent University, Belgium
Ilaria Tiddi	Vrije Universiteit Amsterdam, The Netherlands
Ricardo Usbeck	Paderborn University, Germany
Marieke van Erp	KNAW - Humanities Cluster, The Netherlands
Maria-Esther Vidal	Universidad Simón Bolívar, Venezuela
Ondřej Zamazal	University of Economics, Prague, Czech Republic

PhD Symposium Mentors

Elena Demidova	L3S Research Center, Germany
Andreas Harth	University of Erlangen-Nuremberg, Fraunhofer IIS-SCS, Germany
Olaf Hartig	Linköping University, Sweden
Axel-Cyrille Ngonga Ngomo	Paderborn University, Germany
Heiko Paulheim	University of Mannheim, Germany
Rudi Studer	KIT, Germany
Maria-Esther Vidal	Universidad Simón Bolívar, Venezuela, and Technische Informationsbibliothek (TIB), Germany

PhD Symposium Program Committee

Oscar Corcho	Universidad Politécnica de Madrid, Spain
Elena Demidova	L3S Research Center, Germany
Irini Fundulaki	ICS-FORTH, Greece
Paul Groth	University of Amsterdam, The Netherlands

Andreas Harth	University of Erlangen-Nuremberg, Fraunhofer IIS-SCS, Germany
Olaf Hartig	Linköping University, Sweden
Markus Krötzsch	TU Dresden, Germany
Axel-Cyrille Ngonga Ngomo	Paderborn University, Germany
Heiko Paulheim	University of Mannheim, Germany
Achim Rettinger	Trier University, Germany
Rudi Studer	KIT, Germany
Maria-Esther Vidal	Universidad Simón Bolívar, Venezuela, and Technische Informationsbibliothek (TIB), Germany
Josiane Xavier Parreira	Siemens AG, Austria

Industry Track Program Committee

Artem Revenko	Semantic Web Company GmbH, Germany
Christian Dirschl	Wolters Kluwer, Germany
Jeremy Debattista	Trinity College Dublin, Ireland
Dennis Diefenbach	University Jean Monnet, France
Andreas Wagner	Schaeffler, Germany
Juan F. Sequeda	data.world, USA
Juergen Umbrich	Onlim GmbH, Austria
Dominik Riemer	FZI Research Center for Information Technology, Germany
Maria Esther Vidal	Universidad Simón Bolívar, Venezuela
James Anderson	Datagraph GmbH, Germany
Martin Junghans	IBM, Germany
Nuno Lopes	TopQuadrant, Inc., USA
José María García	University of Seville, Spain
Elias Kärle	STI Innsbruck, Austria
Giorgos Georgiadis	Qamcom Research and Technology AB, Sweden
Simon Steyskal	Siemens AG, Austria
Peter Haase	metaphacts GmbH, Germany
Nelia Lasierra	F. Hoffmann-La Roche AG, Switzerland
Daniel Herzig	metaphacts GmbH, Germany
Anees Mehdi	Bosch, Germany
Andreas Thalhammer	F. Hoffmann-La Roche AG, Switzerland
Maulik R. Kamdar	Elsevier Inc., USA
Gulnar Mehdi	Siemens AG, Austria
Felix Loesch	Robert Bosch GmbH, Germany

Contents

PhD Symposium Papers

Industry Track Papers

Poster and Demo Papers

Towards a Core Ontology for Hierarchies of Hypotheses in Invasion Biology

Alsayed Algergawy[1](✉) , Ria Stangneth[2], Tina Heger[3,4] ,
Jonathan M. Jeschke[4,5,6] , and Birgitta König-Ries[1,7]

[1] Institute for Computer Science, University of Jena, Jena, Germany
{alsayed.algergawy,birgitta.koenig-ries}@uni-jena.de
[2] Institute of Organizational Psychology, University of Jena, Jena, Germany
[3] Biodiversity Research/Systematic Botany, University of Potsdam,
Potsdam, Germany
[4] Berlin-Brandenburg Institute of Advanced Biodiversity Research (BBIB),
Berlin, Germany
[5] Institute of Biology, Free University of Berlin, Berlin, Germany
[6] Leibniz-Institute of Freshwater Ecology and Inland Fisheries (IGB),
Berlin, Germany
[7] German Centre for Integrative Biodiversity Research (iDiv), Leipzig, Germany

Abstract. With a rapidly growing body of knowledge, it becomes more and more difficult to keep track of the state of the art in a research field. A formal representation of the hypotheses in the field, their relations, the studies that support or question them based on which evidence, would greatly ease this task and help direct future research efforts. We present the design of such a core ontology for one specific field, namely invasion biology. We introduce the design of the Hierarchy of Hypotheses (HoH) core ontology to semantically capture and model the information contained in hierarchies of hypotheses created for invasion biology. The proposed core ontology is based on a number of well structured related ontologies, which provide a solid basis for its main entities.

1 Introduction

The work presented in this paper was motivated by efforts by two of its authors, Jeschke and Heger, to advance their field of research, namely invasion biology. This field examines the effects that the introduction of new species has on ecosystems, and which circumstances determine whether a species can establish itself and spread in a new environment. Jeschke and Heger observed that a lack of clear understanding of the hypotheses in this field, their relations, and the evidence supporting or questioning them, considerably hinders scientific progress. Thus, they set out to model their field. This effort resulted in the Hierarchy-of-Hypotheses approach, as shown in Fig. 1, which they applied to sketching possible hierarchies of hypotheses (HoH) for invasion biology [7], (Fig. 2). Overarching ideas branch into more precise, better testable hypotheses at lower levels.

© Springer Nature Switzerland AG 2020
A. Harth et al. (Eds.): ESWC 2020 Satellite Events, LNCS 12124, pp. 3–8, 2020.
https://doi.org/10.1007/978-3-030-62327-2_1

This model, however, has not been rooted in formal semantics. It is thus currently not possible to automatically infer new knowledge. We take a first step to closing this gap by defining a core ontology for the field. We believe that, like the HoH approach, such ontologies are useful in all scientific fields and therefore focus the presentation not on the end result, but on the process. With this, we hope to enable other scientists to develop core ontologies for their fields as well.

In this paper, we propose the design of a core ontology. In general, an ontology is an elegant way to provide tools and methods developing and establishing correct links between data, research questions, and hypotheses towards a more efficient scientific life cycle. Here, we make use of the fusion/merge strategy [10] during the design of the *HoH* core ontology. In particular, a set of collected hypotheses is analyzed and relevant terms are extracted. This set of extracted terms is then used to localize related ontologies that can be reused as a basis for the core ontology design. We employ a module extractor strategy to the selected set of ontologies to reduce the number of selected concepts and properties and to ensure that the core ontology will not contain unneeded concepts making it more complex than necessary. These modules are then combined to form the initial version of the core ontology. Further improvements are made, such as revising the ontology and adding missing concepts.

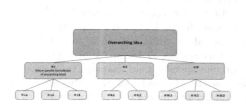

Fig. 1. Basic scheme of HoH

Fig. 2. The enemy release hypothesis

2   Related Work

Core ontologies provide a precise definition of structural knowledge in a specific field that connects different application domains   [3–5,11]. They are located in the layer between upper-level (fundamental) and domain-specific ontologies, providing the definition of the core concepts from a specific field. They aim at linking general concepts of a top-level ontology to more domain-specific concepts from a sub-field. Even though there is a large body of work making use of ontologies as a formal basis to model different aspects of scientific research, such as [3–5], few studies have focused on modeling scientific hypotheses [2,6].

3   The Core Ontology for HoH

To create a core ontology for the hierarchies of hypotheses (HoH) developed for invasion biology [8], we focus on the following issues:

Scenario. Invasion biology is concerned with the question why some species are able to establish and spread in an area where they have not evolved. Over time, the research community has developed several major hypotheses and empirical studies have been performed to test them. Since each hypothesis has been formulated in a general way, suggesting its validity across study systems (e.g., in terrestrial as well as aquatic habitats and across taxonomic groups), empirical tests apply a variety of approaches and produce a wealth of not always consistent results. The Hierarchy-of-Hypotheses (HoH) approach has been introduced as a tool for disclosing the complexity of this research. In an HoH, a major hypothesis can be depicted as a hierarchy of increasingly specific formulations of a broad idea. By assigning empirical tests to sub-hypotheses, it becomes clear that each of them is only addressing a specific aspect of the overall idea. The HoH approach has been applied to twelve major hypotheses in invasion biology [8]. Empirical evidence has been used to assess the validity of these major hypotheses and their sub-hypotheses. So far, however, this has been done manually. A formal representation of the twelve hypotheses and the respective HoHs could provide the basis for future computer-aided updates and expansions. Also, it would allow to reveal the different meanings oftentimes connected to terms, and thus avoid miscommunication and misinterpretation of results.

Strategy. To model the complex structure of knowledge in the hierarchy of hypotheses in the domain of invasion biology, we adopt the fusion/merge strategy [10], where the new ontology is developed by assembling and reusing one or more ontologies. To this end, the proposed pipeline starts by processing the description of each hypothesis extracting relevant terms (with the help of domain experts). Each term can be a noun, verb, or an adjective/adverb. Nouns can be simple or complex nouns. The **Biotic Resistance Hypothesis**, e.g., states that "An ecosystem with high biodiversity is more resistant against exotic species than an ecosystem with lower biodiversity".

Analyzing this hypothesis, the terms "ecosystem, biodiversity, species" can be extracted and identified as main entities of this hypothesis. In order to model the meaning of the hypothesis, additional entities not mentioned in the definition of the hypothesis need to be added. For example, in this domain lower and higher biodiversity are viewed as either related to the number of observed species, or to some index calculated for a specific area within a location. So, we add the "number of species, indices, area, location" entities to the set of extracted terms from the hypothesis, as shown in Fig. 3. After including "area", species can be described as native or exotic species based on their relationship to area. In general, the outcome of this phase are 45 (noun) terms from 12 different hypotheses. We should mention that we consider the extraction of simple and compound terms, e.g. "invasion" and "invasion success". After that we make use of the BioPortal API[1] to look for relevant ontologies that cover the set of extracted terms. We selected the National Center for Biomedical Ontologies (NCBO) BioPortal, since its deployment, it has evolved to become the prevalent repository of biological and biomedical ontologies and terminologies [9].

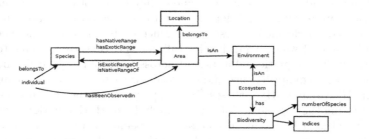

Fig. 3. Entities and relations extracted from the Biotic Resistance Hypothesis

Several challenges arise during this step. First, the same term can be differently represented in several ontologies and we have to select the most suitable one. For example, the term "ecosystem" has been found in 21 ontologies representing different pieces of the domain. The ecosystem concept is defined in the environmental ontology ($ENVO^2$) as an environmental system that includes both living and non-living components, while it is defined within the Interlinking Ontology for Biological Concepts ($IOBC^3$) as an ecological system. Also, in the three invasion biological hypotheses where this term is a main term, it has three different meanings. Another challenge concerning the design of the core ontology is that it needs to satisfy a number of requirements as mentioned in [11]. After having a set of ontologies, for each term we extracted the set of corresponding concepts from different ontologies along with their URIs, labels, and definitions (if they exist). We then asked our domain experts to validate this selection. For example, the term "species" exists in 32 different ontologies, but our experts selected only two ontologies that align with the intended meaning. The term "enemy" exists in two ontologies, but none of them matches our requirements. Thus, we had to define our own concept. After settling on a number of ontologies to be adopted according to the fusion/merge strategy, we applied a module extractor to each ontology to elicit smaller partitions from the selected set of ontologies [1] containing only relevant concepts and those needed to connect them. Finally, these set of partitions were combined and merged to form the initial version of the new ontology.

Outcome. Applying the proposed strategy to the given set of hypotheses resulted in six core concepts in the *HoH* domain, as shown in Fig. 4, where

---

[1] http://bioportal.bioontology.org/.
[2] http://purl.obolibrary.org/obo/ENVO_01001110.
[3] http://purl.jp/bio/4/id/200906003112410894.

each concept has one or more associated concepts. This set of concepts is used to select a set of related ontologies that maximize the coverage of these concepts. The six core concepts together with the associated concepts deliver the basis for semantically modelling twelve major hypotheses in invasion biology. Since these twelve hypotheses are well-known in the research field and regarded as important potential explanation for biological invasions, this core ontology delivers an important first step towards semantically modelling the research field of invasion biology.

All the resources related to the design of the HoH core ontology as well as the first versions of the ontology are accessible online at https://github.com/fusion-jena/HoH_Core_Ontology.

Fig. 4. Core concepts in the HoH domain

Acknowledgments. This work has been funded by the *Deutsche Forschungsgemein-schaft (DFG)* as part of CRC 1076 AQUADIVA. Additional support has been received from the German Federal Ministry of Education and Research BMBF within the Collaborative Project "Bridging in Biodiversity Science - BIBS" (funding number 01LC1501).

References

1. Algergawy, A., König-Ries, B.: Partitioning of bioportal ontologies: an empirical study. In: SWAT4LS (2019)
2. Callahan, A., Dumontier, M., Shah, N.H.: HyQue: evaluating hypotheses using semantic web technologies. J. Biomed. Semant. (2011)
3. Campos, P.M., Reginato, C.C., Almeida, J.P.A.: Towards a core ontology for scientific research activities. In: ER (2019)
4. Fathalla, S., Vahdati, S., Auer, S., Lange, C.: SemSur: a core ontology for the semantic representation of research findings. In: SEMANTICS (2018)
5. Garcia, L.F., Abel, M., Perrin, M., dos Santos Alvarenga, R.: The GeoCore ontology: a core ontology for general use in geology. Comput. Geosci. **135** (2020)
6. Garijo, D., Gil, Y., Ratnakar, V.: The disk hypothesis ontology: capturing hypothesis evolution for automated discovery. In: K-CAP Workshops (2017)
7. Heger, T., et al.: Conceptual frameworks and methods for advancing invasion ecology. AMBIO **42**(5), 527–540 (2013)

8. Jeschke, J.M., Heger, T.: Invasion Biology: Hypotheses and Evidence. CABI, Wallingford (2018)
9. Musen, M.A., et al.: The national center for biomedical ontology. J. Am. Med. Inform. Assoc. **19**(12), 190–195 (2012)
10. Pinto, H.S., Martins, J.P.: Ontologies: how can they be built? Knowl. Inf. Syst. **6**(4), 441–464 (2004)
11. Scherp, A., Saathoff, C., Franz, T., Staab, S.: Designing core ontologies. Appl. Ontol. **6**(3), 177–221 (2011)

Towards Cost-Model-Based Query Execution over Hybrid Linked Data Fragments Interfaces

Amr Azzam[1]([✉]), Ruben Taelman[2], and Axel Polleres[1]

[1] Vienna University of Economics and Business, Vienna, Austria
amr.azzam@wu.ac.at
[2] IDLab, ELIS, Ghent University – imec, Ghent, Belgium
ruben.taelman@ugent.be

Abstract. A multitude of Linked Data Fragments (LDF) server interfaces have been proposed to expose Knowledge Graphs (KGs) on the Web. Each interface leads to different trade-offs when clients execute queries over them, such as how query execution effort is distributed between server and client. There is however no single *silver bullet* that works best everywhere. Each of these interfaces has diverse characteristics that vary the performance based on server load, client resources, and network bandwidth. Currently, publishers can only pick one of these interfaces to expose their KGs on the Web. However, in some cases, multiple interfaces may be suitable for the publisher, and these may even vary over time based on the aforementioned factors. As such, we propose a hybrid LDF interface that can expose multiple interfaces based on a server-side cost model. Additionally, we sketch a negotiation protocol through which clients can determine desirable interfaces during query planning using a client-side cost model. In this paper, we lay out the high-level ideas behind this hybrid framework, and we explain our future steps regarding implementation and evaluation. As such, our work provides a basis for exploiting the trade-offs that exist between different LDF interfaces for optimally exposing KGs on the Web.

1 Introduction

The rapid growth of open and decentralized Knowledge Graphs over the Web has created an immense demand for public Knowledge Graph query services. However, serving live queryable Knowledge Graphs on the Web is difficult due to the low availability [1] and expensive hosting of SPARQL endpoints. As an alternative, publishing data dumps moves query effort to the client, but this may not always be desirable. Recently, the Linked Data Fragments (LDF) [1] framework was introduced to explore the range of Web query interfaces that exist between SPARQL endpoints and data dumps that distribute query execution load between clients and servers.

Several approaches have emerged following this framework such as Triple Pattern Fragments (TPF) [1] and Bindings-Restricted TPF (brTPF) [2], SaGe [3] and smart-KG [4], each offering their own trade-offs. For instance, TPF and brTPF increase server availability at the cost of increased network load. SaGe enhances average query performance at the cost of increased server load for concurrent complex queries. smart-KG increases server availability at the cost of higher client effort. Research shows that

© Springer Nature Switzerland AG 2020
A. Harth et al. (Eds.): ESWC 2020 Satellite Events, LNCS 12124, pp. 9–12, 2020.
https://doi.org/10.1007/978-3-030-62327-2_2

no single optimal approach exists, but they all have their advantages and disadvantages. As such, there is a need for a hybrid LDF approach that determines one or more efficient query approaches based on changing circumstances.

A preliminary hybrid LDF approach [5] investigated the diversity of LDF characteristics [6] that can influence query execution plans. Another proposal [7] provides a different interface based on the current server workload. None of the aforementioned hybrid approaches allow clients and the server to negotiate query interfaces depending on factors such as the executed query, server load, client capabilities, and network bandwidth. In this paper, we propose a negotiation-based hybrid. Using a server-side cost model, the server can expose one or more query interfaces based on its current load, and the query that the client aims to execute. Using a client-side cost model, an efficient query plan over the available interfaces can be determined. This combination of server and client cost model ensure efficient usage of server and client resources to aim for the best possible query performance over the available LDF approaches.

2 Hybrid Framework

The goal of our framework is to expose different server interfaces based on the server load and the queries. Instead of exposing *just one interface* per query, we expose a *collection of interfaces* per query. This allows clients to select a combination of interfaces based on their capabilities, query plans, and other circumstances.

To achieve such a server interface hybrid, a server cost model selects a set of interfaces based on a given query and the server current load. While a client cost model determines a query plan based on the granted interfaces. Figure 1 shows an overview of this framework where client-side query engines start by sending a query q to the server, and receive an answer that contains a token t and a set of allowed interfaces I. Based on the returned interfaces, the client can determine a query plan over these interfaces. These (sub)queries can then be resolved by requesting the appropriate interfaces using the given token.

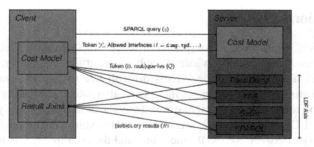

Fig. 1. Overview of client-server communication for a cost-model-based query execution over a hybrid of Linked Data Fragments interfaces.

2.1 Server Component

The server component of our framework consists of a cost model for calculating a set of allowed interfaces, and a token-based wrapper over a set of interfaces.

Cost Model. The goal of this server-side cost model is to ensure the server availability, and to allow queries to be executed as fast as possible. Since the latter goal can sometimes be detrimental to the server availability, for example when many concurrent users are sending highly complex queries, availability must always have priority. Based on these goals, the model should be able to make a suggestion for a set of interfaces based on a given query and a set of internal metrics. For this, we propose a set of internal metrics such as the current CPU usage, memory usage and network I/O. The threshold for these metrics can be configured so that the cost model can estimates the set of interfaces that optimize both goals.

Listing 1 shows the pseudocode of an algorithm that can be used to calculate a set of allowed interfaces. GetValueIncrease would still need a concrete implementation. For this, different possibilities exist, such as heuristics to predict query execution effort based on the number of triple patterns and query operators.

```
GetInterfaces(q, metrics, interfaces, GetValue, GetThreshold)
    allowedInterfaces = []
    FOREACH interface IN interfaces
      validInterface = true
      FOREACH metric IN metrics
        increase = GetValueIncrease(metric, q, interface)
        IF GetValue(metric) + increase > GetThreshold(metric)
          validInterface = false
      IF validInterface
        allowedInterfaces.push(validInterface)
    RETURN allowedInterfaces
```

Listing 1: Algorithm for calculating the allowed interfaces for a given query.

Interface Wrapper. Based on the server-side cost model, the server can wrap over a number of LDF interfaces that the publisher wants to expose. This wrapper is a proxy that accepts SPARQL queries, and replies with a token and a set of granted interfaces that have been estimated for the given query. The token is *required* for performing any requests to any of the wrapped LDF interfaces. This token should be seen as temporary *permission* to make use of a specific set of query capabilities from the data publisher. The server must validates this token upon every request to an LDF interface to prevent the clients from ignoring the set of allowed interfaces and execute queries using the most expressive interface (e.g. SPARQL endpoint).

2.2 Client Component

Usually, the goal of clients is to execute queries as fast as possible. There could however be a number of metrics that can soften this need for fast query execution such as reducing CPU, bandwidth usage or optimizing for early results [8]. Using our server-side hybrid of LDF interfaces, clients will retrieve a set of allowed interfaces based on given query. With respect to the client resources, the client should determine an efficient query plan based on the granted interfaces capabilities. While most client-side query algorithms focus on decomposing queries for execution against a single type of interface, additional algorithms are needed for *intelligently combining interfaces* for certain subqueries [5]. Another metric that influences the selection is the location of dataset fragments, locally [4] or within a network of peers [9].

3 Conclusions

This article outlines our high-level framework. We plan to implement the server and client components, and evaluate different cost models. The client component will be implemented using the Comunica platform [10] as a *Mediator* that can determine optimal interfaces based on the current metrics. This enable us to focus on the cost model of the client, as Comunica supports the majority of the LDF interfaces and SPARQL query operators. Our envisioned cost-model-based framework for enabling query execution over hybrid LDFs is a key element in achieving the vision of a Web where any client can query data over any combination of heterogeneous interfaces.

References

1. Verborgh, R., et al.: Triple pattern fragments: a low-cost knowledge graph interface for the web. J. Web Semant. **37**, 184–206 (2016)
2. Hartig, O., Buil-Aranda, C.: Bindings-restricted triple pattern fragments. In: Proceedings of ODBASE, pp. 762–779 (2016)
3. Minier, T., Skaf-Molli, H., Molli, P.: SaGe: web preemption for public SPARQL query services. In: The World Wide Web Conference, pp. 1268–1278 (2019)
4. Azzam, A., Fernández, J.D., Acosta, M., Beno, M., Polleres, A.: SMART-KG: hybrid shipping for SPARQL querying on the web. In: Proceedings of The Web Conference 2020, pp. 984–994. Association for Computing Machinery, New York (2020)
5. Montoya, G., Aebeloe, C., Hose, K.: Towards efficient query processing over heterogeneous RDF interfaces. In: DeSemWeb@ISWC (2018)
6. Montoya, G., Keles, I., Hose, K.: Analysis of the effect of query shapes on performance over LDF interfaces. In: QuWeDa@ISWC (2019)
7. Khan, H.: Towards more intelligent SPARQL querying interfaces. In: International Semantic Web Conference (2019)
8. Acosta, M., Vidal, M.-E., Sure-Vetter, Y.: Diefficiency metrics: measuring the continuous efficiency of query processing approaches. In: d'Amato, C., et al. (eds.) International Semantic Web Conference, pp. 3–19. Springer, Cham (2017). https://doi.org/10.1007/978-3-319-682 04-4_1
9. Grall, A., Skaf-Molli, H., Molli, P.: SPARQL query execution in networks of web browsers. In: DeSemWeb (2018)
10. Taelman, R., Van Herwegen, J., Vander Sande, M., Verborgh, R.: Comunica: a modular SPARQL query engine for the web. In: Proceedings of the 17th International Semantic Web Conference, pp. 239–255 (2018)

How Good Is This Merged Ontology?

Samira Babalou[1]([✉])[iD], Elena Grygorova[1][iD], and Birgitta König-Ries[1,2][iD]

[1] Heinz-Nixdorf Chair for Distributed Information Systems, Institute for Computer Science, Friedrich Schiller University Jena, Jena, Germany
{samira.babalou,elena.grygorova,birgitta.koenig-ries}@uni-jena.de
[2] Michael-Stifel-Center for Data-Driven and Simulation Science, Jena, Germany

Abstract. With the growing popularity of semantics-aware integration solutions, various ontology merging approaches have been proposed. Determining the success of these developments heavily depends on suitable evaluation criteria. However, no comprehensive set of evaluation criteria on the merged ontology exists so far. We develop criteria to evaluate the merged ontology. These criteria cover structure, function and usability of the merged ontology by evaluating General Merge Requirements (GMR)s, analyzing the intended use and semantics, and considering the ontology and entity annotation, respectively. We demonstrate the applicability of our criteria by providing empirical tests.

Keywords: Semantic web · Ontology evaluation · Ontology merging

1 Introduction

Merging ontologies involves identifying correspondences among the entities in the different ontologies and combining them into a new merged ontology. Given the central role these merged ontologies play in realising real world applications, such as knowledge reusing [1] and query processing [2], there is a strong need to establish evaluation methods that can measure their quality. Existing studies on evaluation of the merged ontology suffer from various drawbacks as detailed in Sect. 2. Automatic merge evaluation can support an expert evaluation along a broad and customizable range of criteria in different aspects.

We adapt evaluation dimensions from well-known ontology evaluation frameworks [3,4] in the context of ontology merging, formulate our evaluation criteria on top of the categories proposed there classified into structural, functional, and usability-profiling measures, and analyze how these dimensions can be evaluated on the merged ontology in practice. Our final contribution is an online ontology merging evaluator, the $\mathcal{C}o\mathcal{M}erger$ tool, which is independent of any merge method.

2 Literature Review

Most ontology merging approaches lack sufficient experimental evaluation on the merged result (cf. [5]). Other ontology merging studies, such as GCBOM [6]

© Springer Nature Switzerland AG 2020
A. Harth et al. (Eds.): ESWC 2020 Satellite Events, LNCS 12124, pp. 13–18, 2020.
https://doi.org/10.1007/978-3-030-62327-2_3

evaluate in terms of the size of created merged ontologies, only. The state of the art is far from providing an adequate benchmark. While [7] provides a benchmark, it includes simple taxonomies only and just compares the number of paths and concepts of a tool-generated merged ontology to a human created one. The benchmark proposed in [8] includes only few and small ontologies and focuses on criteria tailored to the GROM tool [9]. Moreover, user-based evaluation is a complex, time-consuming, and error-prone task. This concludes a need for a comprehensive evaluation, to which we contribute.

3   Proposed Quality Criteria for Evaluating of the Merged Ontology

An ontology merging evaluator measures the quality of the merged ontology $\mathcal{O}_M$ based on a set of source ontologies $\mathcal{O}_S$ and their mapping $\mathcal{M}$ with respect to a set of evaluation criteria. To evaluate the merged ontology in a systematic way, we adapt successful evaluation dimensions from two ontology evaluation frameworks [3,4] and customize them in the context of ontology merging. These two works introduced structural and functional evaluation dimensions. Moreover, in [4] the usability-profiling and in [3] the reliability, operability, and maintainability dimensions are presented. Since the last three mentioned dimensions are not affected by the merge process, we mainly focus on structural, functional and usability-profiling dimensions. We build our criteria on top of these classifications, as follow:

(1) **Measuring the structural dimension.** It focuses on syntax and formal semantics. In this form, the topological and logical properties of an ontology may be measured by means of a metric. To classify the criteria in this dimension, we use the classification of [10], which distinguishes into three dimensions (integrity, logic properties, and model properties) to structure our list of twenty General Merge Requirements (GMR)s.

This list has been build by reviewing publications in three different research areas, including ontology merging methods, benchmarks, and ontology engineering and extracting relevant criteria. Thus, it comprehensively considers all topological properties. Moreover, we consider the consistency aspect from [11], as suggested in [3].

(2) **Measuring the functional dimension.** This dimension is related to the intended use and semantics of a given merged ontology and of its components. Functional measures have been quantified by precision $P = \frac{|TP|}{|TP|+|FP|}$ and recall $R = \frac{|TP|}{|TP|+|FN|}$ in [4], where, TP = True Positive, FP = False Positive, and FN = False Negative. This definition is adapted by choosing an appropriate domain for positive and negative responses from the matching between the ontology structure and the intended usage and meaning. High (low) precision and recall label $\mathcal{O}_M$ as GOOD (WORSE). Low precision and high recall make it LESS GOOD, and vice a versa BAD.

An intended conceptualization corresponds to the expertise of an ontology's intended users [4]. The expertise boundary is provided by the task that should be accomplished with the help of the ontology or at least the schema of that expertise that should be captured. Since expertise is by default in the cognitive "black-box", ontology engineers have to elicit it. Thus, precision and recall of an ontology graph can be measured against experts' judgment, or a data set assumed as a qualified expression of experts' judgment. We find two scenarios to accomplish it:

(i) Using Competency Questions. One of the approaches in [4] to capture the intended use of an ontology is to use Competency Questions (CQ)s. A set of CQs is complete in the sense that if the ontology can provide correct answers to all questions, then the ontology can serve its intended purpose. We determine them in the context of the merged ontology w.r.t. the source ontologies. Thus we define TP, FP, and FN based on the expected answers of the source ontologies.

(ii) Using query scenario. Comparing the individuals and is-a relations queries from merged $\mathcal{O}_M$ and source $\mathcal{O}_S$ ontologies can provide the environment to capture the intended semantic. Thus, we provide a list of queries which the $\mathcal{O}_S$ can or cannot answer, and then compare with the achieved answers from $\mathcal{O}_M$.

(3) Measuring the usability-profile. It focuses on the ontology profile to address the communication context of an ontology. We measure:

- *Annotation about the ontology itself*: It evaluates the existence and correctness of (1) ontology URI, (2) ontology namespace, (3) ontology declaration, and (4) ontology license (requiring modeling compatibility of different licences).
- *Annotation about ontology's entities*: This includes: (1) Label uniqueness to observe whether the created labels are unique [12]. (2) Unify naming to evaluate whether all entity's names follow the same naming conventions in the merged ontology [13]. (3) Entity type declaration to check whether these entities have been explicitly declared [13].

4 Empirical Analysis: Assessments in Practice

The introduced criteria have been implemented in our merge framework *CoMerger* [14] and distributed under an open-source license along with publishing the used merged ontologies. The used patterns and exact algorithms to detect and repair each GMR have been documented in our portal[1]. For the consistency test, we refer to [11]. We have selected[2] a set of well-known ontologies with their available mapping, and created merged ontologies, by combining the corresponding entities and reconstructing their relations, and evaluate our criteria on them. The result of evaluating the structural and usability-profile

---

[1] http://comerger.uni-jena.de/requirement.jsp.
[2] Datasets: https://github.com/fusion-jena/CoMerger/tree/master/EvaluationData set.

dimensions are available in our repository[3]. In this paper, we demonstrate the evaluation of the functional dimension as applicability of our method:

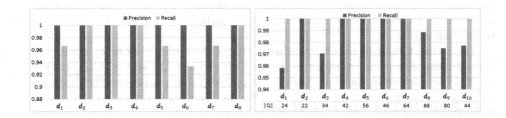

Fig. 1. Left: Functional measure's evaluation for the intended use via CQs; Right: Functional measure's evaluation for intended semantics via queries. Considering high values above 0.5, all tested ontologies achieve "GOOD" labels.

(a) **Test with CQs.** By analyzing user-provided Competency Questions, we aim to observe how the ontology's structure is aligned with the intended use of the created merged ontology. We have provided a list of CQs (available in our portal) for the conference domain datasets. To quantify the precision and recall, we determine positive and negative CQs along with TP, FN, and FP. The *positive CQ* is a CQ that at least one of $\mathcal{O}_S$ can answer. For a *negative CQ*, none of the $\mathcal{O}_S$ can answer it. If $\mathcal{O}_M$ correctly answers a positive query, we mark it as TP, and if it incorrectly answers it, we mark it with FN. If $\mathcal{O}_M$ provides a correct (wrong) answer to a negative query, we mark it as FP (TN). The results are demonstrated in Fig. 1, left, where precision and recall are shown for each dataset. All $\mathcal{O}_M$ evaluated in this test achieved precision 1 because the FP of all of them is zero. If none of the $\mathcal{O}_S$ can answer the negative CQs, the $\mathcal{O}_M$ in our test could not answer it, since no further information than $\mathcal{O}_S$ is added to the $\mathcal{O}_M$ during the merge process. If an $\mathcal{O}_M$ is built by human intervention, that might bring some new knowledge. In this case, non-zero values would be possible for FP. As a whole, the recall of all tested ontologies varied between 0.93 and 1.

(b) **Test with queries.** To evaluate the intended semantics of the merged ontology, we created two types of queries on individuals and is-a relations queries. In the is-a-based queries, for each subclass-of relation like '$A \sqsubseteq B$', we make a true query '$A \sqsubseteq B$?', and a false query like '$A \sqsubseteq C$?'. For each individual c of concept A, we create a positive and negative individual query like '*is c a A?*' and '*is c a B?*'. In both, '$B \neq C$' and '$A \not\sqsubseteq C$'. We expect that the answer from $\mathcal{O}_M$ for the true query is true and for the false query is false. If so, we mark them as intended answers. Otherwise, we mark it as non-intended answers. If $\mathcal{O}_M$ correctly (wrong) answers a non-intended answer, we mark it as FP (TN).

---

[3] https://github.com/fusion-jena/CoMerger/blob/master/EvaluationDataset/result.md.

If $\mathcal{O}_M$ correctly (wrong) answers an intended answer, we mark it as TP (FN). Figure 1, right shows the precision and recall of results from running 500 queries on our used datasets. The test demonstrates that the intended semantics is high.

5 Conclusion

This paper contributes to providing the multi-aspects of evaluating the quality of a merged ontology w.r.t. its source ontologies into structural, functional and usability-profiling dimensions. A practical assessment has been presented. The use case scenario evaluation and meta-evaluation are on our future agenda.

Acknowledgments. S. Babalou is supported by a scholarship from German Academic Exchange Service (DAAD).

References

1. Finke, M.T., Filice, R.W., Kahn Jr., C.E.: Integrating ontologies of human diseases, phenotypes, and radiological diagnosis. J. Am. Med. Inform. Assoc. **26**(2), 149–154 (2019)
2. Livingston, K.M., Bada, M., Baumgartner, W.A., Hunter, L.E.: KaBOB: ontology-based semantic integration of biomedical databases. BMC Bioinform. **16**, 1–21 (2015)
3. Duque-Ramos, A., Fernández-Breis, J.T., Stevens, R., Aussenac-Gilles, N., et al.: OQuaRE: a SQuaRE-based approach for evaluating the quality of ontologies. JRPIT **43**(2), 159 (2011)
4. Gangemi, A., Catenacci, C., Ciaramita, M., Lehmann, J.: Ontology evaluation and validation: an integrated formal model for the quality diagnostic task (2005). http://www.loa-cnr.it/Files/OntoEval4OntoDev_Final.pdf
5. Ju, S.P., Esquivel, H.E., Rebollar, A.M., Su, M.C.: CreaDO-a methodology to create domain ontologies using parameter-based ontology merging techniques. In: MICAI, pp. 23–28. IEEE (2011)
6. Priya, M., Kumar, C.A.: An approach to merge domain ontologies using granular computing. Granular Comput. 1–26 (2019)
7. Raunich, S., Rahm, E.: Towards a benchmark for ontology merging. In: OTM Workshops, vol. 7567, pp. 124–133 (2012)
8. Mahfoudh, M., Forestier, G., Hassenforder, M.: A benchmark for ontologies merging assessment. In: KSEM, pp. 555–566 (2016)
9. Mahfoudh, M., Thiry, L., Forestier, G., Hassenforder, M.: Algebraic graph transformations for merging ontologies. In: Ait Ameur, Y., Bellatreche, L., Papadopoulos, G.A. (eds.) MEDI 2014. LNCS, vol. 8748, pp. 154–168. Springer, Cham (2014). https://doi.org/10.1007/978-3-319-11587-0_16
10. Babalou, S., Konig-Ries, B.: GMRs: reconciliation of generic merge requirements in ontology integration. In: SEMANTICS Poster and Demo (2019)
11. Babalou, S., König-Ries, B.: A subjective logic based approach to handling inconsistencies in ontology merging. In: Panetto, H., Debruyne, C., Hepp, M., Lewis, D., Ardagna, C., Meersman, R. (eds.) OTM, pp. 588–606. Springer, Cham (2019). https://doi.org/10.1007/978-3-030-33246-4_37

12. Noy, N.F., Musen, M.A.: The PROMPT suite: interactive tools for ontology merging and mapping. IJHCS **59**(6), 983–1024 (2003)
13. Poveda-Villalón, M., Gómez-Pérez, A., Suárez-Figueroa, M.C.: Oops! (ontology pitfall scanner!): an on-line tool for ontology evaluation. IJSWIS **10**(2), 7–34 (2014)
14. Babalou, S., Grygorova, E., König-Ries, B.: CoMerger: a customizable online tool for building a consistent quality-assured merged ontology. In: 17th Extended Semantic Web Conference (ESWC 2020), Poster and Demo Track, June 2020

$\mathcal{CoMerger}$: A Customizable Online Tool for Building a Consistent Quality-Assured Merged Ontology

Samira Babalou[1(⊠)] [iD], Elena Grygorova[1] [iD], and Birgitta König-Ries[1,2] [iD]

[1] Heinz-Nixdorf Chair for Distributed Information Systems, Institute for Computer
Science, Friedrich Schiller University Jena, Jena, Germany
{samira.babalou,elena.grygorova,birgitta.koenig-ries}@uni-jena.de
[2] Michael-Stifel-Center for Data-Driven and Simulation Science, Jena, Germany

Abstract. Merging ontologies enables the reusability and interoperability of existing knowledge. With growing numbers of relevant ontologies in any given domain, there is a strong need for an automatic, scalable multi-ontology merging tool. We introduce $\mathcal{CoMerger}$, which covers four key aspects of the ontology merging field: compatibility checking of the user-selected Generic Merge Requirements (GMR)s, merging multiple ontologies with adjustable GMRs, quality assessment of the merged ontology, and inconsistency handling of the result. $\mathcal{CoMerger}$ is freely accessible through a live portal and the source code is publicly distributed.

Keywords: Multiple ontology merging · Generic Merge Requirements · Ontology quality assessment · Ontology inconsistency

1 Introduction

Ontology merging is needed for many Semantic Web applications from a wide variety of domains. Therefore, there is a strong need for efficient, scalable, and customizable ontology merging tools. This has resulted in the development of several merging tools, including [1–6]. However, none of them meets all three requirements: methods in [2–6] are restricted to merging two ontologies at a time and are thus not sufficiently scalable. A set of pre-defined merge requirements is implemented in [5,6] and thus they lack customization. Approaches in [1–5] lack the ability for users to assess the quality of the merged results and do not provide inconsistency handling. Lastly, to the best of our knowledge, none of them are available as web-based applications.

We propose $\mathcal{CoMerger}$ as a first step towards a comprehensive merging tool focussing on four important aspects: (i) compatibility checking of the user-selected Generic Merge Requirements (GMR)s [7], (ii) merging multiple ontologies with adjusting a set of user-selected GMRs [8], (iii) assessing the quality of the merged ontology [9], and (iv) inconsistency handling of the result [10]. This paper presents the architecture of $\mathcal{CoMerger}$ tool and the interaction between the mentioned aspects.

© Springer Nature Switzerland AG 2020
A. Harth et al. (Eds.): ESWC 2020 Satellite Events, LNCS 12124, pp. 19–24, 2020.
https://doi.org/10.1007/978-3-030-62327-2_4

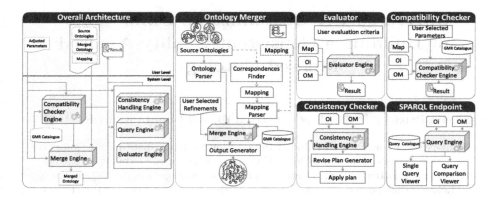

Fig. 1. $\mathcal{C}o\mathcal{M}erger$ architecture and components.

2   Tool Overview

Figure 1 shows the architecture of $\mathcal{C}o\mathcal{M}erger$ components and the interaction between them in distinct boxes. The *Overall Architecture*, the left most box in Fig. 1 depicts the data flow between the $\mathcal{C}o\mathcal{M}erger$ components, in two levels. The *user level* allows a user to interact with the tool through a friendly GUI. In the *system level*, the communication between the components is sketched. The user uploads a set of source ontologies alongside with the respective mappings[1]. If no mapping is given, $\mathcal{C}o\mathcal{M}erger$ automatically detects the correspondences by using embedded ontology matching methods[2]. Moreover, the user is able to select from a set of twenty Generic Merge Requirements (GMR)s, including, e.g., entities preservation, one type restriction, acyclicity, and connectivity. The *Compatibility Checker* engine determines whether it is possible to simultaneously meet all requirements or there are contradictions. For instance, one may want to preserve all classes from the source ontologies in the merged ontology. On the other hand, one could wish to achieve class acyclicity. Likely, these goals conflict. The engine suggests a compatible subset of the GMRs given by the user. After parsing the source ontologies and their mappings, the merged ontology is automatically generated via the *Merge* engine by taking into account the user-selected GMRs.

Afterwards, the quality of the merged ontology can be evaluated via the *Evaluator* engine according to the user-selected evaluation aspects. Furthermore, there is a possibility to evaluate the quality of any given merged ontology independent of the merge process via a separate interface, *Evaluator*. Besides the quality criteria, the *Consistency Handling* engine can validate whether the merged result is consistent and provide support in repairing any issues. Additionally,

---

[1] The tool can read a set of RDF alignment type, containing the similarity relations between entities with at least a given similarity value.

[2] Currently, two ontology matching approaches are embedded in our tool: SeeCOnt method [11] and a string matching based on the Jaccard similarity coefficient [12].

through the embedded SPARQL endpoint of the *Query* engine, the user is able to compare query results on the merged and source ontologies. In the following, we describe the main components of Fig. 1 in more detail.

2.1 Compatibility Checker: A Graph-Based Theory Method

GMRs are a set of Generic Merge Requirements that the merged ontology is expected to achieve. The tool enables the flexible ontology merging process, in which the users can adjust a set of GMRs. However, not all GMRs are compatible. Thus, the compatibility checker component in *CoMerger* verifies which GMRs can be met simultaneously. We utilized a graph-theory based method to capture the maximal compatible superset of user-selected GMRs. Our embedded twenty GMRs with the compatibility checker method have been presented in [7]. Up to now, it is not possible to extend the list of GMRs. Since this list covers all requirements towards merged ontologies mentioned in the literature, we believe that it is unlikely that the need will arise. Should that be the case, the tool could be adapted.

2.2 Ontology Merger: A Partitioning-Based Approach

Our proposed merge method takes as input a set of source ontologies alongside the respective mappings and automatically generates a merged ontology. At first, the n $(n \geq 2)$ source ontologies are divided into k $(k << n)$ blocks and a local refinement is applied to them. After that, the blocks are combined to produce the merged ontology followed by a global refinement. The user can adjust a set of refinement operations via the embedded GMRs. Moreover, the tool logs the knowledge-level of the ontology merging process and the refinement operations, which can be further analyzed by the users. The whole underlying merge method is described in [8] and evaluated on various datasets. We compared the efficiency of our single step merged method with a series of pairwise merges. The results[3] demonstrate the high performance and quality of our method.

2.3 Evaluator: Quality Assessment of the Merged Ontology

The merged ontology plays a central role in a variety of Semantic Web applications. Thus, prior to its usage, the quality and correctness of the merged ontology should be assessed. We provided a comprehensive set of evaluation criteria [9] to cover a variety of characteristics of each individual aspect of the merged ontology in three dimensions: (1) structural criteria via the evaluation of the General Merge Requirement (GMR)s, (2) functional measurements by the intended use and semantics of the merged ontology, and (3) usability-profiling evaluation on ontology and entity annotation. Our evaluation criteria also represent an analytic view on how well the created merged ontology reflects the given source ontologies. Evaluating the merged ontology can be performed even independently of the merge method by the separated interface in *CoMerger*.

---

[3] https://github.com/fusion-jena/CoMerger/blob/master/MergingDataset/result.md.

2.4   Consistency Checker: A Subjective Logic-Based Approach

The merged ontology should be free of any inconsistencies. However, since the encoded knowledge of source ontologies may model different world views, it can easily happen that the merged ontology is inconsistent. It needs to be resolved if one wants to make use of the merged ontology in further applications. Thus, we developed a Subjective Logic-based method in [10] to rank the conflicting axioms, which caused inconsistencies in the merged ontology. The rank function concerns the degree of trustworthiness of the source ontologies knowledge. Upon that, the tool suggests the remedies of changes such as deleting or rewriting a part of conflicting axioms to turn the inconsistent merged ontology into a consistent one. The whole process can be accomplished automatically, or a user can review the system's suggestions and make necessary changes before applying them.

3   Demonstration

In this demo[4], visitors will be able through our friendly GUI (see Fig. 2) specify requirements, ask for their compatibility, obtain suggestions for compatible subsets and a possible suggest compatible set, perform merge obeying the requirements, analyze the quality of the merged result w.r.t. their selected evaluation aspects, and check for consistency of the merged ontology. Users can save the merged ontology and the evaluation's results. For each selected evaluation criteria, they will receive the detailed result of the evaluation, as shown in Fig. 3. We will provide users with example ontologies, but they are also welcome to explore the tool with their own source ontologies. If interested, users can also directly access the source code, which is publicly available[5] and distributed under an open-source license. Our web-based application is supported by many modern web browsers. The host server (VM) for the tool includes 8 cores with CPU 2.39 GHz and 16 GB RAM. The processing time based on the size and number of source ontologies is reasonable. For instance, merging 17 ontologies with 51461 axioms took 140 s with a home internet (44 Mbps speed) in the Firefox 72.0.2 web browser. Users can opt for a local installation of the tool to omit delays due to network communication. We performed an experimental test on a local machine with Intel core i7 with 12 GB internal memory on Windows 7 with Java compiler 1.8. For 7, 22, 55 source ontologies with 3037, 56893, 158567 axioms, the merge method performs in 1.8, 62.3, 150.7 s, respectively. This demonstrates that the merge method in this tool scales well in the number and size of the source ontologies.

4   Related Work

Ontology merging has attracted considerable attention within the research community. Chiticariu et al. [1] proposed a method to enumerate multiple

---

[4] http://comerger.uni-jena.de/.

[5] https://github.com/fusion-jena/CoMerger.

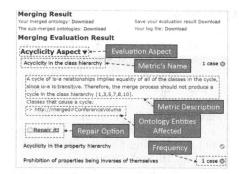

Fig. 2. Ontology merging GUI.   **Fig. 3.** Result of merge and evaluation.

integrated schemas from a set of source schemas by considering all possible choices of merging concepts. GROM [2] uses typed graph grammars with algebraic graph transformations. iPrompt [6] is an interactive ontology merging tool introduced as the Protégé-based implementation. This system leads users to perform merge by suggesting what should be merged. HSSM [3] generates the formal context for the source ontologies and merge the similar concepts within the built concept tree. GCBOM [4] applies the granular computing processes in order to produce the final merged ontology. ATOM [5], at first, creates an intermediate merged result, then refines it based on some of GMRs.

Despite the effort of many research studies, the developed ontology merging systems still suffer specific problems. In [1,6], many user interactions are required, which might not be feasible for large-scale ontologies. iPrompt [6] requires user interaction for all entity merging, and in [1], the enumerated schemas should be manually refined by users. To scale to many sources, the merging systems in [2–6] are insufficient due to merging only two ontologies at a time. No inconsistency handling is provided in [1–5]. In [5,6], a set of fixed GMRs is implemented without user customization. To the best of our knowledge, besides iPrompt, the other mentioned systems are not publicly accessible and reproducible. Moreover, none of them are available as a web-based application.

5 Future Work

In our future work, we plan to extend *CoMerger* with respect to several dimensions: First, we will integrate the possibility to evaluate against a set of Competency Questions in the functional dimension to facilitate many use-case scenarios. Second, embedding other existing matchers in our tool and evaluating the source ontologies before the merge process might give a useful insight to the users. Finally, we plan a user study to evaluate the ease-of-use.

Acknowledgments. S. Babalou is supported by a scholarship from German Academic Exchange Service (DAAD).

References

1. Chiticariu, L., Kolaitis, P.G., Popa, L.: Interactive generation of integrated schemas. In: ACM SIGMOD, pp. 833–846 (2008)
2. Mahfoudh, M., Thiry, L., Forestier, G., Hassenforder, M.: Algebraic Graph Transformations for Merging Ontologies. In: Ait Ameur, Y., Bellatreche, L., Papadopoulos, G.A. (eds.) MEDI, pp. 154–168. Springer, Cham (2014). https://doi.org/10.1007/978-3-319-11587-0_16
3. Priya, M., Ch, A.K.: A novel method for merging academic social network ontologies using formal concept analysis and hybrid semantic similarity measure. Library Hi Tech (2019)
4. Priya, M., Kumar, C.A.: An approach to merge domain ontologies using granular computing. Granular Comput. 1–26 (2019). ISSN: 23644966. https://doi.org/10.1007/s41066-019-00193-3
5. Raunich, S., Rahm, E.: Target-driven merging of taxonomies with atom. Inf. Syst. **42**, 1–14 (2014)
6. Noy, N.F., Musen, M.A.: The prompt suite: interactive tools for ontology merging and mapping. IJHCS **59**(6), 983–1024 (2003)
7. Babalou, S., König-Ries,B.: GMRs: reconciliation of generic merge requirements in ontology integration. In: SEMANTICS Poster and Demo (2019)
8. Babalou, S., König-Ries, B.: Towards building knowledge by merging multiple ontologies with CoMerger: a partitioning-based approach. http://arxiv.org/abs/2005.02659
9. Babalou, S., Grygorova, E., König-Ries, B.: How good is this merged ontology?. In: 17th Extended Semantic Web Conference (ESWC 2020), Poster and Demo Track, June 2020
10. Babalou, S., König-Ries, B.: A subjective logic based approach to handling inconsistencies in ontology merging. In: Panetto, H., Debruyne, C., Hepp, M., Lewis, D., Ardagna, C.A., Meersman, R. (eds.) OTM 2019. LNCS, vol. 11877, pp. 588–606. Springer, Cham (2019). https://doi.org/10.1007/978-3-030-33246-4_37
11. Algergawy, A., Babalou, S., Kargar, M.J., Davarpanah, S.H.: Seecont: a new seeding-based clustering approach for ontology matching. In: ADBIS, pp. 245–258 (2015)
12. Jaccard, P.: Étude comparative de la distribution florale dans une portion des alpes et des jura. Bull Soc. Vaudoise Sci. Nat. **37**, 547–579 (1901)

Semi-automatic RDFization Using Automatically Generated Mappings

Noorani Bakerally[1,2], Cyrille Bareau[3], Fabrice Blache[3], Sébastien Bolle[3], Christelle Ecrepont[2], Pauline Folz[3], Nathalie Hernandez[1(✉)], Thierry Monteil[2], Gilles Privat[3], and Fano Ramparany[3]

[1] IRIT, Toulouse, France
{noorani.bakerally,nathalie.hernandez}@irit.fr
[2] LAAS-CNRS, National Institut of Applied Sciences of Toulouse,
Toulouse 31400, France
{noorani.bakerally,christelle.ecrepont,thierry.monteil}@laas.fr
[3] Orange Labs, Meylan, France
{cyrille.bareau,fabrice.blache,sebastien.bolle,pauline.folz,
gilles.privat,fano.ramparany}@orange.com
http://www.springer.com/gp/computer-science/lncs

Abstract. Most data available on the Web do not conform to the RDF data model. A number of tools/approaches have been developed to encourage the transition to RDF. Manual and automatic tools/approaches tend to be complex and rigid. On the other hand, semi-automatic tools can hide and automate complex tasks while enhancing flexibility by solicitating human experts for decision making purposes. In this paper, we describe a semi-automatic approach to facilitate the transformation of heterogeneous semi-structured data to RDF. The originality of our approach is its ability to generate exhaustive descriptions using entities from several ontologies without requiring end-users to have a knowledge of ontologies. We provide an implementation of our approach and demonstrate its use using a real dataset from an open data portal.

Keywords: RDF · Data transformation · Semi-automatic approach

1 Introduction

To realize the vision of the Semantic Web, the conformance of existing data to the RDF model is a necessary condition. Yet, it is a fact that most of the data available on the Web do not satisfy this requirement. A number of tools have been developed to facilitate the transition to RDF. Much of them are founded on well-defined mapping languages (R2RML [1], RML [2], SPARQL-Generate [3], etc.). Using mapping languages directly is complex. This is because they have a steep learning curve and require knowing the syntax and semantics of the languages in addition to the Semantic Web stack and ontologies that can be used.

Besides mapping languages, there are automatic and semi-automatic RDFizers. We ignore automatic RDFizers (e.g. Direct Mapping [4], Docker2RDF [5],

© Springer Nature Switzerland AG 2020
A. Harth et al. (Eds.): ESWC 2020 Satellite Events, LNCS 12124, pp. 25–31, 2020.
https://doi.org/10.1007/978-3-030-62327-2_5

etc.) as their transformation cannot be customized or they are restricted for specific domain models. The minor category of works (RMLEditor [6], OpenRefine [7], etc.) around semi-automatic RDFizers is our main interest. We focus on this category due to their ability in aiding end-users by automating complex tasks without hindering flexibility by incorporating them for decision making and validation. The main problem with the latter tools is that they mostly only provide a graphical interface with some facilities for searching through ontologies. By doing so, they still rely on end-users with respect to their knowledge about ontologies and data modeling using them.

In this work, our aim is to provide an approach to further facilitate semi-automatic RDFizers by automatically generating mappings without prior knowledge about ontologies, that may then be customized by end-users. The originality of our contribution is that it automatically generates several holistic mappings and try best to provide an exhaustive description for a given type of objects. To ensure exhaustivity, the type of objects can be described with entities defined in several ontologies as long as semantic coherence is maintained. Our approach is not an alternative but complementary to existing tools. In the rest of this paper, we describe our approach and its implementation in Sect. 2 and Sect. 3 respectively. Then, we demonstrate our implementation using a real dataset from open data portal. Finally in Sect. 5, we conclude with limitations of our approach and future works.

2   Our Approach

We use a divide-and-conquer strategy to RDFize non-RDF data. The base case of this strategy occurs when the non-RDF data describes only one type of object. In this paper, our approach is focused on this base case. Our approach to generate final mappings consists of four main steps: **i) Generate Schema Descriptions ii) Generate candidates iii) Generate candidate mappings iv) Refine candidate mappings,** as shown in Fig. 2. The refined mapping selected by the user is then automatically represented in a mapping language and used to generate the RDF representation of the data.

For illustration purposes, we consider a parking dataset[1] from Grenoble open data portal[2]. Figure 1 is part of a preview of that dataset taken directly from the data portal. Moreover, our approach uses an `Ontology repository`, as despicted in Fig. 2. Suppose that it contains the vocabularies MobiVoc[3], Schema.org[4], WGS84[5] and Dublin Core Metadata Terms[6].

---

[1] http://data.metropolegrenoble.fr/ckan/dataset/parkings-de-grenoble/resource/a6919f90-4c38-4ee0-a4ec-403db77f5a4b, last accessed on 7 December 2019.

[2] http://data.metropolegrenoble.fr/, last accessed on 7 December 2019.

[3] https://www.mobivoc.org/, last accessed 10 February 2020.

[4] https://schema.org/, last accessed 10 February 2020.

[5] https://www.w3.org/2003/01/geo/, last accessed 10 February 2020.

[6] https://www.dublincore.org/specifications/dublin-core/dcmi-terms/, last accessed 10 February 2020.

_id	CODE ⌄	LIBELLE	ADRESSE	TYPE	TOTAL	type	id	lon	lat
11	SPR_PKG...	CATANE	RUE AMP...	PKG	490	PKG	SPR_PKG...	5.70503	45.181035
9	QPA_PKG...	CHAVANT	17, BD M...	PKG	394	PKG	QPA_PKG...	5.731463	45.185612
15	PVP_PKG...	ENCLOS...	PLACE V...	PKG	130	PKG	PVP_PKG_...	5.728358	45.188401
16	PVP_PKG...	ENCLOS...	RUE EMI...	PKG	200	PKG	PVP_PKG_...	5.713614	45.194345

Fig. 1. Parking data from Grenoble Open Data Portal

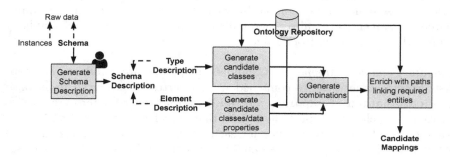

Fig. 2. Mappings Generation Process

Below, we proceed with the descriptions of the steps in our approach.

Generate Schema Description. In our approach, we suppose that the file to be transformed contains only one type of object. We make the difference between the type of object (`Type element`) and its properties (`Schema element`). To capture the background knowledge about the schema used in the raw data, we generate a `Schema description` consisting of a `Type description` and `Elements description`, via a user interface (*cf.* Sect. 3) with the involvement of the end-user.

`Type Description` characterizes the type of objects described by the schema and `Elements descriptions` characterizes the schema elements (e.g. `lon` in Fig. 1). For both, `Type Description` and `Elements Description`, the description can be enriched by `keywords` added by the end-user. The `schema description` may not contain a description for all columns. For example, the schema description of the data in Fig. 1 may omit the description of the column `CODE` as it contains the same information as the column `id`. In this way, uninterested columns may be ignored.

Generate Candidates. Using an `Ontology repository`, and the `Schema description`, a set of candidate classes are generated for typing objects, thanks to `Type description` and a set of candidate data properties or classes are generated for modeling the schema element, thanks to `Elements description`. The `Schema description` is then converted into a pseudo-ontology in OWL and simple ontology matching approaches presented in [8] are used to generate the candidate for the `Type element` and `Schema elements`. Table 1 shows a schema description for the schema of Fig. 1 and generated ontology entities for its elements. For example, the objects' type in Fig. 1 can be described by the keyword 'parking facility'. Using the latter description, the classes `mv:ParkingFacility` and `sc:Park` are generated to type the objects. Similarly, the schema element `TOTAL` is described using the keywords 'capacity' and 'total' using which the class `mv:Capacity` and data property `sc:totalTime` are candidates generated to model it. The candidate proposal `sc:totalTime` is not appropriate to model `TOTAL` as its semantics is not compatible with the latter. To determine the appropriateness of an entity, we also generated a confidence. For the sake of simplicity, we omit this information from Table 1.

Generate Candidate Mappings. Candidate mappings are build in two steps. First, candidate entities are combined with a cartesian product, producing a set of `combination of mappings` where a `combination of mappings` consists of a candidate class for typing the object, that we refer as the `type class`, and a candidate data property or class for each schema elements. Table 2 shows all combinations generated from the candidate entities in Table 1. As we can see, in each combination, there is one candidate entity for the type class and one for each schema element. In a second step, we keep `combination of mappings` where we can assess the existence of a path between the `type class` and candidate entities for the `schema element`. These paths are identified using patterns that we have defined. They exploit the graph structure of ontologies. For example, Fig. 3 shows the first combination from Table 2 and the required paths, illustrated as dotted lines, that will be generated at this step. It is possible that

Table 1. Candidate entities for typing and schema elements

Schema description			Generated entities	
		Keyword	Classes	Data properties
Type description		'parking facility'	`mv:ParkingFacility`, `sc:Park`	
Elements description	id	'identifier'		`dc:identifier`
	LIBELLE	'description'		`sc:description`
	TOTAL	'capacity','total'	`mv:Capacity`	`sc:totalTime`
	lat	'latitude'		`wgs84:lat`
	lon	'longitude'		`wgs84:long`
	ADDRESSE	'address'		`sc:address`

Table 2. Combinations of generated entities for type class and schema elements

	Type class	id	LIBELLE	TOTAL	lat	lon	ADDRESSE
1.	`mv:ParkingFacility`	`dc:identifier`	`sc:description`	`mv:Capacity`	`wgs84:lat`	`wgs84:lon`	`sc:address`
2.	`mv:ParkingFacility`	`dc:identifier`	`sc:description`	`sc:totalTime`	`wgs84:lat`	`wgs84:lon`	`sc:address`
3.	`sc:Park`	`dc:identifier`	`sc:description`	`mv:Capacity`	`wgs84:lat`	`wgs84:lon`	`sc:address`
4.	`sc:Park`	`dc:identifier`	`sc:description`	`sc:totalTime`	`wgs84:lat`	`wgs84:lon`	`sc:address`

more than one path or no path exist between some entities. We then obtain a set of **candidate mappings**.

Generate Final Mapping. A user interface is provided to allow choosing and refining a **candidate mapping** to obtain the **final mapping**. There are cases where a **schema element** may be modeled by a class. In these cases, data properties containing the latter class in their domains may be used to specify the values. Refining consists in choosing the appropriate data property.

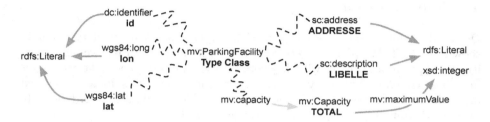

Fig. 3. Candidate mappings for first combination without generated paths

3   Implementation

An overview of our implementation, SAURON, is shown in Fig. 4. Core to SAURON is the **RDFizer** that generate final mappings using the approach described in the previous section. To facilitate human intervention, we provide a graphical **User Interface**. Using the interface, users can upload the raw data in the CSV format and may enrich it with keywords to generate the **Schema description**. The **User Interface** interacts with the **RDFizer** via a **Web Service**. Eventually, on obtaining the candidate mappings, one of them is chosen and refined and validated by the end-user and sent to the web service together with the raw data for transformation to RDF. This is done with SPARQL-Generate in the current implementation.

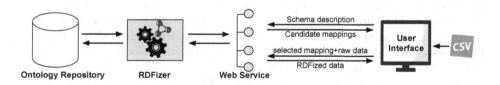

Fig. 4. Overview of SAURON

The user interface is a web application implemented using the JavaScript library *React*[7]. The video available online[8] shows the use of the interface to

---

[7] https://reactjs.org/.
[8] https://youtu.be/LKZH4gs7sNQ.

generate mappings for the CSV parking dataset in Sect. 2. As it can be seen, the user interface has three main parts. The top left part is focused on the raw data that is imported using the import CSV menu item. On clicking on a column, keywords can be entered. The bottom left part shows the candidate mappings and on selecting one of them, its corresponding description graph is rendered on the right part. The end-user can interact with different part of the latter graph and select and validate the paths.

4   Demonstration

During this demonstration, we intend to RDFize Grenoble parking dataset partly shown in Fig. 1. We perform two experiments: NK and WK. In NK, we only specify the type description with keywords. In WK, we also specify keywords for interested columns. These keywords are shown in Table 1. Results are despicted in Table 3. As we can see in Table 3 and the video, adding keywords greatly improve the quality of mappings that are generated.

Table 3. Initial mappings without keywords (NK) and with keywords (WK)

	LIBELLE	ADRESSE	TOTAL	id	lon	lat
NK	–	schema:adress	–	mobivoc:id	–	–
WK	schema:label	schema:adress	mv:Capacity	dc:id	geo:long	geo:lat

5   Conclusion

We have tested our approach on real datasets from open data portals and the results were promising. However, there are three main limitations. Firstly, the success of the approach depends much on the selection of keywords. It may not be easy for the user to define the keywords that will correspond to labels of ontologies entities. An extension of the approach that will suggest keywords according to these labels is currently being implemented. Secondly, as mentioned in Sect. 2, our approach can consider raw data containing only one type of object described by several data properties. However in some cases, the object can be link in its description to other objets. Approaches dealing with entity resolution and entity linking could be used. Thirdly, as of now, there are no alignments between the ontologies in the ontology repository. The existence of these alignments can improve the quality of the generated mappings.

References

1. Das, S., Sundara, S., Cyganiak, R.: R2RML: RDB to RDF Mapping Language, W3C Recommendation. Technical report, 27 September 2012

2. Dimou, A., Vander Sande, M., Colpaert, P., Verborgh, R., Mannens, E., Van de Walle, R.: RML: a generic language for integrated RDF mappings of heterogeneous data. In: LDOW (2014)
3. Lefrançois, M., Zimmermann, A., Bakerally, N.: Flexible RDF generation from RDF and heterogeneous data sources with SPARQL-generate. In: Ciancarini, P., et al. (eds.) EKAW 2016. LNCS (LNAI), vol. 10180, pp. 131–135. Springer, Cham (2017). https://doi.org/10.1007/978-3-319-58694-6_16
4. Arenas, M., Bertails, A., Prud'hommeaux, E., Sequeda, J.: A Direct Mapping of Relational Data to RDF, W3C Recommendation 27 September 2012. W3C Recommendation, World Wide Web Consortium (W3C), September 27 2012
5. Ayed, A.B., Subercaze, J., Laforest, F., Chaari, T., Louati, W., Kacem, A.H.: Docker2RDF: lifting the docker registry hub into RDF. In: 2017 IEEE World Congress on Services (SERVICES), pp. 36–39. IEEE (2017)
6. Heyvaert, P., et al.: RMLEditor: a graph-based mapping editor for linked data mappings. In: Sack, H., Blomqvist, E., d'Aquin, M., Ghidini, C., Ponzetto, S.P., Lange, C. (eds.) ESWC 2016. LNCS, vol. 9678, pp. 709–723. Springer, Cham (2016). https://doi.org/10.1007/978-3-319-34129-3_43
7. Verborgh, R., De Wilde, M.: Using OpenRefine. Packt Publishing Ltd. (2013)
8. Thiéblin, E., Haemmerlé, O., Hernandez, N., Trojahn C.:. Survey on complex ontology matching. Semant. Web (Preprint), 1–39 (2019)

Pini Language and PiniTree Ontology Editor: Annotation and Verbalisation for Atomised Journalism

Guntis Barzdins[1,2,3]([✉]), Didzis Gosko[1,3], Karlis Cerans[1], Oskars F. Barzdins[3],
Arturs Znotins[1], Paulis F. Barzdins[1], Normunds Gruzitis[1], Mikus Grasmanis[2],
Janis Barzdins[1], Uldis Lavrinovics[2], Sinty K. Mayer[3], Intars Students[2],
Edgars Celms[1], Arturs Sprogis[1], Gunta Nespore-Berzkalne[1], and Peteris Paikens[1]

[1] Institute of Mathematics and Computer Science, University of Latvia, Riga, Latvia
{guntis.barzdins,didzis.gosko,karlis.cerans}@lumii.lv
[2] LETA, Marijas Street 2, Riga, Latvia
[3] PiniTree, EU, Jelgava, Latvia

Abstract. We present a new ontology language Pini and the PiniTree ontology editor supporting it. Despite Pini language bearing lot of similarities with RDF, UML class diagrams, Property Graphs and their frontends like Google Knowledge Graph and Protégé, it is a more expressive language enabling FrameNet-style natural language annotation for Atomised journalism use case.

Keywords: Ontology languages and editors · Natural language processing

1 Introduction

We address the problem of describing real-life situations (facts about past, Atomised news [1]) in a formal language close to natural language and easily understandable by the domain experts and end users.

The primary construct necessary in such descriptions is a subject-predicate-object relation, with a possibility to add secondary property-value pairs to the relation.

Basic RDF [3] modelling of this would involve creating a resource for the relation fact, thus bringing the data model far from the linguistic representation.

UML [2], Property Graph [4] and RDF* [8] notations allow for direct property ascriptions to the links (statements in the case of RDF*) in the data model, however, with certain limitations:

- UML, by its design philosophy, allows only one link for a link type (an association class) between an object pair (cf. [2], p. 438),
- Property Graphs allow only scalar values as link attributes, and
- RDF* aggregates all annotations on a subject-predicate-object triple together, thus also excluding several same-predicate links between the same objects.

A. Harth et al. (Eds.): ESWC 2020 Satellite Events, LNCS 12124, pp. 32–38, 2020.
https://doi.org/10.1007/978-3-030-62327-2_6

This paper proposes a new *Pini language* with sentences and paragraphs close to the natural language and a simple data model resembling Wikidata predecessor graphd [9] that do not suffer from the abovementioned data model limitations.

Requirements for the Pini language come from the real-world text modelling experience [7] with the Berkeley FrameNet [6]; the novelty here is to define two frame elements for each considered frame as the subject and object; the other frame elements become secondary properties of the main subject-frame-object relation.

The Pini language is implemented in the *PiniTree* editor (available at *pinitree.com*) tested on LETA News Agency and BBC use-cases – CV extraction from a news archive [7], and Atomised journalism [1] – and demonstrated in this paper.

2 Pini Language

The *Pini language* can represent knowledge about a wide range of domains. The basic element of the Pini language is a *Pini entity,* which represents a discrete object with well-defined boundaries and identity in the physical or imagined world [2, p. 442].

The Pini entity has three attributes: *type, lexical name* and *GUID* represented as:

$$[(\textbf{type}) \textbf{ LexicalName (GUID)}]$$

The *type* denotes a class to which the Pini entity belongs, such as *person, organization, place, relation.* It helps disambiguating the lexical name of the Pini entity, as "Paris" could be either a *location* or a *person* name.

The *lexical name* is a canonical name by which the Pini entity could be referenced in natural language, for example *Peter, Nokia, Finland, located_in.*

The *GUID* values are globally unique random identifiers (unlike the globally coordinated URIs for resource identification) by which Pini entity is uniquely referenced.

Pini entities are subdivided into *item entities* and *link entities.* Item entities exist on their own and they represent objects like *Finland* and *Nokia.* Link entities represent a concrete relationship between two other Pini entities, as, e.g., in the Pini triples:

$$<[(org)\textbf{ Nokia }(\ldots)], [(relation)\textbf{ located\_in }(45af23\ldots)], [(place)\textbf{ Finland }(\ldots)]>$$

$$<[(org)\textbf{ Ericsson }(\ldots)], [(relation)\textbf{ located\_in }(7e53b4\ldots)], [(place)\textbf{ Sweden }(\ldots)]>$$

Note that although the relation lexical name "*located_in*" is the same in both examples, these relations are different Pini entities since their GUIDs are different.

The *Pini triple* is an ordered list of three Pini entities referred to as *<subject, predicate, object>* respectively, where the predicate must be a link entity and the object must be an item entity (the subject can be either an item entity or a link entity).

The *Pini ontology* is a set of Pini triples, where every link entity appears as a predicate in exactly one Pini triple. A Pini ontology can be visualized as a graph in which all Pini entities with the same GUID are collapsed in the same node (cf. Fig. 1).

Pini sentence is a fragment of the Pini ontology starting with a single Pini triple

$$<[subject\text{-}entity], [predicate\text{-}entity], [object\text{-}entity]>$$

and it includes all secondary Pini-triples in which the above *predicate-entity* shows up as the subject entity. With well-chosen lexical names such Pini sentences easily map to a natural language sentence such as *"Steve Jobs wife was Laurene Powell and they married in 1991 at Yosemite National Park."* (see Fig. 2).

The *Pini paragraph* is a set of all Pini sentences sharing the same focus-entity (see Pini paragraph for the focus-entity *Steve Jobs* in Fig. 2).

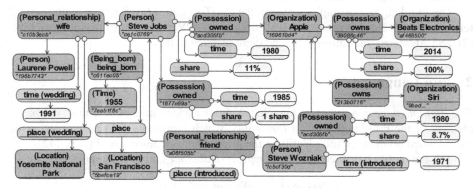

Fig. 1. Example Pini ontology. Note two separate triples *<Steve Jobs, owned, Apple>* with different attributes. (Color figue online)

Pini literal is syntactic sugar for self-describing item entities appearing only in the object of some Pini triple, like "184 cm" in:

$$<[(person)\ \textbf{Peter}\ (\ldots)],\ [(relation),\ \textbf{height},\ (4bv15f\ \ldots)],\ [(literal)\ \textbf{184}\textbf{\textit{cm}}\ (\ldots)]>$$

Pini literals can be included in the lexical name of the relation to omit the object:

$$<[(person)\ \textbf{Peter}\ (\ldots)],\ [(relation),\ \textbf{height}:\textbf{184}\textbf{\textit{cm}},\ (4bv15f\ \ldots)],\ ->$$

Pini literals are depicted light blue in Fig. 1 and Fig. 2.

3   PiniTree Ontology Editor

PiniTree is an editor implementing the Pini language for the Atomised journalism use-case. As shown in Fig. 2 it has two distinct panes: the right pane is the Pini ontology editor and the left pane is the Atomised journalism workbench. The left pane displays *Pini documents* (text with images) resembling Wikipedia articles while the right pane allows navigating and editing the ontology resembling DBpedia. But unlike DBpedia, which integrates with Wikipedia only on the article level, PiniTree editor integrates the Pini ontology and Pini documents on the word and sentence level by means of Pini mentions.

Pini mention is a feature of the PiniTree editor enabling referencing Pini document segments from Pini entities as a source of attribution – a grounding feature missing

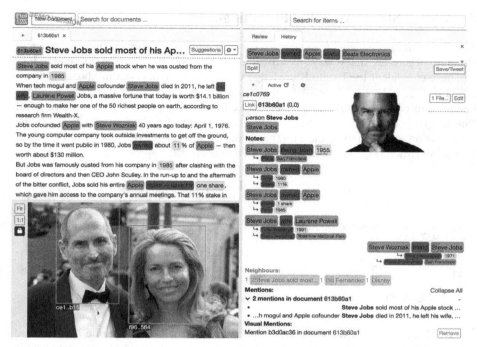

Fig. 2. Pini ontology fragment in the PiniTree ontology editor. (Color figure online)

e.g. in Google Knowledge Graph [5]. Pini documents are accumulated as read-only objects in the PiniTree editor and are assigned a unique Pini item (GUID 613b60a1... in Fig. 2) holding the document metadata. Document GUIDs along with the segment offset serve as the Pini mention target. Besides manual disambiguated entity mention annotation assisted through the entity spelling *aliases*, the PiniTree editor also suggests entity mentions similarly to Google search using neural contextual word embeddings and neural face recognition. Link entities are suggested based on frequently co-occurring neighbouring item entities (e.g. "Disney" in Fig. 2). GUIDs and aliases rather than Wikipedia page names stimulate broad synset use as Pini entities.

Pini ontology editor in the right pane assumes that human perception of the Pini ontology naturally is based on sequential navigation through the neighbouring Pini paragraphs. A Pini paragraph is the unit of information one can perceive simultaneously as the episodic memory. Navigating through Pini paragraphs forms a linear history of focus-entities in the short-term memory to be re-accessed easily.

The Pini ontology graph in Fig. 1 can't deliver this experience as in real applications it may become very large and incomprehensible. Instead the PiniTree editor represents Pini paragraphs as illustrated in Fig. 2. It supports navigation between the Pini entities by clicking on them like in a web browser; unlike the browser "back" button the entire browsing history is accessible at the top-right pane. The browsing history often resembles a short story and can be saved in a new Pini document as the blue-print for the Atomised journalism output.

4   Adding Structure to the Pini Language

The Pini ontology in Fig. 1 and Fig. 2 is easily understandable because it has clear structure. There are many ways to structure a Pini ontology – e.g., an alternative Pini structure equivalent to Google Knowledge Graph [5] or Wikipedia infoboxes is illustrated in Fig. 4. But for journalistic use-cases we need more granular n-ary relations better captured by the Berkeley FrameNet (see Frame example in Fig. 3a) requiring full Pini language expressivity for secondary attributes (see *SanFrancisco* in Fig. 2). The visualisation and editing in the PiniTree editor is universal and supports infobox and FrameNet structuring, as well as unstructured "linked data" approaches.

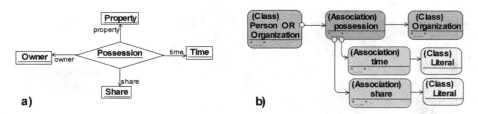

Fig. 3. Frames in PiniTree: FrameNet notation (a) and Pini frame notation (b).

We define a *Pini frame* to be a FrameNet frame in which two frame-elements are identified as a binary subject-predicate-object *core association*, where predicate type is the frame-name. Other frame-elements attach to the predicate of the core association as subject – these we will regard as secondary roles (see Fig. 3b). Pini sentences are instances of such Pini frames. Formally, a Pini frame is a Pini ontology with the meta-types *Class* and *Association*. Pini frames constitute the terminological part of the Pini ontology and are stored in the separate *Ontology* meta-type used by PiniTree editor to soft-constrain the regular Pini entity types.

Fig. 4. PiniTree view of the Google Knowledge Graph or WikiPedia infobox data.

The example ontology in Fig. 1 and Fig. 2 uses Pini frames derived from the corresponding FrameNet frames: *Possession, Personal_relationship*, and *Being_born*. The core association among the roles constituting the frame is identified by studying the syntactic realization and valence patterns of the frame, which are part of the FrameNet dataset derived from large manually annotated text corpora.

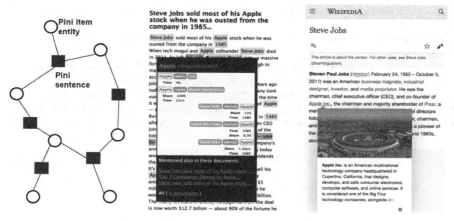

Fig. 5. Pini WoIB structure and end user view resembling Wikipedia page preview popup.

5   Discussion and Conclusions

The three FrameNet frames used in above example are insufficient for the LETA and BBC use-cases. In the LETA use-case [7] we found that seven FrameNet frames *Being_born, Death, Personal_relationship, Education_teaching, Being_employed, Membership, Possession* are sufficient for their use-case of extracting politician CVs from their news archive. On top of these 7 frames the BBC Atomised journalism use-case [1] also requires *Participation* and *Statement* frames, as daily news typically revolve around events and their participants along with any notable statements made by political influencers.

The end user Web of infoboxes (WoIB) view in Fig. 5 illustrates the Pini enriched web page with navigation popup resembling a Wikipedia page preview with the Pini infobox and mentions. We are optimistic that the described approach can be further extended with neural question answering [10] and reasoning.

Acknowledgments. The research leading to these results has received funding also from the ERDF project 1.1.1.1/18/A/045 at IMCS, University of Latvia, and from the project "Competence Centre of Information and Communication Technologies" of EU Structural funds, No. 1.2.1.1/18/A/003, Research No. 2.4 "Platform for the semantically structured information extraction from the massive Latvian news archive".

References

1. Rhianne, J., Bronwyn Jones, J.: Atomising the news: the (in)flexibility of structured journalism. Digital Journal. **7**(8), 1157–1179 (2019)
2. Rumbaugh, J., Jacobson, I., Booch, G.: The Unified Modeling Language Reference Manual, 2nd edn. Addison-Wesley, Boston (2005)
3. Resource Description Framework (RDF). http://www.w3.org/RDF. Accessed 05 May 2020
4. Robinson, I., Webber, J., Eifrem, E.: Graph Databases. O'Reilly Media, Sebastopol (2013)

5. Google Knowledge Graph. https://developers.google.com/knowledge-graph. Accessed 05 May 2020
6. Fillmore, C.J., Johnson, C.R., Petruck, M.R.L.: Background to FrameNet. Int. J. Lexicogr. **16**, 235–250 (2003)
7. Barzdins, G., Gosko, D., Rituma, L., Paikens, P.: Using C5.0 and exhaustive search for boosting frame-semantic parsing accuracy. In: LREC2014, pp. 4476–4482 (2014)
8. Hartig, O.: Reconciliation of RDF* and Property Graphs. arXiv:1409.3288 (2014)
9. FreeBase graphd Repository. https://github.com/google/graphd. Accessed 05 May 2020
10. Dhingra, B., et al.: Differentiable reasoning over a virtual knowledge base. In: ICLR (2020)

Semantic Artificial Neural Networks

Sotirios Batsakis[1,2]([✉]), Ilias Tachmazidis[1], George Baryannis[1],
and Grigoris Antoniou[1]

[1] University of Huddersfield, Huddersfield, UK
{s.batsakis,i.tachmazidis,g.bargiannis,g.antoniou}@hud.ac.uk
[2] Technical University of Crete, Chania, Greece

Abstract. Neural networks have achieved in recent years human level
performance in various application domains, including critical applications where accountability is a very important issue, closely related to the
interpretability of neural networks and artificial intelligence in general.
In this work, an approach for defining the structure of neural networks
based on the conceptualisation and semantics of the application domain
is proposed. The proposed approach, called Semantic Artificial Neural
Networks, allows dealing with the problem of interpretability and also
the definition of the structure of neural networks. In addition, the resulting neural networks are sparser and have fewer parameters than typical
neural networks, while achieving high performance.

1 Introduction

Neural networks have been an important machine learning method for many
decades but impressive results in recent years have brought them to the spotlight of artificial intelligence (AI) research and the wider discussion around
AI's impact in society. Since AI is applied on critical domains, interpretability,
accountability and legal compliance become significant requirements. Although
neural networks achieve impressive performance, they are problematic with
respect to these requirements and are commonly characterised as a "black
box" approach [2]. Instead, interpretable machine learning approaches can be
employed, such as linear and logistic regression, Bayes classifiers and decision
trees [3]. These approaches are often efficient but not always as performing as
non-interpretable ones, such as Support Vector Machines and neural networks.
Extracting interpretation rules from noisy data when employing machine learning is also an alternative approach [4], applied after the creation of a neural
network.

In this work, a knowledge graph based approach is proposed for achieving
interpretability as in regression methods, while still employing neural networks
and thus taking advantage of related work and advances (e.g. in deep learning) in
this very prolific research area. The main idea, presented in detail in Sect. 2, is to
construct the network in such a way that dataset features correspond to inputs
and outputs, and the nodes of hidden layers correspond to concepts associated
with inputs and outputs in a domain conceptualisation represented in graph
form.

A. Harth et al. (Eds.): ESWC 2020 Satellite Events, LNCS 12124, pp. 39–44, 2020.
https://doi.org/10.1007/978-3-030-62327-2_7

Algorithm 1. Semantic Artificial Neural Networks Construction

---

Require: Dataset D,

Require: Ontology (Domain Conceptualization) O

 1: Create empty Neural Network Graph G

 2: **for all** output features $o_j \in D$ **do**

 3:     Map $o_j \in D$ to concepts or attributes $c_j^o \in O$

 4:     Add corresponding $c_j^o \in O$ into G

 5: **end for**

 6: **for all** input features $i_j \in D$ **do**

 7:     Map $i_j \in D$ to concepts or attributes $c_j^i \in O$

 8:     Add corresponding $c_j^i \in O$ into G

 9: **end for**

10: **while** $\exists\ c_j^o \in G$ not connected to $c_j^i \in G$ **do**

11:     **for all** nodes $c_j \in G$ **do**

12:         Find concept(s) $c_k \in O$ connected to node(s) $c_j \in G$

13:         Add node(s) c_k in G

14:         Add arc(s) connecting c_j, c_k

15:     **end for**

16: **end while**

17: **return** Graph G

---

2   Semantic Artificial Neural Networks

The proposed method is based on the construction of a neural network by mapping its structure to an existing or purposely created conceptualisation or ontology in graph form, containing definitions of inputs and outputs of the neural network. Dataset features that correspond to the nodes of the input and output layers of the neural network are mapped to ontology concepts and attributes. Additional concepts within the ontology form the hidden layers of the neural network. This is based on the observation that both ontologies and neural networks are represented using a graph structure. This allows neural network nodes to be mapped to concepts and their properties in the ontology. If properly constructed, the semantics of nodes in the resulting Semantic Artificial Neural Network (SANN) can be determined directly.

The dataset to analyse and the corresponding domain conceptualisation are necessary in order to construct an SANN. Specifically, the dataset consists of samples and a set of features D. The conceptualisation or ontology O consists of a set of nodes V corresponding to features/attributes and a set of edges E connecting related concepts/attributes in V. All features in D correspond to nodes in V. Notice that, instead of using existing conceptualisations and ontologies, users can develop task-specific ontologies when defining the structure of the neural network. The SANN construction process is shown in Algorithm 1 and is defined as follows: given a conceptualisation or an ontology graph O, the properties corresponding to the output features in D are mapped to an output layer node in the neural network G (lines 2–5). Input properties in D correspond to input layer nodes in G (lines 6–9) and intermediate nodes appearing in the path between input and output in G form the hidden layers (lines 10–16).

The proposed SANN approach can be applied even when a formal domain ontology is not available. In this case the structure can defined using methods as in knowledge engineering, based on the stakeholders' understanding and conceptualization of the domain and an analysis of related concepts. This can be achieved by slightly modifying Algorithm 1, specifically lines 3, 7 and 12: instead of mapping dataset features to ontology concepts or attributes, such concepts or attributes have to be defined. We expect that defining the network structure is a simpler task compared to a typical knowledge engineering task, because network inputs and outputs are given in advance in the form of dataset features. Thus, it is only necessary to define concepts connecting or associating inputs with outputs, instead of creating a complete domain conceptualisation.

3 Evaluation

In this section the performance of SANNs is compared with that of typical dense neural networks. Several diverse datasets are used for comparison for both classification and regression tasks. Specifically, ten datasets covering diverse domains are used (8 of which are from the UCI machine learning collection [1]), with five datasets used for classification and five for regression. The classification datasets are: UCI diabetes [6][1], UCI heart disease[2], UCI Iris[3], UCI credit card default[4] and the prostate cancer dataset[5]. For regression the datasets are: UCI Auto-mpg[6], UCI wine quality[7], UCI real estate valuation[8], UCI Istanbul stock exchange[9] and the graduate admissions dataset[10]. Min-max normalization was performed on all input features in the datasets.

We present indicatively the SANN created for the UCI diabetes dataset [6] by combining lexical description of inputs and DBpedia concepts. Note that similar SANNs have been created for all 10 datasets but are not shown here due to space limitations. The UCI diabetes dataset contains the following 8 attributes: number of times pregnant (*preg*), plasma glucose concentration after 2 h in an oral glucose tolerance test (*plas*), diastolic blood pressure in mm Hg (*pres*), triceps skin fold thickness in mm (*skin*), 2-h serum insulin in mu U/ml (*insu*), body mass index measured as weight in kg/(height in m)^2 (*mass*), diabetes pedigree function (*pedi*) and age in years (*age*). The diabetes pedigree function (*pedi*)

---

[1] https://www.kaggle.com/uciml/pima-indians-diabetes-database.

[2] https://www.kaggle.com/ronitf/heart-disease-uci.

[3] https://www.kaggle.com/uciml/iris.

[4] https://www.kaggle.com/uciml/default-of-credit-card-clients-dataset.

[5] https://www.kaggle.com/multi8ball/prostate-cancer.

[6] https://www.kaggle.com/uciml/autompg-dataset/.

[7] https://www.kaggle.com/uciml/red-wine-quality-cortez-et-al-2009.

[8] https://archive.ics.uci.edu/ml/datasets/Real+estate+valuation+data+set.

[9] https://www.kaggle.com/uciml/istanbul-stock-exchange/.

[10] https://www.kaggle.com/mohansacharya/graduate-admissions.

provides data on diabetes mellitus history in relatives and the genetic relationship of those relatives to the patient. Of these features *preg*, *pedi* and *age* are grouped together as attributes directly associated with the *person* concept in DBpedia. Skin thickness (*skin*) and BMI mass indicators (*mass*) are associated with *anatomy/physiology* of the person's body while *plas*, blood pressure (*pres*) and *insul* are attributes of a person's blood, hence they are grouped together under the label *blood*. DBpedia and Linked Open Data were used for selecting proper concepts and relations when building the Semantic Artificial Neural Network. The resulting network is presented in Fig. 1.

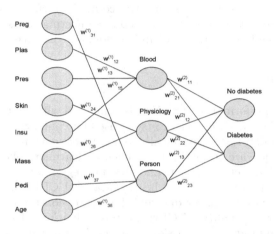

Fig. 1. Semantic Artificial Neural Network for UCI Diabetes dataset - classification.

After constructing SANNs for all datasets, the Weka machine learning software [5] was used for performance evaluation, based on default hyperparameters. The multilayer perceptron implementation was used for implementing SANNs by modifying the network construction phase. Specifically, instead of automatically selecting a predefined structure (typically fully connected networks) provided by Weka, the structure is defined manually for each dataset using the semantics of the related input/output features. Apart from the definition of the network structure, all other components of the SANN implementation are identical to those of the multilayer perceptron implementation in Weka. In addition, for the experimental evaluation all hyperparameters of SANNs and multilayer perceptrons were identical and set to the default hyperparameters of multilayer perceptrons of Weka. This ensures that the evaluation focuses on the effects of the network topology of SANNs: all other things being equal, determine the effects in performance of the network topology defined using Algorithm 1 and the one produced by Weka.

The average performance over five classification and five regression experiments for SANNs and dense multilayer perceptrons using Weka is reported in

Table 1. For classification, the performance metric is accuracy, while for regression, the performance metric is correlation coefficient. The best performing algorithm for a given metric is highlighted in bold.

Table 1. Comparison between SANNs and dense neural networks - average performance for classification (5 datasets) and regression (5 datasets)

Task/Metric	Multilayer perceptron	Semantic Artificial Neural Network
Classification/Accuracy	**81.94**	81.76
Regression/Correlation coefficient	0.659	**0.697**

The experiments indicated that no algorithm was dominant in terms of performance, with dense neural networks slightly outperforming SANNs on average in case of classification and SANNs achieving better average performance in case of regression. Overall, the performance of SANNs compared with fully connected Neural Networks was comparable if not superior on average. This is a quite positive result considering the additional advantages afforded by SANNs: explainability, reduced number of weights and reduced overall complexity.

4   Conclusion

In this work a novel approach for constructing neural networks, called Semantic Artificial Neural Networks, is proposed. The structure of the network reflects the conceptualisation of the application domain by means of a knowledge graph with the objective to create networks that are easy to interpret. Since lack of interpretability is a major issue of neural networks, the proposed approach can be used to create networks where hidden layer nodes correspond to specific concepts and have a specific meaning. In addition, the resulting networks are typically sparse and have fewer parameters, which is typically an advantage during training. Compared with fully connected neural networks with the same number of layers, Semantic Artificial Neural Networks are interpretable, have fewer parameters to train and achieve comparable and, in many cases, better performance.

In future work, we intend to further explore the applicability of SANNs, by also considering the effect of selecting different conceptualisations, which, in its essence, is a knowledge representation problem. For instance, we will compare the different SANNs created based on generic or domain specific ontologies and complex versus minimalist taxonomies.

References

1. Asuncion, A., Newman, D.: UCI machine learning repository (2007)
2. Castelvecchi, D.: Can we open the black box of AI? Nat. News **538**(7623), 20 (2016)
3. Došilović, F.K., Brčić, M., Hlupić, N.: Explainable artificial intelligence: a survey. In: 2018 41st International Convention on Information and Communication Technology, Electronics and Microelectronics (MIPRO), pp. 0210–0215. IEEE (2018)
4. Evans, R., Grefenstette, E.: Learning explanatory rules from noisy data. J. Artif. Intell. Res. **61**, 1–64 (2018)
5. Frank, E., et al.: Weka-a machine learning workbench for data mining. In: Maimon, O., Rokach, L. (eds.) Data Mining and Knowledge Discovery Handbook, pp. 1269–1277. Springer, Boston (2009). https://doi.org/10.1007/978-0-387-09823-4_66
6. Smith, J.W., Everhart, J., Dickson, W., Knowler, W., Johannes, R.: Using the ADAP learning algorithm to forecast the onset of diabetes mellitus. In: Proceedings of the Annual Symposium on Computer Application in Medical Care, p. 261. American Medical Informatics Association (1988)

Market and Technology Monitoring Driven by Knowledge Graphs

Andreas Belger[1]([✉]) [iD], Renato Budinich[1], Ralph Blum[1], Martin Zablocki[2], and Roland Zimmermann[3] [iD]

[1] Fraunhofer SCS, Nordostpark 93, 90411 Nuremberg, Germany
{andreas.belger,renato.budinich,ralph.blum}@iis.fraunhofer.de
[2] Trivadis AG, Elisabethenanlage 9, 4051 Basel, Switzerland
martin.zablocki@trivadis.com
[3] Technische Hochschule Nuernberg Georg Simon Ohm,
Kesslerplatz 12, 90489 Nuremberg, Germany
roland.zimmermann@th-nuernberg.de

Abstract. In this paper, we describe an ongoing research project that aims to detect and trace trends for markets and technologies, hidden behind the vast amount of diverse information populated through the whole world. Our goal is to detect and follow upcoming and ongoing trends in a domain-agnostic and automatized fashion. In this paper we describe our experiences from the initial project steps and our approach using a continuously growing Knowledge Graph. We use a general model that allows us to capture identified mentions and relationships and resolve them into a number of entity and fact classes. Based on two business use cases we present first results where we already gained new insights into various technological developments without the intervention of human domain experts.

Keywords: Knowledge graph · Semantic web · Text mining · Market and technology monitoring

1 Introduction

The idea of this research project is to work on tools, which reveal lines of timely developments by analyzing a "stream" of publicly available information, usually issued on a daily, weekly or monthly basis in public domains. More specifically the focus is on timely monitoring of technologies readiness (or maturity). Those technologies are propelled by a variety of stake holders (as e.g. universities, research institutes and tech companies) in certain market or branch surroundings. Chronologically, such information is first viewed in the form of patents, scientific publications, domain publications and, with some delay in general news relating technologies to market applications and distinctive use cases. In this paper, we describe an ongoing joint research project of Fraunhofer Supply Chain Services (SCS), Technische Hochschule Nueremberg (THN) and Trivadis AG to retrieve such information from different sources continuously whenever it discloses. The project considers continuously information starting from 2018, which report on the e-mobility

A. Harth et al. (Eds.): ESWC 2020 Satellite Events, LNCS 12124, pp. 45–49, 2020.
https://doi.org/10.1007/978-3-030-62327-2_8

domain and retrieve information from those sources to answer the following sample questions:

A. *Which companies may constitute potential acquisition targets or sales leads in the e-mobility market?*
B. *In what stage of development are the existing technologies and which are emerging in the e-mobility market?*

In the early stage of the project we tested Latent Dirichlet Allocation (LDA) [1] to group different documents into topics. Regardless of how well LDA works, there was still a significant amount of manual work required to interpret these results, e.g. by characterizing resulting topics. We further utilized the word2vec method for word embedding [2], leveraging the semantical properties of the resulting vector space to find other companies and technologies that are similar or related to few manually selected ones. Nevertheless, we were faced with the challenge of manually keeping track of the provenance and source text of each entity of interest, since word2vec is agnostic about these details.

Reconsidering these experiences, we decided to use text analysis methods in combination with Semantic Web technologies. The representation of such information as a knowledge graph (KG), by means of the Resource Description Framework (RDF), allows not only to model complex networks of information, but also to infer latent structures [3]. However, constructing a KG form unstructured data, such as written text and providing a common interface for the business end-users is a challenging task.

First, we describe the approach of a general model to integrate entities and relations in a KG and how we extract these entities and relations from a continuous data flow by applying state-of-the-art Natural Language Processing (NLP). Secondly, we analyse the automatically built KG including 3,9 million entities and 54 million relations by applying the sample questions. Finally, we close with open questions targeted to the community.

2 Methods

For market and technology monitoring, we define a temporal development through the three following stages: (I) research: as description of functionality, (II) prototype: demonstration of functionality and (III) market solution: deployment on the commercial market. Different actors and events can describe each of these stages. For example, stage (I) is dominated by actors such as universities and research institutions. The relevant events are described by verbs like study, develop, observe. The focus is not on interpreting each text correctly, but rather on drawing conclusions from the entire stream of data. We use an easy-to-understand model, which is expressive enough to capture the described aspects and reduce complexity to being able to interact with the KG. This approach ensures that on the one hand we are able to disambiguate relationships from different sources, which actually represent the same thing, and merge them by means of a domain-specific ontology. On the other hand, information is made unambiguous without losing the provenance of the information. In addition, temporal changes should be mapped so that trends can be derived.

Figure 1 illustrates our simplified RDF model representing three main components: (1) input documents, (2) identified mentions, (3) retrieved facts. Each component includes metadata such as timestamps and trustworthiness regarding the method that was used to derive the RDF Triples from unstructured text. *Mentions* represent the particular appearances of an entity as a substring of the text, while *Concepts* represent a general disambiguated version of them. The relation between these concepts describes how they relate to each other. In order to merge similar relations and reduce their number, we clustered all relations based on the ones we need as *Facts*. We differentiate between mentions and concepts in order to be able to use a Named Entity Recognition (NER) tool, which can find new instances of specific types of entities in the texts without relying on Named Entity Linking (NEL) or the databases in the LOD it refers to.

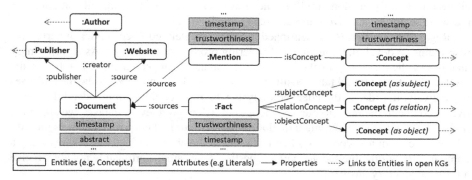

Fig. 1. A simplified RDF model for market and technology monitoring

We collected a list of 1,082 potentially relevant RSS feeds in the field of e-mobility. From these we incrementally gather the new abstracts and integrate them into our KG. While processing the abstracts we are storing the metadata of the documents (such as source and title) in the KG. We then pass the texts through the publicly available Spotlight API [4] which links any recognized mention m to its DBpedia [5] concept c_m and store them in the KG. See also Fig. 1.

For the fact extraction we are currently employing a rule-based approach: we manually choose a set $V = \{v_1, ..., v_n\}$ of verbs of interest (e.g. buy, sell, produce,...) and look at their neighbors when considering the graph of synonyms built from WordNet [6]. This way we build $C_1, ..., C_k$ classes of verbs with similar meaning to ones representing events meaningful for market and technology monitoring. To detect the three stages of technologies' lifecycles described in the opening of this section we used k = 3, with C_1 being a similarity class for the verb "develop", C_2 for "test" and C_3 for "order". We then use NLTK's part-of-speech tagger [7] to identify in the text corpus triples of the form s, v_j, o, where s and o are mentions that have the grammatical function of subject and object in the sentence while v_j is an element of V. We can finally create the corresponding *Fact* of the form c_s, $C(v_j)$, c_o, where $C(v_j)$ is the class of verb v_j, and reinsert this into the graph, for example in the form depicted in Fig. 1. This allows us to query for facts between relevant entities somewhat independently of the particular formulation used to describe them in the original text.

For interacting and monitoring the temporal changes, we define Sparql queries which are made available via a REST API of the KG database to a standard Business Intelligence Frontend. Due to the general model, the interacting remains small in its output triple size for monitoring at larger scales.

3   Insights and Future Research

In this section, we report our first results produced out of 452,549 abstracts about e-mobility from April to September 2019.

To answer question A, we analyzed data such as type and size of a company, which was provided by the disambiguated DBpedia concepts. The Semantic Web structure allowed us to analyze along multiple meaningful dimensions, e.g. find all companies in the same sector as any given (already recognized) company.

Regarding question B, as mentioned in Sect. 2 we defined three classes of verbs corresponding to developing, testing and ordering product technologies. As a preliminary analysis of the efficiency of the method, we manually checked a small number of the produced facts and found false-positive rates of 15%, 39% and 14% for the three classes respectively. In order to do a deeper analysis where we could compute also false negatives, and due to the lack (to our knowledge) of a domain relevant dataset, we are in the process of manually annotating a random sample of our text corpus. The labels identify whether a certain text contains a fact from one of the above defined classes involving a company. Regarding the second part of question B, we are unfortunately not able to give a fully satisfactory answer yet.

Our current plans for future research aim at extending into further market domains and on the technical side to enrich the structure of the KG. We are currently working on including new sources (such as social media), separating NEL and NER steps using tools such as Flair [8], SpaCy [9] and Agdistis [10] to detect also entities that have no current entry in DBpedia. To extract relations between entities in a more automated way, we consider investigating FRED [11] and PIKES [12]. FRED is a service that extracts semantic representations from natural language text offering a REST API and Python library for querying. PIKES is a Java-based suite for Knowledge Extraction that automatically extracts entities of interest and facts about them from text. Regarding the analysis, aside from the data contained in the KG, we want to start leveraging the structure of the KG itself: which methods from social networks analysis could be adapted in order to detect different types of node neighborhoods that could signal relevant features? How can we further integrate and exploit temporal aspects and dynamical changes? How can we define a semantic model which captures something like a "trend" as part of the graph and enables us to detect new and emerging ones?

We provide further information about the presented research project on the website: www.th-nuernberg.de/future-engineering.

References

1. Blei, D.M., et al.: Latent Dirichlet allocation. J. Mach. Learn. Res. **3**(4–5), 993–1022 (2003)

2. Mikolov, T. et al.: Efficient estimation of word representations in vector space. arXiv preprint arXiv:1301.3781 (2013)
3. Kertkeidkachorn, N., Ichise, R.: T2KG: An end-to-end system for creating knowledge graph from unstructured text. In: The AAAI 2017 Workshop on Knowledge-Based Techniques for Problem Solving and Reasoning, pp. 743–749 (2017)
4. Daiber, J., et al.: Improving efficiency and accuracy in multilingual entity extraction. In: Proceedings of the 9th International Conference on Semantic Systems (I-Semantics), Graz, Austria (2013)
5. DBpedia. https://wiki.dbpedia.org/. Accessed 10 Mar 2020
6. Miller, G.A.: WordNet: a lexical database for English. Commun. ACM **38**(11), 39–41 (1995)
7. Natural Language Toolkit. https://www.nltk.org/book/ch05.html. Accessed 10 Mar 2020
8. Akbik, A., et al.: Contextual string embeddings for sequence labeling. In 27th International Conference on Computational Linguistics, pp. 1638–1649 (2018)
9. SpaCy. https://spacy.io/models. Accessed 15 Jan 2020
10. Usbeck. R, et al.: AGDISTIS - agnostic disambiguation of named entities using linked open data. In: ECAI 2014, pp. 1113–1114 (2014)
11. Gangemi, A., et al.: Semantic web machine reading with FRED. Semant. Web J. **8**(6), 873–893 (2017)
12. Corcoglioniti, F., et al.: Frame-based ontology population with PIKES. IEEE Trans. Knowl. Data Eng. **28**(12), 3261–3275 (2016)

A Collection of Benchmark Data Sets for Knowledge Graph-Based Similarity in the Biomedical Domain

Carlota Cardoso[1]([✉]), Rita T. Sousa[1], Sebastian Köhler[2], and Catia Pesquita[1]

[1] LASIGE, Faculdade de Ciências da Universidade de Lisboa, Lisbon, Portugal
{cmacardoso,risousa,clpesquita}@ciencias.ulisboa.pt
[2] Ada Health GmbH, Berlin, Germany
http://monarchinitiative.org

Abstract. The ability to compare entities within a knowledge graph is a cornerstone technique for several applications, ranging from the integration of heterogeneous data to machine learning. It is of particular importance in biomedical applications such as prediction of protein-protein interactions, associations between diseases and genes, cellular localization of proteins, among others. However, building a gold standard data set to support their evaluation is non-trivial, due to size, diversity and complexity of biomedical knowledge graphs.

We present a collection of 21 benchmark data sets that aim at circumventing the difficulties in building benchmarks for large biomedical knowledge graphs by exploiting proxies for biomedical entity similarity. These data sets include data from two successful biomedical ontologies, the Gene Ontology and the Human Phenotype Ontology, and explore proxy similarities based on protein and gene properties. Data sets have varying sizes and cover four different species at different levels of annotation completion. For each data set we also provide semantic similarity computations with state of the art representative measures. Available at: https://github.com/liseda-lab/kgsim-benchmark.

1 Introduction

Nearly all domains of human endeavour are responsible for producing large amounts of complex data, and the life sciences domain is a good example of this: high throughput techniques in genomics and proteomics produce large amounts of complex and unstructured data about the function, regulation and interaction of genes and proteins. This was a strong motivator for the adoption of ontologies, as the result of tremendous effort to make data understandable by both humans and machines. The ability to describe complex entities resorting to ontologies supports the computation of semantic similarity (SS) between entities. Several tasks can be supported by these metrics, in fact, entity similarity is an integral part of many machine learning techniques. For instance, SS has been successfully applied to prediction of protein-protein interaction [8] and clustering [5]. A semantic similarity measure (SSM) is a function that, given two ontology

© Springer Nature Switzerland AG 2020
A. Harth et al. (Eds.): ESWC 2020 Satellite Events, LNCS 12124, pp. 50–55, 2020.
https://doi.org/10.1007/978-3-030-62327-2_9

classes or two sets of classes describing two individuals, returns a numerical value reflecting the closeness in meaning between them [11]. There are several measures available [11] and each formalizes similarity in a slightly different way. However, determining the best measure for each application is still an open question since there is no gold standard. One possible solution is to compare SSMs to proxies of similarity that compare entities through different lenses. For instance, two proteins can be compared via their sequence, structure or common metabolic pathways. These can be used to assess how well SSMs capture entity similarity.

We present a collection of 21 benchmark data sets that aim at circumventing the difficulties in building benchmarks for large biomedical knowledge graphs (KGs) by exploiting proxies for biomedical entity similarity. These data sets are grouped according to the KG and proxy measures they are based on and have a wide range of sizes, from a few hundreds to over 150 thousand pairs.

2   Related Work

Building a gold standard data set to support semantic similarity evaluation is not trivial. Accomplishing this manually is extremely time consuming and existing manual gold standards are very small compared to the size of the ontologies they correspond to. For instance, Pedersen et al. [9] created a set of only 30 term pairs extracted from a universe of over 1 million of biomedical concepts from UMLS. To mitigate this challenge, some semantic web related applications have turned to crowd-sourcing (e.g.. ontology matching [4]), which brings with it a series of new challenges. The evaluation task can be inherently biased towards a particular viewpoint of the domain and is highly dependent on the ability to provide crowd-sourced workers with enough information to make a decision.

In previous works, we developed CESSM [12], a tool for the evaluation of new SSMs through comparison with previously published ones, and considering their relation to different similarity proxies. CESSM has been adopted by the community and used to evaluate several novel SSMs. Overtime some limitations of its use have been identified, namely being limited to a single ontology and being focused on a single functional perspective (molecular function similarity).

Finally, there are related contributions in the area of benchmark data for link prediction [3] and classification in KGs [13]. KG-based SS can be applied in these contexts, but these benchmark data sets do not support a direct evaluation of SSMs.

3   Building the Benchmark Data Sets

Each benchmark data set is made up of several pairs of biomedical entities (e.g. proteins or genes) and their respective state of the art SS and proxy similarity values. In building them, the first step is to select features for the entities and pairs. Entities should be as thoroughly described within the context of the ontology as possible, while pairs should capture the full spectrum of similarity values throughout.

Calculating the SS between entities described by sets of ontology classes usually combines a measure of the information content (IC) of a class (i.e. a measure of its specificity) and an approach to calculate similarity between all the classes. 2 different approaches for the calculation of entity SS were combined with 2 methods for IC calculation [11] to arrive at four state of the art SSMs employed in the data sets: BMA_{Resnik}, BMA_{Seco}, $simGIC_{Resnik}$ and $simGIC_{Seco}$.

3.1   Protein Benchmark Data Sets

The majority of research into SSMs in bioinformatics is applied to the Gene Ontology (GO) [10], the most widely adopted ontology by the life sciences community, which covers three distinct aspects of gene product's roles: molecular function, cellular component and biological process [2]. We built two types of protein benchmark data sets: one based on molecular functional similarity and another based on protein-protein interactions (PPIs). To ensure enough information, the data sets are constituted by protein pairs, in which each protein is sufficiently annotated with GO classes and with the necessary information to compute proxy similarity[1]. This results in two annotation levels: *One aspect*, where all proteins are well annotated in at least one GO aspect; and its subset, *All aspects*, where all proteins are well annotated in all GO aspects.

We employ three proxies of protein similarity based on their biological properties: (1) **sequence similarity** measures the relationship between two protein sequences; (2) **molecular function similarity** compares the functional regions that exist in each protein sequence; and (3) **protein-protein interaction** that determines if the proteins interact or not. In the molecular function similarity data sets, we employ (1) and (2), whereas in the protein-protein interactions data sets, we employ (1) and (3). The proposed methodology was employed to produce the data sets described in Table 1.

Table 1. Summary of the Protein benchmarks

Species	Protein-protein interaction				Molecular function			
	One aspect		*All aspects*		*One aspect*		*All aspects*	
	Proteins	Pairs	Proteins	Pairs	Proteins	Pairs	Proteins	Pairs
D. melanogaster	481	397	335	270	7.494	53.797	5.810	52.460
E. coli	371	738	264	428	1.250	4.623	748	1.813
H. sapiens	7.644	44.677	7.149	42.204	1.3604	60.176	12.487	60.163
S. cerevisae	3.874	34.772	2.959	21.577	4.783	42.192	3.660	30.747
All	12.370	80.584	10.707	64.479	27.131	158.512	22.705	142.736

---

[1] PPI information retrieved from the data sets used in [14]. Molecular function similarity is based on Pfam [6] assignments to proteins.

Table 2. Pearson correlation coefficient between semantic similarity ($simGIC_{Seco}$) and biological similarity proxies for *H.sapiens*

Data set	One aspect		All aspects	
	sim_{Seq}	sim_{Pfam}	sim_{Seq}	sim_{Pfam}
Molecular function	0.723	0.612	0.732	0.620
PPI	0.536	0.422	0.546	0.421
Disease-Phenotype	0.482			

3.2 Genes-Phenotypes Benchmark Data Set

The Human Phenotype Ontology (HPO), another widely used biomedical ontology, provides a standardized vocabulary of phenotypic abnormalities encountered in human diseases [7]. The HPO KG integrates the links between human genes and their associated HPO classes. Human genes without sufficient and specific annotations, or the necessary information to compute proxy similarity were filtered. The similarity proxy selected for this data set is **phenotypic series similarity**, computed by comparing the phenotypic series (groups of identical or similar phenotypes [1]) related to each gene. After selecting the eligible genes, pairs were filtered to ensure the same number of pairs with null, not-null and full phenotypic series similarity. Following this methodology resulted in a data set with 2026 distinct human genes and 12000 pairs.

Table 2 shows correlation values for all *H. sapiens* data sets with $simGIC_{Seco}$.

4 Conclusions

The collection of benchmark data sets we present aims at supporting the large-scale evaluation of KG-based SS. All data sets and KG data used to compute the SSMs are available online[2]. This allows for a direct comparison with the pre-computed semantic similarity measures, as well as facilitates the direct comparison between different works using this resource. For this reason, the benchmark will purposefully remain static for a few years, following the approach used by CESSM [12], released in 2009 and updated in 2014. Parallel updates to the benchmark data sets will include new KGs, with updated attributes for entity selection and new similarity proxies.

The benchmark supports simple evaluation metrics, such as computing Pearson's correlation coefficient between the SSMs and the similarity proxies, but it also supports more complex evaluations. For instance, the PPI data sets also support prediction of protein-protein interaction based on semantic similarity, as done in Sousa et al. [14]. Despite being domain-specific, we expect this collection to be useful beyond the biomedical domain. Similarity computation within

---

[2] https://github.com/liseda-lab/kgsim-benchmark.

KG is a fundamental building block of many semantic web applications ranging from data integration to data mining, meaning the benchmark data sets can be used for the evaluation of SSMs developed outside the biomedical domain. Alternatively, the general approach developed for the creation of the data sets is generalizable to any domain where a similarity proxy can be created, making the development of analogous benchmark data sets outside the biomedical domain a possibility.

Acknowledgements. CP, CC and RTS were funded by the Portuguese FCT through the LASIGE Research Unit (UIDB/00408/2020 and UIDP/00408/2020), and also by the SMILAX project (PTDC/EEI-ESS/4633/2014). RTS was also funded by SFRH/BD/145377/2019.

References

1. Amberger, J.S., Bocchini, C.A., Schiettecatte, F., Scott, A.F., Hamosh, A.: Omim.org: online mendelian inheritance in man (OMIM®), an online catalog of human genes and genetic disorders. Nucleic Acids Res. **43**(D1), D789–D798 (2014)
2. Ashburner, M., et al.: Gene ontology: tool for the unification of biology. Nat. Genet. **25**(1), 25–29 (2000)
3. Bordes, A., Usunier, N., Garcia-Duran, A., Weston, J., Yakhnenko, O.: Translating embeddings for modeling multi-relational data. In: Advances in Neural Information Processing Systems, pp. 2787–2795 (2013)
4. Cheatham, M., Hitzler, P.: Conference v2. 0: an uncertain version of the OAEI conference benchmark. In: International Semantic Web Conference, pp. 33–48 (2014)
5. Chen, J., Liu, Y., Sam, L., Li, J., Lussier, Y.: Evaluation of high-throughput functional categorization of human disease genes. BMC Bioinform. **8**(Suppl 3), S7 (2007)
6. El-Gebali, S., Mistry, J., Bateman, A., Eddy, S.R., Luciani, A., et al.: The Pfam protein families database in 2019. Nucleic Acids Res. **47**(D1), D427–D432 (2018)
7. Köhler, S., Carmody, L., Vasilevsky, N., Jacobsen, J.O.B., Danis, D., et al.: Expansion of the Human Phenotype Ontology (HPO) knowledge base and resources. Nucleic Acids Res. **47**(D1), D1018–D1027 (2018)
8. Maetschke, S.R., Simonsen, M., Davis, M.J., Ragan, M.A.: Gene ontology-driven inference of protein-protein interactions using inducers. Bioinformatics **28**(1), 69–75 (2011)
9. Pedersen, T., Pakhomov, S.V., Patwardhan, S., Chute, C.G.: Measures of semantic similarity and relatedness in the biomedical domain. J. Biomed. Inform. **40**(3), 288–299 (2007)
10. Pesquita, C.: Semantic similarity in the gene ontology. In: Dessimoz, C., Škunca, N. (eds.) The Gene Ontology Handbook, pp. 161–173. Humana Press, New York (2017)
11. Pesquita, C., Faria, D., Falcao, A.O., Lord, P., Couto, F.M.: Semantic similarity in biomedical ontologies. PLoS Comput. Biol. **5**(7) (2009)
12. Pesquita, C., Pessoa, D., Faria, D., Couto, F.: CESSM: collaborative evaluation of semantic similarity measures. In: JB2009: Challenges in Bioinformatics, vol. 157, p. 190 (2009)

13. Ristoski, Petar., de Vries, Gerben Klaas Dirk, Paulheim, Heiko: A collection of benchmark datasets for systematic evaluations of machine learning on the semantic web. In: Groth, P., et al. (eds.) ISWC 2016. LNCS, vol. 9982, pp. 186–194. Springer, Cham (2016). https://doi.org/10.1007/978-3-319-46547-0_20
14. Sousa, R.T., Silva, S., Pesquita, C.: Evolving knowledge graph similarity for supervised learning in complex biomedical domains. BMC Bioinformatics **21**(1), 6 (2020)

REWARD: Ontology for Reward Schemes

Ioannis Chrysakis[1,3]([✉]), Giorgos Flouris[1], Theodore Patkos[1],
Anastasia Dimou[2], and Ruben Verborgh[2]

[1] FORTH, Institute of Computer Science, Heraklion, Greece
{hrysakis,fgeo,patkos}@ics.forth.gr
[2] IDLab, Department of Electronics and Information Systems, UGent – imec,
Ghent, Belgium
{anastasia.dimou,ruben.verborgh}@ugent.be
[3] UGent – imec, Ghent, Belgium
ioannis.chrysakis@ugent.be

Abstract. Rewarding people is common in several contexts, such as
human resource management and crowdsourcing applications. However,
designing a reward strategy is not straightforward, as it requires considering different parameters. These parameters include, for example,
management of rewarding tasks and identifying critical features, such
as the type of rewards and possibilities such as gamification. Moreover,
the lack of a common terminology introduces the problem of communication among experts and prevents integration among different reward
strategies. An ontology can offer a common understanding among domain
experts and flexible management of rewarding parameters. Apart from
that, an ontology can also help in the interrelationship and integration
between different reward schemes employed by different service providers.
In this paper, we present REWARD, a general-purpose ontology for capturing various common features of diverse reward schemes. This ontology is a result of the CAP-A European project and its application to the
crowdsourcing domain, but it is designed to cover different needs and
domains.

1 Introduction

Rewarding is a common strategy for improving people's effectiveness in different
domains, such as business[1], games [5], applications and services [2], or organizational workflows [7]. A successful reward strategy significantly improves the
engagement of the applied target audience [1]. For example, by rewarding specific
tasks' accomplishment, user loyalty increases[2], and continuous growth, recurring
engagement and personal or team improvement are ensured [5].

Although studies analyze features of successful reward strategies [6,9], most
are tailor-made for specific target audience needs. Domain experts design a
reward strategy from scratch, even though it is not straightforward as it requires

---

[1] https://www.shopify.com/enterprise/ecommerce-loyalty-programs.
[2] https://www.justuno.com/blog/how-to-effectively-use-loyalty-programs-to-increas
e-customer-retention/.

© Springer Nature Switzerland AG 2020
A. Harth et al. (Eds.): ESWC 2020 Satellite Events, LNCS 12124, pp. 56–60, 2020.
https://doi.org/10.1007/978-3-030-62327-2_10

redesigning and adapting to the specific target audience. Moreover, the lack of a common terminology introduces the problem of communication among experts and prevents integration among different reward strategies.

A *conceptual model* [10] can help domain experts in the design process, by setting a well-defined terminology, and in the combination of reward strategies. One way of implementing a conceptual model is to build an ontology. An ontology helps as well in the flexible adaptation of new features in any applied reward strategy and can enable integration among different service providers. Thus, a general-purpose ontology affects different beneficiaries, from service providers to end users. Service providers benefit from the flexibility and interoperability in the design process and actual application. End users may transfer features from one service provider to another (e.g., by exchanging points).

In this paper, we present REWARD, a general-purpose ontology that implements a conceptual model designed to represent a reward strategy. The ontology is published at https://w3id.org/reward-ontology/.

REWARD enhances and facilitates employing a reward strategy, by adopting common features of reward strategies, and casting them to a well-defined terminology. The ontology's concepts and relationships can give an extra level of common understanding, expressiveness and flexible knowledge manipulation through exploiting semantic web technologies. Thus, our proposed ontological engineering process requires appropriate (minor) changes at schema or instance level for applying any reward strategy. REWARD can help improve interoperability and integration among different reward schemes employed by different service providers and define a uniform process for creating reward strategies.

2 The REWARD Ontology

We build a general-purpose ontology that describes concepts employed by reward strategies, such as *Tasks, Points, Badges, Tiers* and *Rewards* [1,5,7,9,11]. For each concept we created a respective class (Fig. 1). Tasks are related to actions to reach conditions to earn a reward. Thus, instances of the class *Task* capture information about the applied rewarding actions per reward strategy.

Tasks can be distinguished to *Platform-Based* and *Point-based* following a platform and user-centric approach respectively [11]. The former is related to the users' interaction with the applied system (platform) that is initiated by the service provider. In this case the rewarding is based on exclusive user's interaction with this platform, by following specific workflow scenarios. The latter is accomplished by the user to earn points due to execution of defined tasks. This distinction allows us to support tasks that are not necessarily bound to the applied platform or do not require a specific workflow of execution. Moreover, platform-based tasks allow the service provider to define specific tasks that are critical for the optimal performance of the system, and assign them to specific users; this differentiates platform-based tasks from point-based ones, which are freely selected by users without any prompt or encouragement by the system. These categories of tasks are represented as respective subclasses (*is-a* relationship) of the class Task. To support different levels of tasks according to various

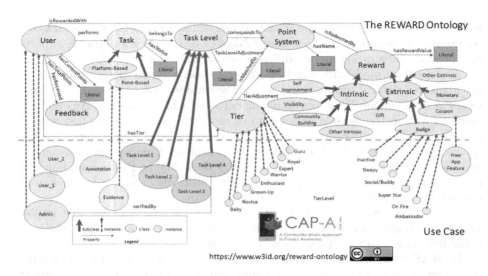

Fig. 1. The REWARD Ontology (top) and the CAP-A implementation (bottom)

parameters such as difficulty of execution we introduce the class of *Task Level* which is connected with the Task class (via property: *belongsTo*).

Points quantify users' effort and as such they are related with the tasks [8]. In any reward strategy, a *Point System* classifies each user to a *Tier* according to currently earned points [8] and defines the redemption process, which determines the types of rewards users can claim with their points. Specifically, this information is ensured to the ontology through the properties *isMatchedTo* and *isRedeemedBy* respectively. Through multiple instantation, REWARD can support different reward schemes per user by applying a different point system. In this case we need to define different adjustment values for instances of Tier and Task Level class through the properties *TaskLevelAdjustment* and *TierAdjustment* respectively. For each point system the ontology keeps a name through the property *hasName*. Apart from the current points used for redemption, the ontology models the total acquired points for capturing users' activity through the respective properties: *hasCurrentPoints* and *hasTotalPoints*.

The users' activity is related to the defined *Badges* which represent the degree of user recognition [4] and is a type of Rewards. *Rewards* can be *intrinsic*, if users' effort is recognized based on internal motivation parameters, such as curiosity and self improvement, or *extrinsic*, if the motivation is based on external motivation parameters, such as earning a badge, a gift or a coupon [5].

Rewards are modeled under *Intrinsic* or *Extrinsic* class [5]. Intrinsic rewards are categorized in three general subclasses: *Self Improvement, Community Building and Visibility* [5,8] and *Other Intrinsic* class to capture rest cases. These can be ensured through the application of playful tasks that enable community commitment and increase peer recognition among all users.

Badges are implemented as subclass of the *Extrinsic* class, which also contains other subclasses (*Monetary, Gift, Coupon*) [8] and *Other Extrinsic class* to capture rest cases. Badges and tiers are modeled as instances of Badge and Tier class respectively. For any critical notification the user receives feedback captured in the respective Feedback class, a fundamental feature for reward strategies [8].

The ontology supports various types of queries allowing the extraction of basic information regarding reward strategies. We present a set of representative competency queries that can be easily answered through REWARD: *(i) What is the tier of a user U? (ii) What rewards has user U gained? (iii) What is the level of task T? (iv) Which types of tasks have been completed and how many are they? (v) What type of rewards have already been redeemed by users? (vi) How many active points does user U have for the point system P? (vii) Given a minimum defined reward value, which point system(s) support any type of reward?*

3   Application

We present a use case implemented in the context of CAP-A project[3] (Fig. 1, bottom part). The REWARD Ontology is used as a general-model for building the rewarding framework of CAP-A which aims to engage users in participating in crowdsourcing tasks for improving privacy awareness on mobile applications [3].

We define *instances* of the *Point Based* class related to the privacy context, that lead to rewarding, such as *Annotation* on Term of Service documents and adding of *Evidence* on a privacy topic. Four task levels are defined to facilitate task management. Each of them represents different level of difficulty and captured in the ontology as *subclasses* of the *Task Level* class (*Task Level 1, Task Level 2, Task Level 3, Task Level 4*). Furthermore, each task level subclass determines the task's visibility and applicability according to the user's tier and the *Point System*. User's tier is calculated according to the earned points.

In the CAP-A project, we use the following tiers: *Baby, Grown-Up, Novice, Enthusiast, Warrior, Expert, Guru, Royal* which are implemented as instances of *Tier class*. Rewards are stored as *instances* of the respective *Reward* class and include free features on mobile applications or acquirement of specific Badges. CAP-A Badges are modeled as *instances* of the *Badge* class (*Inactive, Sleepy, Social/Buddy, Super Star, On Fire, Ambassador*), while the free app features are modeled as instances of the *Coupon* class. The badges are given to users based on their activity in terms of specific task accomplishments, continuous work or gained expertise, but we skip further details due to lack of space.

The Rewarding Loyalty Programs by Air flight companies is another use case where the REWARD ontology can be used. An instance of a travel task belongs to *Point-Based* class. Tasks can be defend depending on the loyalty program, such as booking accommodation, renting a car, shopping etc., and with two levels of difficulty, depending om whether they require verification by service providers (e.g., Reclaim miles). The *Point System* denotes the appropriate

---

[3] https://www.cap-a.eu.

lower point bounds for promoting users to different tiers (e.g., blue, silver, gold tier). The rewards are mostly *extrinsic*, in terms of free tickets, discounts and coupons. Frequent Travelers are instances of *User* class that uses the specific loyalty program.

Consequently, we conclude that REWARD can be adapted easily to these different domains as it is designed to be. Our future plans include evaluation of the ontology in more use-cases and domains. Finally, as REWARD provides a generic model for designing any reward scheme, it leaves room for collaboration among service providers by offering more features on their common end users. The first step for service providers would be to try matching their existing reward schemes to REWARD in order to incorporate features such as consolidation of points or offering combined rewards.

Acknowledgements. This work has been supported by the CAP-A project which has received funding from the European Union's Horizon 2020 research and innovation programme under the NGI_TRUST grant agreement no 825618. Ruben Verborgh is a postdoctoral fellow of the Research Foundation – Flanders (FWO). The authors wish to thank Yannis Roussakis, Elias Tzortzakakis and Elisjana Ymeralli for contributions in the validation process of CAP-A use case.

References

1. Antikainen, M.J., Vaataja, H.K.: Rewarding in open innovation communities-how to motivate members. Int. J. Entrepreneurship Innov. Manage. **11**, 440–456 (2010)
2. Detwiller, D., Sparks, R.: Rewarding users for sharing digital content (2012). uS Patent App. 13/306,917
3. Flouris, G., et al.: Towards a collective awareness platform for privacy concerns and expectations. In: Panetto, H., et al. (eds.) OTM 2018. LNCS, vol. 11229, pp. 135–152. Springer, Cham (2018). https://doi.org/10.1007/978-3-030-02610-3_8
4. Hamari, J., Eranti, V.: Framework for designing and evaluating game achievements. In: Digra Conference. Citeseer (2011)
5. Kavaliova, M., Virjee, F., Maehle, N., Kleppe, I.A.: Crowdsourcing innovation and product development: Gamification as a motivational driver. Cogent Bus. Manage. **3**(1), 1128132 (2016)
6. Morschheuser, B., Hamari, J., Koivisto, J.: Gamification in crowdsourcing: a review. In: 49th Hawaii International Conference on System Sciences. IEEE (2016)
7. Prendergast, C.: The provision of incentives in firms. J. Econ. Lit. **37**(1), 7–63 (1999)
8. Landers, R.N., Bauer, K.N., Callan, R.C., Armstrong, M.B.: Psychological theory and the gamification of learning. In: Reiners, T., Wood, L.C. (eds.) Gamification in Education and Business, pp. 165–186. Springer, Cham (2015). https://doi.org/10.1007/978-3-319-10208-5_9
9. Scekic, O., Truong, H.L., Dustdar, S.: Incentives and rewarding in social computing. Commun. ACM **56**, 72–82 (2013)
10. Wand, Y., Storey, V.C., Weber, R.: Analyzing the meaning of a relationship. ACM Trans. Database Syst. **24**, 494–528 (1999)
11. Yang, D., Xue, G., Fang, X., Tang, J.: Crowdsourcing to smartphones: incentive mechanism design for mobile phone sensing. In: Proceedings of the 18th Annual International Conference on Mobile Computing and Networking. ACM (2012)

STILTool: A Semantic Table Interpretation evaLuation Tool

Marco Cremaschi[1(✉)], Alessandra Siano[1], Roberto Avogadro[1],
Ernesto Jimenez-Ruiz[2,3], and Andrea Maurino[1]

[1] University of Milan - Bicocca, Milan, Italy
{marco.cremaschi,alessandra.siano,roberto.avogadro,
andrea.maurino}@unimib.it
[2] City, University of London, London, UK
ernesto.jimenez-ruiz@city.ac.uk
[3] University of Oslo, Oslo, Norway

Abstract. This paper describes STILTool, an open-source tool for the automatic evaluation of the quality of semantic annotations computed by semantic table interpretation approaches. STILTool provides a graphical interface allowing users to analyse the correctness of the annotations of tabular data. The tool also provides a set of statistics in order to identify the most common error patterns.

Keywords: Semantic web · Ontology · Linked data · Knowledge graph · Semantic table interpretation · Semantic annotations · Tabular data

1 Introduction and Motivation

Much information is conveyed within tables. Just think of the relational databases or tables present on the Web pages. In order to size the spread of tabular data, 2.5M tables have been identified within the Common Crawl repository[1] [3]. The current snapshot of Wikipedia contains more than 3.23M tables from more than 520k Wikipedia articles [1]. The tables may contain high-value data, but due to the lack of contextual information or meta-data, they can be challenging to understand, both for humans and for machines. In order to solve this problem, several techniques have been proposed in the state-of-the-art whose aim is the semantic annotation of tabular data using information extracted from a Knowledge Graph (KG) (*e.g.*, DBpedia[2]). Inside a Semantic Table Interpretation (STI) process, it is possible to identify three main tasks:

1. assigning a semantic type (*e.g.*, a KG class) to a column ((CTA));
2. matching a cell to a kg entity (Cell Entity Annotation (CEA));
3. assigning a KG property to the relationship between two columns ((CPA)).

---

[1] commoncrawl.org.
[2] wiki.dbpedia.org.

© Springer Nature Switzerland AG 2020
A. Harth et al. (Eds.): ESWC 2020 Satellite Events, LNCS 12124, pp. 61–66, 2020.
https://doi.org/10.1007/978-3-030-62327-2_11

Although several approaches deal with semantic annotations on tabular data, there are limited Gold Standards (GSs) for the assessment of the quality of these annotations. The main ones are T2Dv2, Limaye, Musicbrainz, IMBD, Taheryan 2015 and SemTab 2019. Table 1 shows statistics for these GSs..

T2Dv2[3] Gold Standard (GS) consists of a manually annotated dataset of 779 Web tables extracted from Web Table Corpora[4]. Inside this dataset, only 234 tables share at least one instance with DBpedia.

Limaye [4] consists of over 6,000 tables extracted from Wikipedia and the general Web. Entities in the tables are annotated with links to Wikipedia articles; columns and relations between columns are annotated by concepts and properties from the YAGO KG[5]. Limaye 200 [6] is a subset of the Limaye dataset; it is composed of 200 tables annotated using a manual and an automatic process. LimayeAll [6] is another version of Limaye, re-annotated through an automatic process. It contains 6,310 tables and the annotations are extracted from Freebase.

MusicBrainz [6] is composed of a set of annotated tables extracted from MusicBrainz record label webpages[6]. Each MusicBrainz record label webpage contains a table listing the music released by a production company. The reference KG is Freebase.

The IMDB [6] is composed of annotations related to a dataset of 7,416 tables about film extracted from a set of web pages of the IMDB[7].

Taheriyan 2016 [5] is composed of two datasets manually annotated. The first dataset contains 29 tables related to museum works annotated through two different ontologies (*i.e.*, CIDOC-CRM and the European Data Model, EDM). In the second, there are 15 tables about weapons interpreted using the Schema.org ontology.

The SemTab[8] challenge [2] presents a common framework to conduct a systematic evaluation of tabular data to KG matching systems. SemTab is composed of several evaluation rounds and relies on an automated method to generate benchmark datasets. The target KG in 2019 was DBpedia, but other KGs will be used in future editions of SemTab (*e.g.*, Wikidata[9] will be introduced in the 2020 edition).

The discrepancy between the KG used for annotations, the structure of the tables, the various storage formats (*e.g.*, CSV, JSON, XML, HTML) and the absence of some types of annotations makes it challenging to use these datasets for the evaluation of STI approaches. Besides, in the state-of-the-art, there are only two scripts[10] to automate the evaluation. One provides only a command-line

---

[3] webdatacommons.org/webtables/goldstandardV2.html.
[4] webdatacommons.org/webtables/.
[5] github.com/yago-naga/yago3.
[6] musicbrainz.org/label/13a464dc-b9fd-4d16-a4f4-d4316f6a46c7.
[7] www.imdb.com.
[8] www.cs.ox.ac.uk/isg/challenges/sem-tab/.
[9] www.wikidata.org/.
[10] *(i)* Web Data INTEgRation Framework: github.com/olehmberg/winter; and *(ii)* SemTab evaluator: github.com/sem-tab-challenge/aicrowd-evaluator.

Table 1. Statistics for the most common gold standards. '-' indicates unknown.

GS		Tables	Columns	Rows	Classes	Entities	Predicates	KG
T2Dv2		234	1,157	27,996	39	-	154	DBpedia
Limaye		6,522	-	-	747	142,737	90	Wikipedia and Yago
LimayeAll		6,310	28,547	135,978	-	227,046	-	Freebase
Limaye200		200	903	4,144	615	-	361	Freebase
MusicBrainz		1,406	9,842	-	9,842	93,266	7,030	Freebase
IMDB		7,416	7,416	-	7,416	92,321	-	Freebase
Taheriyan		29	2,467	16,006	-	-	-	CIDOC-CRM EDM Model Schema.org
SemTab 2019	Round 1	64	320	9,088	120	8,418	116	DBpedia
	Round 2	11,924	59,620	298,100	14,780	463,796	6,762	
	Round 3	2,161	10,805	153,431	5,752	406,827	7,575	
	Round 4	817	3,268	51,471	1,732	107,352	2,747	

interface, the other, instead, has been integrated into a multi-purpose platform[11] which aims to propose real-world problems as challenges to find collaborative solutions; in this case, the evaluation is provided only in the form of scores.

For this reason, we have implemented STILTool[12], a web application to automate the quality assessment of the annotations produced by STI approaches.

2 Overview of **STILTool**

The purpose of STILTool is to provide a reliable tool for the evaluation of annotations. The evaluation is carried out by comparing the semantic annotations with one or more GSs.

It is developed as a web application with the Python-based Django framework[13] and MongoDB[14] as a database. The code is freely available through a Git repository[15]. In order to achieve the scalability of the application, and therefore improve efficiency and to facilitate the deployment on servers, STILTool has been installed in a Docker container.

An authentication system has been integrated to allow users to have their own set of annotations and GS stored privately.

STILTool is composed of three main parts: (i) loading data, (ii) evaluate annotations, and (iii) compare results.

---

[11] www.aicrowd.com.
[12] zoo.disco.unimib.it/stiltool/.
[13] www.djangoproject.com.
[14] www.mongodb.com.
[15] bitbucket.org/disco_unimib/stiltool/.

Loading Data. STILTool allows users to upload both a set of annotations and GSs. A GS is composed at least by the annotations for one of the three main STI tasks (*i.e.*, CTA, CPA, CEA) in CSV format; a score criterion is automatically defined based on the task and the type of annotation.

Furthermore, a GS has to define its availability to other users: it can be *(a) private* - it is accessible only for the owner, or *(b) public* - it is accessible for all users. A *public GS* has an additional configuration parameter to define how users can access it: *(a) score mode* - user gets only the score from the evaluation (*e.g.*, during a challenge where GS annotations should not be provided to participants); or *(b) info mode*: user gets the score and some detailed statistics and info about the evaluation.

Uploading annotations (in CSV format) require the user to select the STI task to evaluate and the GS for the comparison.

Evaluate Annotations. This section provides some detailed information and statistics about the annotations provided; it is only available for annotations compared against a *private GS* or *public-info mode GS*. Data displayed are grouped by three main categories: *(i)* global info, *(ii)* most recurrent errors, and *(iii)* side by side comparison of the user and GS annotations.

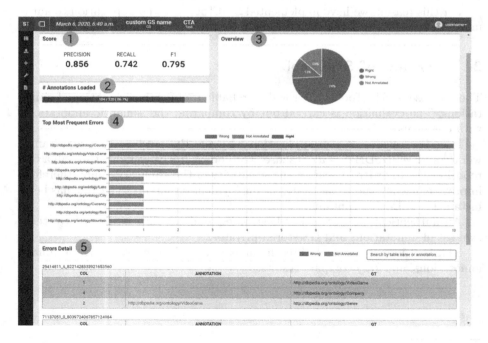

Fig. 1. STILTool "Evaluate Annotations" section: Global Info (1. score, 2. number of annotations loaded, 3. right/wrong/missing annotations chart), 4. Most recurrent errors, 5. Side by side comparison

Global Info. To give the user an overall overview of the annotation evaluations results, some general info such as the obtained score (Fig. 1(1)), the total loaded annotations (Fig. 1(2)) or the percentage of right/wrong/missing annotations (Fig. 1(3)) is displayed.

Most Recurrent Errors. A list of the ten most wrong and missing annotations is displayed using a bar chart, as showed in Fig. 1(4); this visualisation allows the user to visually identify the common error patterns that occur in the annotations.

Side by Side Comparison. To allow a detailed data analysis, the wrong or missing annotations are displayed side by side with the GS ones, grouped by table (Fig. 1(5)).

Compare Results. All loaded annotations sets are displayed grouped by GS and task. For each, some global info is displayed (*i.e.*, the obtained score and the completeness of the annotations against the target GS). A line chart is used to display the score across the different uploads to allow a comparison of the results in time. The data displayed in the chart can be filtered.

3 Conclusion

STILTool is a web application which aims to automate the quality assessment of semantic annotations produced by STI approaches. It offers a graphical interface to analyse in detail the results of the evaluation and to track how a STI approach improves in time. Using the different settings provided by the tool, it can be used as a generic evaluation tool or as the underlying platform for a STI challenge. Regarding this, STILTool will be tested during the SemTab 2020 challenge.

As a future development, we could consider extending the functionality of the tool to cover different fields that use similar Gold Standards and metrics or integrate the system with other evaluation tools.

Acknowledgments. Special thanks to Andrea Barazzetti and David Chieregato for their support during the development of the project. EJR was supported by the SIRIUS Centre for Scalable Data Access (Research Council of Norway).

References

1. Fetahu, B., Anand, A., Koutraki, M.: TableNet: an approach for determining fine-grained relations for Wikipedia tables. In: The World Wide Web Conference (WWW), pp. 2736–2742 (2019)
2. Jiménez-Ruiz, E., Hassanzadeh, O., Efthymiou, V., Chen, J., Srinivas, K.: SemTab 2019: resources to benchmark tabular data to knowledge graph matching systems. In: Harth, A.A., et al. (eds.) ESWC 2020. LNCS, vol. 12123, pp. 514–530. Springer, Cham (2020). https://doi.org/10.1007/978-3-030-49461-2_30
3. Lehmberg, O., Ritze, D., Meusel, R., Bizer, C.: A large public corpus of web tables containing time and context metadata. In: Proceedings of the 25th International Conference Companion on World Wide Web, pp. 75–76 (2016)

4. Limaye, G., Sarawagi, S., Chakrabarti, S.: Annotating and searching web tables using entities, types and relationships. Proc. VLDB Endow. **3**(1–2), 1338–1347 (2010)
5. Taheriyan, M., Knoblock, C.A., Szekely, P., Ambite, J.L.: Leveraging linked data to discover semantic relations within data sources. In: Groth, P., Simperl, E., Gray, A., Sabou, M., Krötzsch, M., Lecue, F., Flöck, F., Gil, Y. (eds.) ISWC 2016. LNCS, vol. 9981, pp. 549–565. Springer, Cham (2016). https://doi.org/10.1007/978-3-319-46523-4_33
6. Zhang, Z.: Effective and efficient semantic table interpretation using TableMiner+. Semant. Web **8**(6), 921–957 (2017)

A Parthood Approach for Modeling Tangible Objects' Composition TOC - An Application on Cultural Heritage

Fatima Danash[1,2](✉), Danielle Ziebelin[1,2], and Emilie Chalmin-Aljanabi[3]

[1] Université Grenoble Alpes, Grenoble, France
{fatme.danash,danielle.ziebelin}@univ-grenoble-alpes.fr
[2] Laboratoire d'Informatique de Grenoble, Grenoble, France
[3] Laboratory of Environments, Dynamics and Mountain Territories,
Le Bourget-du-Lac, Chambéry, France
emilie.chalmin-aljanabi@univ-savoie.fr

Abstract. Several semantic web approaches tackle the problem of integrating multidisciplinary rich content using Linked Open Data. Cultural heritage (CH) is a multidisciplinary domain that contains a massive heterogeneous content that varies distinctly by types and properties. Various semantic web approaches have been proposed in the context of CH, and at multiple integration levels (local, national, international). These approaches focus on metadata schemata integration but give no significant importance to the representation of a tangible cultural heritage object, as a whole entity, and the different parts that compose it. Targeting the goal of the preservation and restoration of CH artifacts, we aim at modeling the CH content focusing on the composition of a CH object. We thus illustrate here an approach of using a part-whole and spatial relations to model the composition of a tangible object in general, and a CH object in particular. To do this, we introduce parthood concepts and properties for representing the composition mechanism, and 7 cases of parthood/spatial relations in tangible objects, with their corresponding logical/ontological relation(s). We implement our approach using OWL2 as the ontological language for our linked open data approach.

Keywords: Conceptual modeling · Composition relations · Part-whole relations · Spatial relations · Cultural heritage

1 Introduction

Cultural Heritage: CH gives high importance for studies on the restoration and preservation of the physical pieces of evidence of the past i.e. CH artifacts. Despite the distinct variation of the CH content, it is semantically richly interlinked. Several semantic web approaches have been proposed, built and implemented to model this content, and at multiple integration levels (local, national, and international). Examples include the Europeana data model [1] (aiming at

© Springer Nature Switzerland AG 2020
A. Harth et al. (Eds.): ESWC 2020 Satellite Events, LNCS 12124, pp. 67–72, 2020.
https://doi.org/10.1007/978-3-030-62327-2_12

greater flexibility and expressiveness for designing a metadata schemata), the CIDOC CRM [2] (focusing on objects' types and 3 main composition relations: consists of, is composed of, and defines typical parts of), FRBRoo [3] (establishing a formal ontology for bibliographic information), cultural heritage integrated into the framework of INSPIRE [4,5] (creating an abstract model of 3 main parts, and representing a cultural material/non-material entity), ABC Ontology [6] (to research models that describe the variety of content -including CH content- that is increasingly populating the web), CultureSampo [7] (a prototype system for integrating the context of the national Finnish culture).

However, most approaches have tackled the problem of schema integration focusing on modeling a metadata schemata [8]. But, they do not consider a CH object itself, its composition, and its different parts.

Our Approach: Hence, we address the goal of preservation and restoration of CH artifacts by building a complete representation of a tangible CH object, and studying its evolution with time and space constraints. For the former part, the representation of a tangible object is illustrated through modeling the composition of it using part-whole relations between entities. The idea is to offer rich top-level semantic contextualization for the composition of tangible objects in general, with the application to cultural heritage objects in particular, using part-whole concepts and properties and spatial relations. This will enable complex semantic and spatial inferences on these objects.

Part-Whole Relations: The study of part-whole relations between entities has been an active area of research in several domains [14]: conceptual and object-oriented modeling [9,10], knowledge representation and reasoning about objects, spatial representations [11,12], cognitive sciences, linguistics, and philosophy [13]. Here in our proposed approach, we plan to use a combination of part-whole relations based on Winston's part-whole relations taxonomy and properties [13], Bittner's and Donnelly's ontological/spatial aspect [11] along with RCC8, the qualitative spatial aspect [12]. The choice is based on the context's needs and the part-whole relations that would best represent it.

2　TOC Ontology

The TOC ontology is a conceptual ontology for the representation of tangible object's composition. It allows the modeling of the composition of any type of valuable entity according to the TOC automaton, that uses parthood concepts and properties. Furthermore, the parthood relations specialize the parthood properties according to the type of the domain and range entities.

2.1　Ontology Formalization in OWL2

As OWL does not provide any built-in primitives for part-whole relations [15], we aim at filling this gap through the TOC ontology. An initial implementation of the ontology is built using OWL2 in Protégé. An OWLdoc documentation is available at the following URI http://lig-tdcge.imag.fr/steamer/patrimalp/TOC-ontology.

2.2 TOC Components

The TOC ontology introduces two main parent-concepts, *ParthoodConcept* and *ValuableEntity*, and two main parent-properties, *ParthoodProperty* and *ParthoodRelation*. Together, they form the main components of the TOC ontology that are used as the elements of the *TOC automaton*. Due to the limitation of space, for further explanation of concept in this section, refer to the online documentation http://lig-tdcge.imag.fr/steamer/patrimalp/TOC-ontology.

ParthoodConcept: It is the parent-concept of the part-whole concepts of the TOC ontology. It encompasses the two primitive classes *Whole* and *Part*, and their subclasses *PartWhole*, *AbsolutePart*, and *AbsoluteWhole*. As the fact of being a part or not being a part is a matter of the perspective upon which an entity is viewed, we base our approach on relativeness. That is an entity A can be viewed as a part with respect some entity B ($\exists isPartOf.B$), and as a whole with respect to another entity C ($\exists hasPart.C$). Thus, an entity is referred to be one of the parthood concepts based on its role in the composition mechanism (compositional function), rather than its nature as an entity. Moreover, one can say that an entity can always be part of a bigger entity, and thus it will be always both; a whole and a part. However, the composition mechanism that we model is based on the closed-world-assumption. That is, for an entity to be a *Whole* or/and a *Part*, it should be explicitly expressed that it has the relation *hasPart* or/and *PartOf* respectively.

ParthoodProperty: It is the parent-property of the part-whole properties of the TOC ontology. It encompasses the two primitive properties *hasPart* and *isPartOf* which are inverse properties. More specifically, depending on the domain's and range's types as roles in the composition mechanism, the sub-properties are *hasAbsolutePart*, *hasRelativePart*, *isAbsolutePartOf*, and *isRelativePartOf*.

ValuableEntity: It is the parent-concept of the entity types in the TOC ontology. We refer to the hierarchy of valuable entities built in CHARM [17], the Cultural Heritage Abstract Reference Model. We extend it by generalizing some terms and presenting it as an infrastructure ontology of entity types in TOC.

ParthoodRelation: It is the parent-property of the part-whole relations of the TOC ontology expressing not only relations between whole and part entities, but also the spatial position of the part with respect to whole. It specializes 7 cases of part-whole and spatial relations depending on the domain's and range's entity-types. Out of which, 5 relations are based on Winston's linguistic taxonomy of part-whole relations (1, 4, 5, 6, & 7) and reused, and 2 proposed ones (2 & 3).

1-Area-Place: is the meronymic relation between two spatial entities. RCC8, the qualitative spatial representation and reasoning calculus, is used as the ontological family of relations to represent the area-place parthood relation.

2-Place-Object: is the relation between a spatial entity and a material or methodological entity. In our model, 4 ontological relations are used to it: contained-in, located-in, located-on, and includes-stratigraphy.

3-Sequence-Unit: is the relation between a group of entities having order (functional spatial/temporal relation) and an entity of this group. Two ontological relations are used to represent it: object-stratum-of and deposit-stratum-of.

4-Mass-Portion: is the relation between portions and masses, extensive objects, or physical dimensions. In our model, we choose two ontological relations to represent it: sample-of and fragment-of.

5-Integral Object-Component: is the meronymic relation between components and the object to which they belong. In our model, the ontological relation sub-object-of is used to represent it.

6-Object-Stuff: is the meronymic relation representing what an object is made of. The ontological relation has-material-composition is used to represent it.

7-Collection-Member: is the relation between an abstract group of entities and an entity of this group i.e. membership. In our model, the ontological relation member-of is used to represent it.

TOC Automaton: A graph representation of the composition mechanism using nodes and arcs to represent the parthood concepts and properties respectively (Fig. 1).

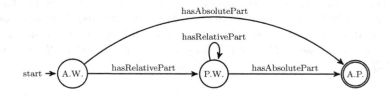

Fig. 1. The TOC automaton

2.3   Discussion of the Model's Application

For the overall structure of the application of the model, our approach is a "Global as View" approach [16] presenting a global ontology, the TOC ontology. TOC uses generic and domain-independent vocabularies that make it applicable in more than one domain. It can be used as a language representing objects' composition, and to which local ontologies -of different domains- can be linked. This link can be seen as an instantiation of local models from the global one. An example of a local model is an archaeological CH model representing the composition of a CH site in general, and Rocher du Chateau site in particular.

For the usage of the model's components, Fig. 2 illustrates an example of the composition of an entity X. On the one side, each entity is classified, according to its nature, to a valuable entity type upon which the corresponding part-whole relation is used. On the other side, according to the occurrences of the *isPartOf* and *hasPart* properties of each entity, it will be classified into a parthood concept representing its function in the composition mechanism.

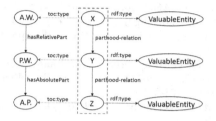

Fig. 2. An example of the usage of TOC's main components

2.4 Evaluating Ontological Decisions Using OntoClean

For evaluating the correctness and consistency of the ontology's taxonomy, we use the OntoClean methodology [18]. OntoClean is used in Protégé with OWL and its reasoner based on the OntOWLClean approach [19]. According to the tutorial of applying OntoClean in Protégé [20], three tasks were performed: punning the TOC ontology, assigning meta-properties to classes of the TOC ontology, and running the reasoner to discover the inconsistencies. This resulted in no inconsistencies which validates the correctness of our taxonomy. The built TOC-with-OntoClean ontology is available at the URI http://lig-tdcge.imag.fr/steamer/patrimalp/TOC-with-OntoClean.

3 Conclusion and Future Work

In this paper, we illustrated the work done in the CH context and highlighted the gap of focusing on the preservation and restoration of a CH entity. Then, we proposed the approach of modeling the composition of tangible entities using part-whole and spatial relations. After that, we presented the TOC ontology and provided an OWL2 based implementation. We also discussed the model's application using an example from the CH domain. For the ontological evaluation of the model, we showed the validity of its taxonomy using Ontoclean.

References

1. Doerr, M., Gradmann, S., Hennicke, S., Isaac, A., Meghini, C., Van de Sompel, H.: The Europeana data model (EDM). In: 76th IFLA General Conference and Assembly, Sweden (2010)

2. Le Boeuf, P., Doerr, M., Ore, C.E., Stead, S.: Definition of the CIDOC conceptual reference model, version 6.2.6, May 2019
3. Le Boeuf, P., Doerr, M.: The FRBRoo, version 0.8.1. https://web.archive.org/web/20070616033312/http:/cidoc.ics.forth.gr/frbr_inro.html
4. Generic Conceptual Model of the INSPIRE data specifications, version 3.4rc3, 05 April 2013
5. Parcero-Oubiña, C., et al.: Conceptual basis for a cultural heritage data model for INSPIRE, January 2013
6. Lagoze, C., Hunter, J.: The ABC Ontology and Model, Tokyo, Japan (2001)
7. Mäkelä, E., Hyvönen, E., Ruotsalo, T.: How to deal with massively heterogeneous cultural heritage data - lessons learned in CultureSampo. Semant. Web J. **3**(1), 85–109 (2012)
8. Doerr, M.: Ontologies for cultural heritage. In: Staab, S., Studer, R. (eds.) Handbook on Ontologies. IHIS, pp. 463–486. Springer, Heidelberg (2009). https://doi.org/10.1007/978-3-540-92673-3_21
9. Varzi, A.: Standford Encyclopedia of Philosophy: Mereology. https://plato.stanford.edu/entries/mereology/
10. Odell, J.J.: Advanced Object-Oriented Analysis & Design using UML. Cambridge University Press, Cambridge (1998)
11. Bittner, T., Donnelly, M.: Computational ontologies of parthood, componenthood, and containment, In: Kaelbling, L. (ed.) Proceedings of the Nineteenth International Joint Conference on Artificial Intelligence 2005 (IJCAI05), pp 382–387 (2005)
12. Randell, D.A., Cui, Z., Cohn, A.G.: A spatial logic based on regions and connections. In: 3rd International Conference on Knowledge Representation and Reasoning. Morgan Kaufmann (1992)
13. Winston, M.E., Chaffin, R., Herrmann, D.: A taxonomy of part-whole relations. Cogn. Sci. **11**, 417–444 (1987)
14. Keet, M.: Introduction to part-whole relations: mereology, conceptual modelling and mathematical aspects. KRDB06-3, 2 October 2006
15. https://www.w3.org/2001/sw/BestPractices/OEP/SimplePartWhole/
16. Ekaputra, F.J., Sabou, M., Serral, E., Kiesling, E., Biffl, S.: Ontology-based data integration in multi-disciplinary engineering environments: a review. Open J. Inf. Syst. (OJIS) **4**(1), 1–26 (2017)
17. Gonzalez-Perez, C.: Information Modelling for Archaeology and Anthropology, Software Engineering Principles for Cultural Heritage. Springer, New York (2018). https://doi.org/10.1007/978-3-319-72652-6
18. Guarino, N., Welty, C.: Evaluating ontological decisions with ontoclean. Commun. ACM **45**(2), 61–65 (2002)
19. Welty, C.: OntOWLClean: cleaning OWL ontologies with OWL. In: Proceedings of the Fourth International Conference, FOIS (2006)
20. Mahlaza, Z., Keet M.: OntoClean in OWL with a DL reasoner – a tutorial (2019)

LandCover2RDF: An API for Computing the Land Cover of a Geographical Area and Generating the RDF Graph

Jordane Dorne[1,2], Nathalie Aussenac-Gilles[1], Catherine Comparot[1], Romain Hugues[2], and Cassia Trojahn[1(✉)]

[1] Institut de Recherche en Informatique de Toulouse, Toulouse, France
{jordane.dorne,nathalie.aussenac-gilles,
catherine.comparot,cassia.trojahn}@irit.fr
[2] Thales Alenia Space, Toulouse, France
romain.hugues@thalesaleniaspace.com

Abstract. Land cover classifications are recognised to be a fundamental source of data to characterise Earth surface and to support change detection analyses. Land cover maps have been produced from different sources as a result of massive time-series image processing. This paper proposes a REST API (and a web user interface) that allows for computing the percentage of land cover classes of a geographic area according to a given map. The computed data is then represented as an RDF graph based on an ontology dedicated to this kind of data focusing on their temporal and spatial dimensions. We illustrate the use of the API to study the evolution of Land Cover on a French geographical area.

Keywords: Satellite images · Computed data · Land cover · RDF

1 Introduction

Earth Observation (EO) is a domain that has rapidly evolved in the past few years. Since 2015, the European Space Agency has launched the Sentinel satellites, which deliver between 8 and 10 TB of data per day, promoting emerging applications, from agriculture to forestry, environmental monitoring to urban planning and climate domains. One fundamental type of data required for these applications and available thanks to EO images is the Earth surface coverage (e.g., water, croplands, urban) or "land cover". Land cover is available as maps produced by different services as a result of massive time-series image processing under different resolutions [4]. Examples of such classifications are the Global Land Cover Share (GLC-SHARE), the European Corine Land Cover (CLC), and the French CESBIO Land Cover. A further step to make use of land cover is to compute the percentage of each type of land cover on a given area (i.e., agricultural parcel), so as to identify the main land cover on this area. Land cover data can then be useful to study crop evolution, the progress of urban areas or the

© Springer Nature Switzerland AG 2020
A. Harth et al. (Eds.): ESWC 2020 Satellite Events, LNCS 12124, pp. 73–78, 2020.
https://doi.org/10.1007/978-3-030-62327-2_13

impact of natural hazards. Moreover the semantic representation of land cover data has been exploited for image annotation improving semantic search [2,3].

In this paper, we propose a REST API (together with a web user interface) that allows for computing on-demand the percentage of land cover classes of a geographic area, according to a given classification. These percentages are represented as RDF triples according to an ontology representing this kind of data together with its temporal and spatial dimensions. While previous works concentrated on using specific land cover classifications (e.g., CLC in [3] or GLC-SHARE in [1]), we propose a modular ontology to accommodate different land cover classifications. Close to our study, the CLC has been pre-calculated and exposed in RDF in different projects, such as the Greece Land Cover[1] and the H2020 Copernicus App Lab[2]. However, to the best of our knowledge, a REST API able to generate an RDF graph describing the land cover from a give polygon of a specific area does not exist. This API can be further exploited in a range of EO semantic-oriented data integration applications. We illustrate the use of the API in a case-study on the evolution of land cover (CESBIO) on a French geographical area. The RDF graph generated thanks to this service is then stored into a local RDF triple store.

2   Land Cover Ontology

In order to represent land cover classes, together with spatial and temporal dimensions, we propose a two-layers ontology. The first layer (top in Fig. 1) forms a core ontology and the second one (bottom in Fig. 1) extends this core in order to represent any EO computed data (e.g. land cover data).

Core Ontology. Spatio-temporal dimensions of data are represented using the GeoSPARQL and OWL-Time standards, respectively. The class *EOFeature* represents geographic areas (i.e. entities associated to a geometry, a closed polygon defined by GPS coordinates) linked to an EO computed dataset (property *hasE-OFeature*). This dataset brings together all the EO data computed on the same geographic area from the same source at the same time. The temporal property of the data set (i.e. the period corresponding to the validity time of the data) is also associated to the dataset (property *hasTime* from OWL-Time). EO datasets are associated to their respective computed data (property *hasData*).

Land Cover Representation. Several proposals addressed the semantic representation of land cover categories using dedicated ontologies, as in [3] where CLC classes are represented with concepts (e.g., ConiferousForest) within a taxonomy, or in the SmOD INSPIRE vocabulary[3] that represents the CLC Nomenclature in SKOS[4]. Here, we selected two land covers with different resolutions:

---

[1] http://linkedopendata.gr/dataset/corine-land-cover-of-greece.
[2] https://www.app-lab.eu/linked-data/.
[3] https://www.w3.org/2015/03/inspire/.
[4] https://www.w3.org/2015/03/corine.

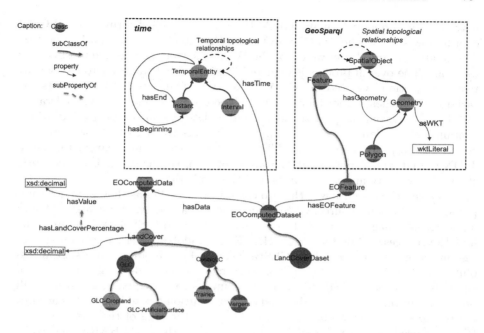

Fig. 1. The proposed ontology: the core reuses standard vocabularies (upper boxes) extended with a specialisation to represent the land cover data.

a global one, GLC-SHARE[5], and a local (French) one, CESBIO[6]. GLC-SHARE is produced by FAO and the last version is dated 2014. It has 11 aggregated land cover classes (e.g., cropland, snow and glaciers, and water bodies). CES-BIO nomenclature contains 17 classes (such as artificial, agricultural and semi-natural surfaces). Our API associates the percentage of the different classes of a given classification to a specific area. To do so, each land cover classification specialises the *LandCover* class with a hierarchy of classes. All the calculated values (linked to a *LandCover* using a *hasLandCoverPercentage* relation) for the same geographic area (an *EOFeature* with a *Geometry*, i.e. a polygon) from the same source (i.e a given Land Cover) are grouped in a *LandCoverDataset*.

3   Proposed API

Land cover classifications are provided as raster images (maps) linked to a text file containing the naming convention of classes associated to pixel values in the image. Each category in the text is given a value that allows for linking the number of pixel contained in this category for a given area. These raster files

---

[5] http://www.fao.org/land-water/land/land-governance/land-resources-planning-toolbox/category/details/en/c/1036355.
[6] http://www.cesbio.ups-tlse.fr/.

may come in different formats. GLC-SHARE uses GeoTiff format and WGS84 coordinates system whereas CESBIO uses JPEG200 format with a Lambert 93 coordinates system. Here, we chose the WGS84 system as it is the most widely used one. The overall process is depicted in Fig. 2. First, in order to change the raster projection, we used the GDAL[7] library. It translates and reprojects the rasters in the chosen coordinate system. The output format is a virtual raster (VRT). The second step is to define a template file in Turtle format which contains all the land cover class names and links them to the corresponding classes of the proposed ontology. The last step is to define a parameter file in JSON format which contains all the values of the pixels associated to each class, the period validity and the resolution of the land cover.

Moreover the resolution of the two classifications differ as they were not computed from the same source. CESBIO is provided annually, and is mainly based on Sentinel-2 images acquired all year long, whereas GLC-SHARE combines various EO sources. While the GLC-SHARE has a global coverage, with a spatial resolution of $1000\,m^2$ per pixel, CESBIO covers France only with a spatial resolution of $10\,m^2$. The resolution is important in order to determine the area of the polygon to be studied. If a polygon contains too few pixels, the result will not be accurate. That is why the land cover resolution has to be selected according to the size of the studied area. For instance, the area of the French city of Blagnac (used in our use case) is about $17\,km^2$; with GLC-SHARE land cover this corresponds to 17 pixels, which are not enough to determine an accurate value of the land cover in percent of this area. CESBIO resolution fits better.

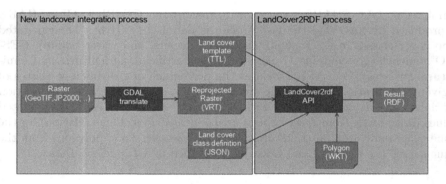

Fig. 2. Process pipeline for land cover integration and RDF generation.

The proposed REST API exposes a service implemented as a Django module in Python[8]. The service has a REST interface, it accepts as a parameter a WKT polygon. The service crops the original land cover image with the given polygon and then it computes the percentage of each class with the number of pixels.

[7] https://gdal.org/.

[8] http://melodi.irit.fr/share/demo_landcover2RDF_curl.mp4.

The response of the server is a JSON document containing the percentage of each land cover class for the area. This JSON document is then used as input of a JSON to RDF transformation process that relies on the ontology above. A web interface[9] can be used for accessing the API (Fig. 3).

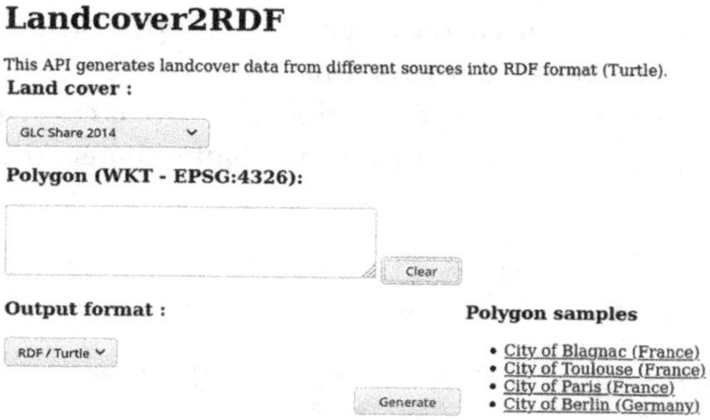

Landcover2RDF

This API generates landcover data from different sources into RDF format (Turtle).
Land cover :

GLC Share 2014   ⌄

Polygon (WKT - EPSG:4326):

Clear

Output format :

RDF / Turtle ⌄

Generate

Polygon samples

- City of Blagnac (France)
- City of Toulouse (France)
- City of Paris (France)
- City of Berlin (Germany)

Fig. 3. Web user interface for generating the RDF graph from a polygon.

4   Use Case

We used the proposed API to compute the percent of CESBIO classes of the city of Blagnac (FR)[10]:

```
curl --data "datasetId=land_cover_cesbio_2017" --data "wkt=POLYGON((1.3473654876713013
43.63352225951501, ...))" http://melodi.irit.fr/rasterStats
```

An extract of the RDF graph with specific prefixes is as follows:

```
@prefix lci: <http://melodi.irit.fr/ontologies/lci.owl#> .
@prefix g-lci: <http://melodi.irit.fr/lod/lci/> .

g-lci:landcover_cesbio_2017_area_dataset a lci:LandCoverDataset .
g-lci:landcover_cesbio_2017_area_dataset lci:hasEOFeature g-lci:landcover_cesbio_2017_area .
g-lci:landcover_cesbio_2017_area_dataset time:hasTime g-lci:interval_1514764799.
g-lci:landcover_cesbio_2017_area_dataset lci:hasData g-lci:landcover_cesbio_2017_area_cultureEte.
g-lci:landcover_cesbio_2017_area a lci:EOFeature .
g-lci:lc_cesbio_2017_area geo:hasGeometry g-lci:lc_cesbio_2017_area_geo .
g-lci:lc_cesbio_2017_area_geo geo:asWKT "POLYGON((1.3473654876713013 43.63352225951501, ...))" .
g-lci:interval_1514764799 time:hasBeginning g-lci:instant_1483228801 .
g-lci:interval_1514764799 time:hasEnd g-lci:instant_1483228802 .
g-lci:instant_1483228801 time:inXSDDateTime "2017-01-01T00:00:01"^^xsd:dateTime .
g-lci:instant_1483228802 time:inXSDDateTime "2017-12-31T23:59:59.999000"^^xsd:dateTime .
g-lci:landcover_cesbio_2017_area_cultureEte a lci:CESBIO-CultureEte .
g-lci:landcover_cesbio_2017_area_cultureEte lci:hasLandCoverPercentage "3.9903"^^xsd:decimal .
```

We use the API for retrieving the RDF graph for the specific entity (geometry of the city of Blagnac in our use case) and store it into an RDF triplestore. Then,

---

[9] http://melodi.irit.fr/share/demo_landcover2rdf.webm.
[10] Full query at http://melodi.irit.fr/rasterStats?query-blagnac.

thanks to its geometry, we linked the corresponding entity to the one in INSEE dataset and generate an OWL *sameAs* relation).

To study the land cover evolution in terms of vegetation and urban cover we chose some classes for vegetation such as *Culture Ete, Culture Hiver, Foret Conifere, Foret Feuillus*, and for urban such as *Urbain Dense, Urbain Diffus*. By grouping these classes and by integrating the land cover maps from 2016 and 2017 we query the computed data with SPARQL and show the evolution of the vegetation and urbanisation over one year for Blagnac (Fig. 4). We can observe a decrease in vegetation coverage while the urban cover percentages have increased, which can be corroborated by the urban expansion in this area.

lcTimeStart	lcTimeEnd	adminInsee	name	totalVegetationCESBIO	totalUrbanCESBIO
2016-01-01T00:00:01	2016-12-31T23:59:59.999	http://id.insee.fr/geo/commune/31069	"Blagnac"@fr	33.0485	59.4996
2017-01-01T00:00:01	2017-12-31T23:59:59.999	http://id.insee.fr/geo/commune/31069	"Blagnac"@fr	31.3683	62.988

Fig. 4. Result of the SPARQL query for the CESBIO over the geometry of Blagnac.

5   Conclusions

Computing land cover percentages on selected areas is of interest in a large range of semantic applications exploiting EO observations. We designed an API that implements such a service using the land cover classification selected by the user according to the country under study and to the size of the areas of interest. This flexibility is obtained thanks to an ontology that represents land cover classes, their location and dates. The calculated land cover values are represented as RDF triples using this ontology. For future work, we plan to other classifications such as CLC and to align the various classifications versions. A new feature of the API will allow the user to add a new land cover of his choice. The user shall provide a template file that contains the different land cover classes and the associate values in order to integrate it in the API.

References

1. Arenas, H., Aussenac-Gilles, N,. Comparot, C., Trojahn, C.: Relations topologiques pour l'intégration sémantique de données et images d'observation de la terre. In: Actes du XXXVIème Congrès INFORSID, pp. 63–78 (2018)
2. Dumitru, C., Schwarz, G., Datcu, M.: Land cover semantic annotation derived from high-resolution SAR images. IEEE J. Sel. Top. Appl. Earth Obs. Remote. Sens. 9(6), 2215–2232 (2016)
3. Espinoza-Molina, D., et al.: Very-high-resolution SAR images and linked open data analytics based on ontologies. IEEE J. Sel. Top. Appl. Earth Obs. Remote. Sens. 8(4), 1696–1708 (2015)
4. Lambin, E., Geist, H.: Land-Use and Land-Cover Change. Springer, Heidelberg (2006). https://doi.org/10.1007/3-540-32202-7

N3X: Notation3 with SPARQL Expressions

Matthias Farnbauer-Schmidt[(✉)] [ID], Victor Charpenay [ID], and Andreas Harth [ID]

Chair of Technical Information Systems,
Friedrich-Alexander Universität Erlangen-Nürnberg, Nuremberg, Germany
{matthias.farnbauer-schmidt,victor.charpenay,andreas.harth}@fau.de

Abstract. Writing calculations with many intermediate steps in Notation3 (N3) rules is complex and verbose. This issue is addressed by extending N3 with SPARQL expressions. In this paper, we introduce and evaluate the syntax of this approach, called N3X. In our examples N3X reduces the number of triples in calculation heavy N3 rules by 30%, the number of triples with a *math:**-predicate by 65% and the number of non-blank characters by 24.4% on average.

Keywords: Notation3 · N3X · SPARQL expressions

1 Introduction

Notation3 (N3) is a logical framework for the Semantic Web [2]. Originally designed as a more readable syntax for humans (compared to RDF/XML). It also includes N3 Logic, an extension to RDF by universally quantified variables and quoted graphs. The latter, called formulae, allow to express statements about graphs. Existentially quantified variables are already included in RDF as blank nodes. The combination of quoted graphs, universally quantified variables and the predicate *log:implies* enables users to express first-order logic in N3. In addition, predicates for logical relationships and for retrieving information from the Web are given.

The serialization format Turtle, derived from N3, is nowadays widely used to present RDF in an human-readable way. However, the adoption of N3 Logic lags behind [1].

The adoption of the Semantic Web in the Internet of Things causes an increase of numeric data in RDF graphs [5]. However, writing arithmetic calculations in N3 is cumbersome. Besides *log:implies*, N3 provides further built-in predicates to perform calculations during rule evaluation. The use of predicates dictates that for each calculation step one statement must be provided. For complex expressions, this becomes increasingly error-prone and verbose.

In this paper we tackle this issue by extending the definition of N3 terms to SPARQL expressions [4]. This extension, called Notation3 Expressions (N3X), allows one to nest expressions and write less triples overall. Furthermore, this supports N3's objective of human-readability.

© Springer Nature Switzerland AG 2020
A. Harth et al. (Eds.): ESWC 2020 Satellite Events, LNCS 12124, pp. 79–83, 2020.
https://doi.org/10.1007/978-3-030-62327-2_14

Listing 1. Distance between two 2D points as N3 rule.

```
1  { ?p1 :x ?x1; :y ?y1. ?p2 :x ?x2; :y ?y2.
2    ?p1 log:notEqualTo ?p2.
3    (?x1 ?x2) math:difference ?dx.
4    (?y1 ?y2) math:difference ?dy.
5    (?dx 2) math:exponentiation ?dx2.
6    (?dy 2) math:exponentiation ?dy2.
7    (?dx2 ?dy2) math:sum ?sum.
8    ?sum math:sqrt ?sqrt. }
9  => { :result :value ?sqrt. }.
```

To illustrate the syntactic discrepancies between N3 and N3X we use the example presented in Listing 1. It is a rule to calculate the distance between two points in a 2D Cartesian coordinate system. The prefixes of *cwm*, a N3-engine, built-in predicates[1] *math:* and *log:* are used.

The semantics of N3X requires little change compared to N3. In fact, every N3X document can be translated back into N3. Formal semantics are out of the scope of this paper.

In the next section we present alternative approaches to simplify expressions in N3. Then, in Sect. 3 we present the syntax of N3X. An evaluation of how N3X affects the length of rules is given in Sect. 4. Finally, we give a conclusion and an outlook for N3X's future in Sect. 5.

2   Comparable Approaches

In fact, N3's path syntax ! can be used to nest expressions in a similar fashion to postfix notation. For example, line 5 of Listing 1 could be written as:

```
((?x1 ?x2)!math:difference 2) math:exponentiation ?dx2.
```

However, this contradicts the objective of human-readability, especially for deeper nested expressions.

Another approach is implemented in the N3-engine EYE which is based on Prolog [6]. It provides a built-in predicate *e:calculate* that takes an arithmetic expression provided as string, substitutes given variables and passes this to the underlying Prolog instance for evaluation. EYE's test suite makes extensive use of *e:calculate* in computation heavy tests. In fact, this shows that there is a need for a more simple way to write complex expressions in N3.

3   Syntax of N3X

The syntax of SPARQL expressions is taken almost as-is in N3X, up to two exceptions: SPARQL's comparators = and <= are also defined in N3 as predicate

---

[1]   https://www.w3.org/2000/10/swap/doc/CwmBuiltins.

Listing 2. Distance between two 2D points as N3X rule.

```
1  { ?p1 :x ?x1; :y ?y1. ?p2 :x ?x2; :y ?y2.
2    ?p1 log:notEqualTo ?p2.
3    ?x1 - ?x2 = ?dx. ?y1 - ?y2 = ?dy. }
4  => { :result :value math:sqrt(?dx*?dx + ?dy*?dy). }.
```

shorthands, the comparators are replaced by == and =< respectively to avoid ambiguity between expressions and other terms.

In fact, SPARQL's comparison and N3's built-in comparators overlap in their semantics but are not the same. In SPARQL the meaning of a comparator is defined by the values compared [4], whereas the function of N3's comparators only consider the lexical values of literals regardless of datatypes (see Footnote 1). The alignment of both is a matter for future improvements.

The translation of the example in Listing 1 to N3X is shown in Listing 2. The number of triples is reduced from 12 to 8 (−33%) and the number of non-blank characters is reduced from 242 to 126 (−48%).

In Listing 2 the triples using predicates from the *math:* namespace are rewritten to N3X expressions. Instead, of using a *math:**-predicate to create a new variable binding N3's shorthand = for *owl:sameAs* is used. In this context, N3 creates a binding to ?dx (or ?dy) with the evaluation's result of the left-hand side expression.

4 Evaluation

We used EYE's test suite[2] to evaluate N3X's gain in conciseness compared to N3. There are 13 tests in the suite that include nested N3 calculations. To name a few, these range from calculating Pi over calculating the date of Easter to calculating the distance between GPS coordinates up to accounting. In addition, there are 6 tests making extensive use of *e:calculate* that we could not translate due to use of built-in Prolog predicates. Furthermore, we added the example of Listing 1 and 2, a rule to iteratively calculate square root and one for Fibonacci numbers. The results of rewriting those 16 examples are shown in Fig. 1. On average we reduced the number of triples by 30%, the number of triples with *math:**-predicates by 65.2% and the number of non-blank characters by 24.4%. In general, *math*-comparators can not be removed by N3X as they are used to filter solutions rather than calculating new values.

N3X can only remove those triples with a functional predicate but never adds one. Accordingly, N3X is never longer than N3 and the more functional predicates are included, the more can be reduced. In some cases it was even possible to remove all *math:**-predicates (see Fig. 1 cases 6, 8 and 11).

---

[2] https://github.com/josd/eye/tree/master/reasoning/.

The full grammar of N3X and the evaluation's documentation can be found at http://github.com/MattesWhite/n3x.

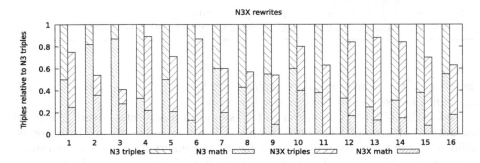

Fig. 1. Results of evaluation. Comparison of triples in rules. Included are the number of triples with a *math:**-predicate.

5 Conclusion and Future Work

N3X introduces SPARQL expressions to N3. Compared to N3, rules become shorter, depending on the number of functional statements included. The basics of the syntax for this extension was presented.

In the future, we will provide formal semantics for N3X based on the *core logic* presented in [1]. With syntax and semantics defined, we will implement a prototype N3X-engine to compare it with existing N3-engines and Prolog implementations.

N3 includes the built-in predicate *log:semantics* which allows engines to fetch and parse documents from the Web to extend their knowledge base. N3X introduces explicit function calls. We plan to leverage this as a hook to retrieve functions from the Web, e.g. in the form of Web Assembly (WASM) modules [3].

References

1. Arndt, D., Schrijvers, T., De Roo, J., Verborgh, R.: Implicit quantification made explicit: how to interpret blank nodes and universal variables in Notation3 Logic. J. Web Semant. **58**, 100501 (2019). https://doi.org/10.1016/j.websem.2019.04.001
2. Berners-Lee, T., Connolly, D.: Notation3 (N3): A readable RDF syntax. W3C team submission, W3C, March 2011. https://www.w3.org/TeamSubmission/2011/SUBM-n3-20110328/
3. Rossberg, A.: Webassembly core specification. W3C recommendation, W3C, December 2019. https://www.w3.org/TR/2019/REC-wasm-core-1-20191205/
4. Seaborne, A., Harris, S.: SPARQL 1.1 query language. W3C recommendation, W3C, March 2013. http://www.w3.org/TR/2013/REC-sparql11-query-20130321/

5. Szilagyi, I., Wira, P.: Ontologies and semantic web for the internet of things - a survey. In: IECON 2016–42nd Annual Conference of the IEEE Industrial Electronics Society, pp. 6949–6954, October 2016. https://doi.org/10.1109/IECON.2016.7793744

6. Verborgh, R., De Roo, J.: Drawing conclusions from linked data on the web: the EYE reasoner. IEEE Softw. **32**(3), 23–27 (2015). https://doi.org/10.1109/MS.2015.63. Conference Name: IEEE Software

CounQER: A System for Discovering and Linking Count Information in Knowledge Bases

Shrestha Ghosh[(✉)], Simon Razniewski, and Gerhard Weikum

Max Planck Institute for Informatics, Saarland Informatics Campus,
66123 Saarbruecken, Germany
{ghoshs,srazniew,weikum}@mpi-inf.mpg.de

Abstract. Predicate constraints of general-purpose knowledge bases (KBs) like Wikidata, DBpedia and Freebase are often limited to sub-property, domain and range constraints. In this demo we showcase Coun-QER, a system that illustrates the alignment of *counting predicates*, like `staffSize`, and *enumerating predicates*, like `workInstitution`$^{-1}$. In the demonstration session, attendees can inspect these alignments, and will learn about the importance of these alignments for KB question answering and curation. CounQER is available at https://counqer.mpi-inf.mpg. de/spo.

Keywords: Knowledge bases · semantics · count information

1 Introduction

Motivation and Problem. Detecting inter-predicate relations in Knowledge Bases (KBs) beyond inheritance can lead to a better semantic understanding that can be leveraged for important tasks such as KB curation and question answering (QA). In this work we focus on set predicates and their alignment. Set predicates describe the relation between an entity and a set of entities through two variants - i) *counting predicates* which relate an entity to a count (of a set of other entities) and, ii) *enumerating predicates* which relate an entity to multiple entities.

Consider a list of counting predicates, {`numberOfChildren`, `staffSize`}, which take only integer count values as objects and a list of enumerating predicates, {`child`, `employer`$^{-1}$, `workInstitution`$^{-1}$}, which take only entity values. Identifying set predicates pairs across the two variants, aligned by their semantic relatedness, such as {`numberOfChildren` ↔ `child`}, {`staffSize` ↔ `employer`$^{-1}$}, {`staffSize` ↔ `workInstitution`$^{-1}$}, has two major benefits.

1. *KB curation* - We can discover incompleteness and/or inconsistencies in KBs through alignments [7,9]. For instance, if the value of `numberOfChildren` exceeds the count of `child` entities of a subject, then the `child` statements for that subject may be incomplete. Alternately, if the value of

© Springer Nature Switzerland AG 2020
A. Harth et al. (Eds.): ESWC 2020 Satellite Events, LNCS 12124, pp. 84–90, 2020.
https://doi.org/10.1007/978-3-030-62327-2_15

`numberOfChildren` is less than the count of `child` entities, there may be inconsistent enumerations. An empty instantiation is also an indication of incompleteness.

2. *QA enhancement* - Set predicate alignments can aid in KB query result debugging and enrichment [1,2]. Even in an event of empty result, for instance, when an entity has no `numberOfChildren` predicate instantiations, but, has `child` predicate instances, we can enumerate the object entities of `child` instead. Set predicate alignments highlight the variation in predicate usage for the same concept. For instance, the `staffSize` of an entity has related results on employees through `employer`$^{-1}$ as well as `workInstitution`$^{-1}$.

Approach. CounQER (short for "**Coun**ting **Q**uantifiers and **E**ntity-valued P**R**-edicates") uses a two-step approach. First it identifies the counting and enumerating predicates with supervised classification and then aligns set predicate pairs, one from each variant, according to ranking methods and statistical and lexical metrics. For further details refer to [3]. The classification and alignment steps are executed offline. We use the obtained results in our demonstrator for count-related SPO queries on three KBs[1] - Wikidata-truthy and two variants of DBpedia based on mapped and raw extractions.

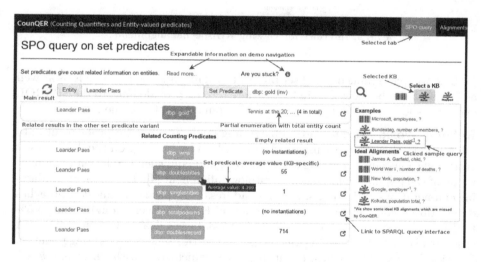

Fig. 1. The interface for SPO queries showing results on an example query. (Color figure online)

Figure 1 shows the interface with results on an example query on the DBpedia-raw KB. The query is on the events where the entity, *Leander Paes*, wins gold (`dbp: gold`$^{-1}$). The main result (set predicate in blue) is succeeded by

---

[1] https://tinyurl.com/wikidata-truthy,   https://tinyurl.com/dbpedia-mappings, https://tinyurl.com/dbpedia-raw

related results on ranked and aligned set predicates (in orange). Enumerations expand on hovering and we show up to 1000 enumerations. A user can check the actual query fired for each row by following the link to the SPARQL query endpoint. Also, KB-specific predicate statistics show up while hovering over the predicate buttons. On clicking a set predicate from the related results, a new query is fired on the same subject and the new clicked predicate.

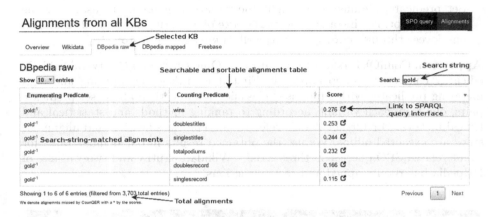

Fig. 2. Interface for viewing KB-specific alignments.

The complete ranked list of set predicate alignments for the three KBs as well as Freebase can be viewed as in Fig. 2. Here too, we provide links to the SPARQL endpoint showing the subjects that have populated facts for the alignments.

Related Work. Schema and ontology alignment is a classic problem in data integration, which in the semantic web is tackled by focusing on the dynamics of entity relations across ontologies [8]. Subset and equivalence relation alignment is one of the popular approaches to ontology alignment [4]. The problem of aligning enumerations with counts, which we address is atypical since most approaches do not target completeness and correctness of KBs [6]. Even though between 5% to 10% of questions in popular TREC QA datasets deal with counts [5], QA systems like AQQU [1] and QAnswer [2] only perform ad-hoc count aggregation function to deal with typical count questions, which start with *"How many..?"*.

2   System Description

SPO Query. The SPO query function provides two input fields, *Entity* and *Set Predicate*, and a KB selection button. The first field provides real-time entity suggestions from the selected KB, based on the input prefix, to the user to choose from. Next, the user selects a set predicate from the set predicate input field. The predicate choices are KB-specific and ordered by i) whether they are

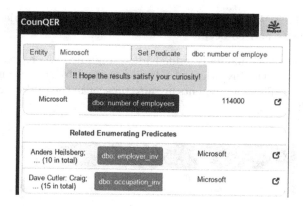

Fig. 3. Query results on the number of employees in Microsoft (DBpedia-mapped).

populated and have alignments, ii) they are populated but without alignments, and iii) they are unpopulated.

Upon execution, the input parameters are sent to our server, where we determine the variant of the user-selected set predicate - counting or enumerating. Then from the KB-specific alignments containing the queried predicate, we shortlist the top-five highest scoring pairs to obtain related set predicate facts. If there are no alignments we do not generate any related query. The server then fires the main query to the SPARQL endpoint of the corresponding KB followed by the SPARQL queries for the aligned set predicates, if present. Once these results are obtained, the server returns the results along with KB-specific predicate statistics, i.e., the average value that the counting predicates take and the average number of entities per subject that the enumerating predicates take.

Alignments. CounQER provides an option of viewing all alignments across the four KBs along with their alignment scores. A user can go through the list ordered by the alignment score or, use the search bar to filter matching set predicates and view their corresponding alignments. Each alignment has a link to SPARQL query API where the user can view the list of subjects for which the predicate pair co-occur.

The main features of the interface are as follows.

1. *Predicate suggestions* - Set predicates are ordered based on whether they are populated for the selected entity and whether alignments exist for them.
2. *Empty results* - If the main query returns an empty result, but, the predicate has populated alignments, CounQER shows the related results. Conversely, if the set predicate in the main query is populated and alignments exist for this predicate, we show the related results regardless of them being empty, thus highlighting potential incompleteness in the KB, w.r.t the queried entity.
3. *Links to SPARQL queries* - Every row in the results contains a link to the SPARQL endpoint, which a user can follow to check the actual query that was fired and also view enumerations of size more than 1000. Alignment tables

also link to the SPARQL endpoint with queries which list subjects for which the set predicate pair co-occur.

We also show some manually added ideal alignments, *i.e.,* the alignments which are present in the investigated KBs but missed by the automated Coun-QER methodology. These alignments are also present in the table with a fictitious score between $[0.9-1]$.

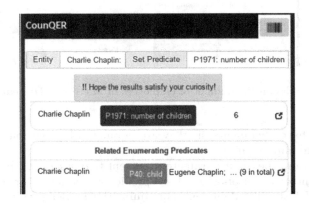

Fig. 4. Query results on the number of children of Charlie Chaplin (Wikidata).

3   Demonstration Experience

Scenario 1 - QA. In a query about the number of employees at Microsoft, CounQER finds the main result from the queried KB, DBpedia-mapped, to be $114,000$ employees. In addition, CounQER returns instantiated facts on interesting enumerating predicates, such as, employer^{-1} and occupation^{-1} (see Fig. 3).

Scenario 2 - KB Curation. Consider the example in Fig. 4, where the user searches for the number of children of the British comic actor, Charlie Chaplin. The alignment results reveal inconsistent information in Wikidata-truthy. While the value for number of children is 6, there are 9 statements for the enumerating predicate child.

Next, we investigate the winning titles of Roger Federer in DBpedia-raw (Fig. 5). Even though a query on the golds won by Federer returns no main results, unlike the query on the golds won by Leader Paes in Fig. 1, the counting predicates doublestitles (2nd) and singlestitles (3rd) give the number of doubles and singles titles won by Federer.

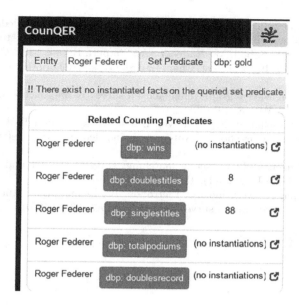

Fig. 5. Query results on golds won by Roger Federer (DBpedia-raw).

4   Conclusion

We demonstrate how set predicate alignments highlight redundancies in the KB schema, enhance question answering by providing supporting counts and/or enumerations and help in KB curation. Utilizing KB alignments to automatically flag inconsistent SPO facts for resolution and highlight SPO facts needing completions is a possible future work. Analysing multi-hop alignments and extending KB alignments towards open information extraction is also worth exploring.

References

1. Bast, H., Haussmann, E.: More accurate question answering on Freebase. In: Proceedings of the 24th ACM International Conference on Information and Knowledge Management, CIKM (2015)
2. Diefenbach, D., Migliatti, P.H., Qawasmeh, O., Lully, V., Singh, K., Maret, P.: QAnswer: a question answering prototype bridging the gap between a considerable part of the LOD cloud and end-users. In: The World Wide Web Conference, WWW (2019)
3. Ghosh, S., Razniewski, S., Weikum, G.: Uncovering hidden semantics of set information in knowledge bases. arXiv:2003.03155. Under revision at Journal of Web Semantics 2020
4. Koutraki, M., Preda, N., Vodislav, D.: Online relation alignment for linked datasets. In: Blomqvist, E., Maynard, D., Gangemi, A., Hoekstra, R., Hitzler, P., Hartig, O. (eds.) ESWC 2017. LNCS, vol. 10249, pp. 152–168. Springer, Cham (2017). https://doi.org/10.1007/978-3-319-58068-5_10

5. Mirza, P., Razniewski, S., Darari, F., Weikum, G.: Enriching knowledge bases with counting quantifiers. In: Vrandečić, D., Bontcheva, K., Suárez-Figueroa, M.C., Presutti, V., Celino, I., Sabou, M., Kaffee, L.-A., Simperl, E. (eds.) ISWC 2018. LNCS, vol. 11136, pp. 179–197. Springer, Cham (2018). https://doi.org/10.1007/978-3-030-00671-6_11
6. Paulheim, H.: Knowledge graph refinement: a survey of approaches and evaluation methods. Semant. Web **8**, 489–508 (2017)
7. Razniewski, S., Suchanek, F., Nutt, W.: But what do we actually know? In: Proceedings of the 5th Workshop on Automated Knowledge Base Construction AKBC (2016)
8. Shvaiko, P., Euzenat, J.: Ontology matching: state of the art and future. IEEE Trans. Knowl. Data Eng. **25**(1), 158–176 (2013)
9. Zaveri, A., Rula, A., Maurino, A., Pietrobon, R., Lehmann, J., Auer, S.: Quality assessment for linked data: a survey. Semant. Web **7**, 63–93 (2016)

EventKG+BT: Generation of Interactive Biography Timelines from a Knowledge Graph

Simon Gottschalk[1]([✉])[ID] and Elena Demidova[2][ID]

[1] L3S Research Center, Leibniz Universität Hannover, Hanover, Germany
gottschalk@L3S.de
[2] Data Science and Intelligent Systems Group, University of Bonn, Bonn, Germany
elena.demidova@cs.uni-bonn.de

Abstract. Research on notable accomplishments and important events in the life of people of public interest usually requires close reading of long encyclopedic or biographical sources, which is a tedious and time-consuming task. Whereas semantic reference sources, such as the EventKG knowledge graph, provide structured representations of relevant facts, they often include hundreds of events and temporal relations for particular entities. In this paper, we present EventKG+BT – a timeline generation system that creates concise and interactive spatio-temporal representations of biographies from a knowledge graph using distant supervision.

1 Introduction

Wikipedia, with more than one million articles dedicated to famous people, as well as other encyclopedic or biographical corpora on the Web, are rich sources of biographical information. These sources can help to answer questions like *"What were the notable accomplishments in the life of George Washington?"*, and to learn about the life of people of public interest. Researchers who analyse event-centric cross-lingual information (in particular, computer scientists, information designers, and sociologists) prefer to approach such questions by exploiting concise representations, rather than by close reading of long articles [3].

In this paper, we introduce *EventKG+BT*[1] – a system that enables exploration of personal biographies based on concise biography timelines. In [6], we have shown how to automatically extract biography timelines from EventKG, an event-centric and temporal knowledge graph [4], using a distant supervision approach. In this approach, we trained an SVM classifier to predict the relevance of the potential timeline entries to a biography. We obtained training data through the mapping of facts extracted from biographical articles to the temporal relations in the EventKG knowledge graph.

We demonstrate the *EventKG+BT* system that implements the distant supervision approach to biography timeline generation presented in [6] and presents the results of this approach on an interactive biography timeline. We

---

[1] http://eventkg-biographies.l3s.uni-hannover.de.

© Springer Nature Switzerland AG 2020
A. Harth et al. (Eds.): ESWC 2020 Satellite Events, LNCS 12124, pp. 91–97, 2020.
https://doi.org/10.1007/978-3-030-62327-2_16

illustrate how biography timelines generated by *EventKG+BT* can help to obtain a concise overview of a biography, alleviating the burden of time-consuming reading of long biographical or encyclopedic articles.

2   Biography Timelines

We assume a use case where the user task is to gain insights into the life of a person of interest, e.g., to get the first impression and a rough understanding of that person's role in history, the notable accomplishments, and to obtain a starting point for further in-depth research. To this extent, *EventKG+BT* shows a *biography timeline* to the user as the core of the visualisation. As defined in [6], a biography timeline is a chronologically ordered list of temporal relations involving the person of interest:

Definition 1. *A biography timeline $TL(p, bio) = (r_1, \ldots, r_n)$ of a person of interest p is a chronologically ordered list of timeline entries (i.e. temporal relations involving p), where each timeline entry r_i is relevant to the person biography bio.*

2.1   *EventKG+BT* Components

EventKG+BT consists of several components that together enable interaction with the biography timeline. Figure 1 presents an example of the generated biography timeline for John Adams, the second president of the United States.

Wikipedia Biography. On top, a brief textual biography and the person's Wikipedia link is shown next to the person's image.

Event Map. An interactive map displays the locations of timeline entries and events in the person's life.

Biography Timeline. The actual biography timeline is displayed in the centre. At first glance, the user can see the person's life span, as well as relevant phases in the person's life. Among other timeline entries, the example timeline indicates the birth of Adams' child, as well as his term as US president. The user can interact with the timeline to obtain additional information.

Related People. Below the timeline, a list of people relevant to the selected person is shown to enable the exploration of further biography timelines.

Events. A chronological list of events in the person's life is presented.

2.2   User Interaction and Data Export

The different components of *EventKG+BT* are connected and are highly interactive. For example, a click on a timeline entry leads to the selection of the associated location, event and people.

EventKG+BT does also offer an export option for the events and relations that underline the timeline generation, which provides access to the timeline facts in a JSON file. Moreover, the exported file contains all the temporal relations that were judged as non-relevant by our model. That way, we envision that *EventKG+BT* can facilitate further research on biography timeline generation from the knowledge graph.

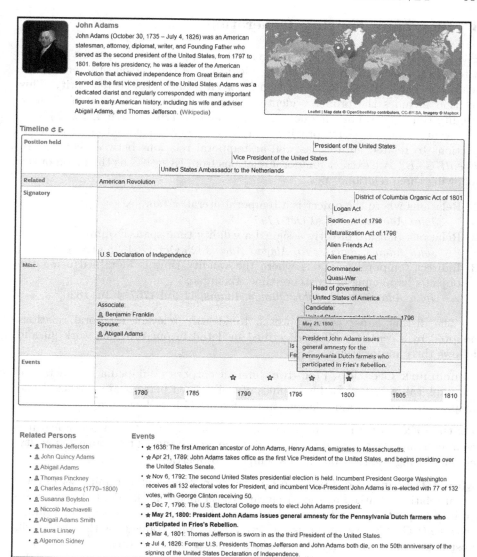

Fig. 1. Biography timeline of John Adams, showing a short textual biography, a map, the generated biography timeline, related people and events. If possible, the timeline entries are grouped by property labels of the underlying temporal relations (e.g., "Position held" and "Signatory", plus "Misc." for all properties only covered in the timeline once). The "Events" section shows textual events related to John Adams, e.g. a sentence about amnesty for farmers.

3   Biography Timeline Generation

The goal of the biography timeline generation approach is to predict whether a temporal relation is relevant to the biography of the person of interest p. A temporal relation is a binary relation between p and a connected entity. This relation includes the property identifier (e.g., "child" or "marriedTo") and a validity time interval or time point (e.g., "March 4, 1797–March 4, 1801").

EventKG does not only provide information about events but also their connections to related entities, as well as temporal relations between entities. In *EventKG+BT*, we extract temporal relations from EventKG as the union of the following three relation types:

1. Relations where the object is a temporal literal. Example:
   – *John Adams, born, 30 Oct 1735*
2. Relations that are directly assigned a validity time span. Example:
   – *John Adams, marriedTo, Abigail Adams* [25 Oct 1764–28 Oct 1818]
3. Indirect temporal relations where the validity time is identified using the object's happening or existence time. Example:
   – *John Adams, child, John Quincy Adams* [11 Jul 1767–4 Jul 1826][2]

The distant supervision approach to identify relevant temporal relations adopted by *EventKG+BT* is described in detail in our previous work [6] and follows three major steps:

Benchmark Creation. From two different corpora (Wikipedia abstracts and biographical websites[3,4]), biographies of well-known persons are extracted and mapped to the temporal relations in the EventKG knowledge graph.

Feature Extraction. From each temporal relation, we extract a set of features characterising the person type, indicating the importance of the connected entity, characterising the relation and its temporal properties.

Model Training and Timeline Generation. Based on a training set of temporal relations marked as (non-)relevant to the benchmark, SVM classifiers are trained to predict the relevance of a temporal relation for a person's biography. In *EventKG+BT*, we make use of two SVMs, one trained on the Wikipedia abstracts and another one trained on the biographical websites.

In addition, *EventKG+BT* also provides textual events (e.g., "President John Adams issues general amnesty for the Pennsylvania Dutch farmers who participated in Fries's Rebellion") that are queried from EventKG.

---

[2] John Quincy Adams was born on July 11, 1767 and his father died on July 4, 1826.
[3] https://www.biography.com/.
[4] https://www.thefamouspeople.com/.

4   Datasets and Implementation

EventKG+BT relies on models pre-trained on Wikipedia and biographical websites, temporal relations extracted on-the-fly from EventKG and additional information obtained from Wikipedia (the brief textual biography and image). The user can generate biography timelines for nearly 1.25 million persons. The pre-trained models were learnt on a benchmark consisting of 2,760 persons and more than 750 thousand biography entries that is also publicly available[5] [6].

EventKG+BT[6] is accessible as an HTML5 website implemented using the Java Spark web framework[7]. The biography timelines are visualised through the browser-based Javascript library vis.js[8], the maps are generated through the Leaflet Javascript library[9], and pop-overs showing detailed information are based on Bootstrap[10]. EventKG data is queried through its SPARQL endpoint[11], and Wikipedia information is retrieved via the MediaWiki action API[12]. To reduce the number of calls to the SPARQL endpoint, biography timelines are cached.

5   Demonstration

In our demonstration, we will show how *EventKG+BT* works and how users can use it to generate biography timelines. We will give the users the option to select any person of interest, but also prepare a diverse set of people with interesting timelines (e.g., John Adams, Angelina Jolie, Albert Einstein, Lionel Messi). By comparison with Wikipedia articles, we will demonstrate how *EventKG+BT* gives a particularly fast first impression of a person's life.

6   Related Work

Timeline Generation and Entity Summarisation. The biography timelines shown in *EventKG+BT* are based on our previous work on automated biography timeline generation using distant supervision on relations identified in textual biographies [6]. In contrast, the biography timelines of Althoff et al. are created based on an optimisation task with hand-crafted constraints and features [1]. In a similar setting, traditional entity summarisation (e.g. [2]) aims at the identification of relevant facts given a query concept. While entity summarisation approaches also utilise semantic information given in knowledge graphs, they are not considering temporal information.

---

[5] http://eventkg.l3s.uni-hannover.de/timelines.html.
[6] http://eventkg-biographies.l3s.uni-hannover.de.
[7] http://sparkjava.com/.
[8] http://visjs.org/timeline_examples.html.
[9] https://leafletjs.com.
[10] https://getbootstrap.com/.
[11] http://eventkg.l3s.uni-hannover.de/sparql.html.
[12] https://www.mediawiki.org/wiki/API:Main_page.

Biography and Timeline Visualisation. Few systems exist that provide visualisations of biography timeline extracted from knowledge graphs: BiographySampo [7] provides Finnish textual biographies that a user can explore using network exploration and maps. The TimeMachine by Althoff et al. [1] gives a compact overview of only a few related entities but does not provide time intervals, or any further information. EventKG+TL [5] is another system built on top of EventKG that provides event timelines. BiographySampo and TimeMachine are limited to a pre-selected set of person entities. *EventKG+BT* offers different views for nearly 1.25 million persons that are accessible through a common interactive interface. Also, *EventKG+BT* focuses on the provision of relevant information: there is no restriction on a limited amount of relations, but *EventKG+BT* also does not overwhelm the user with all possible information available.

7　Conclusion

In this paper, we discussed how knowledge graphs could facilitate research on notable accomplishments and essential events in the life of people of public interest. We presented *EventKG+BT* that generates a concise overview of a person's biography on an interactive timeline from the EventKG knowledge graph.

Acknowledgements. This work was partially funded by the EU Horizon 2020 under MSCA-ITN-2018 "Cleopatra" (812997), and the Federal Ministry of Education and Research, Germany (BMBF) under "Simple-ML" (01IS18054).

References

1. Althoff, T., Dong, X.L., Murphy, K., Alai, S., Dang, V., Zhang, W.: TimeMachine: timeline generation for knowledge-base entities. In: Proceedings of the ACM SIGKDD 2015, pp. 19–28 (2015). https://doi.org/10.1145/2783258.2783325
2. Diefenbach, D., Thalhammer, A.: PageRank and generic entity summarization for RDF knowledge bases. In: Gangemi, A., et al. (eds.) ESWC 2018. LNCS, vol. 10843, pp. 145–160. Springer, Cham (2018). https://doi.org/10.1007/978-3-319-93417-4_10
3. Gottschalk, S., Bernacchi, V., Rogers, R., Demidova, E.: Towards better understanding researcher strategies in cross-lingual event analytics. In: Méndez, E., Crestani, F., Ribeiro, C., David, G., Lopes, J.C. (eds.) TPDL 2018. LNCS, vol. 11057, pp. 139–151. Springer, Cham (2018). https://doi.org/10.1007/978-3-030-00066-0_12
4. Gottschalk, S., Demidova, E.: EventKG: a multilingual event-centric temporal knowledge graph. In: Gangemi, A., et al. (eds.) ESWC 2018. LNCS, vol. 10843, pp. 272–287. Springer, Cham (2018). https://doi.org/10.1007/978-3-319-93417-4_18
5. Gottschalk, S., Demidova, E.: EventKG+TL: creating cross-lingual timelines from an event-centric knowledge graph. In: Gangemi, A., et al. (eds.) ESWC 2018. LNCS, vol. 11155, pp. 164–169. Springer, Cham (2018). https://doi.org/10.1007/978-3-319-98192-5_31

6. Gottschalk, S., Demidova, E.: EventKG-the hub of event knowledge on the web-and biographical timeline generation. Semant. Web **10**(6), 1039–1070 (2019). https://doi.org/10.3233/SW-190355

7. Hyvönen, E., et al.: BiographySampo – publishing and enriching biographies on the semantic web for digital humanities research. In: Hitzler, P., et al. (eds.) ESWC 2019. LNCS, vol. 11503, pp. 574–589. Springer, Cham (2019). https://doi.org/10.1007/978-3-030-21348-0_37

Toward OWL Restriction Reconciliation in Merging Knowledge

Elena Grygorova[1]([✉]) [iD], Samira Babalou[1] [iD], and Birgitta König-Ries[1,2] [iD]

[1] Heinz-Nixdorf Chair for Distributed Information Systems,
Institute for Computer Science, Friedrich Schiller University Jena, Jena, Germany
{elena.grygorova,samira.babalou,birgitta.koenig-ries}@uni-jena.de
[2] Michael-Stifel-Center for Data-Driven and Simulation Science, Jena, Germany

Abstract. Merging ontologies is the standard way to achieve interoperability of heterogeneous systems in the Semantic Web. Because of the possibility of different modeling, OWL restrictions from one ontology may not necessarily be compatible with those from other ontologies. Thus, the merged ontology can suffer from restriction conflicts. This problem so far has got little attention. We propose a workflow to detect and resolve the OWL restriction conflicts within the merged ontology. We reconcile "one type" conflicts by building a subsumption hierarchy. We tackle cardinality restriction conflicts with least upper and greatest lower bound methods. By utilizing the semantic relatedness between two classes, we overcome value restriction conflicts.

Keywords: Semantic web · Ontology merging · OWL restriction conflict

1 Introduction and Related Work

Ontology merging [1] is the process of creating a merged ontology $\mathcal{O}_M$ from a set of source ontologies $\mathcal{O}_S$ based on given mappings. In ontologies, OWL classes are described through class expressions to represent real-world constraints, such as type, cardinality or value restrictions. However, two ontology developers may model the same or overlapping entities to describe the common real-world objects with different restrictions. When two different restrictions are combined in the merged ontology, conflict can happen easily. Finding a compromise between restrictions in the merged ontology is introduced as one of the Generic Merge Requirements (GMR)s in [2]. Representing conflicts has been considered as a significant challenge for integration methodologies for a while. Existing approaches address either data-level conflicts [3], or schema-level conflicts [4], or structural conflicts [5], only.

We develop a workflow that detects and resolves OWL restriction conflicts. We build a subsumption hierarchy over datatypes to reconcile "one type" conflicts. To detect and resolve OWL cardinality and value restriction conflicts, we build an attribute restriction graph. Cardinality restriction conflicts are tackled

© Springer Nature Switzerland AG 2020
A. Harth et al. (Eds.): ESWC 2020 Satellite Events, LNCS 12124, pp. 98–103, 2020.
https://doi.org/10.1007/978-3-030-62327-2_17

with least upper and greatest lower bound methods. By utilizing the semantic relatedness between two classes, we overcome value restriction conflicts.

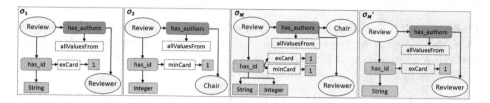

Fig. 1. Fragments of $\mathcal{O}_1$ and $\mathcal{O}_2$, the conflicting $\mathcal{O}_M$, and the repaired $\mathcal{O}'_M$.

2 Proposed Reconciliation Method

Datatype and object properties in an ontology represent the context and the semantics of concepts. They obey a set of restriction rules. Putting them together in the merged ontology can result in either a *compatible* or a *conflicting* merged ontology with the following definition:

Definition 1. *The merged ontology is* **compatible** *if no conflicts exist. If there is at least one conflict over its restrictions, we have a* **conflicting** *merged ontology.*

Conflicting merged ontologiy contains a set of restriction conflicts: (i) "one type" conflicts, (ii) value and cardinality restriction conflicts.

(i) "One type" Conflicts: Detection and Solution. A datatype property should have at most one range. This has been called the one-type restriction [1]. A conflict can happen in the merged ontology when two corresponding entities from different source ontologies have different data types[1]. For example, in the ontology fragments in Fig. 1, has_id from $\mathcal{O}_1$ and $\mathcal{O}_2$ contain two different datatypes: String and Integer. In the merged result $\mathcal{O}_M$, the two corresponding has_id are integrated into one entity. However, the type entities remain separate, so has_id is the origin of two type relationships, which indicates a "one type" conflict.

The first step toward reconciling "one type" conflicts is to determine which alternative data type can be used in the merged ontology. We build a *Subsumption Hierarchy* $\mathcal{SH}$ over all supported datatypes in OWL Full. The subsumption relations between the datatypes in $\mathcal{SH}$ are built based on the general data types conversions[2]. Starting from depth zero at the root, the most general datatype

---

[1] The one type conflict can happen only on datatype properties.

[2] We assumed the OWL/RDF data types could be mapped to Java data types and considered the general data types conversions from: https://docs.oracle.com/javase/specs/jls/se7/html/jls-5.html#jls-5.5.

comes on the next level. After that, more precise datatypes are considered. The depth of each datatype $depth(v_i)$ shows its level in the $\mathcal{SH}$. For example, the depth of Float in $\mathcal{SH}$ is less than the depth of Double because Double is more precise than Float.

Definition 2. *Two data types are* **compatible** *if there is a path in $\mathcal{SH}$ between them that does not go through the root. Otherwise, they are* **incompatible.** *Substitution of two compatible data types $v_i, v_j \in \mathcal{SH}$ with $depth(v_i) < depth(v_j)$, is the type of v_i, since v_i is a more general type in $\mathcal{SH}$.*

If v_i and v_j are compatible and have the same depth, e.g., are siblings, the substitution is the parent type of both in $\mathcal{SH}$. If v_i and v_j are incompatible, then no substitution can be performed on them. In this case, we follow the proposed solution in the early work of the schema merging aspects in [6]. This resolution creates a completely new type that inherits from both data types and replaces the two type-of relationships from the respective property by one type-of relationship to the new type. Thus, for two contradicting values, an **instantiation** of them is a new inherited type of both. The proposed approach is valid when the values of the restrictions are data types, i.e., String, Integer, Float. If they are class types (e.g., Man, Woman, Person), we follow the semantic relatedness strategy, which we will discuss in the next part.

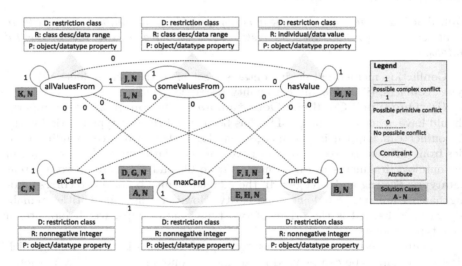

Fig. 2. The attributed Restriction Graph $\mathcal{RG}$ for six OWL Restriction types, showing the interaction and solution cases.

(ii) Value and Cardinality Restriction Conflicts: Detection and Solution. An ontology may restrict the maximum or a minimum number of occurrences that a given entity can take part in a relationship or enumerate the possible values of properties. However, when the source ontologies place restrictions on a property's values, the merged ontology may exhibit conflicts [2]. To detect and reconcile value and cardinality restriction conflicts, we build an attributed Restriction Graph $\mathcal{RG}$ for the six OWL restrictions (see Fig. 2). A $\mathcal{RG} = (V, E)$ is an undirected labeled graph, where V is a set of vertices, and E is a set of edges. The vertices correspond to the values and cardinality restrictions, while the edges show the interactions between the vertices. Each vertex holds three attributes: Domain (D), Range (R), and the properties (P) on which the constraint can be applied. A constraint links a Domain to a Range and can be applied on object or datatype properties. Domain (D) and Properties (P) attributes for our vertices have the same values. Thus, we construct the edges based on the Range (R) attribute, as given by Definition 3 and 4. The interactions between vertices can reveal three different states: (1) no conflict (isolated), (2) primitive, or (3) complex conflict.

Definition 3. *If the Range (R) attributes of two vertices in the $\mathcal{RG}$ are the same, depending on their values and ranges, there is a possibility of **conflict** for them. However, two restrictions with different Range (R) attributes are **isolated** from each other and can not have any conflicts.*

When there is a possible conflict between vertices, the edge between these two vertices holds label 1. Otherwise, labels of the edges are 0.

Definition 4. *A **primitive** conflict is a possible conflict between the same restriction types. A possible conflict over different restriction types is called a **complex** conflict.*

In the $\mathcal{RG}$ depicted in Fig. 2, all recursive violet-colored edges are types of possible primitive conflicts. Orange edges between two vertices in $\mathcal{RG}$ depict possible complex conflicts. Each primitive or complex conflict on the values or cardinality constraints requires a reconciliation method. We developed such methods and derived a detailed solution[3] to all 21 interaction restriction cases given by the cases A-N in Fig. 2. A summary of the resolution is:

- **Cardinality restriction conflicts solution**: We use greatest lower and least upper bound methods adapted to the individual cases.
- **Value restriction conflicts solution**: When the value restriction is on a data property, we follow the approach described in Sect. 2-(i). If the value restriction is related to an object property, we apply the *semantic relatedness* solution, in this way, if two values are semantically related, following the generalization of them, we choose the super class out of them. If the values are siblings, we select the parent value of them. When there is no semantic relatedness for two values (i.e., they are not on the same hierarchy), no automatic reconciliation can be made.

---

[3] https://github.com/fusion-jena/CoMerger/blob/master/Restriction/solution.md.

3   Use Case Study

We have provided a preliminary evaluation of our proposed method. To this end, we conducted an experimental test on three pairs of ontologies adapted from the *conference* domain of the OAEI benchmark[4] provided by the OntoFarm project [7]. We observed how easily the small ontologies can cause conflicts when being merged, as they are augmented with many properties and constraints. We apply our strategy to solve existing conflicts. We then compare the conflicting merged ontology with the revised one with a set of Competency Questions[5]. The merged ontology that was revised by our approach could achieve homogenous answers, whereas the conflicting one returns contradicting answers. This test demonstrates that applying our method on the conflicting merged ontology can provide homogenous answers and shows the applicability of our method in practice.

4   Conclusion

Differences in modeling common entities can cause different types of conflicts when merging ontologies. In this paper, we tackled (i) "one type" conflicts by building a subsumption hierarchy on data types and performing substitution or instantiation on them, (ii) cardinality restriction conflicts with least upper and greatest lower bound method, (iii) value restriction conflicts by utilizing the semantic relatedness. A preliminary evaluation on a use case study shows the feasibility of our method. We plan to extend our experiments on the large scale ontologies in different domains such as biomedicine. Analyzing the effect of caused conflict on the instance level is on our future agenda.

Acknowledgement. S. Babalou is supported by a scholarship from German Academic Exchange Service (DAAD).

References

1. Pottinger, R.A., Bernstein, P.A.: Merging models based on given correspondences. In: VLDB, pp. 862–873 (2003)
2. Babalou, S., König-Ries, B.: GMRs: reconciliation of generic merge requirements in ontology integration. In: SEMANTICS Poster and Demos (2019)
3. Sonsilphong, S., Arch-int, N., Arch-int, S., Pattarapongsin, C.: A semantic interoperability approach to health-care data: resolving data-level conflicts. Expert. Syst. **33**(6), 531–547 (2016)
4. Batista, M.d.C.M., Salgado, A.C.: Information quality measurement in data integration schemas. In: QDB, pp. 61–72 (2007)
5. Fahad, M.: Merging of axiomatic definitions of concepts in the complex owl ontologies. Artif. Intell. Rev. **47**(2), 181–215 (2017)

---

[4] http://oaei.ontologymatching.org/2019/conference/index.html.

[5] https://github.com/fusion-jena/CoMerger/blob/master/Restriction/caseStudy.md.

6. Buneman, P., Davidson, S., Kosky, A.: Theoretical aspects of schema merging. In: Pirotte, A., Delobel, C., Gottlob, G. (eds.) EDBT 1992. LNCS, vol. 580, pp. 152–167. Springer, Heidelberg (1992). https://doi.org/10.1007/BFb0032429
7. Zamazal, O., Svátek, V.: The ten-year ontofarm and its fertilization within the onto-sphere. J. Web Semant. **43**, 46–53 (2017)

Linked Data Creation with ExcelRDF

Karl Hammar[✉][iD]

Jönköping University, Jönköping, Sweden
karl.hammar@ju.se

1 Introduction

Constructing an RDF-based knowledge graph requires designing a data model (typically an OWL ontology) and transforming one's data into an RDF representation that is compliant with said model. There are a multitude of tools built to support these two tasks, and of the ones addressing the first task, several that are specifically intended to enable less experienced users to construct, maintain, or analyse ontologies easily and with confidence: these include WebProtégé [8], VOWL-based visualizations [5], CoModIDE [7], etc.

The second task, transforming existing data into RDF representation, can either be carried out in a batch manner (e.g., using OpenRefine, or an R2RML-based [2] transformation tool like DB2Triples), or at query time (e.g., using databases that provide RDF views over relational data, again typically employing R2RML mappings). Neither is easy for a linked data beginner. In the former case they must typically learn a non-trivial mapping tool and its vocabulary; in the latter case, a server daemon needs to be setup (and possibly licensed), a mapping definition needs to be defined, etc. In neither case is the user guided on how to create RDF data in accordance with a specific ontology.

By contrast, Microsoft Excel is a well-established and well-understood software for data wrangling in industry. It is installed on a large number of desktop machines already, and office workers tend to navigate and use its basic functionalities with minimal, if any, training. Integrating user-friendly ontology-based RDF creation functionalities in Excel enables this group of users to easily contribute to knowledge graph construction; that is the intuition behind the ExcelRDF[1] tool. ExcelRDF was created in the Building Knowledge project, where it is used by real estate owners to populate knowledge graphs using the RealEstateCore [3] smart buildings ontology. Its key design criteria are that it should:

- Be easy to install, update, and start; no IT support should be required.
- Employ a transparent syntax for mapping cells to RDF constructs; nothing should be "hidden" in the underlying Excel file format.
- Support users in creating said mappings from a source ontology.
- Generate Excel files that can be shared across an organisation, even by users who do not have ExcelRDF installed, without the RDF mappings being lost.
- Provide simple and direct data export from spradsheet to RDF graph; any data transformation can be done in Excel itself.

---

[1] https://dev.realestatecore.io/ExcelRDF/.

© Springer Nature Switzerland AG 2020
A. Harth et al. (Eds.): ESWC 2020 Satellite Events, LNCS 12124, pp. 104–109, 2020.
https://doi.org/10.1007/978-3-030-62327-2_18

2   Related Work

There are several tools that enable spreadsheet-to-RDF translation, but to my knowledge, none that emphasize the ExcelRDF design criteria described above.

XLWrap [4] and Spread2RDF[2] operate on spreadsheets and translate these (batch-based or at query time) using custom mapping languages. DB2Triples[3] and D2RQ [1] do the same, but employ mapping languages that have been standardised (the R2RML and D2RQ languages, respectively). These tools are geared toward users who are already quite famphrasehmilar with linked data and who are comfortable with writing their own mapping rules.

OpenRefine[4] is a well-established tool for data transformation and its RDF plugin supports GUI-based mapping of tabular data (e.g., from Excel) to an RDF graph structure. Users can modify their data using both GUI approaches (e.g., merging or splitting columns, filtering values, etc.) and for more fine-grained data manipulation on cell-by-cell level, through the GREL language. However, OpenRefine does not allow for easy sharing of work, as each participant needs to import the shared project into their own on-machine OpenRefine install; and installing it, and the RDF extension, is non-trivial.

TabLinker[5] uses spreadsheet styling to indicate the mapping of cells, rows, and columns to values, types, properties, etc. A spreadsheet that has been annotated using TabLinker styles can be shared and edited by multiple users before being run through the command line script that exports RDF. Compared with ExcelRDF, TabLinker however lacks an ontology import feature, so users need the develop style-based mappings by hand.

Other approaches to bring ontology structures into spreadsheets include RightField [9] (for Excel) and OntoMaton [6] (for Google Spreadsheets). These tools allow for the annotation of spreadsheet data by terms in an ontology; but they do not include RDF export functionality.

3   System Design and Features

ExcelRDF is implemented as a .NET-based Microsoft Office VSTO Add-In. The .NET underpinnings allows ExcelRDF to reuse the DotNetRDF[6] library, saving significant development effort. The VSTO plugin infrastructure also provides a dead-simple deployment mechanism, "ClickOnce", which generates a user-friendly installer, and provides automated Internet-based updates.

Using ExcelRDF consists of three distinct steps. First, the user loads an ontology, and through a friendly GUI selects which classes and properties from that ontology that they intend to use (Fig. 1) – based on their selection, the tool creates corresponding works sheets and column headers in an otherwise

---

[2] https://github.com/marcelotto/spread2rdf.
[3] https://github.com/antidot/db2triples.
[4] http://openrefine.org/.
[5] https://github.com/Data2Semantics/TabLinker.
[6] https://www.dotnetrdf.org/.

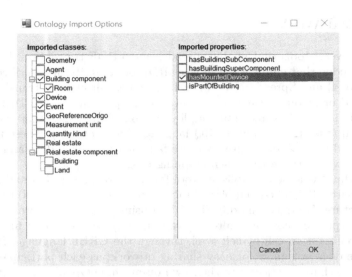

Fig. 1. Ontology import dialog

empty Excel skeleton file. Second, the user fills out this skeleton file with their data, using standard Excel tools and existing workflows. Third, once the data is complete the user exports it into RDF that is compliant with the initially loaded ontology – a simple GUI is provided to configure data namespaces and prefixes (Fig. 3). Each of these steps is described in detail below.

OWL Import. The ExcelRDF ontology import GUI (Fig. 1) is launched from the "Data" ribbon menu. The user is asked to select an on-disk OWL ontology file[7]. The named classes in this file are parsed and added to the class selection GUI; the properties for each such class (i.e., that have the class asserted as `rdfs:domain`) are added to the property selection GUI for that class. The user selects the classes and properties that they wish to use for their data, and the tool then constructs one work sheet (i.e., Excel tab) per selected class, and for each such work sheet adds columns corresponding to the selected properties. Additionally, a special identifier column is inserted and used for IRI minting. For examples of the complete structure, see Figs. 4a and 4b.

The header row cells on each generated work sheet are marked up with Excel notes that describe the properties that underlie each column; these notes (see Fig. 2a for an example) act as instructions for the RDF exporter. Optionally, the user may when importing an ontology select to embed anonymous individuals on a work sheet, spanning over several columns; when doing so, the cells of these columns will correspond with nested objects through an intermediate anonymous node. In the latter case, the RDF exporter instructions become a little more complex: see Fig. 2b for an example.

---

[7] Supported serializations: XML/RDF, Turtle, JSON-LD, NTriples, NQuads, and TriG.

```
<https://w3id.org/rec/core/associatedWithDevice>
<http://www.w3.org/2002/07/owl#ObjectProperty>
<https://w3id.org/rec/core/Device>
```

```
<https://w3id.org/rec/core/hasRealEstateComponent>
<http://www.w3.org/2002/07/owl#ObjectProperty>
<https://w3id.org/rec/core/RealEstateComponent>
<http://www.w3.org/2000/01/rdf-schema#label>
<http://www.w3.org/2002/07/owl#AnnotationProperty>
<http://www.w3.org/2001/XMLSchema#string>
```

(a)   Column   representing   the associatedWithDevice property.

(b) Column representing the label of a nested individual of the type RealEstateComponent.

Fig. 2. RDF generator instructions embedded in Excel skeleton

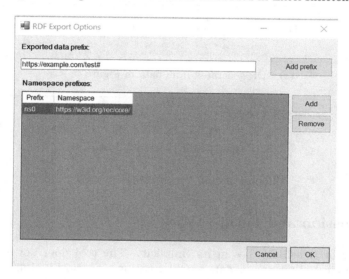

Fig. 3. Ontology import dialog

RDF Export. Once the user has populated the spreadsheet with data, they launch the RDF export GUI (Fig. 3). ExcelRDF extracts URI namespaces from the classes and properties mentioned in the note objects, and suggests that these be added to the namespace prefix mapping in the same GUI; additionally, the user is asked for a data namespace, that will be prepended to the identifiers that the user has given in the identifier column.

ExcelRDF generates an RDF graph[8] using the aforementioned notes objects it finds in the work sheet headers. Every cell on the sheet will generate an RDF statement where the subject is the row identifier, the predicate is the column header, and the object is the literal value held in the cell, or in the case of an object property, is a URI with that value as local name (Fig. 4c); unless if the embedded anonymous individuals feature has been used, in which case a more complicated structure such as the one in Fig. 4d is generated instead.

---

[8] Supported serializations: RDF/XML, Turtle, and NTriples.

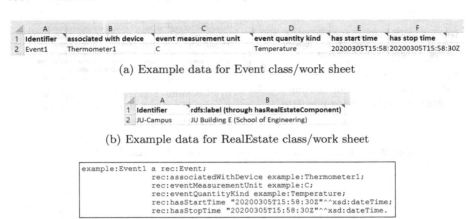

(a) Example data for Event class/work sheet

(b) Example data for RealEstate class/work sheet

```
example:Event1 a rec:Event;
               rec:associatedWithDevice example:Thermometer1;
               rec:eventMeasurementUnit example:C;
               rec:eventQuantityKind example:Temperature;
               rec:hasStartTime "20200305T15:58:30Z"^^xsd:dateTime;
               rec:hasStopTime "20200305T15:58:30Z"^^xsd:dateTime.
```

(c) RDF generated from data in Figure 4a

```
example:JU-Campus a rec:RealEstate;
               rec:hasRealEstateComponent [
                        a rec:RealEstateComponent ;
                        rdfs:label "JU Building E (School of Engineering)"^^xsd:string].
```

(d) RDF generated from data in Figure 4b

Fig. 4. Excel and generated RDF data

4   Discussion and Future Work

The beauty of ExcelRDF lies in its simplicity. The tool does not purport to enable complicated schema or data transformation scenarios; it simply provides a round-trip translation from ontology to spreadsheet and back to RDF graph. This enables data owners to maintain and user their existing Excel-based tools or workflows. Since the RDF exporter instructions are embedded in the generated Excel file itself, these files can be shared through the organisation and data collated from multiple sources by users who may not have ExcelRDF installed. And, since the RDF generation instructions are stored in a transparent manner using Excel notes, modifying them is easy.

New features being considered for the future roadmap include:

1. Support for `owl:Imports` – At present, the tool only operates on an ontology file loaded from disk. Adding imports resolution (possibly over the Internet) adds significant complexity, and arguably, an ontologist could anyway integrate imports in a pre-processing step, e.g., using Protégé. That said, as an optional feature, imports support may be very useful.
2. Pre-loading A-box from ontology – The tool ignores any A-box entities (i.e., `owl:NamedIndividual`) in the imported ontology. In some use cases it is useful to have a base set of individuals already in the ontology; I am considering how they should be represented in the generated Excel file.

3. Type checking of values – The tool does not validate that the types of values provided in cells are correct with regard to the `rdfs:range` of the column's underlying property. Such checking should raise an error if, for instance, the user has entered a string in a cell that should generate an XSD integer object.

Additionally, while ExcelRDF has been used successfully in the Building Knowledge project, it has not been rigorously evaluated in a more formal setting; this remains to be done in the near future.

Finally, it should be noted that since ExcelRDF is based on the VSTO architecture, it will run only on Excel for Windows. Microsoft provides an alternate add-in-architecture that is platform-agnostic, based on web technologies; but since ExcelRDF depends on .NET-based libraries this architecture has until recently not been available to use. However, with the uptake of WebAssembly, it may in the not so distant future be possible to compile those .NET libraries into WASM that can be executed in a web environment, in which case ExcelRDF could certainly be re-engineered to also become entirely platform-agnostic, running anywhere Excel runs (including in the browser, on macOS, iOS, etc.).

References

1. Bizer, C., Seaborne, A.: D2RQ – treating non-RDF databases as virtual RDF graphs. In: Poster at the 3rd International Semantic Web Conference, Hiroshima, Japan, November 2004
2. Das, S., Sundara, S., Cyganiak, R.: R2RML: RDB to RDF Mapping Language, September 2012. https://www.w3.org/TR/r2rml/
3. Hammar, K., Wallin, E.O., Karlberg, P., Hälleberg, D.: The RealEstateCore ontology. In: Ghidini, C., et al. (eds.) ISWC 2019. LNCS, vol. 11779, pp. 130–145. Springer, Cham (2019). https://doi.org/10.1007/978-3-030-30796-7_9
4. Langegger, A., Wöß, W.: XLWrap – querying and integrating arbitrary spreadsheets with SPARQL. In: Bernstein, A., et al. (eds.) ISWC 2009. LNCS, vol. 5823, pp. 359–374. Springer, Heidelberg (2009). https://doi.org/10.1007/978-3-642-04930-9_23
5. Lohmann, S., Negru, S., Haag, F., Ertl, T.: Visualizing ontologies with VOWL. Semant. Web **7**(4), 399–419 (2016). http://dx.doi.org/10.3233/SW-150200
6. Maguire, E., González-Beltrán, A., Whetzel, P.L., Sansone, S.A., Rocca-Serra, P.: OntoMaton: a bioportal powered ontology widget for Google spreadsheets. Bioinformatics **29**(4), 525–527 (2013). https://doi.org/10.1093/bioinformatics/bts718
7. Shimizu, C., Hammar, K.: CoModIDE - The comprehensive modular ontology engineering IDE. In: ISWC 2019 Satellites. CEUR Workshop Proceedings, vol. 2456, October 2019. http://urn.kb.se/resolve?urn=urn:nbn:se:hj:diva-46397
8. Tudorache, T., Nyulas, C., Noy, N.F., Musen, M.A.: WebProtégé: a collaborative ontology editor and knowledge acquisition tool for the Web. Semant. Web **4**(1), 89–99 (2013). http://dx.doi.org/10.3233/SW-2012-0057
9. Wolstencroft, K., et al.: RightField: embedding ontology annotation in spreadsheets. Bioinformatics **27**(14), 2021–2022 (2011). https://doi.org/10.1093/bioinformatics/btr312

Publishing and Using Legislation and Case Law as Linked Open Data on the Semantic Web

Eero Hyvönen[1,2](✉) , Minna Tamper[1,2] , Esko Ikkala[1] , Sami Sarsa[1] ,
Arttu Oksanen[1,3] , Jouni Tuominen[1,2] , and Aki Hietanen[4]

[1] Semantic Computing Research Group (SeCo), Aalto University, Espoo, Finland
{eero.hyvonen,minna.tamper,esko.ikkala,sami.sarsa,
arttu.oksanen,jouni.tuominen}@aalto.fi
[2] HELDIG – Helsinki Centre for Digital Humanities, University of Helsinki,
Helsinki, Finland
[3] Edita Publishing Ltd., Helsinki, Finland
[4] Ministry of Justice, Helsinki, Finland
aki.hietanen@om.fi
https://seco.cs.aalto.fi, https://heldig.fi,
https://www.editapublishing.fi, https://oikeusministerio.fi

Abstract. Legislation and case law are widely published on the Web
as documents for humans to read. In contrast, this paper argues for
publishing legal documents as Linked Open Data (LOD) on top of which
intelligent legal services for end users can be created in addition to just
providing the documents for close reading. To test and demonstrate this
idea, we present work on creating the Linked Open Data service SEMAN-
TIC FINLEX for Finnish legislation and case law and the semantic portal
prototype LAWSAMPO for serving end users with legal data. SEMANTIC
FINLEX is a harmonized knowledge graph that is created automatically
from legal textual documents and published in a SPARQL endpoint on
top of which the various applications of LAWSAMPO are implemented.
First applications include faceted semantic search and browsing for 1)
statutes and 2) court decisions, as well as 3) a service for finding court
decisions similar to a given one or free text. A novelty of LAWSAMPO
is the provision of ready-to-use tooling for exploring and analyzing legal
documents, based on the "Sampo" model.

Keywords: Linked data · Case law · Legislation · Semantic portal

1 Semantic Finlex Linked Open Data Service

Finnish legislation and case law have been published as web documents since
1997 in the Finlex Data Bank[1]. Although the Finlex service is widely used by
the public, it does not provide machine-readable legal information as open data,

---

[1] http://www.finlex.fi.

A. Harth et al. (Eds.): ESWC 2020 Satellite Events, LNCS 12124, pp. 110–114, 2020.
https://doi.org/10.1007/978-3-030-62327-2_19

on top of which services and analyses could be built by the ministry or third parties. The first version of SEMANTIC FINLEX based on Linked Data was published in 2014 [4]. The data included 2413 consolidated statutes, 11904 judgments of the Supreme Court, and 1490 judgments of the Supreme Administrative Court. In addition, some 30000 terms used in 26 different thesauri were harvested for a draft of a consolidated vocabulary. During the work, shortcomings of the initial RDF data model became evident as well as the need for using the then emerging new standards for EU level interoperability: ELI European Legislation Identifier [3] and ECLI European Case Law Identifier [2]. The dataset also consisted of only one version (2012) of the statutory law and was not updated, as new legislation and case law was published in Finlex. The issues were resolved in the new version of SEMANTIC FINLEX [10] that currently hosts a dataset comprising approximately 28 million triples. The data was enriched by automatic annotation to named entities (judges mentioned in the court decisions) and references to legal texts (such as EU law transposed by the statutes and statutory citations appearing in court cases), vocabularies, and data sources, such as DBpedia, by utilizing different named entity linking tools [10,13].

The Semantic Finlex service adopts the 5-star Linked Data model[2], extended with two more stars, as suggested in the Linked Data Finland model and platform [7]. The 6th star is obtained by providing the dataset schemas and documenting them. Semantic Finlex schemas can be downloaded from the service and the data models are documented under the data.finlex.fi domain. The 7th star is achieved by validating the data against the documented schemas to prevent errors in the published data. Semantic Finlex attempts to obtain the 7th star by applying different means of combing out errors in the data within the data conversion process. The service is powered by the Linked Data Finland[3] publishing platform that along with a variety of different datasets provides tools and services to facilitate publishing and re-using Linked Data. All URIs are dereferenceable and support content negotiation by using HTTP 303 redirects. In accordance with the ELI specification, RDF is embedded in the HTML presentations of the legislative documents as RDFa[4] markup. In addition to the converted RDF data, the original XML files are also provided. To support easier use by programmers without knowledge of SPARQL or RDF, a simplified REST API is provided, too. As the underlying triplestore, Apache Jena Fuseki[5] is used as a Docker container, which allows efficient provisioning of resources (CPU, memory) and scaling.

2   LAWSAMPO Semantic Portal

To demonstrate the use of SEMANTIC FINLEX in applications, the semantic portal LAWSAMPO is being developed. LAWSAMPO is a new member in the

---

[2] https://www.w3.org/DesignIssues/LinkedData.html.

[3] http://ldf.fi.

[4] http://www.w3.org/standards/techs/rdfa.

[5] https://jena.apache.org/documentation/fuseki2/.

Sampo[6] series of semantic portals, based on the "Sampo model" [6], where the data is enriched through a shared ontology and Linked Data infrastructure, multiple application perspectives are provided on a single SPARQL endpoint, and faceted search and browsing is integrated with data-analytic tooling. The faceted search and tooling are implemented using the Sampo-UI framework[7] [8]. The Sampo portals[8] have had millions of end users on the Web suggesting that it is a promising model to create useful semantic portals.

The landing page of the LawSampo portal offers different application perspectives: **1. Statutes.** By clicking on Statutes, a faceted search interface [14] for searching and browsing statutes is opened. The facets on the left include document type (with seven subtypes), statute type, year, and related EU regulation. After filtering out a set of documents (or a particular document) of interest, the user is provided with two options. First, the user can select a document from the result list and a "homepage" of the document opens, showing not only the document but also linked contextual information related to it such as the referred EU regulations linked to EU CELLAR[9] or other documents from Semantic Finlex referring to it. For example, court decisions in which the statute has been applied can be shown. Second, it is possible to do data analysis based on the filtered documents. For example, a histogram can be created showing the dates of the filtered documents. **2. Case Law.** In the Case Law perspective, a similar faceted search interface opens for searching and browsing court decisions. In this case, the facets include court, judge, and keywords characterizing the subject matter of the judgement. **3. Case Law Search.** The third perspective is an application, where a law case judgement, or more generally any document or text, can be used for finding similar other case judgements. For example, if one gets a judgement from a court, this application can be used to find out what kind of similar judgements have been made before. Several methods for finding similar cases were tested when implementing this application including TF-IDF, Latent Dirichlet Allocation (LDA), Word2Vec, and Doc2vec [11,12]. **4. Life Events.** In addition, a fourth perspective is being implemented by which legal materials can be searched for based on the end user's life situation problem at hand (e.g., divorce).

---

[6] In Finnish mythology and the epic Kalevala, "Sampo" is a mythical artefact of indeterminate type that gives its owner richness and good fortune, an ancient metaphor of technology.

[7] Cf. homepage for more info: https://seco.cs.aalto.fi/tools/sampo-ui/.

[8] Including, e.g., CultureSampo (2008) for cultural heritage, TravelSampo (2011) for tourism, BookSampo (2011) for fiction literature, WarSampo (2015) for military history, BiographySampo (2018) for prosopography, and NameSampo (2019) for toponomastic research. Cf. homepage: https://seco.cs.aalto.fi/applications/sampo/.

[9] https://data.europa.eu/euodp/en/data/dataset/sparql-cellar-of-the-publications-office.

3   Related Work and Contributions

Our work on legal Linked Data services was influenced by the MetaLex Document Server[10] [5] that publishes Dutch legislation using the CEN Metalex XML and ontology standards. Other Metalex ontology based implementations include legislation.gov.uk[11] and Nomothesia[12] that also implements ELI-compliant identifiers. Various ELI implementations and prototypes have also been implemented in existing legal information portals nationally, e.g., in Luxembourg[13], France[14], and Norway[15]. Many countries already produce ECLI-compliant case law documents to be indexed by the ECLI search engine[16]. A prominent example of publishing EU Law and publications as linked data is the CELLAR system. Previous related works in the U.S. include, e.g., the Legal Linked Data project aiming at enhanced access to product regulatory information [1].

LawSampo aims to widen the focus of these related works by providing both legislation and case law to end users through intelligent user interfaces, such as semantic faceted search and document similarity-based search. The documents are automatically enriched with contextual linked data, and the end user is also provided with ready-to-use data-analytic tooling for analyzing the documents and their relations. In the future, we plan to expand the related enriching datasets to include, e.g., related parliamentary documents and discussions[17], in the spirit of [15]. In order to be able to publish more legal documents in cost-efficient way, we also work on semi-automatic pseudonymization of court judgements [9] and automatic annotation of legal documents [13].

Acknowledgments. Our work was funded by the Ministry of Justice; CSC – IT Center for Science, Finland, provided computational resources for the work.

References

1. Casellas, N., et al.: Linked legal data: improving access to regulations. In: Proceedings of the 13th Annual International Conference on Digital Government Research (dg.o 2012), pp. 280–281 (2012). Association for Computing Machinery
2. Council of the European Union: Council conclusions inviting the introduction of the European Case Law Identifier (ECLI) and a minimum set of uniform metadata for case law. In: Official Journal of the European Union, C 127, 29.4.2011, pp. 1–7. Publications Office of the European Union (2011)
3. Council of the European Union: Council conclusions inviting the introduction of the European Legislation Identifier (ELI). In: Official Journal of the European

---

[10] http://doc.metalex.eu.
[11] http://legislation.gov.uk.
[12] http://legislation.di.uoa.gr.
[13] http://legilux.public.lu/editorial/eli.
[14] http://www.eli.fr/en/constructionURI.html.
[15] http://lovdata.no/eli.
[16] https://e-justice.europa.eu/content_ecli_search_engine-430-en.do.
[17] The ParliamentSampo system: https://seco.cs.aalto.fi/projects/semparl/en/.

Union, C 325, 26.10.2012, pp. 3–11. Publications Office of the European Union (2012)

4. Frosterus, M., Tuominen, J., Hyvönen, E.: Facilitating re-use of legal data in applications-Finnish law as a linked open data service. In: Proceedings of JURIX 2014, Kraków, Poland, pp. 115–124. IOS Press (2014)

5. Hoekstra, R.: The MetaLex document server. In: Aroyo, L., et al. (eds.) ISWC 2011. LNCS, vol. 7032, pp. 128–143. Springer, Heidelberg (2011). https://doi.org/10.1007/978-3-642-25093-4_9

6. Hyvönen, E.: Using the semantic web in digital humanities: shift from data publishing to data-analysis and serendipitous knowledge discovery. Semant. Web 11(1), 187–193 (2020)

7. Hyvönen, E., Tuominen, J., Alonen, M., Mäkelä, E.: Linked data Finland: a 7-star model and platform for publishing and re-using linked datasets. In: Presutti, V., Blomqvist, E., Troncy, R., Sack, H., Papadakis, I., Tordai, A. (eds.) ESWC 2014. LNCS, vol. 8798, pp. 226–230. Springer, Cham (2014). https://doi.org/10.1007/978-3-319-11955-7_24

8. Ikkala, E., Hyvönen, E., Rantala, H., Koho, M.: Sampo-UI: A Full Stack JavaScript Framework for Developing Semantic Portal User Interfaces (2020). https://seco.cs.aalto.fi/publications/2020/ikkala-et-al-sampo-ui-2020.pdf. Submitted

9. Oksanen, A., Tamper, M., Tuominen, J., Hietanen, A., Hyvönen, E.: ANOPPI: a pseudonymization service for Finnish court documents. In: Proceedings of JURIX 2019, Madrid, Spain, pp. 251–254. IOS Press (2019)

10. Oksanen, A., Tuominen, J., Mäkelä, E., Tamper, M., Hietanen, A., Hyvönen, E.: Semantic finlex: transforming, publishing, and using Finnish legislation and case law as linked open data on the web. In: Peruginelli, G., Faro, S. (eds.) Knowledge of the Law in the Big Data Age, Frontiers in Artificial Intelligence and Applications, vol. 317, pp. 212–228. IOS Press (2019)

11. Sarsa, S.: Information retrieval with Finnish case law embeddings. Master's thesis, University of Helsinki, Department of Computer Science (2019)

12. Sarsa, S., Hyvönen, E.: Searching case law judgements by using other judgements as a query. In: Proceedings of the 9th Conference Artificial Intelligence and Natural Language. AINL 2020, Helsinki, Finland, 7–9 October 2020. Springer-Verlag (2020)

13. Tamper, M., Oksanen, A., Tuominen, J., Hietanen, A., Hyvönen, E.: Automatic annotation service APPI: named entity linking in legal domain. In: Proceedings of ESWC 2020, Posters and Demos. LNCS, vol. 12124, pp. 208–213. Springer, Heidelberg (2020)

14. Tunkelang, D.: Faceted Search. Morgan & Claypool Publishers, San Rafae (2009)

15. Van Aggelen, A., Hollink, L., Kemman, M., Kleppe, M., Beunders, H.: The debates of the European parliament as linked open data. Semant. Web 8(2), 271–281 (2017)

cqp4rdf: Towards a Suite for RDF-Based Corpus Linguistics

Maxim Ionov[1]([⊠])[iD], Florian Stein[1][iD], Sagar Sehgal[2][iD],
and Christian Chiarcos[1][iD]

[1] Applied Computational Linguistics Lab, Goethe University Frankfurt,
Frankfurt, Germany
{ionov,chiarcos}@informatik.uni-frankfurt.de, flo@stein-software.com
[2] Indian Institute of Information Technology, Sri City, India
sagar.r16@iiits.in

Abstract. In this paper, we present cqp4rdf, a set of tools for creating and querying corpora with linguistic annotations. cqp4rdf builds on CQP, an established corpus query language widely used in the areas of computational lexicography and empirical linguistics, and allows to apply it to corpora represented in RDF.

This is in line with the emerging trend of RDF-based corpus formats that provides several benefits over more traditional ways, such as support for virtually unlimited types of annotation, linking of corpus elements between multiple datasets, and simultaneously querying distributed language resources and corpora with different annotations.

On the other hand, application support tailored for such corpora is virtually nonexistent, leaving corpus linguist with SPARQL as the query language. Being extremely powerful, it has a relatively steep learning curve, especially for people without computer science background. At the same time, using query languages designed for classic corpus management software limits the vast possibilities of RDF-based corpora.

We present the middle ground aiming to bridge the gap: the interface that allows to query RDF corpora and explore the results in a linguist-friendly way.

Keywords: Linguistic linked data · Corpus linguistics · SPARQL · CQP

1 Background

Corpora with annotations for features of morphology, grammar or semantics are fundamental to modern-day lexicography, linguistics, language technology and digital philology. Along with their broad range of uses, many different types of annotations emerged, leading to diverse and/or complicated data models, often with tool-specific data formats and a limited degree of interoperability. This interoperability challenge has long been recognized as an obstacle to scientific progress in the field, and has been the basis for developing language resource

A. Harth et al. (Eds.): ESWC 2020 Satellite Events, LNCS 12124, pp. 115–121, 2020.
https://doi.org/10.1007/978-3-030-62327-2_20

standards, e.g., the Linguistic Annotation Framework [12]. LAF implements the common insight that every form of linguistic annotation can be modelled as a labelled, directed multi-graph. More recently, the application-specific stand-off XML formats previously developed in the language resource community to represent such graphs have been largely replaced by RDF-based data models, especially for annotations on the web or using web services [11,15]. RDF is also applied to static language resources, e.g., machine-readable dictionaries [8] and terminologies [9], subsequently leading to the emergence of a linked data cloud of linguistic resources. Linked Data is a well-established paradigm for representing different types of data on the Semantic Web [1]. Linguistic Linked Open Data [3] describes the application of LOD principles and methodologies for modeling, sharing and linking language resources in various text- and knowledge-processing disciplines. For these areas, a number of benefits of LLOD and the underlying RDF technology over traditional representation formalisms have been identified [6]. Most notable for corpus linguistics, this includes:

1. Representation: linked graphs can represent any kind of linguistic annotation.
2. Interoperability: Different RDF graphs can be used together in a single query.
3. Ecosystem: broad support by off-the-shelf database technology.

The application of RDF and linked data technology to linguistic corpora is to be seen in this context and has been worked on for more than a decade, already [2,10]. Despite the relevance, RDF is not well supported by existing corpus technology. Its current role in corpus linguistics is currently restricted to that of a publication format [14]. But aside from representing corpora, querying with Linked Data technology allows to query several resources in a single query, harmonizing different tagsets, creating intermediate annotations with annotation integration and flexible linking with other annotations, lexical resources (e.g. dictionaries or wordnets) and knowledge graphs as well as the linking (and querying) across concurrent annotations of the same text. Still, user- (i.e., linguist-) friendly interfaces to this technology are largely absent. This paper describes an effort to address this gap.

In our previous work, [4], we introduced a research methodology that uses these advantages in a typological linguistic study that relies heavily on corpora. Even though we found the approach valid, there was a downside: SPARQL is much more complex than traditional corpus query languages. This allows for more nuanced queries but makes the process of writing them more complicated: In addition to linguistic expertise required to know what to query, researchers need to have experience in SPARQL, or to work in tandem with semantic web professionals.[1]

In this paper, we introduce the new component of our methodological approach: `cqp4rdf`,[2] a collection of tools that allows querying corpora represented in RDF with CQP, a query language that is widely used for querying corpora

---

[1] Total time spent on writing all the necessary queries for [4] was more than a week, it was done by a developer in tandem with a linguist.

[2] https://purl.org/liodi/cqp4rdf.

with linguistic annotations, increasing the usability and visibility of Linked Data corpora resources, making it possible to use them for corpus linguists unfamiliar with Semantic Web technologies. We briefly summarize the syntax of CQP with the additions we introduced to make it suitable for RDF data, and show the basic corpus manager interface that utilizes this.

2   CQP

CQP, the Corpus Query Processor, is a tool developed initially for the IMS Corpus Workbench [7]. It uses a query language which is also usually called *CQP*, or *CQP query language*.[3] Since its development, several major corpus management systems adopted it as a query language. The most prominent of them is *(no)SketchEngine* [13].

CQP is mainly intended for querying corpora with morphosyntactic annotations even though it has a possibility to query for segments if there are such annotations in corpora.

The query can consists of the three main types of expressions:

1. words and sequences of words filtered by attributes: [], [word="cat"], []+, [word="c.*"], 1:[]
2. segment names: <s/>, <p/>
3. special constructions: (not) containing and (not) within
4. global conditions: & 1.lemma = 2.lemma

The first group matches consecutive words (tokens) that can be filtered using logical expressions that use token attributes, such as a part of speech or a lemma, e.g. [word="comment" and pos="V"]. They can be labeled, as demonstrated on the last example. The second group matches the whole structural segment. The presence of these segments depends on the annotations available in a corpus. The third group are operators between two sub-queries (which can contain one of these operators in turn). Finally, the last group allows to set constraints between tokens.

The non-standard feature we introduced to CQP are namespaces: all attributes and all segments should contain a prefix which correspond to a SPARQL prefix: conll:WORD, nif:Sentence. The list of recognised prefixes is defined in the configuration file. With this, there are no limitations on the vocabularies that are used in the corpus representation and there are no limitations on the list of properties that can be used to query corpora.

3   cqp4rdf

Currently, the tool set consists of a query conversion service, a backend which connects to a triple store to query for data and a frontend which provides a

---

[3] Sometimes there is a confusion with *CQL*, which is another query language, still, some systems use *CQL* as the name for *CQP*.

web interface. All these elements are packaged as a Docker container. There are two steps required to set up the corpus: putting the data into a triple store and providing basic information about it in the YAML configuration file which stores configurations for all the corpora accessible for the `cqp4rdf` instance. The Docker container starts a triple store but it is possible to use an external one.

For the query conversion, we have implemented a eBNF grammar and used a parse tree of a query as a basis for further transformation to SPARQL. For this demonstration, it is adapted for corpora with CoNLL-RDF data model [5] which, in turn, relies on NIF [11], but adaptation to other data models can be achieved by modifying SPARQL templates which are used to generate queries.

On top of the conversion, we implemented an API that provides endpoints **/api/info** and **/api/query**. The former provides all the attributes of a token by its URI and the latter returns a list of results, transforming the input query and executing the SPARQL query returning a list of results for a specified page encoded in JSON. The output is limited to a number specified in the configuration file. Next sets of results can be retrieved with another request. The endpoint and the list of prefixes are specified in the configuration file as well.

This API is meant to be a backend, allowing to create tailored frontends for the specific needs or to adapt existing corpus management systems to use it. Currently, we implemented a minimalistic corpus interface[4] that allows to enter a CQP query and get a list of results in a KWIC[5] format (see Fig. 1). Every word in the output can be clicked to see the full information about this word.

Additionally, a user can construct the query using the user interface. The list of attributes and their possible values are specified in a configuration file. Note that there is no limitation on the attributes that can be used in a query, so users may still specify any additional attributes manually.

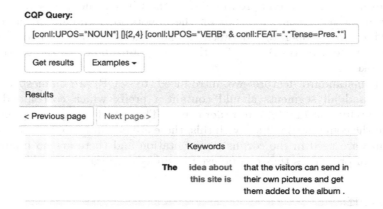

Fig. 1. Search results for a query that extracts contexts with a noun and a verb in present tense with 2 to 4 words in between.

---

[4] http://purl.org/liodi/cqp4rdf/ud.

[5] Key-word in context.

To compare the complexity of CQP and SPARQL queries, consider the query on the Fig. 1,[6] which returns contexts with a noun and a verb in a present tense with 2 to 4 words in between:

```
1  [ conll:UPOS="NOUN" ]
   []{2,4}
   [ conll:UPOS="VERB" &
     conll:FEAT=".*Tense=Pres.*" ]
```

Listing 1.1. CQP version of the query

```
 1  SELECT DISTINCT ?noun ?verb
    WHERE
    {
       ?w_1  a  nif:Word ;
             conll:HEAD* ?sent ;
 6           conll:WORD ?noun ;
             conll:UPOS ?w_1_pos ;
             nif:nextWord{2,4} ?w_2 .

       ?w_2  a  nif:Word ;
11           conll:HEAD* ?sent ;
             conll:UPOS ?w_2_pos ;
             conll:FEAT ?w_2_feats ;
             conll:WORD ?verb .

16     FILTER(REGEX(?w_2_feats ,
         ".*Tense=Pres.*") &&
         ?w_1_pos = "NOUN" &&
         ?w_2_pos = "VERB")
    }
```

Listing 1.2. SPARQL version of the query

The CQP representation, while may seem unfamiliar, is compact and intuitive, even for people with a limited knowledge of CQP. The corresponding SPARQL query is much more verbose and require knowledge of the underlying data model, whereas for the CQP query it is only required to know corpus attributes and a tagset (which is a prerequisite for using a corpus anyway).[7]

At the same time, corpus linguists can benefit from the underlying RDF format. For example, it is possible for a token to have multiple tags from different tagsets and combine them in the same query, or to have annotation provenance or other additional information stored and queried.

Even the minimalistic interface presented in this section allows to navigate through RDF corpora, increasing its usability, giving people unfamiliar with Semantic Web technologies the possibility to use the data quite efficiently.

4 Outlook

We showed our service for querying linguistic corpora represented in RDF with a common corpus query language, CQP. This approach increases the usability of RDF-based corpora, at the same time leaving the possibility to use the

---

[6] For brevity, we use non-normative SPARQL 1.1 Property Path (W3C Working Draft 26.01.2010), which is supported by some triple stores as an extension.

[7] This is, of course, not a problem of SPARQL but a result of using an intermediate conversion, which hides the data model under the hood.

whole arsenal of Semantic Web technologies when needed, for instance, to add intermediate annotations or to link elements to external vocabularies.

We see our work as a proof of concept implementation, and a basis for further studies. A number of open questions remain. First and foremost, the universality of such approach: How universal can be this service in terms of data models and vocabularies? Our next goal is to find the optimal middle ground between usability and expressiveness. Additionally, performance and scalability of the approach: corpus managers use highly optimized search mechanisms which require indexing data whereas in our approach the flexibility is prioritized over speed. Preliminary experiments with relatively small corpora shows that it does not cause problems but more benchmarks are required to test whether this can work for larger corpora.

References

1. Berners-Lee, T.: Linked data. Technical report, W3C Design Issue (2006)
2. Burchardt, A., Padó, S., Spohr, D., Frank, A., Heid, U.: Formalising multi-layer corpora in OWL/DL - Lexicon modelling, querying and consistency control. In: Proceedings of the IJCNLP-2008 (2008)
3. Chiarcos, C., Nordhoff, S., Hellmann, S. (eds.): Linked Data in Linguistics. Representing Language Data and Metadata. Springer, Heidelberg (2012). https://doi.org/10.1007/978-3-642-28249-2
4. Chiarcos, C., Donandt, K., Sargsian, H., Ionov, M., Schreur, J.W.: Towards LLOD-based language contact studies. A case study in interoperability. In: Proceedings of the LREC 2018 (2018)
5. Chiarcos, C., Fäth, C.: CoNLL-RDF: linked corpora done in an NLP-friendly way. In: Gracia, J., Bond, F., McCrae, J.P., Buitelaar, P., Chiarcos, C., Hellmann, S. (eds.) LDK 2017. LNCS (LNAI), vol. 10318, pp. 74–88. Springer, Cham (2017). https://doi.org/10.1007/978-3-319-59888-8_6
6. Chiarcos, C., McCrae, J., Cimiano, P., Fellbaum, C.: Towards open data for linguistics: linguistic linked data. In: Oltramari, A., Vossen, P., Qin, L., Hovy, E. (eds.) New Trends of Research in Ontologies and Lexical Resources. NLP. Springer, Heidelberg (2013). https://doi.org/10.1007/978-3-642-31782-8_2
7. Christ, O.: The IMS corpus workbench technical manual. Institut für maschinelle Sprachverarbeitung, Universität Stuttgart (1994)
8. Cimiano, P., McCrae, J., Buitelaar, P.: Lexicon model for ontologies. Technical report, W3C Community Report (2016)
9. Farrar, S., Langendoen, D.T.: A linguistic ontology for the semantic web. GLOT Int. **7**(3), 97–100 (2003)
10. Frank, A., Ivanovic, C.: Building literary corpora for computational literary analysis-a prototype to bridge the gap between CL and DH. In: Proceedings of the LREC 2018 (2018)
11. Hellmann, S., Lehmann, J., Auer, S., Brümmer, M.: Integrating NLP using linked data. In: Alani, H., et al. (eds.) ISWC 2013, Part II. LNCS, vol. 8219, pp. 98–113. Springer, Heidelberg (2013). https://doi.org/10.1007/978-3-642-41338-4_7
12. ISO: ISO 24612:2012. Language resource management - linguistic annotation framework. Technical report (2012)

13. Kilgarriff, A., et al.: The sketch engine: ten years on. Lexicography **1**, 7–36 (2014). https://doi.org/10.1007/s40607-014-0009-9
14. Mazziotta, N.: Building the syntactic reference corpus of medieval French using NotaBene RDF annotation tool. In: Proceedings of the 4th Linguistic Annotation Workshop (LAW) (2010)
15. Sanderson, R., Ciccarese, P., Young, B.: Web annotation data model. Technical report, W3C Recommendation 23 February 2017 (2017)

Elas4RDF: Multi-perspective Triple-Centered Keyword Search over RDF Using Elasticsearch

Giorgos Kadilierakis[1,2], Christos Nikas[1,2], Pavlos Fafalios[1(✉)],
Panagiotis Papadakos[1,2], and Yannis Tzitzikas[1,2]

[1] Information Systems Laboratory, FORTH-ICS, Heraklion, Greece
{cnikas,fafalios,papadako,tzitzik}@ics.forth.gr
[2] Computer Science Department, University of Crete, Heraklion, Greece
kadilier@csd.uoc.gr

Abstract. The task of accessing knowledge graphs through structured query languages like SPARQL is rather demanding for ordinary users. Consequently, there are various approaches that attempt to exploit the simpler and widely used keyword-based search paradigm, either by translating keyword queries to structured queries, or by adopting classical information retrieval (IR) techniques. This paper demonstrates `Elas4RDF`, a keyword search system over RDF that is based on `Elasticsearch`, an out-of-the-box document-centric IR system. `Elas4RDF` indexes and retrieves *triples* (instead of entities), and thus yields more refined and informative results, that can be viewed through different perspectives. In this paper we demonstrate the performance of the `Elas4RDF` system in queries of various types, and showcase the benefits from offering different perspectives for aggregating and visualising the search results.

1 Motivation and Novelty

The Web of Data contains thousands of RDF datasets available online, including cross-domain KBs (e.g., DBpedia and Wikidata), domain specific repositories (e.g., DrugBank and MarineTLO), as well as Markup data through schema.org (see [5] for a recent survey). These datasets are queried through complex structured query languages, like SPARQL. Faceted Search is a user-friendlier paradigm for interactive query formulation, however the systems that support it (see [7] for a survey) need a keyword search engine as an entry point to the information space. Consequently, and since plain users are acquainted with web search engines, an effective method for keyword search over RDF is indispensable.

At the same time we observe a widespread use of out-of-the-box IR systems (e.g., `Elasticsearch`) in different contexts. To this end we investigate how these, document-centric Information Retrieval Systems (IRSs), can be used for enabling keyword search over arbitrary RDF datasets. This endeavor raises various questions revolving around: (a) how to index an RDF dataset, (b) what to rank and how, and (c) how the search results should be presented.

© Springer Nature Switzerland AG 2020
A. Harth et al. (Eds.): ESWC 2020 Satellite Events, LNCS 12124, pp. 122–128, 2020.
https://doi.org/10.1007/978-3-030-62327-2_21

This paper demonstrates `Elas4RDF`, a keyword search system over RDF that is based on the popular IR system `Elasticsearch`. Our main research question, as elaborated in the conference paper [4], was: *"Can Elasticsearch be configured to offer a retrieval performance comparable to that of dedicated keyword search systems for RDF?"*. Here, we describe and demonstrate a system that is based on that approach, that additionally focuses on the presentation/aggregation of the search results. Specifically, the retrieved RDF triples are displayed through various *perspectives* (each corresponding to a separate tab) that provide different presentations and visualisations of the search results and can satisfy different information needs. Since interaction is of prominent importance in information retrieval [1], we propose a perspectives' switching interaction that is familiar to all users (Web search engines offer various tabs for images, videos, news, etc.).

The most relevant work to ours is the LOTUS system [3], a keyword search system over RDF data that is also based on `Elasticsearch`. However, its main focus is on scalability, while we focus on effectiveness (see [4]) and the support of various types of search through different views. With respect to user-friendly interfaces, there are systems focusing on particular aspects (e.g., faceted search). To the best of our knowledge though, there are no available prototypes that offer keyword access and multiple methods for inspecting the search results.

2   Indexing, Retrieval, and Evaluation

As detailed in the conference paper [4], we opt for high flexibility and thus consider *triple* as the retrieval unit. A triple is more informative than an entity. It can be viewed as the simplest representation of a fact that verifies the correctness of a piece of information for Q&A tasks. Furthermore, it offers flexibility on how to structure and present the final results, which is the focus of this work.

For *indexing*, we evaluated variations of two main approaches on what data to consider for each *virtual document* (triple in our case). The *baseline* approach considers only data from the triple itself (i.e., text extracted from the subject, object and predicate). The *extended* approach exploits information in the neighbourhood of the triple's resource elements, like one or more descriptive properties such as *rdfs:label* and *rdfs:comment*. Regarding the *retrieval process* we have experimented with various *query types*, *weighting methods* and *similarity models* that are offered by `Elasticsearch`.

We have *evaluated* the above using the DBpedia-Entity test collection[1], which is based on a DBpedia dump of 2015-10. The collection contains a set of heterogeneous keyword queries that cover four categories: i) named-entity queries (e.g., "Brooklyn bridge"), ii) IR-style keyword queries (e.g., "electronic music genre"), iii) natural language questions (e.g., "Who is the mayor of Berlin?"), and iv) entity-list queries (e.g., "professional sports teams in New York)". In total, over 49K query-entity pairs are labelled using a three-point scale; 0 for irrelevant, 1 for relevant, and 2 for highly relevant.

---

[1] https://iai-group.github.io/DBpedia-Entity/.

The key results from the evaluation are the following: i) all triple components contribute to the system's performance; ii) object keywords seem to be more important than subject keywords, thus giving higher weight to the object fields can improve performance; iii) extending the index with additional descriptive information about the triple URIs improves performance; however, including all available information (all outgoing properties) introduces noise and drops performance; iv) the default similarity model of `Elasticsearch` (BM25) performs satisfactory; v) using `Elasticsearch` for keyword search over RDF data is almost as effective as task- and dataset-oriented systems built from scratch. For more details the interested reader should refer to [4].

3   The `Elas4RDF` Search System

3.1   Indexing Service and Search REST API

For enabling the community and other interested parties to use our approach over arbitrary RDF datasets, we have made publicly available two dedicated `Elas4RDF` services.

Elas4RDF-index Service.[2] This service creates an index of an RDF dataset based on a given configuration (e.g., using the baseline/extended approaches described in [4]). The index can then be queried by the `Elas4RDF-search` service.

Elas4RDF-search Service.[3] This service exploits an `Elas4RDF-index` and initialises a REST API which accepts keyword queries and returns results in JSON format. Apart from the *query*, the list of parameters optionally includes: i) the *size* of the answer, ii) the name of the *index* to consider (from `Elas4RDF-index`), iii) the *type* of the answer (triples, entities, both), iv) the index *field* over which to evaluate the query (e.g., only over the subject), and v) a *body* parameter through which one can express a complicated DSL query.[4]

The `Elas4RDF-search` service is used by the `Elas4RDF` search system for retrieving the results of a keyword query and presenting them to the user through different visualisation methods (more details below). One can easily configure it to use the search service over another dataset. A demo of the `Elas4RDF` system over DBpedia is available at: https://demos.isl.ics.forth.gr/elas4rdf/.

3.2   Multi-perspective Presentation of Search Results

The presentation and visualisation of RDF data is challenging due to the complex, interlinked, and multi-dimensional nature of this type of data [2]. An established method on how to present RDF results for arbitrary query types does not exist yet, and it seems that a single approach cannot suit all possible requirements.

---

[2] https://github.com/SemanticAccessAndRetrieval/Elas4RDF-index.
[3] https://github.com/SemanticAccessAndRetrieval/Elas4RDF-search.
[4] https://www.elastic.co/guide/en/elasticsearch/reference/current/query-dsl.html.

A core design characteristic of `Elas4RDF` is that the retrieval unit is *triples*. This decision enables us to offer a *multi-perspective* approach, by providing different methods to organise and present the retrieved relevant triples. Specifically, *multiple perspectives*, each presented as a separate *tab*, are used for the presentation of the keyword search results, where each one stresses a different aspect of the hits. The user can easily inspect all tabs and get a better overview and understanding of the search results. Figure 1 shows the search results for the query "`El Greco paintings`", as presented in each of the four currently-supported perspectives. Below, we give more details for each perspective/tab.

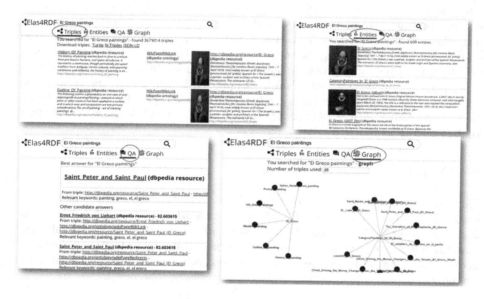

Fig. 1. Search results for the query "El Greco paintings".

Triples Tab. A ranked list of triples is displayed to the user, where each triple is shown in a different row. For visualising a triple, we create a *snippet* for each triple component (subject, predicate, object). The snippet is composed of: i) a title (the text indexed by the baseline method), ii) a description (the text indexed by the extended index; if any), and iii) the URI of the resource (if the element is a resource). If the triple component is a resource, its title is displayed as a hyperlink, allowing the user to further explore it. We also retrieve and show an image of the corresponding entity (if any), which is usually provided in cross-domain knowledge bases like DBpedia and Wikidata.

Entities Tab. Here the retrieved triples are *grouped* based on entities (subject and object URIs), and the entities are *ranked* following the approach described in [4], which considers the discounted gain factor of the ranking order of the triples in which the entities appear. Then, a ranked list of entities is displayed to the user, where each entity is shown in a different row. For visualising an entity, we create the same snippet like previously. The title is displayed as a hyperlink, since the entities are resources, allowing the user to further explore the entity.

Graphs Tab. Here the retrieved triples are visualised as a graph enabling the user to see how the 15 top-ranked triples *are connected*, however the user can increase or reduce this number. Moreover, the nodes that correspond to resources are clickable, pointing to the corresponding DBpedia pages. The current implementation uses the JavaScript InfoVis Toolkit[5].

Question Answering (QA) Tab. Here we attempt to interpret the user's query as a question and provide a *single compact answer*. The challenge is to retrieve the most relevant triple(s) and then extract natural language answers from them. QA over structured data is a challenging problem in general and currently only a few kinds of questions are supported by this "under-development" tab. It returns the more probable answer accompanied by a score, plus a list of other possible answers. In our running example, this tab returns the title of one painting of El Greco, while for the query "Who developed Skype?" it returns as more probable answer "Microsoft" and the next possible answer is "Skype Technologies".

4   Demonstration Scenarios

We will showcase the functionality of the system through queries of various kinds, like "fletc.her bounty", "drugs containing aloe", "Which cities does the Weser flow through?", "Rivers of Greece". Below we briefly discuss the added value that each perspective brings for the indicative query $q =$ Crete and Mars (as it involves more than two entities, and words with different meanings).

- **Triple's Tab**: This tab is generally the most useful one since the user can inspect all components of each triple, and understand the *reason why* that triple is returned. The addition of images helps to easily understand which triples involve the same entities. For the query q the user gets more than 600K triples that involve the name Crete (island) and Mars (mythical god, planet, etc.).
- **Entities' Tab**: If the user is interested in *entities*, and not in particular facts, this view provides the main entities. For the query q the returned entities include the island of Crete, an area of Mars whose name is related to Crete, Administration Area of Crete, Battle of Crete, and others.
- **Graph's Tab**: This tab allows the user to inspect a large number of triples without having to scroll down. Moreover this view reveals the *grouping* of triples, and whether there is one or more poles and interesting insights. For example, for the query q the user can see the connection of Crete (island) with Mars (mythology), through a resource about the Battle of Crete: Mars was

---

the mythical codename of a group of the Operation Mercury (Nazi's invasion to Crete in WWII).

- **Q&A Tab**: The result of this view for the query q is "Icaria Planum" which is a region on Mars whose name is based on the land where Icarus lived (Crete). This is what the current implementation of QA estimated as the more probable compact answer that connects Crete and Mars. In this particular query, this answer corresponds to the top ranked entity, however for other queries this is not the case: for the query "Tesla birth place" the entities' tab return first the resource about Nikola Tesla, while the QA tab returns "Obrenovac" which is the area where the largest Serbian thermal power plant "TPP Nikola Tesla" is located. The correct birth place of Nicola Tesla (Smiljan, Croatia) is shown in the first page of results.

5 Closing Remarks

`Elas4RDF` is a triple-centric keyword search system over RDF data. It can be applied to a plethora of RDF datasets since it is schema agnostic, it can be configured easily, and "inherits" the maturity and scalability features of `Elasticsearch`. The multi-perspective presentation of the search results enables tackling various kinds of information needs and allows users to explore the information space through the prisms of triple, entities, graph and Q&A tabs.

More perspectives will be added in the near future, e.g. for supporting *Faceted Search* as well as the formulation of SPARQL queries for advanced users. We also plan to advance the QA perspective for recognising the query type, enabling in this way the prioritisation of the perspectives, and to test the system over the domain specific knowledge repositories of GRSF [8] and ClaimsKG [6].

Acknowledgements. This work has received funding from the European Union's Horizon 2020 innovation action BlueCloud (Grant agreement No 862409).

References

1. Croft, W.B.: The importance of interaction for information retrieval. In: Proceedings of the 42nd International ACM SIGIR Conference on Research and Development in Information Retrieval, pp. 1–2. ACM (2019)
2. Dadzie, A.S., Pietriga, E.: Visualisation of linked data-reprise. Semantic Web **8**(1), 1–21 (2017)
3. Ilievski, F., Beek, W., van Erp, M., Rietveld, L., Schlobach, S.: LOTUS: adaptive text search for big linked data. In: Sack, H., Blomqvist, E., d'Aquin, M., Ghidini, C., Ponzetto, S.P., Lange, C. (eds.) ESWC 2016. LNCS, vol. 9678, pp. 470–485. Springer, Cham (2016). https://doi.org/10.1007/978-3-319-34129-3_29
4. Kadilierakis, G., Fafalios, P., Papadakos, P., Tzitzikas, Y.: Keyword search over rdf using document-centric information retrieval systems. In: Harth, A., et al. (eds.) ESWC 2020. LNCS, vol. 12123, pp. 121–137. Springer, Cham (2020). https://doi.org/10.1007/978-3-030-49461-2_8

5. Mountantonakis, M., Tzitzikas, Y.: Large-scale semantic integration of linked data: a survey. ACM Comput. Surv. (CSUR) **52**(5), 103 (2019)
6. Tchechmedjiev, A., et al.: ClaimsKG: a knowledge graph of fact-checked claims. In: Ghidini, C., et al. (eds.) ISWC 2019. LNCS, vol. 11779, pp. 309–324. Springer, Cham (2019). https://doi.org/10.1007/978-3-030-30796-7_20
7. Tzitzikas, Y., Manolis, N., Papadakos, P.: Faceted exploration of RDF/S datasets: a survey. J. Intell. Inf. Syst. **48**(2), 329–364 (2016). https://doi.org/10.1007/s10844-016-0413-8
8. Tzitzikas, Y., et al.: Methods and tools for supporting the integration of stocks and fisheries. In: Salampasis, M., Bournaris, T. (eds.) HAICTA 2017. CCIS, vol. 953, pp. 20–34. Springer, Cham (2019). https://doi.org/10.1007/978-3-030-12998-9_2

Answering Controlled Natural Language Questions over RDF Clinical Data

Naouel Karam[1]($\boxtimes$), Olga Streibel[2], Aray Karjauv[1], Goekhan Coskun[2],
and Adrian Paschke[1]

[1] Fraunhofer FOKUS, Berlin, Germany
{naouel.karam,aray.karjauv,adrian.paschke}@fokus.fraunhofer.de
[2] Bayer AG, Berlin, Germany
{olga.streibel,goekhan.coskun}@bayer.com

Abstract. Clinical trial data requires a lot of processing before it can be submitted in accordance with its standardization requirements. After its processing, data has to be stored carefully, often in different systems and formats. Integrating this data without information loss and enabling easy retrieval for later analysis is a highly challenging task. In this demo, we present our system for answering controlled Natural Language questions over RDF clinical data. Questions entered by a user through the proposed interface are annotated on the fly and suggestions are displayed based on an ontology driven auto-completion system. This approach assures a high level of usability and readability while preserving semantic correctness and accuracy of entered questions.

Keywords: Question answering · Controlled Natural Language · Clinical study ontology · RDF knowledge base · Clinical data

1 Introduction

Research practice has become more and more data-intensive, clinical studies are no exception, dealing with large amounts of data spread through a multitude of sources and stored in different formats. Research in this field is primarily data-driven and in order to enable cross-study analysis there is a permanent need for data integration. Since decades, multiple standardisation instances are trying to respond to those challenges by developing standards for clinical trials data exchange. Among many others, SDTM[1] (Study Data Tabulation Model) and ADaM[2] (Analysis Dataset Model) are the most prominent ones. Those standards come with inherent challenges. These are due to their two dimensional (tabular) nature, limiting their ability to represent relationships, as well as their lack of intrinsic metadata and linking to other standards. PhUSE[3], an independent, not-for-profit organisation run by clinical professionals, initiated the Clinical Trials Data as RDF project [6] to investigate the ability of Semantic Web technologies to address these challenges. The project goal is the creation of high-quality, highly compliant SDTM clinical

---

[1] cdisc.org/standards/foundational/sdtm.
[2] cdisc.org/standards/foundational/adam.
[3] phuse.eu.

© Springer Nature Switzerland AG 2020
A. Harth et al. (Eds.): ESWC 2020 Satellite Events, LNCS 12124, pp. 129–134, 2020.
https://doi.org/10.1007/978-3-030-62327-2_22

data, by converting it to RDF, based on an ontological model. The developed ontology and all deliverable of the project are available in the project Github repository[4].

In this work we have been exploring a novel retrieval mechanism that support clinical data scientists in finding relevant information for their research activities. We transformed clinical data coming from different sources and systems into RDF using the PhUSE ontologies. The resulting Knowledge Base (KB) serves as an integrated view to answer queries spreading over all required data. The majority of data analysts in the area of clinical data processing are neither familiar with SPARQL nor with Semantic Web technologies, hence the need to provide a user-friendly interface for querying the KB. A Natural Language (NL) interface was the solution of choice enabling scientists to easily pose their questions over the clinical data. They could be interested for instance in finding the number of subjects that were treated with a specific drug and who have been facing a serious adverse event[5].

Answering NL questions over Semantic Web resources is a very challenging and widely studied problem [3]. In order to reduce the complexity due to complex NL constructed sentences, Controlled Natural Language (CNL) approaches have been proposed lately [2, 5]. As stressed out in [1], using CNL improves considerably the usability of user interfaces to Semantic Web resources, by avoiding the ambiguity and vagueness of full Natural Language, while still preserving readability. Questions entered trough the interface produce more accurate and complete answers which in our case is a priority over question formulation flexibility.

Although our systems show case applied to the clinical domain, the system is conceived to be flexible and can be connected to any kind of RDF KB with an underlying OWL ontology. For instance, in our previous work on a linked data model for infectious disease reporting systems [7], we could conclude that a Natural Language query system would be of great value also for scientists working on epidemiological data.

In this demonstration, we present our system for querying RDF clinical data called askTONI. This paper describes the functionality of our system, its architecture and the showcase for end users in the clinical domain. A demo video can be found at: https://owncloud.fokus.fraunhofer.de/index.php/s/5GWk6sG50UggI9o.

2   Overview of askTONI

askTONI enables enterprise users to enter questions over their clinical data graph in a guided way. In the clinical domain, scientists are interested in retrieving fast answers to their questions over the scattered study data. By fast, we mean retrieval which does not involve any long query writings or any query language at all. An example of such a question could be "Give me enrolled subjects treated with placebo and afflicted by a serious adverse event." or "Give me adaptive design studies having age group equals to elderly 60.".

The process of question construction is based on the finite state machine depicted in Fig. 1. We propose an extension of the automaton, initially introduced to answer questions over DBpedia [5], with more complex ontological constructs and the possibility

---

[4] github.com/phuse-org/CTDasRDF.
[5] An experience associated with the use of a medical product in a study subject.

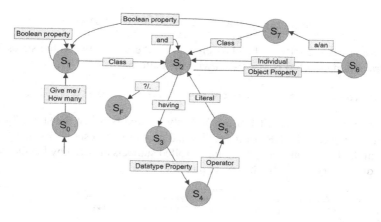

Fig. 1. askTONI finite state machine

of combined and embedded questions. The original solution defined the states S_1 to S_5 and operated on KB resources like entities, classes and properties. askTONI makes the distinction between datatype and object properties, individuals, classes and literals. In addition to the ontological constructs, operators (like "equals to", "less than", etc.) and nominal phrases (like "how many", "having", "a/an", etc.) are used to formulate the NL questions.

When a user starts entering a question like: "Give me enrolled subjects treated with placebo." (Q1) or "Give me adaptive design studies having age group equals to elderly 60." (Q2), the automaton is in the initial state (S_0). The user can choose between "Give me" and "How many", moving the automaton to state S_1. At S_1, the system can accept a class ("enrolled subjects" in Q1) and moves to S_2 or a boolean (yes/no) property ("add on" in Q2) and loops in S_1, then accepts a class (studies) to move to S_2. In S_2, a point or a question mark can be accepted leading to the final state where the generated query is executed. Alternatively, the user can enter a restriction using either an object property ("treated with" in Q1) or the NL phrase "having" and a datatype property ("age group" in Q2), leading to S_6 and S_4 respectively. From S_4, using an operator and a literal ("equals to elderly 60" in Q2) and from S_7 an individual ("placebo" in Q1), the systems goes back to S_2, which ends our example questions Q1 and Q2.

From S_7, the user can also choose the NL phrases ("a" or "an") and then either a class or a Boolean property which can be used to express a question like "Give me enrolled subjects afflicted by an adverse event?" or "Give me enrolled subjects afflicted by a serious adverse event?", serious being a boolean property for adverse events.

In S_2, we added the possibility to select "and" to enable users to select as many restrictions about the first class as desired. If the user do not enter "and" at state S_2, the restrictions apply to the last selected class. For instance, in "Give me enrolled subjects participating in a study having blinding equals to double blind.", the restriction on the blinding type applies to study and not to enrolled subject.

The SPARQL query is generated on the fly. Each transition is associated with a query pattern that is added to the where clause of the query. For instance, the transition $(S_1)(S_2)$ is associated with the pattern:

$$[\texttt{class-variable}] \ \texttt{rdf:type} \ <[\texttt{class12}]>. \qquad (1)$$

where `class12` is the URI of the class entered by the user between the states S_1 and S_2. The transition $(S_6)(S_2)$ is associated with the pattern:

$$[\texttt{class-variable}] \ <[\texttt{property26}]> \ <[\texttt{individual62}]>. \qquad (2)$$

where `property26` is the URI of the property entered between the states S_2 and S_6 and `individual62` the URI of the individual given by the user between S_6 and S_2. As an example, for the question "Give me enrolled subjects afflicted by Erythema?" the corresponding query would be the one depicted in Listing 1.

```
PREFIX study: <https://w3id.org/phuse/study#>
PREFIX cdiscpilot01: <https://w3id.org/phuse/cdiscpilot01#>
SELECT distinct ?c12
WHERE {
    ?c12 rdf:type study:EnrolledSubject.
    ?c12 study:afflictedBy cdiscpilot01:AE5_Erythema.
}
```

Listing 1. SPARQL query for question:"Give me enrolled subjects afflicted by Erythema?"

3   System Architecture

Figure 2 shows the main components of our system architecture. It consists of 3 docker containers:

1. **NodeJS server** is the main node and represents an intermediate layer between the user interface and the triple store. It communicates with other components over HTTP.
2. **Virtuoso server** is the triple store server storing all RDF data.
3. **OWL2VOWL converter** [4] is a service for converting RDF into JSON which is used to display a graph describing the ontology parts related to the query.

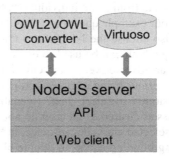

Fig. 2. Service architecture

Since all these components are decoupled, they can be deployed on different servers. The NodeJS server can be then configured so that it can access RESTful services. For security reasons, the web client can only communicate with the API. This makes it impossible for the user to access Virtuoso directly.

The user interface (Fig. 3) consists of a search field with an auto-suggest functionality. When entering a question, an auto-complete menu suggests terms and NL phrases based on which state the system is in. Depending on the current state (c.f. Fig. 1), the system sends the suitable request to the API and the list of returned terms are displayed to the user in an auto-complete drop-down list. The colors in the search field differentiate between types of terms: gray for NL phrases, green for concepts, aubergine for properties and yellow for instances. Once the system reaches the final state (i.e. the user have selected "?" or "."), the system generates the SPARQL query that is sent to Virtuoso for execution. The query results are returned to the web client as JSON and displayed in the UI as a list with corresponding properties. The user can browse the results set using pagination, he can switch between two presentation modes, tabular form and vignettes. The tool also generates the RDF to be converted into JSON using the OWL2VOWL converter and sent to the visualisation component to be displayed as a force-directed graph. The "show chart" button displays the VOWL visualisation of the parts of the ontology the query is based on.

Fig. 3. askTONI user interface

4   Demonstration

In this demonstration, visitors will be able to use the interface to type questions and will be guided by the system through suggestions. We will provide guidance and example questions. For those more adventurous, they are more than welcome to explore on their own. For user more interested in the models and RDF data behind the demo, we can also provide access to the PhUSE ontologies visualisation and the SPARQL endpoint.

Acknowledgements. This work was partially funded by the German Federal Ministry of Education and Research (BMBF) through the project QURATOR (grant no. 03WKDA1A).

References

1. De Coi, J.L., Fuchs, N.E., Kaljurand, K., Kuhn, T.: Controlled English for reasoning on the semantic web. In: Bry, F., Małuszyński, J. (eds.) Semantic Techniques for the Web. LNCS, vol. 5500, pp. 276–308. Springer, Heidelberg (2009). https://doi.org/10.1007/978-3-642-04581-3_6
2. Ferré, S.: squall2sparql: a translator from controlled English to full SPARQL 1.1. In: Forner, P., Navigli, R., Tufis, D., Ferro, N. (eds.) CEUR Workshop Proceedings of Working Notes for CLEF 2013 Conference, Valencia, Spain, vol. 1179, 23–26 September 2013. CEUR-WS.org (2013)
3. Höffner, K., Walter, S., Marx, E., Usbeck, R., Lehmann, J., Ngonga Ngomo, A.-C.: Survey on challenges of question answering in the semantic web. Semantic Web 8(6), 895–920 (2017)
4. Lohmann, S., Negru, S., Haag, F., Ertl, T.: Visualizing ontologies with VOWL. Semantic Web 7(4), 399–419 (2016)
5. Mazzeo, G.M., Zaniolo, C.: Answering controlled natural language questions on RDF knowledge bases. In: Pitoura, E., et al. (eds.) Proceedings of the 19th International Conference on Extending Database Technology, EDBT 2016, Bordeaux, France, 15–16 March 2016, pp. 608–611 (2016)
6. Oliva, A., Williams, T.: Transforming clinical trials with linked data. In: Pharmaceutical Users Software Exchange US 2018, Raleigh, North Carolina, 3–6 June 2018
7. Streibel, O., Kybranz, F., Kirchner, G.: Linked data and ontology reference model for infectious disease reporting systems. In: Panetto, H. et al. (eds.) On the Move to Meaningful Internet Systems. Lecture Notes in Computer Science. OTM 2017 Conferences - Confederated International Conferences: CoopIS, C&TC, and ODBASE 2017, Rhodes, Greece, 23–27 October 2017, Part II, vol. 10574, pages 109–124. Springer, Cham (2017). https://doi.org/10.1007/978-3-319-69459-7_8

Training NER Models: Knowledge Graphs in the Loop

Sotirios Karampatakis[(✉)] [iD], Alexis Dimitriadis, Artem Revenko,
and Christian Blaschke

Semantic Web Company, Neubaugasse 1, 1070 Vienna, Austria
{sotiris.karampatakis,alexis.dimitriadis,artem.revenko,
christian.blaschke}@semantic-web.com
http://www.semantic-web.com

Abstract. Motivated by the need of annotated data for training named entity recognition models, in this work we present our experiments on a distantly supervised approach using domain specific vocabularies and raw texts in the same domain. In the experiments we use MeSH vocabulary and a random sample of PubMed articles to automatically create an annotated corpus and train a named entity recognition model capable to identify diseases in raw text. We evaluate method against the manually curated CoNLL-2003 corpus and the NCBI-disease corpus.

Keywords: Named Entity Recognition · Machine learning · Linked data · Vocabulary · Knowledge graph

1 Introduction

Named Entity Recognition (NER) is a sub-task of information extraction with the objective to identify and classify named entities mentioned in unstructured text. [7,10] NER is commonly approached as a supervised classification problem. This means that annotated training materials are required. Annotated training corpora are obtainable for common NER types like Person, Location and Organization, but training NER models of other named entity types often requires an additional manual effort to annotate texts.

We aim at producing annotated data semi-automatically. As the pre-requisite we require an incomplete vocabulary for a domain. These vocabularies are often produced manually, for example, as a result of terminology extraction. The effort to produce such an incomplete domain specific vocabulary is significantly smaller than manually annotating a corpus. Most of the existing methods either use gazetteers as additional input to the NER model [2–4] or introduce new mechanisms to completely automate the task [6,8]. In this paper we investigate a different task of training an NER model with the help of Knowledge Graphs in the form of vocabularies. We reuse existing NER methods and use the vocabulary to create a training set. We investigate how well the modern NER methods can cope with the errors introduced by automatic annotation and if this procedure could be used to also make the domain vocabularies more complete.

A. Harth et al. (Eds.): ESWC 2020 Satellite Events, LNCS 12124, pp. 135–139, 2020.
https://doi.org/10.1007/978-3-030-62327-2_23

2   Methodology

Automatic Annotations. For getting the automatically annotated training corpus we have conducted the following steps.

First, we obtain or create a fixed vocabulary of a domain (for instance, chemical compound names, animal species, or geographic locations) to extract entity mentions from texts, i.e. to automatically annotate texts. The vocabulary should be sufficiently large, covering the majority of entity mentions in the training set, in order to reduce obscure entities during entity extraction. Instead of using a plain gazetteer, we structure the vocabulary using the SKOS data model [5] as it is easier to maintain and among with other benefits, it can be reused for additional NLP tasks, such as Entity Linking and Entity Disambiguation.

Second, we obtain a sizeable collection of raw texts (without annotations) for the domain of interest. Entity extraction is run on texts to identify occurrences of the vocabulary items. In particular, words in a text undergo morphological analysis and are matched against the contents of the vocabulary, meaning that only terms in the vocabulary can be recognized. As the result we obtain the **automatically annotated** training set. We use PoolParty Semantic Suite[1] as the automatic annotation tool. PoolParty is a tool that is used in many different enterprise use cases, therefore the quality of annotation is assumed to be high. We publish the resulting annotated dataset at https://github.com/semantic-web-company/ner-corpora.

Third, the automatically annotated corpus is then used to train an NER model, which draws on contextual cues to recognize Named Entities that are similar to the training vocabulary. The new classifier is then able to recognize new entities that are not in the training vocabulary.

Human Annotations. The human annotations are the original annotations manually done by the creators of the dataset. We train the same NER model also on human annotations and then evaluate it on the test set.

3   Experiments

Description of Datasets. The **CoNLL-2003** shared task corpus [9] is used as a standard benchmark for the NER task. It consists of human annotated text based on the Reuters News. It is annotated by four NE types: Person, Organization, Location and Miscellaneous. The **NCBI-disease** corpus [1] is a collection of 793 PubMed abstracts fully annotated at the mention and concept level to serve as a NER benchmark in the biomedical domain. The public release of the NCBI disease corpus contains 6892 disease mentions, which are mapped to 790 unique disease concepts.

---

[1] www.poolparty.biz.

Table 1. Evaluation results of OpenNLP NER on human annotated test corpora. Annotation method refers to the training corpora in each case. ΔF_1 is the difference in F_1 scores between automatic and human annotations. Vocabulary identifies how the controlled vocabulary for automatic annotations was created: either already provided human annotations were collected and used for automatic re-annotation or *Disease* branch of MeSH-2019.

Dataset	Vocabulary	Entity type	Annotation method						ΔF_1
			Human			Automatically			
			PR	RE	F_1	PR	RE	F_1	
CoNLL-2003	Extracted	Person	96.2	86.2	90.9	90.7	72.1	80.3	−10.6
CoNLL-2003	Extracted	Location	94.9	89.1	91.9	81.2	78.3	79.8	−12.2
CoNLL-2003	Extracted	Organization	94.2	65.4	77.2	55.1	70.2	61.7	−15.5
NCBI-disease	Extracted	Disease	82.7	62.1	70.9	75.6	67.1	71.1	0.2
NCBI-disease	MeSH-2019	Disease	82.7	62.1	70.9	55.5	27.7	36.9	−34.0

Set Up. To set a baseline for our evaluation, we used the human annotated training corpora to train models and then used the evaluation corpora for each dataset to evaluate the models in terms of Precision (PR), Recall (RE) and F_1 score (F_1). For each of the NE types, we created a Concept Scheme based on the labels of the NE found on the training corpora and re-annotated the raw training corpus using the PoolParty Extractor API, configured to use the corresponding Concept Scheme for each of the NE types. Finally, we used this corpus to train NER models for OpenNLP and evaluated the new models using the human annotated evaluation corpus for each. Results are summarized in Table 1.

Results. As presented in Table 1 models trained on automatically annotated corpus can achieve comparable results to models trained on human annotated corpus. Regarding the CoNLL-2003 corpus, an average difference of 12.8% indicates that we can actually create high quality training corpus for NER models. The process allowed us to identify common pitfalls in the automated annotation task. For instance homographs, words with the same spelling but different meaning, led to a large number of erroneous annotations on the training corpus. This induced a noisy training corpus for the classifier and as a result a considerable number of misclassified entities reducing both precision and recall. Hiding those entities from the annotator improved the results. In other cases, the annotator missed the correct bounds of the entity. In the case of the NCBI-disease corpus we conducted an additional experiment. For the automatic annotation part, instead of using extracted annotations from the manually curated training corpus, we used the *Disease* branch of the MeSH vocabulary. In this case, the coverage of the vocabulary was not complete to the annotations in the training corpus, leading to unidentified entities and reducing dramatically the performance of the classifier. Additionally, MeSH contains labels of the entities in an inverted form, for instance "Adenoma, Hepatocellular". This form confuses the annotator in an entity reach sentence leading to incorrect bounds of annotation and thus reduced quality of the training corpus. Normalizing the labels improved the quality.

Case Study. We wanted to test if we can produce an improved NER model for diseases. The corpus we used for this experiment consists of 10.000 abstracts (100k sentences) harvested from articles published in PubMed[2], filtered in the domain of diseases.

We used the MeSH vocabulary[3] (2019 update) as the target taxonomy to automatically annotate the corpus. We merged the automatically annotated corpus from PubMed with the manually curated NCBI-disease training corpus and then used OpenNLP to train an NER model for diseases. Finally we evaluated the produced model against the NCBI-disease test corpus. The scores of this model are PR 82.2%, RE 74.7% and F_1 78.2%, an improvement of 7.3% in F_1 and 12.5% in recall and 0.5% decline in recall.

4   Conclusion

The performance of the NER models for each specific NE type is dependant on the quality of the training corpus. Manual curated corpus gives the best results, though in this work we presented that it is feasible to produce comparable results using automatically annotated corpus. The quality of the corpus in this case depends on the quality of the vocabulary or Knowledge Graph used. Additionally the case study showed that we can combine a rather small manually curated training corpus with an automatically annotated training corpus to increase the performance of the model.

Acknowledgements. This work has been partially funded by the project LYNX which has received funding from the EU's Horizon 2020 research and innovation programme under grant agreement no. 780602, see http://www.lynx-project.eu.

References

1. Doğan, R.I., Leaman, R., Lu, Z.: NCBI disease corpus: a resource for disease name recognition and concept normalization. J. Biomed. Inf. **47** (2014). http://www.sciencedirect.com/science/article/pii/S1532046413001974
2. Liu, A., Du, J., Stoyanov, V.: Knowledge-augmented language model and its application to unsupervised named-entity recognition, pp. 1142–1150. Association for Computational Linguistics (2019). https://doi.org/10.18653/v1/n19-1117
3. Liu, T., Yao, J.G., Lin, C.Y.: Towards improving neural named entity recognition with gazetteers. In: Proceedings of the 57th Annual Meeting of the Association for Computational Linguistics, pp. 5301–5307 (2019)

---

[2] https://www.ncbi.nlm.nih.gov/pubmed/.

[3] Provided by National Library of Medicine https://www.nlm.nih.gov/mesh/meshhome.html.

4. Magnolini, S., Piccioni, V., Balaraman, V., Guerini, M., Magnini, B.: How to use gazetteers for entity recognition with neural models. In: Proceedings of the 5th Workshop on Semantic Deep Learning (SemDeep-5), pp. 40–49 (2019)
5. Miles, A., Bechhofer, S.: SKOS simple knowledge organization system reference. W3C recommendation 18, W3C (2009). https://www.w3.org/TR/skos-reference/
6. Nadeau, D., Turney, P.D., Matwin, S.: Unsupervised named-entity recognition: generating gazetteers and resolving ambiguity. In: Lamontagne, L., Marchand, M. (eds.) AI 2006. LNCS (LNAI), vol. 4013, pp. 266–277. Springer, Heidelberg (2006). https://doi.org/10.1007/11766247_23
7. Peng, M., Xing, X., Zhang, Q., Fu, J., Huang, X.: Distantly supervised named entity recognition using positive-unlabeled learning. In: Proceedings of the 57th Annual Meeting of the Association for Computational Linguistics, Florence, Italy, pp. 2409–2419. Association for Computational Linguistics, July 2019. https:// www.aclweb.org/anthology/P19-1231
8. Štravs, M., Zupančič, J.: Named entity recognition using gazetteer of hierarchical entities. In: Wotawa, F., Friedrich, G., Pill, I., Koitz-Hristov, R., Ali, M. (eds.) IEA/AIE 2019. LNCS (LNAI), vol. 11606, pp. 768–776. Springer, Cham (2019). https://doi.org/10.1007/978-3-030-22999-3_65
9. Tjong Kim Sang, E.F., De Meulder, F.: Introduction to the CoNLL-2003 shared task: language-independent named entity recognition. In: Proceedings of the Seventh Conference on Natural Language Learning at HLT-NAACL 2003, CONLL 2003, USA, vol. 4, pp. 142–147. Association for Computational Linguistics (2003). https://doi.org/10.3115/1119176.1119195
10. Wang, X., Zhang, Y., Li, Q., Ren, X., Shang, J., Han, J.: Distantly supervised biomedical named entity recognition with dictionary expansion. In: Yoo, I., Bi, J., Hu, X. (eds.) IEEE International Conference on Bioinformatics and Biomedicine, BIBM 2019, San Diego, CA, USA, 18–21 November 2019, pp. 496–503. IEEE (2019). https://doi.org/10.1109/BIBM47256.2019.8983212

ABECTO: An ABox Evaluation and Comparison Tool for Ontologies

Jan Martin Keil$^{(\boxtimes)}$ (iD)

Heinz Nixdorf Chair for Distributed Information Systems,
Institute for Computer Science, Friedrich Schiller University Jena, Jena, Germany
jan-martin.keil@uni-jena.de

Abstract. Correctness and completeness of ontologies on the schema and the instance level are important quality criteria in their selection for an application. Due to the general lack of gold standard data sources, the determination of these criteria, especially on the instance level, is challenging. The direct comparison of candidate data sources enables the approximation of these criteria. We introduce ABECTO, an ABox evaluation and comparison tool for ontologies. ABECTO provides a framework for the comparison of different semantic data sources in the same domain on the instance level.

Keywords: Ontology ABox · Ontology comparison · Ontology evaluation · Ontology quality · Ontology selection

1 Introduction

Ontologies can be valuable sources of domain knowledge for various applications. However, the selection of appropriate ontologies requires particular attention. The ontologies must provide a sufficient degree of entity coverage (*population completeness* in [1,2]) and a sufficient level of detail (*schema completeness* in [1,2]) [3]. Besides that, the faultless operation of applications also relies on the correctness (*accuracy* in [1,2]) and sufficient value coverage (*property completeness* and *interlinking completeness* in [1] or *column completeness* in [2]) of the ontologies. To verify the correctness and completeness of a candidate ontology, modeled facts must be compared to actual facts. These actual facts would be contained in a gold standard data source. Classical ontology engineering methodologies use competency questions to specify requirements and to verify requirement compliance. Expected answers to competency questions for the verification of correctness or completeness of facts in ontologies would implicitly also represent a gold standard data source. However, the existence of a gold standard data source for real world data is almost impossible. Due to this general lack of gold standard data sources, we proposed the direct comparison of multiple independent candidate ontologies to approximate their correctness

The original version of this chapter was revised: this chapter was previously published non-open access. The correction to this chapter is available at
https://doi.org/10.1007/978-3-030-62327-2_48

A. Harth et al. (Eds.): ESWC 2020 Satellite Events, LNCS 12124, pp. 140–145, 2020.
https://doi.org/10.1007/978-3-030-62327-2_24

and completeness [4]. Measures of the correctness and completeness could then support the selection of appropriate ontologies that fulfill the requirements of a certain project. As an example, consider two candidate ontologies containing 100 and 150 relevant entities respectively for a text annotation service. The first contains 100 English and 100 Spanish labels, the second 140 English and 130 Spanish labels. A comparison reveals that 90 of the entities are contained in both ontologies and detects deviations between the ontologies in 40 Spanish labels, caused by errors in the second ontology. Depending on the focused languages, this allows a more profound choice of the ontology.

The term *ontology comparison* is used with different meanings in the literature: (a) The comparison of entire ontologies regarding certain aspects to evaluate or select ontologies, (b) the comparison of different versions of one ontology to highlight changes, (c) the comparison of single entities or sets of entities to calculate recommendations of entities, or (d) the calculation of the similarity of single or a few entities from different ontologies to match or merge these ontologies [4]. In this paper, we focus on Variant (a), only.

We introduce ABECTO, an ABox evaluation and comparison tool for ontologies. ABECTO implements a framework for comparing multiple ontologies in the same domain. To the best of our knowledge, this is the first software tool for the comparison of ontologies on ABox level to approximate their correctness and completeness. In the remainder of this article, we will introduce the functionality of ABECTO in Sect. 2, explain our strategy to handle different modeling approaches in Sect. 3, describe the implementation of ABECTO in Sect. 4, and describe the demonstration in Sect. 5.

2 System Overview

ABECTO implements our framework for ontology ABox comparison described in [4]. The framework consists of five components, as shown in Fig. 1: (a) A *source* component to load ontologies, (b) a *transformation* component to add deduced axioms to the ontologies in preparation of further processing, (c) a *mapping* component to map the resources of the ontologies, (d) a *comparison* component to provide measurements of the ontologies, and (e) an *evaluation* component to identify potential mistakes in the ontologies.

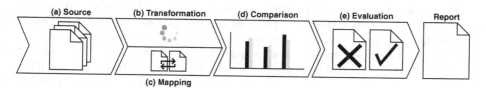

Fig. 1. Schematic of the comparison framework implemented in ABECTO. The order of the transformation and mapping processes is up to the user.

For each component, ABECTO provides a couple of *processors*, which provide a specific functionality. These processors can be arranged by the users into a processing pipeline to define the comparison process.

3   Handling of Different Modeling Approaches

The comparison of the ABoxes requires identifying corresponding facts of the ontologies. However, different ontologies of the same domain might use different approaches to model certain aspects of this domain. For example, there might be (a) properties corresponding to a chain of properties, (b) anonymous individuals corresponding to named individuals, (c) data properties corresponding to annotation properties, or (d) classes corresponding to individuals [4].

To meet this challenge, the sets of resources and their comparable properties are described with so-called *categories*. A category is defined by a SPARQL GroupGraphPattern [5] (the WHERE clause) for each ontology. The variable with the same name as the category represents the resource to compare. The bindings of all other equally named variables will be compared. This enables the definition of the facts to compare in a way that meets all mentioned cases: (a) Resource and variables can be linked by properties as well as complex property paths, (b) unambiguous IRIs can be created using key properties values, (c) resource and variables can be linked by data properties as well as annotation properties, and (d) the resource might represent a class as well as a individual. In the further processing, these patterns will be used to obtain the facts for ontology comparison.

4   Implementation

ABECTO is implemented as a Java HTTP REST service based on Apache Jena[1] and Spring[2] to provide a convenient interface for user interfaces or other applications. The size of compared ontologies is mainly limited by the memory required to represent the ontologies. Therefore, we expect ABECTO to be able to process large ontologies on appropriate hardware. A Python module provides handy functions to use ABECTO inside a Jupyter notebook[3], hiding the raw HTTP requests. This allows an easy setup of reproducible ontology comparison projects. However, the result presentation in the Jupyter Notebook interface for ABECTO is only suitable for smaller ontologies. To support large ontologies, an independent interface like a stand-alone web application would be needed. The sources of ABECTO are publicly available under the Apache 2.0 license [6].

In ABECTO, the ontologies will be compared inside of a project. A project consists of several ontologies and a processing pipeline. Each node of the pipeline represents a processor with a particular configuration. A processor is a Java class with specified methods to generate an output RDF model. The start nodes of the pipeline are the nodes representing a *source processor*, which loads an RDF model from an external source. To support modularized ontologies, multiple source nodes might belong to one ontology. Nodes of other processors require at least one input node. These processors can be divided into (a) *transformation*

---

[1] https://jena.apache.org/.
[2] https://spring.io/.
[3] https://jupyter.org/.

processors, which extend the input RDF model, (b) *mapping processors*, which provide resource mappings of the input RDF models of different ontologies, and (c) *meta processors*, which calculate comparative meta data from the input RDF models. The comparative meta data include *measurements*, like resource counts, identified *deviations* of mapped resources, *issues*, like an encountered literal when a resource was expected, and *categories*, which define the sets of resources and their properties to compare. The output RDF models of source and transformation processors belong to a certain ontology, whereas the output RDF models mapping and meta processors do not belong to a certain ontology. Therefore, they will be treated differently by the subsequent processors. The following processors are already available in ABECTO:

RdfFileSourceProcessor: Loads an RDF document from the local file system.

JaroWinklerMappingProcessor: Provides mappings based on Jaro-Winkler Similarity [7] of `string` property values using our implementation from [8].

ManualMappingProcessor: Enables users to manually adjust the mappings by providing or suppressing mappings.

RelationalMappingProcessor: Provides mappings based on the mappings of referenced resources.

OpenlletReasoningProcessor: Infers the logical consequences of the input RDF models utilizing the Openllet Reasoner[4] to generate additional triples.

SparqlConstructProcessor: Applies a given SPARQL Construct Query to the input RDF models to generate additional triples.

CategoryCountProcessor: Measures the number of resources and property values per category.

LiteralDeviationProcessor: Detects deviations between the property values of mapped resources as defined in the categories.

ManualCategoryProcessor: Enables users to manually define resource categories and their properties.

ResourceDeviationProcessor: Detects deviations between the resource references of mapped resources as defined in the categories.

We plan to add further processors in the near future, including:

- A mapping processor that employs the well known matching libraries using the Alignment API [9].
- A mapping processor that reuses mappings contained in the ontologies.
- A mapping processor that provides transitive mappings based on results of other mappings.
- A meta processor that utilizes mark and recapture techniques [10] to measure the completeness of ontologies.
- A source processor that loads an RDF document from a URL.
- A source processor that imports triples of a specified scope from a SPARQL endpoint.
- A source processor that utilizes SPARQL Generate [11] to load comparison data from non-RDF documents.

---

[4] https://github.com/Galigator/openllet.

Category Count Report

Category	Variable	Ontology 1	Ontology 2	Ontology 3
person		2	3	4
person	boss	2	2	
person	label	2	3	4
person	pnr	2		4

Deviation Report

Category: person

	Ontology 1			Ontology 2	
http://example.org/a/alice	boss	<http://example.org/a/bob>	<http://example.org/b/alice>	boss	http://example.org/b/alice
http://example.org/a/bill	label	Bill	William	label	http://example.org/b/william

	Ontology 1			Ontology 3	
http://example.org/a/alice	pnr	45678^^http://www.w3.org/2001/XMLSchema#integer	12345^^http://www.w3.org/2001/XMLSchema#integer	pnr	http://example.org/c/P001

Issue Report

Ontology: Ontology 2

Issue Type	Affected Entity	Message
UnexpectedValueType	http://example.org/b/william	Value of property "boss" is not a resource.

Fig. 2. Screenshot of an example report generated in a Jupyter Notebook. The report shows one type of measurement (number of resources and property values per category), encountered deviations, and encountered issue of a comparison of three ontologies.

The meta data models generated by the nodes can be used to generate reports. These reports might contain the calculated *measurements*, *deviations* and *issues*. Figure 2 shows an example report generated in a Jupyter Notebook.

5 Demonstration

We will demonstrate how users can utilize ABECTO to compare and evaluate ontologies. We will provide sets of real world RDF documents with prepared project definitions and category descriptions. The projects are managed inside of Jupyter notebooks. A tutorial notebook is available and can be executed online[5] using Binder [12]. Users will be able to manipulate and execute the project pipelines and examine the resulting comparison and evaluation reports.

Acknowledgments. Many thanks to the three anonymous reviewers, to my supervisor Birgitta König-Ries, and to my colleagues Alsayed Algergawy, Felicitas Löffler, and Samira Babalou for very helpful comments on earlier drafts of this manuscript.

---

[5] https://mybinder.org/v2/zenodo/10.5281/zenodo.3786194/?filepath=abecto-tutorial.ipynb (live preview loading might take a few minutes).

References

1. Zaveri, A., Rula, A., Maurino, A., et al.: Quality assessment for linked data: a survey. Seman. Web **7**(1), 63–93 (2016). https://doi.org/10.3233/SW-150175
2. Färber, M., Bartscherer, F., Menne, C., Rettinger, A.: Linked data quality of DBpedia, Freebase, OpenCyc, Wikidata, and YAGO. Seman. Web **9**(1), 77–129 (2018). https://doi.org/10.3233/SW-170275
3. Heist, N., Hertling, S., Ringler, D., Paulheim, H.: Knowledge graphs on the web - an overview. arXiv: 2003.00719v2 [cs.AI] 2 March 2020
4. Keil, J.M.: Ontology ABox comparison. In: Gangemi, A., et al. (eds.) ESWC 2018. LNCS, vol. 11155, pp. 240–250. Springer, Cham (2018). https://doi.org/10.1007/978-3-319-98192-5_43
5. SPARQL 1.1 Query Language. Recommendation. W3C, 21 March 2013. https://www.w3.org/TR/2013/REC-sparql11-query-20130321/
6. Keil, J.M.: ABECTO. https://doi.org/10.5281/ZENODO.3786194
7. Winkler, W.E.: String comparator metrics and enhanced decision rules in the Fellegi-Sunter model of record linkage. In: Proceedings of the Section on Survey Research, pp. 354–359. American Statistical Association (1990). http://eric.ed.gov/?id=ED325505
8. Keil, J.M.: Efficient bounded Jaro-Winkler similarity based search. In: Grust, T., Naumann, F., Böhm, A., et al. (eds.) BTW 2019. Gesellschaft für Informatik, Bonn, pp. 205–214 (2019). https://doi.org/10.18420/btw2019-13
9. David, J., Euzenat, J., Scharffe, F., dos Santos, C.T.: The alignment API 4.0. Seman. Web **2**(1), 3–10 (2011). https://doi.org/10.3233/SW-2011-0028
10. Razniewski, S., Suchanek, F.M., Nutt, W.: But what do we actually know? In: Pujara, J., Rocktäschel, T., Chen, D., Singh, S. (eds.) Proceedings of the 5th Workshop on Automated Knowledge Base Construction, AKBC@NAACL-HLT 2016. The Association for Computer Linguistics, pp. 40–44 (2016). https://doi.org/10.18653/v1/W16-1308
11. Lefrançois, M., Zimmermann, A., Bakerally, N.: A SPARQL extension for generating RDF from heterogeneous formats. In: Blomqvist, E., Maynard, D., Gangemi, A., Hoekstra, R., Hitzler, P., Hartig, O. (eds.) ESWC 2017. LNCS, vol. 10249, pp. 35–50. Springer, Cham (2017). https://doi.org/10.1007/978-3-319-58068-5_3
12. Project Jupyter, Bussonnier, M., Forde, J., et al.: Binder 2.0 - reproducible, interactive, sharable environments for science at scale. In: Akici, F., Lippa, D., Niederhut, D., Pacer, M. (eds.) Proceedings of the 17th Python in Science Conference 2018, pp. 113–120. https://doi.org/10.25080/Majora-4af1f417-011

LinkedPipes Applications - Automated Discovery of Configurable Linked Data Applications

Jakub Klímek$^{(\boxtimes)}$ (ID), Altynbek Orumbayev, Marzia Cutajar, Esteban Jenkins, Ivan Latták, Alexandr Mansurov, and Jiří Helmich (ID)

Department of Software Engineering, Faculty of Mathematics and Physics, Charles University, Malostranské náměstí 25, 118 00 Praha 1, Czech Republic
klimek@ksi.mff.cuni.cz
https://jakub.klímek.com

Abstract. Consumption of Linked Data (LD) is a far less explored problem than its production. LinkedPipes Applications (LP-APPs) is a platform enabling data analysts and data journalists to easily create LD based applications such as, but not limited to, visualizations. It builds on our previous research regarding the automatic discovery of possible visualizations of LD. The approach was based on the matching of classes and predicates used in the data, e.g. in a form of a data sample, to what an application or visualization expects, e.g. in a form of a SPARQL query, solving potential mismatches in data by dynamically applying data transformers. In this demo, we present a platform that allows a data analyst to automatically discover possible visualizations of a given LD data source using this method and the applications contained in the platform. Next, the data analyst is able to configure the discovered visualization application and publish it or embed it in an arbitrary web page. Thanks to the configuration being stored in their Solid POD, multiple analysts are able to collaborate on a single application in a decentralized fashion. The resulting visualization application can be kept up to date via scheduling an ETL pipeline, regularly refreshing the underlying data.

Keywords: Linked data · Consumption · Visualization · Application · Solid

1 Introduction

Nowadays, there are many linked data (LD) sources available, either within enterprise knowledge graphs, or as linked open data (LOD) publicly available on the Web. There has been a lot of research done on how to create LD. It is created either by transforming legacy data, e.g. by defining ETL processes [9] or

This work was supported by the Czech Science Foundation (GAČR), grant number 19-01641S.

A. Harth et al. (Eds.): ESWC 2020 Satellite Events, LNCS 12124, pp. 146–151, 2020.
https://doi.org/10.1007/978-3-030-62327-2_25

by building declarative mappings [3], or by producing LD natively, e.g. from IoT sensors in a form of RDF streams [1], etc. Note that an ETL (extract-transform-load) process is a data transformation paradigm, where data is first *extracted* from its original location, *transformed* by the data processing system and *loaded* to the target database. Once a LD dataset is created and accessible, either as an RDF dump, in a SPARQL endpoint, through IRI dereference or as a Linked Data Fragments server [13], there is an issue regarding its discoverability, i.e. how do the users find it. Partially, the issue of discoverability is tackled by, e.g. the Linked Open Data Cloud[1], or by a recently initialized list of known SPARQL endpoints[2]. This is, however, still far from ideal, as we show in [10]. Let us now assume that the potential consumer of the published dataset manages to find it.

Once an LD dataset is found by the consumer, they need to figure out how to work with it. This may include studying the dataset documentation, if available, or browsing through the dataset using one of the publisher provided data browsers such as the OpenLink Virtuoso Faceted Browser[3] or the more sophisticated Linked Data Reactor [8], if deployed. Typically, the process of getting to know a new dataset comes down to querying the data using dataset-independent exploratory SPARQL queries, such as:

1. Discover classes used in the data
2. Pick a few instances of the interesting classes
3. Discover predicates used by the picked instances

Only after the user gets to know the data, they are able to use it, e.g. in their own applications or visualizations. This is a critical part of the dataset consumption process when the user needs to extract the data relevant for the desired application and match the format to their tool of choice. However, there is information present in an LD dataset, such as the used classes and predicates, which could be exploited by an LD-enabled tool to match the data to its possible visualizations or other usages automatically.

In this demonstration, we present LinkedPipes Applications (LP-APPs) - a platform offering an alternative approach to the discovery of visualization applications applicable to a given LD data source, exploiting semantic information present in LD datasets and descriptions of expected input by applications in the platform. The discovered applications can be configured for better presentation to end users and published or embedded in a web page. The visualization configuration itself is stored in Solid PODs, which we exploit to provide collaboration capabilities. In case the source data changes over time, it might be necessary to periodically re-create the visualizations to keep them up to date, which is also supported by the platform. A Solid POD [11] is a personal online datastore, based on standard web technologies and separated from any applications, which can access and modify the stored data based on the users' permissions.

---

[1] https://lod-cloud.net/.

[2] https://github.com/OpenLinkSoftware/lod-cloud.

[3] http://vos.openlinksw.com/owiki/wiki/VOS/VirtFacetBrowserInstallConfig.

2   LinkedPipes Applications (LP-APPs)

The LP-APPs platform has a goal of easing creation and configuration of LD based visualizations in form of interactive applications. It supports two principal user roles. The first user role is the analyst, or journalist, who wants to prepare an LD based interactive application, which can be published or embedded in a news article. The second user role is the end user who can view the application and play with its interactive controls, such as filters. While the applications are created to be used by the end users, the platform focuses mainly on the analysts, to whom it offers features easing the creation of such interactive applications based on LD. LP-APPs builds on our previous research regarding automatic discovery of ways to visualize a given LD datasource [6,12], and focuses on the application configuration and publishing part of the process. The LP-APPs platform is open-source, hosted on GitHub[4] and can be run simply via Docker compose. From the point of view of the analyst, this is the typical workflow using the platform:

1. *WebID login.* Since all the visualization configurations are stored in the analysts' Solid PODs, the user needs to do login using their WebID first.
2. *Choice of LD data source.* From the dashboard, the user starts with selecting a LD data source. This can be either a SPARQL endpoint or an RDF dump - either via a direct file upload, or via a URL. There is also a set of showcase data sources for various application types.
3. *Automatic discovery of supported visualization techniques.* In this step, the platform uses the automated discovery process described in [12]. This is why, in addition to the data source, a small, but structurally representative data sample is required. For small datasets, the sample can be the same as the dataset, which is enough for the purpose of this demonstration. For larger datasets, the data sample can be created manually e.g. by separating one representative entity instance from the dataset. It could also be obtained automatically using techniques for dataset profiling [4], but this is not implemented yet. This step could also be substituted for a step generating an artificial data sample based on pre-existing metadata describing the dataset, e.g. using the VoID Vocabulary [5]. However, these descriptions, when present, are often inaccurate and outdated.
4. *Choice of desired technique in case of multiple options.* When multiple applications can be applied to the selected data source, the analyst chooses the desired one. This step is skipped, if there is only one application supported.
5. *Actual data transformation using LinkedPipes ETL.* Now that it is known which application is to be applied to the input data, a set of LinkedPipes ETL [9] data transformation pipelines is constructed automatically. Each pipeline takes the input data, and applies a set of data transformations, which lead to data compatible with the chosen application. If there is more than one possibility of how to transform the input data for the selected application,

---

[4] https://github.com/linkedpipes/applications.

the user chooses one. This step is skipped, if there is only one transformation available.

6. *Initial visualization in selected application.* Once the input data is transformed to a form consumable by the chosen application, the application is opened and the analyst can see the data in it.

7. *Configuration of application.* In this phase, the analyst can specify, which interactive controls such as filters and their values will be available to the end users. This is because a generic visualization might need to be, for instance, limited, to show only what is relevant to the end users. The application configuration is stored in the analyst's Solid POD [11], which also facilitates collaboration with other analysts and propagation of updates of the application configuration to the end users.

8. *Application publication or embedding.* Once the analyst is happy with the application configuration, they can publish it, i.e get its public URL, or generate an embedding snippet using HTML's `iframe`.

9. *Data refresh scheduling.* If the source data is regularly updated, and the analyst wishes to update the resulting application accordingly, they can schedule regular updates of the underlying data via scheduling of the LinkedPipes ETL pipeline.

3   Demonstration

The demonstration will be performed on our live demo instance running on https://applications.linkedpipes.com/. The source code is hosted on GitHub https://github.com/linkedpipes/applications.

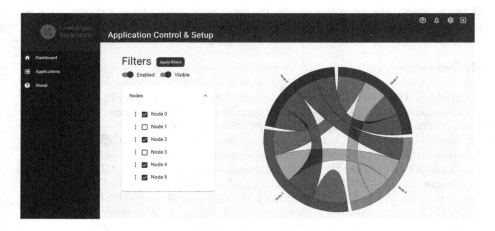

Fig. 1. Chord visualization application in LinkedPipes Applications

We will go through the basic workflow described in Sect. 2, resulting in applications in a form of chord visualization (see Fig. 1), Treemap visualization and a Timeline visualization.

In addition, we will demonstrate the benefits of the application configuration being stored in a Solid POD. Besides the usual benefits of the decentralized storage approach, we will show how the analysts can collaborate on configuration of a single visualization application thanks to the configurations being stored in Solid PODs.

4   Conclusions and Future Work

This demonstration shows how LP-APPs can be used to provide configurable visualization applications based on data in a linked data source. However, the platform is not limited to visualization applications. Using the same mechanism, any application such as a contact list manager or statistical data cube tool can be matched to a given data source. This is, as in the demonstration, provided that the data source contains data, which can either directly, or through a data transformation pipeline work with the application. A similar approach could also be adapted to match applications to data in Solid PODs.

On the other hand, the approach has some drawbacks. Mainly, even if LP-APPs finds a match of an application to a data source based on its data sample, it does not always mean that the actual data contains what is necessary for the application to work. Also, given that the approach is based on ETL, it does not work well for larger datasets. An alternative approach could be based on rewriting of SPARQL queries. A query used by the application to query data could be gradually rewritten in the opposite direction of the ETL pipeline, to match the data in the original data source. This could allow us to process even larger datasets. Finally, the Solid specification and implementation is quite live at the moment, changing frequently, breaking existing implementations. This is, however, to be expected at this stage of development.

References

1. Barbieri, D.F., Braga, D., Ceri, S., Valle, E.D., Grossniklaus, M.: C-SPARQL: a continuous query language for RDF data streams. Int. J. Seman. Comput. **4**(1), 3–25 (2010). https://doi.org/10.1142/S1793351X10000936
2. Bizer, C., Heath, T., Auer, S., Berners-Lee, T. (eds.): Proceedings of the Workshop on Linked Data on the Web Co-located with the 23rd International World Wide Web Conference (WWW 2014), Seoul, Korea, 8 April 2014, CEUR Workshop Proceedings, vol. 1184. CEUR-WS.org (2014). http://ceur-ws.org/Vol-1184
3. Dimou, A., Sande, M.V., Colpaert, P., Verborgh, R., Mannens, E., de Walle, R.V.: RML: a generic language for integrated RDF mappings of heterogeneous data. In: Bizer, et al. [2]. http://ceur-ws.org/Vol-1184/ldow2014_paper_01.pdf
4. Ellefi, M.B., et al.: RDF dataset profiling - a survey of features, methods, vocabularies and applications. Seman. Web **9**(5), 677–705 (2018). https://doi.org/10.3233/SW-180294
5. Hausenblas, M., Cyganiak, R., Alexander, K., Zhao, J.: Describing Linked Datasets with the VoID Vocabulary. W3C note, W3C, March 2011. https://www.w3.org/TR/2011/NOTE-void-20110303/

6. Helmich, J., Potoček, T., Klímek, J., Nečaský, M.: Towards easier visualization of linked data for lay users. In: Akerkar, R., Cuzzocrea, A., Cao, J., Hacid, M. (eds.) Proceedings of the 7th International Conference on Web Intelligence, Mining and Semantics, WIMS 2017, Amantea, Italy, 19–22 June 2017, pp. 12:1–12:9. ACM (2017). https://doi.org/10.1145/3102254.3102261

7. Indrawan-Santiago, M., Steinbauer, M., Salvadori, I.L., Khalil, I., Anderst-Kotsis, G. (eds.): Proceedings of the 19th International Conference on Information Integration and Web-based Applications & Services, iiWAS 2017, Salzburg, Austria, 4–6 December 2017. ACM (2017). https://doi.org/10.1145/3151759

8. Khalili, A., de Graaf, K.A.: Linked data reactor: towards data-aware user interfaces. In: Proceedings of the 13th International Conference on Semantic Systems. p. 168–172. Semantics 2017, Association for Computing Machinery, New York, NY, USA (2017). https://doi.org/10.1145/3132218.3132231

9. Klímek, J., Škoda, P.: LinkedPipes ETL in use: practical publication and consumption of linked data. In: Indrawan-Santiago et al. [7], pp. 441–445. https://doi.org/10.1145/3151759.3151809

10. Klímek, J., Škoda, P., Nečaský, M.: Survey of tools for linked data consumption. Seman. Web **10**(4), 665–720 (2019). https://doi.org/10.3233/SW-180316

11. Mansour, E., et al.: A demonstration of the solid platform for social web applications. In: Proceedings of the 25th International Conference Companion on World Wide Web. WWW 2016 Companion, International World Wide Web Conferences Steering Committee, Republic and Canton of Geneva, CHE, pp. 223–226 (2016). https://doi.org/10.1145/2872518.2890529

12. Nečaský, M., Helmich, J., Klímek, J.: Platform for automated previews of linked data. In: Indrawan-Santiago et al. [7], pp. 395–404. https://doi.org/10.1145/3151759.3151769

13. Verborgh, R., Sande, M.V., Colpaert, P., Coppens, S., Mannens, E., de Walle, R.V.: Web-scale querying through linked data fragments. In: Bizer et al. [2]. http://ceur-ws.org/Vol-1184/ldow2014_paper_04.pdf

MedTable: Extracting Disease Types from Web Tables

Maria Koutraki$^{(\boxtimes)}$ and Besnik Fetahu

L3S Research Center, Leibniz University of Hannover, Hannover, Germany
{koutraki,fetahu}@l3s.de

Abstract. Diseases and their symptoms are a frequent information need for Web users. Diseases often are categorized into sub-types, manifested through different symptoms. Extracting such information from textual corpora is inherently difficult. Yet, this can be easily extracted from semi-structured resources like tables. We propose an approach for *identifying* tables that contain information about *sub-type classifications* and their *attributes*. Often tables have *diverse* and *redundant* schemas, hence, we align *equivalent* columns in disparate schemas s.t. information about diseases are accessible through a *unified* and a *common* schema. Experimental evaluation shows that we can accurately identify tables containing disease sub-type classifications and additionally align equivalent columns.

1 Introduction

Publicly available medical resources like PubMed[1], or MedQuad [1] (a Q&A dataset about *disease information*), serve as a training ground for Q&A systems with use cases such as symptoms and disease identification [2]. Yet, these repositories are mostly unstructured and require extensive efforts for reasoning over concepts like disease, or different types that diseases or genetic syndromes may have.

On the other hand, for structured resources, like the Disease Ontology (DO)[2] or the classification schema International Classification of Diseases (ICD)[3], accessing information is trivial, however, coverage is limited. DO uses up to seven features to describe a disease (e.g. ID, name, description) while ICD provides only a textual description and a link to the parental disease in the taxonomy.

Recent efforts, focused on harnessing information from Web tables, show that tables are rich in information coverage (e.g. more than 4k medical articles in Wikipedia). Often, tables can be interlinked with each other according to their topic similarity [6], thus, producing even a richer landscape of information that can be extracted from tables.

---

[1] https://www.ncbi.nlm.nih.gov/pubmed/.

[2] https://disease-ontology.org/.

[3] https://www.who.int/classifications/icd/en/.

© Springer Nature Switzerland AG 2020
A. Harth et al. (Eds.): ESWC 2020 Satellite Events, LNCS 12124, pp. 152–157, 2020.
https://doi.org/10.1007/978-3-030-62327-2_26

In this work, our main aim is to harness information from tables containing medical information about *disease sub-type* classifications (e.g. `Arthritis` has two common types `Osteoarthritis` and `Rheumatoid Arthritis`) and their *characteristics* and *symptoms*, to enrich existing medical corpora like MedQuad, such that Q&A application can provide more faceted answers from the rich table structures, contrary to the short and ambiguous summaries in MedQuad dataset.

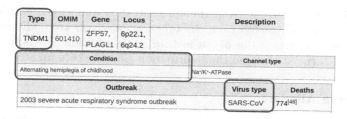

Fig. 1. Examples of three different disease tables with equivalent columns marked in green. (Color figure online)

To do so, we address two problems. First, from the tables' corpus, TableNet [6], we *identify* tables that contain information about disease *sub-type classifications*, and second, due to diversity of table schemas, we *align* related or equivalent columns. These steps ensure our goal to provide a common schema, which allows for a unified access to all tables containing disease classification related information. In this paper, we make the following contributions:

- an approach for identifying tables about disease types or genetic syndromes;
- an approach for aligning columns that refer to equivalent or related concepts;
- a corpus under a common schema for tables related to disease type classifications.

2   MedTable: Table Identification and Column Alignment

In this section, we present our approach *MedTable* and describe the two main steps for generating the corpus of tables containing disease classification related information.

2.1   Table Identification

Our testbed for tables is the TableNet [6], with more than 3M tables. However, only a small portion of tables is of interest, namely, containing information related to possible (-sub)types of a disease. In the following, we describe the features that we construct for building a supervised machine learning model for classifying tables into either containing *(-sub)types* of diseases or *not*. Since our tables' corpus consists of tables and the corresponding Wikipedia articles from where they are extracted, we consider the following two feature categories.

Article Level Features. The choice of article features is to consider the context in which a table occurs. This is necessary as some tables are under-specified and the actual information can be interpreted only in conjunction with the article information [4,5]. We consider the Wikipedia *article name*, *section label*, and the *average word representation* of a section's text [11]. Contextual information is necessary as the models learn to distinguish between tables that have similar structures, but topically are highly divergent.

Table Related Features. Even though context is important, another set of crucial features are extracted from the tables themselves. We additionally consider the *column names* as one of our features. The intuition here is that column names provide crucial hints on the information that the column stores.

2.2 Column Alignment

After having classified tables whether they contain (sub-)type diseases information, the objective here is to *align* columns that are semantically related or equivalent. This is a necessary step, as table schemas across tables are not standardized and often columns with the same information are named differently (cf. Fig. 1). Furthermore, column names are ambiguous, and as such a simple lexical match is insufficient.

For that reason we follow a similar approach to those used on schema matching for knowledge graphs [3,8,9]. For a column pair $\langle c_i, c_j \rangle$ from two disparate table schemas, we extract features from the columns, namely the cell values from the respective tables they are extracted, and train a supervised model that classifies them into either *equivalent* or *not*.

We consider the following column features. First, from the *column heading* we construct an average word representation based on GloVe pretrained embeddings [11], correspondingly, we measure the cosine similarity of such representations for the columns c_i and c_j. Second, since column names can be ambiguous, hence, we consider features that are computed based on the column cell values. For columns whose cell values are already interlinked to Wikipedia entities, we consider the average node embedding representation from all instances, by training the graph embeddings based on node2vec [7] on the Wikipedia's anchor graph. That is, for the pair $\langle c_i, c_j \rangle$, we compute the cosine similarity of such representations. Third, for cell values that are simple literals (i.e. numbers, strings etc.), we consider the jaccard similarity of the corresponding values, and in the case of numerical values, we compute the Kullback-Leibler divergence from the corresponding probability distributions of the cell values.

3   Evaluation

The evaluation setup and approach of this work is available for download[4].

3.1 Dataset and Ground Truth

Diseases Dataset. We collect all the Wikidata (WD)[5] instances of class *Disease* (wd:Q12136), resulting in 11k instances. From the resulting subset, we consider only those that have a corresponding article in the English Wikipedia (WP) resulting in 4386 pages, out of those 327 contain tables. We additionally investigated the diseases' ontology from the BioSNAP Datasets [10], resulting in an additional 17 diseases that did not exist in the WD corpus. Finally, our dataset consists of 344 WP disease articles.

TableNet – Data. From the 344 WP pages, we extract 764 tables from the TableNet [6], consisting of 5,738 rows in total, with 990 distinct columns.

Ground Truth. We manually constructed the ground-truth for both classification steps in our approach. For the first step, **table classification.**, we annotated all the 764 tables of our dataset, resulting in 190 relevant tables, and the remainder are not related to (sub-)type disease classification. Whereas, for the second step, **column alignment.**, we randomly sampled a set of 350 column pairs from the tables to assess which columns can be aligned, which resulted in 66 aligned column pairs, whereas the remainder of column pairs did not represent equivalent columns.

3.2 Results and Discussion

In this section we discuss the obtained results for both steps in our approach. In both cases, we train a *logistic regression* model based on the described feature sets in Sect. 2.1 and 2.2. We evaluate the performance of our models based on evaluation metrics such as: *precision* – P, *recall* – R and F1. Evaluation results in Table 1 and 2 correspond to 5-fold cross validation.

Table 1. Table classification results.

	P	R	F1
Article features	0.82	0.68	0.74
Table features	0.86	0.53	0.66
All	**0.87**	**0.73**	**0.80**

Table 2. Column alignment results.

	P	R	F1
equiv.	0.867	0.703	0.78
non-equiv.	0.922	0.970	0.95

Table Classification. Table 1 shows the results of the table classification step, and the feature ablation. Note how the two feature sets are complementary, in that, article features provide better coverage, which was our initial intuition as well by capturing contextual information from the articles which describe the diseases listed in a table. On the other hand, table features are more accurate predictors of tables that contain (sub-)type disease information. This is mostly attributed to specific columns that are often to describe disease classifications

---

[5] Accessed 17.04.2019.

and describing their symptoms (e.g. *"Type"* the table contains relevant information to (sub-)types of the disease). Jointly, the model is able to achieve high classification performance with an overall score of $F1 = 0.80$.

Column Alignment. Table 2 shows the classification results for the column alignment step. Note here that the two classes are highly imbalanced, with the `equiv` class representing only 18% of the dataset. The achieved results are highly satisfactory, reaching a high F1 score of 0.78. This allows us to align columns that are equivalent across disparate table schemas, and thus, offer a unified way to access the disease (sub-)type classifications and their descriptions through a common schema.

4   Conclusions

We present MedTable, an approach for identifying tables about (sub-)types of diseases and correspondingly aligning columns that represent equivalent concepts. We performed an evaluation on the TableNet corpus, where we evaluated on manually constructed ground-truth. We identified nearly 200 relevant tables and were able to align 18% of columns as equivalent. The generated corpus will be made publicly available and can serve for Q&A approaches in the medical domain.

References

1. Abacha, A.B., Demner-Fushman, D.: A question-entailment approach to question answering. arXiv e-prints, January 2019. https://arxiv.org/abs/1901.08079
2. Abacha, A.B., Shivade, C., Demner-Fushman, D.: Overview of the MEDIQA 2019 shared task on textual inference, question entailment and question answering. In: BioNLP (2019)
3. Biswas, R., Koutraki, M., Sack, H.: Exploiting equivalence to infer type subsumption in linked graphs. In: Gangemi, A., et al. (eds.) ESWC 2018. LNCS, vol. 11155, pp. 72–76. Springer, Cham (2018). https://doi.org/10.1007/978-3-319-98192-5_14
4. Biswas, R., Koutraki, M., Sack, H.: Predicting Wikipedia infobox type information using word embeddings on categories. In: Proceedings of the EKAW 2018 Posters and Demonstrations Session (2018)
5. Biswas, R., Türker, R., Moghaddam, F.B., Koutraki, M., Sack, H.: Wikipedia infobox type prediction using embeddings. In: Proceedings of the First Workshop on Deep Learning for Knowledge Graphs and Semantic Technologies (DL4KGS) (2018)
6. Fetahu, B., Anand, A., Koutraki, M.: Tablenet: An approach for determining fine-grained relations for Wikipedia tables. In: The World Wide Web Conference, WWW 2019 (2019)
7. Grover, A., Leskovec, J.: node2vec: scalable feature learning for networks. In: KDD (2016)
8. Koutraki, M., Preda, N., Vodislav, D.: SOFYA: semantic on-the-fly relation alignment. In: Proceedings of the 19th International Conference on Extending Database Technology, EDBT 2016, Bordeaux, France, 15–16 March 2016 (2016)

9. Koutraki, M., Preda, N., Vodislav, D.: Online relation alignment for linked datasets. In: Blomqvist, E., Maynard, D., Gangemi, A., Hoekstra, R., Hitzler, P., Hartig, O. (eds.) ESWC 2017. LNCS, vol. 10249, pp. 152–168. Springer, Cham (2017). https://doi.org/10.1007/978-3-319-58068-5_10

10. Zitnik, M., Rok Sosič, S.M., Leskovec, J.: BioSNAP Datasets: Stanford biomedical network dataset collection, August 2018. http://snap.stanford.edu/biodata

11. Pennington, J., Socher, R., Manning, C.D.: Glove: global vectors for word representation. In: EMNLP (2014)

Can a Transformer Assist in Scientific Writing? Generating Semantic Web Paper Snippets with GPT-2

Albert Meroño-Peñuela[1]([envelope]), Dayana Spagnuelo[1], and GPT-2[2]

[1] Vrije Universiteit, Amsterdam, The Netherlands
{albert.merono,d.spagnuelo}@vu.nl
[2] OpenAI Inc., San Francisco, CA, USA

Abstract. The Semantic Web community has produced a large body of literature that is becoming increasingly difficult to manage, browse, and use. Recent work on attention-based, sequence-to-sequence Transformer neural architecture has produced language models that generate surprisingly convincing synthetic conditional text samples. In this demonstration, we re-train the GPT-2 architecture using the complete corpus of proceedings of the International Semantic Web Conference since 2002 until 2019. We use user-provided sentences to conditionally sample paper snippets, therefore illustrating cases where this model can help at addressing challenges in scientific paper writing, such as navigating extensive literature, explaining the Semantic Web core concepts, providing definitions, and even inspiring new research ideas.

Keywords: Natural language generation · Semantic Web papers · Scholarly communication

1 Introduction

A current scientific crisis revolves around the unmanageable pace at which new papers are being published. Studies show that over the past decades the number of published scientific papers has climbed by 8–9% each year; only in biomedicine 2 papers per minute are published in PubMed [6]. This causes problems to the traditional workflows of scientists, who lack resources for keeping up. The added load on an already resource-scarce scientific environment creates additional challenges: navigating scientific literature; writing papers; and getting new ideas becomes even harder. Moreover, humans have inherent limitations, such as not being systematic, introducing errors, having biases, and writing poor reports [3]. The use of AI to address these limitations has been identified as essential [5].

The Semantic Web, a research community that had its first international conference in 2002, is also exposed to these challenges. Only in 2019 its proceedings contained 1,377 pages and 569,371 words [4]; the complete 2002–2019 series contains 21,337,067 words. As time progresses, the entry cost to the knowledge and insights contained in these proceedings raises.

© Springer Nature Switzerland AG 2020
A. Harth et al. (Eds.): ESWC 2020 Satellite Events, LNCS 12124, pp. 158–163, 2020.
https://doi.org/10.1007/978-3-030-62327-2_27

Language models have seen a spectacular improvement due to the introduction of deep neural architectures for long short-term memory [1]. Specifically, neural architectures based on the attention-based, sequence-to-sequence transformers such as BERT [2] and GPT-2 [8] have produced language models that generate surprisingly convincing synthetic conditional text samples. These models have been applied *e.g.*, to generate PubMed/MEDLINE abstracts[1] and investigate imaginary and unexplored hypotheses around climate change [7].

Here, we leverage the language learning and generation capabilities of GPT-2 for Semantic Web literature, and we re-train its small model (117M parameters) using the full corpus of International Semantic Web Conference (ISWC) proceedings. We focus on GPT-2 mainly due to its emphasis on auto-regression rather than the context of both sides of a word. Our goal is to investigate how AI and natural language generation can support the increasingly challenging task of writing Semantic Web papers. To do this, we first gather all ISWC proceedings volumes in PDF format, and we transform and prepare them in text form (Sect. 2). Then, we use this representation as training set for GPT-2, and we study the conditional samples it generates at given inputs (Sect. 3). We build a web-based interface on top of the model in order to demonstrate our approach (Sect. 4). Finally, we draw some conclusions and reflect on future work (Sect. 5).

2   Dataset

Our dataset is generated from the electronic version of the International Semantic Web Conference[2] (ISWC) proceedings. There are 18 proceedings ranging from the year of 2002, until 2019, with those after 2010 split into two parts due to their extensive length. This amounts into a total of 28 files processed by us.

We have converted each PDF file into TXT using the `pdftotext` command line tool. The tool can transcribe files while roughly maintaining their original physical layout, in the case of ISWC, the Lecture Notes in Computer Science (LNCS) template. Nonetheless, the tool is not precise, and introduces some conversion errors. These make the generated text, at times, meaningless to human readers. We have cleaned up most of these errors, and some other elements (*e.g.*, list of authors, table of contents, page headers) which disrupt the training of language models. In the following, we describe our data cleaning process.

2.1   Data Cleaning

We clean the transcribed proceedings by leveraging from the LNCS template and its layout components. We use them to build regular expressions[3] which help us locate and remove unwanted content, in this particular order: 1. cover pages and meta information about the book; 2. running headers with authors and paper titles; 3. the list of organisation committee and sponsors, and the table

---

[1] https://twitter.com/DrJHoward/status/1188130869183156231.
[2] Latest edition at time of writing: https://iswc2020.semanticweb.org/.
[3] Script available at: https://github.com/dayspagnuelo/lncs_template_cleaner.

of contents; 4. copyright footnotes; 5. list of references; and 6. author index. We also conduct some cleanings to help structuring better the output text, they clean some but not all instances of: 7. tables; 8. extra spaces and indentation (which also covers figures, algorithms, and formulae); and 9. extra lines. For the sake of brevity, we select a few components to give more explanation.

Cover Pages. The initial pages of the proceedings contain the cover, and mostly information about the book and its printing. We remove everything found before the heading "Preface" as it does not contain scientific text on Semantic Web. We decided to include the preface in our dataset as it is also written by members of the Semantic Web community.

Running Headers. Running headers contain authors' names, paper titles and page numbers. They are the first content in most pages of the proceedings (except first page of each paper), which means they break the flow of natural text. We identify running headers by the presence of a *page break* character.

References. We remove references as they do not represent natural text. In order to remove the list of references of each paper we select content from the heading "References" until the next *page break* character.

The order of the cleaning steps is relevant. For instance, removing running headers before references. For short references sections that fit within one page, the next *page break* represents the beginning of the next paper. However, for longer ones taking more than one page, we must first remove the running headers, which also removes the page breaks characters in between the reference list.

Some automatic steps do not clean all the instances in a proceeding. One example are the Figures, which sometimes contain textual elements that get transcribed as disconnected words spaced in a random fashion. Building unambiguous regular expressions for those is challenging. We chose instead to search for extra spaces and indentation in the text, which normally includes figures and their captions. Some instances may remain, but the results of the last cleaning steps (7–9) help giving our dataset a natural text structure.

3 Training GPT-2 with Semantic Web Papers

Using the output of the clean ISWC text proceedings, we retrain GPT-2 using the 117M model as a basis in a 32 core Intel(R) Xeon(R) CPU E5-2630 v3 @ 2.40 GHz with 252 GB of RAM. We use the framework provided directly by OpenAI[4]. First, we encode the dataset to prepare it for multiple runs (118 s, 21,337,067 tokens). Then, we run the training process for 68,280 iterations and 332,533.83 s (92.37 h, average of 4.87 s/it). The average loss at this point is 2.19 (with the last loss being 2.10). We then use the resulting model to generate conditional samples using various input texts. The following examples show the synthetic conditional samples generated by the model (in italics) at the provided input sentences (between quotes):

---

[4] https://github.com/openai/gpt-2

Example 1 (Explaining related work). "Reasoning with OWL ontologies at scale has proven to be a difficult problem in the Semantic Web. As shown by van Harmelen et al." *[1], the task of OWL reasoning involves the problem of identifying the relations between entities in a knowledge base. In this paper we present a series of approaches to the discovery of such relations. In particular, we focus on the problem of OWL reasoning by defining a set of axioms (or concepts) that can be used to classify knowledge bases.*

Example 2 (Definitions). "The Semantic Web is" *a rich and evolving web of interconnected resources with many different types of content, such as web pages, blogs, videos, music plays, and so on.*

Example 3 (Acknowledgements). See Acknowledgements below.

Example 4 (Explaining topics). "Decentralised querying on the Semantic Web with SPARQL has a number of advantages." *First, the presence of RDF graphs (i.e., named graphs) in the data, along with the possibility of querying them with SPARQL, allows the user to retrieve relevant data from the data cloud. Second, with the large amount of available data, the application is able to scale up to a large number of data sources.*

Example 5 (Suggesting novel ideas). "Many of the challenges of the Semantic Web have been partially solved using deep learning techniques based on embeddings. In this paper," *we present a system that generates a deep neural network (Deep Convolutional Network) from a set of neural networks and integrates it with a subset of the ontology that is used to model features of the text. Such neural networks are applied to model the textual content of the text, and the features are used to compute the semantic similarity between these features. The user-defined features can then be used to compute semantic features for the textual content of the text. Figure 2 shows the implementation of this class of features for the text in the system.*

Example 6 (Structured language). "PREFIX rdf: <http://www.w3.org/ 1999/02/22-rdf-syntax-ns#> SELECT * WHERE {" *?entity ?name . ?entity ?name . ?entity . ?entity . ?entity . ?entity . ?entity }*

Example 7 (Exploring research alternatives). "A number of different approaches investigate the problem of ontology matching in the Semantic Web. For example," *the work on ontology matching by Euzenat [5] is an example of a model of matching. Recently, a new approach for ontology matching has been proposed that addresses the problem of ontology alignment based on the problem of ontology matching. The problem of ontology alignment based on similarity of concepts is described by similarity of classes and property.*

Example 8 (Paper structure). "The main contributions of this paper are" *as follows: – The first is a set of rules for the classification of relational data schemas. These rules are designed to be based on the following categories of data: – Datatypes: These are data that are the subject of at least one triple pattern and are considered to be an instance of schema. – Classes: These are either datatypes that are a subclass of data types, or datatypes that are not datatypes.*

Example 9 (Scientific hypotheses). "In this paper, our hypothesis is" *that a new ontology can be derived from an existing one. The key idea is to combine ontology-based and knowledge-based approaches, which are designed to provide reasoning and reasoning-based services that allow to perform reasoning tasks.*

Example 10 (Scientific research questions). "Therefore, our research question in this paper is" *how do we build a system that is able to learn and use such knowledge in a real context and that can answer this question in a way that is representative of a real problem.*

Example 11 (Providing explanations, Web-scale reasoning). "A simple explanation for the difficulty of solving large scale ontology reasoning is" *that we tend to solve small problems by imposing very big and complex rules. We often end up with very large portions of ontologies that cannot be represented using standard reasoners.*

Example 12 (Providing explanations, entity linking methods). "Machine learning techniques are used for the task of entity linking because" *it is a challenging task for the user. Therefore, we propose a novel method that is scalable to large knowledge bases with a high number of facts and a high accuracy.*

4   Demonstration

A web-based demonstrator of the trained model through conditional sampling is available at http://swgpt2.amp.lod.labs.vu.nl/. As parameters for conditional sampling, we set the temperature at 1 and the diversity at 40. After the service loads the required libraries, a `Model prompt` is displayed. The user can then type the sentence, followed by the enter key, that will be used as input to the model for conditional sampling. After a few seconds, the model outputs a sample.

The demonstration on the floor will make use of this prompt for conditional sampling. Users will be instructed to provide contexts of various lengths, as well as finished and unfinished sentences. The guidance for the input sentences, as well as the generated content, will include: (a) Semantic Web topics (*e.g.*, knowledge graph construction, querying, ontologies, APIs, reasoning, etc.); (b) Structured and unstructured content (*e.g.*, RDF vs natural language); (c) Outlines, citations, and other scholarly features; (d) Well-known authors in the community.

5   Conclusion and Future Work

In this paper, we describe a demonstration that uses the GPT-2 transformer architecture to learn a language model for a cleaned corpus of 2002–2019 ISWC proceedings, and leverages this model to generate samples conditioned on input. The demonstration is available as a public Web interface. Our findings are that the model can be used to generate meaningful texts that can be used for various scientific writing tasks, such as explaining related work, providing definitions, or proposing hypotheses. We think this work can be used for scientific writing assistance, as well as inspire new research directions through human-machine brainstorming.

From the social perspective, we are aware of the ethical implications of using natural language generation and AI for scientific writing, including the need for accountability, the shared responsibility of all contributors (humans or machines), and the requirement on these contributors to fully understand what they report on. In this sense, we see this work more as an assistance and a tool for human writers, as seen in *e.g.*, Gmail's auto-complete, rather than a substitute.

We foresee various possibilities to continue this work in the future. First, we plan to to retrain GPT-2 adding the whole collection of ESWC papers, increasing the scale of the experiment and testing the robustness of our dataset cleaning strategy. Second, we will investigate methods for dynamically generating this cleaning strategy, and reusing the training set for different user-specific goals. Third, we want to expand our approach by leveraging the knowledge already available in Knowledge Graphs, and generate the seed conditioning sentences by querying Knowledge Graphs to effectively guide the text generation through real-world models and semantic pathways. Fourth, we plan on using this language model for downstream tasks other than text generation, *e.g.*, finding similar papers by using alternative wordings.

Acknowledgements. "This paper would not have been possible without the support of several persons and institutions. GPT-2 would like to thank" *all of the members of the GPT-1 technical committee.* The authors want to thank Frank van Harmelen, Paul Groth, and the anonymous reviewers for their valuable comments. This work is partly supported by the CLARIAH project funded by NWO.

References

1. Cho, K., et al.: Learning phrase representations using RNN encoder-decoder for statistical machine translation. arXiv:1406.1078 (2014)
2. Devlin, J., Chang, M., Lee, K., Toutanova, K.: BERT: pre-training of deep bidirectional transformers for language understanding. CoRR abs/1810.04805 (2018). http://arxiv.org/abs/1810.04805
3. Garijo, D., et al.: Quantifying reproducibility in computational biology: the case of the Tuberculosis Drugome. PloS One **8**(11), e80278 (2013)
4. Ghidini, C., et al.: The Semantic Web-ISWC 2019. Springer, Cham (2019). https://doi.org/10.1007/978-3-030-30796-7
5. Gil, Y.: Thoughtful artificial intelligence: forging a new partnership for data science and scientific discovery. Data Sci. **1**(1–2), 119–129 (2017)
6. Landhuis, E.: Scientific literature: information overload. Nature **535**(7612), 457–458 (2016)
7. Pearce, W., Niederer, S., Özkula, S.M., Sánchez Querubín, N.: The social media life of climate change: platforms, publics, and future imaginaries. Wiley Interdiscip. Rev. Climate Change **10**(2), e569 (2019)
8. Radford, A., Wu, J., Child, R., Luan, D., Amodei, D., Sutskever, I.: Language models are unsupervised multitask learners. OpenAI Blog **1**(8), 9 (2019)

Assessing the Quality of RDF Mappings with EvaMap

Benjamin Moreau[1,2(✉)] and Patricia Serrano-Alvarado[2]

[1] Opendatasoft, Paris, France
`Benjamin.Moreau@opendatasoft.com`
[2] Nantes University, LS2N, CNRS, UMR6004, 44000 Nantes, France
`{Benjamin.Moreau,Patricia.Serrano-Alvarado}@univ-nantes.fr`

Abstract. Linked Data (LD) is a set of best practices to publish reusable data on the web in RDF format. Despite the benefits of LD, many datasets are not published as RDF. Transforming structured datasets into RDF datasets is possible thanks to RDF Mappings. But, for the same dataset, different mappings can be proposed. We believe that a tool capable of evaluating the quality of an RDF mapping would make the creation of mappings easier. In this paper, we present EvaMap, a framework to assess the quality of RDF mappings. The demonstration shows how EvaMap can be used to evaluate and improve RDF mappings.

1 Introduction and Motivation

Linked Data (LD) is a set of best practices to publish reusable data on the web in RDF format. Despite the benefits of LD, many datasets are not published as RDF. Transforming structured datasets into RDF datasets is possible thanks to *RDF Mappings*.

An RDF mapping consists in a set of rules that maps data from an input dataset to RDF triples. Languages like R2RML[1] and RML[2] are widely used to define machine-readable mappings. In this work, we use YARRRML, a human-readable representation of RDF mappings.

Making a relevant RDF mapping for a dataset is a challenging task because it requires to answer several questions:

1. What are the different resources described in the dataset (e.g., cars, persons, cities, places, etc.)?
2. What are the attributes of these resources (e.g., price, age, etc.)?
3. How should the IRI of resources be defined?

---

[1] https://www.w3.org/TR/r2rml/.
[2] https://rml.io/specs/rml/.

© Springer Nature Switzerland AG 2020
A. Harth et al. (Eds.): ESWC 2020 Satellite Events, LNCS 12124, pp. 164–167, 2020.
https://doi.org/10.1007/978-3-030-62327-2_28

4. What are the possible relations between the different resources (e.g., the city is the birthplace of the person)?
5. Which ontology, classes, and properties should be used?

In addition to possible errors by the user, different answers are possible for some of these questions and, thus, different RDF mappings are possible for the same dataset.

For example, Fig. 1 represents two possible mappings for the dataset in Table 1. Unlike mapping Fig. 1(a), mapping Fig. 1(b) does not include a class description in resource IRIs and does not reference the *Birth Province* column.

Table 1. Excerpt from a structured dataset describing Roman emperors.

Name	Birth	Birth City	Birth Province
Augustus	0062-09-23	Rome	
Caligula	0012-08-31	Antitum	
Claudius	0009-08-01	Lugdunum	Gallia Lugdunensis
...	...	...	...

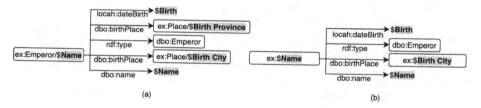

Fig. 1. Two RDF mappings for the Roman emperors dataset. Bold text starting with $ are references to a column in the dataset.

Given a structured dataset, how to help users to create RDF mappings without errors automatically, and how to choose the best mapping from a set of RDF mappings?

We believe that a tool capable of evaluating the quality of an RDF mapping would make the creation and the choice of RDF mappings easier. [1] proposes a framework that assesses and refines RML mappings. However, authors focus on logical errors due to incorrect usage of ontologies (e.g., violation of domain, range, disjoin classes, etc.). [3] proposes a framework to assess the quality of RDF datasets through metrics. Metrics are organized in dimensions evaluating different aspects of a dataset (e.g., availability, interlinking, etc.). But, [3] does not propose to assess the quality of an RDF mapping. In our work, like in [1], we evaluate metrics on the RDF mapping instead of on the resulting RDF dataset. This choice allows us to identify errors at the beginning of the publishing process and saves time.

Based on the framework proposed in [3], we propose **EvaMap**. EvaMap is a framework to **Eva**luate RDF **Map**pings. The goal is to control the quality of the resulting dataset through its mapping without having to generate the RDF dataset.

2   EvaMap: A Framework to Evaluate RDF Mappings

EvaMap uses a set of metrics organized in 7 dimensions. Each metric is evaluated on the RDF mapping or on the resulting RDF dataset when instances are needed. For example, the *available resource IRIs* metric needs RDF dataset to check if generated IRIs are dereferenceable. In this case, EvaMap generates a sample such that applying each mapping rule to the entire input dataset is not necessary. Table 2 describes each dimension of EvaMap. These dimensions are based on [3]. From these dimensions, we propose the *Coverability* one that detects the lose of data between the input dataset and the resulting RDF dataset. We also introduce four new metrics described in Table 3.

Table 2. Dimensions used by EvaMap.

Dimension	Description
Availability	Checks if IRIs are dereferenceable
Clarity	Checks human-readability of the mapping and the resulting dataset
Conciseness	Checks if the mapping and the resulting dataset is minimal while being complete
Consistency	Checks if the mapping is free from logical errors
Metadata	Checks metadata quality (license, date, creator, etc.)
Connectability	Checks if links exist between local and external resources
Coverability	Checks if the RDF mapping is exhaustive compared to the initial dataset

Table 3. New metrics proposed in EvaMap.

Dimension	Metric	Description
Conciseness	Redundant rule	Checks if multiple rules generate the same triples
Connectability	Local links	Checks if resources described in the mapping are connected
Consistency	Datatype inheritance	Checks if datatypes in the mapping correspond to datatypes in the initial dataset
Metadata	License compatibility	Checks if the license of the initial dataset is compatible with the license of the resulting dataset

In order to compute the quality of a mapping, M_i applied on a raw dataset D, we propose a function $q(M_i, D) \in [0, 1]$ that is the weighted mean of the quality of each metric $m_j(M_i, D)$:

$$q(M_i, D) = \frac{\sum_{j=1}^{n} w_j . m_j(M_i, D)}{\sum_{j=1}^{n} w_j}$$

We use the same function to compute the score for a specific dimension. To do that, we only consider the subset of metrics for the corresponding dimension.

Weights w_j associated with metrics can be used to give more or less importance to each metric. For example, the user does not always want to generate RDF triples for all data in the input dataset. Thus, weights associated with *coverability* metrics can be lowered or set to zero.

3   Demonstration

We implemented EvaMap to evaluate YARRRML [2] mappings for datasets of the OpenDataSoft's data network[3]. Our tool is available as a web service at https://evamap.herokuapp.com/. The source code of our tool[4] and web service[5] are available on GitHub under the MIT license.

During the demonstration, attendees will be able to select different mappings and use EvaMap to compare them. For each mapping, the global quality score will be computed as well as the quality score for each dimension. Our tool will also give feedback to improve RDF mapping.

In our tool, users can assess two mappings for the dataset *football-ligue*. Users can see that the mapping *football-ligue* obtains a worse global score than the mapping *football-ligue-fixed*. In the detailed report, users can analyze by dimension why these scores are different.

Acknowledgments. Authors thank Chanez Amri, Alan Baron, and Marion Hunault (Master students of the University of Nantes) for their participation in this work.

References

1. Dimou, A., et al.: Assessing and refining Mappingsto RDF to improve dataset quality. In: Arenas, M., et al. (eds.) ISWC 2015. LNCS, vol. 9367, pp. 133–149. Springer, Cham (2015). https://doi.org/10.1007/978-3-319-25010-6_8
2. Heyvaert, P., De Meester, B., Dimou, A., Verborgh, R.: Declarative rules for linked data generation at your fingertips!. In: Gangemi, A., et al. (eds.) ESWC 2018. LNCS, vol. 11155, pp. 213–217. Springer, Cham (2018). https://doi.org/10.1007/978-3-319-98192-5_40
3. Zaveri, A., Rula, A., Maurino, A., Pietrobon, R., Lehmann, J., Auer, S.: Quality assessment for linked data: a survey. J. Semant. Web **7**, 63–93 (2016)

---

[3] https://data.opendatasoft.com.

[4] https://github.com/benjimor/EvaMap.

[5] https://github.com/benjimor/EvaMap-Web.

LODsyndesis$_{IE}$: Entity Extraction from Text and Enrichment Using Hundreds of Linked Datasets

Michalis Mountantonakis[1,2] and Yannis Tzitzikas[1,2(✉)]

[1] Institute of Computer Science - FORTH-ICS, Heraklion, Greece
{mountant,tzitzik}@ics.forth.gr
[2] Computer Science Department, University of Crete, Heraklion, Greece

Abstract. We shall demonstrate LODsyndesis$_{IE}$, which is a research prototype that offers Entity Extraction from text and *Entity Enrichment* for the extracted entities, using several Linked Datasets. LODsyndesis$_{IE}$ exploits widely used Named Entity Extraction and Disambiguation tools (i.e., DBpedia Spotlight, WAT and Stanford CoreNLP) for identifying the entities of a given text, and enriches each identified entity with hyperlinks to LODsyndesis, which offers various services for millions of entities by leveraging hundreds of Linked Datasets. LODsyndesis$_{IE}$ brings several benefits to the entity extraction task: the user can a) annotate the entities of a given text by selecting different entity recognition tools, b) retrieve all the URIs and facts of each recognized entity from multiple datasets, and c) discover the K most relevant datasets (e.g., datasets containing the most facts) for each entity. The demo is available at https://demos.isl.ics.forth.gr/LODsyndesisIE/.

Keywords: Information Extraction · Linked data · Multiple datasets

1 Introduction

There is a large proliferation of approaches that perform named entity extraction (or recognition), linking and disambiguation [1,13] from textual sources, which is an important task of any *Information Extraction* (IE) process. These approaches use pure NLP methods (e.g., Stanford CoreNLP [8]), methods based on a knowledge base (KB), e.g., DBpedia Spotlight [9], and others [1]. They usually associate each recognized entity with links (i.e., URIs) either to a single or to a few KBs (see more details in a recent survey [1]), i.e., for reasons of disambiguation and/or for extracting more information from the corresponding KB. For instance, *DBpedia Spotlight* [9] annotates each entity with a link to DBpedia [2] and WAT [12] provides links to Wikipedia. Since these approaches link each entity to a few number of knowledge bases, it is not trivial to find all the related URIs (and to collect all the triples) for each entity from multiple sources, e.g., for aiding users to select the URI that is more desirable for a given task or the URI that corresponds to the desired meaning of the word occurrence. This could

© Springer Nature Switzerland AG 2020
A. Harth et al. (Eds.): ESWC 2020 Satellite Events, LNCS 12124, pp. 168–174, 2020.
https://doi.org/10.1007/978-3-030-62327-2_29

be achieved by using approaches such as LODsyndesis [11] and sameAs.cc [3], which provide all the available URIs for an entity. However, such systems are not connected with *Entity Extraction* tools, therefore the user has to use two or more systems: one *Entity Extraction* tool and one system that provides all the URIs of a given entity.

For facilitating this process, we present LODsyndesis$_{IE}$ (*IE* stands for Information Extraction), which provides fast access to all data related to a recognized entity by leveraging data coming from 400 RDF datasets. The approach is depicted in Fig. 1. It takes as input a text of any length, like the text about the greek writer "Nikos Kazantzakis". As an output, it offers a) the initial text enriched with hyperlinks to LODsyndesis for each entity, by using three popular *Entity Recognition* tools (i.e., DBpedia Spotlight, WAT and Stanford CoreNLP), and b) an HTML table containing links to LODsyndesis, for extracting more information for each entity (e.g., related URIs and facts) from 400 RDF datasets. The output of LODsyndesis$_{IE}$ is offered in several formats (e.g., RDF, JSON, and HTML), either through its web interface, or by using its REST API. As we shall see, many tasks could be benefited from LODsyndesis$_{IE}$, including *Data Enrichment, Annotation, Data Integration, Data Discovery* and *Data Veracity*.

The rest of this demo paper is organized as follows: Sect. 2 describes related work, Sect. 3 introduces the steps of LODsyndesis$_{IE}$, and Sect. 4 reports use cases for demonstration. Finally, Sect. 5 concludes the demo paper.

2   Related Work

First, there are available several *Entity Extraction* systems over knowledge graphs, i.e., see a recent survey for more details [1], whereas a comparison of such approaches (through the benchmark *GERBIL*) is given in [13]. Moreover, there are tools such as *WDAqua* [4] and *LODQA* [5], which support *Entity Extraction* for offering Question Answering over Knowledge bases (more tools are surveyed in [6]). Comparing to these approaches, we neither focus on proposing a new *Entity Extraction* system (e.g., [8,9,12]) nor a new Question Answering system (e.g., [4,5]). We focus on combining existing *Entity Extraction* tools and LODsyndesis [11] for facilitating the extraction of *more* information for the entities of a given text from hundreds of linked datasets.

3   The Steps of LODsyndesis$_{IE}$

LODsyndesis$_{IE}$ consists of two major steps, i.e., *Entity Recognition* (see Sect. 3.1) and *Entity Enrichment* (see Sect. 3.2).

3.1   Entity Recognition Step

The user can select to use *DBpedia Spotlight, Stanford CoreNLP, WAT*, or any combination of these tools (see Step 2 of Fig. 1). Concerning *DBpedia Spotlight*

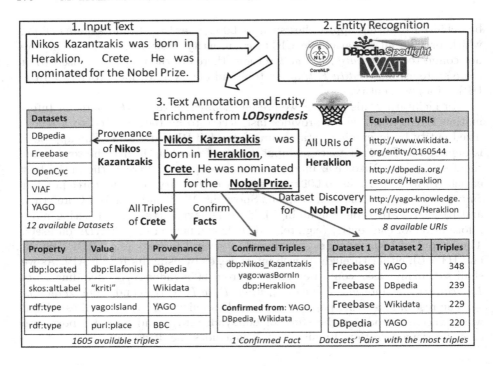

Fig. 1. The process of LODsyndesis$_{IE}$

and *WAT*, both tools produce a set of entity-URI pairs. In particular, for each recognized entity *DBpedia Spotlight* provides its corresponding DBpedia URI [2], whereas *WAT* offers its corresponding *Wikipedia* URI. However, for being able to compare the URIs derived from these tools, we replace each *Wikipedia* URI with its equivalent DBpedia URI. On the contrary, *Stanford CoreNLP* produces just a unique word for each entity (and not a URI to a knowledge base). For this reason, we take such words and we use LODsyndesis to find the most relevant DBpedia URI for each of these words (this approach is described in [5]), and then we create the desired set of entity-URI pairs. When the user has selected to use two or more tools, we take the union of all the recognized entity-URI pairs, produced by these tools. In case of conflicts and for reasons of disambiguation, i.e., if two or more tools identified different DBpedia URIs for the same entity *e*, we just keep the URI whose suffix, i.e., the last part of the URI (e.g., the suffix of "http://dbpedia.org/resource/Crete" is "Crete"), has the minimum Levenhstein distance with *e*. Therefore, in all cases the output of this step is a single entity-URI pair, for each recognized entity.

3.2   Entity Enrichment Step

For the set of recognized entity-URI pairs, we replace the URI of each entity with a hyperlink to LODsyndesis (i.e., we annotate the text with this hyperlink), for making it feasible to browse all the available triples for the given entity (i.e., see step 3 of Fig. 1), whereas we also retrieve and show an image for each recognized entity. Moreover, the user can extract more information for each entity through LODsyndesis, which supports cross-dataset identity reasoning (i.e., computation of transitive and symmetric closure of owl:sameAs relationships), for offering semantics-aware indexes and services for 400 Linked Datasets, 412 million entities and 2 billion triples.

LODsyndesis$_{IE}$ exploits the aforementioned indexes and services and offers six options for the user, which can be accessed either through its web interface, or by using its REST API. In particular, one can browse or download (in JSON and RDF format), i) the URLs of the datasets containing each recognized entity e, ii) all the URIs that refer to e, and iii) all the triples (and their provenance) for e. Moreover, iv) LODsyndesis$_{IE}$ exploits the *Dataset Discovery* service of LODsyndesis for discovering for each entity e, "the K datasets maximizing the number of triples for e", and "the K datasets having the most common triples that contain e". The results of the aforementioned service can be exported in CSV format. For instance, we can provide answers for queries like "Give me the 4 datasets (i.e., quad of datasets) that maximize the number of triples for Nikos Kazantzakis". Since the number of possible combinations of datasets (e.g., quads) is given by the binomial coefficient formula, our services rely on incremental algorithms that are quite efficient for such a problem [11]. Moreover, the user is able to use these services for all the recognized entities together, e.g., one can download the triples of all the recognized entities in a single RDF file.

The user can also v) verify the correctness of the facts that are included in the text, i.e., LODsyndesis$_{IE}$ shows all the triples that connect the "key" entity of the text with any of the rest entities, e.g., ⟨"Nikos Kazantzakis","was born in","Heraklion"⟩. By default, the "key" entity is the entity which was recognized first in the text (e.g., "Nikos Kazantzakis" in Fig. 1), however, the user can select any other entity, as the "key" one. In this way, it is feasible to find all the relationships between any pair of recognized entities. Finally, one can vi) export the annotated text in *HTML+RDFa* format, i.e., we store for each entity in the output file, its DBpedia URI, its type (e.g., "Person"), its corresponding URI to LODsyndesis, and all its related URIs, by using the *schema.org* vocabulary [7].

Example. Figure 1 shows an example of the output offered by LODsyndesis$_{IE}$, for each of the four recognized entities of the input text, i.e., "Nikos Kazantzakis", "Heraklion", "Crete" and "Nobel Prize". In this example, we selected to find all the datasets for "Nikos Kazantzakis" (12 datasets contain triples for this entity from the 400 available ones), all the URIs of "Heraklion" (8 URIs), all the triples for "Crete" (in total 1,605 triples), and the pairs of datasets offering the most triples for the entity "Nobel Prize". In particular, the union of {*FreeBase*, *YAGO*} offers 348 triples for this entity. Moreover, we can see that the fact "Nikos Kazantzakis was born in Heraklion" is verified from 3 datasets.

Demo and REST API. The demo is accessible at https://demos.isl.ics.forth. gr/LODsyndesisIE/. For making it feasible to integrate LODsyndesis$_{IE}$ with external services, the demo website also offers a REST API and a REST client for JAVA. The backend of this website is implemented using Java technologies, whereas the front-end is based on common web technologies (Javascript). Finally, a demo video is available at https://youtu.be/i52hY57dRms.

4   Demonstration of Use Cases

We present four use cases, the first one corresponds to the *Entity Recognition* step, and the three remaining ones to the *Entity Enrichment* step.

Use Case 1. Comparison of Entity Recognition Tools. By exploiting LODsyndesis$_{IE}$, it is feasible to compare the effectiveness of each tool performing *Entity Recognition* (or any combination of them) for different scenarios, i.e., for different texts.

Use Case 2. Data Integration and Enrichment. Suppose that a user wants to integrate data for one or more entities of the given text, for enriching their content, e.g., for creating either a Mediator or a Semantic Warehouse. In the case of Mediator (i.e., the data remain at their sources [10]), the user can collect and use any subset of the available URIs for each entity (e.g., through the RDFa file), or can find which datasets contain information about these entities (and probably their SPARQL endpoints). On the contrary, for constructing a Semantic Warehouse (i.e., the data should be pre-collected [10]), one can directly download and use all (or any subset of) the available triples for each entity.

Use Case 3. Dataset Discovery and Selection. The number of available datasets for a single or multiple entities can be large, e.g., for the entity "Greece" there are 40 available datasets in LODsyndesis. However, in many cases the user desires to keep only K (e.g., five) datasets, since the cost of integrating several datasets, can be huge as the number of datasets grows [10]. LODsyndesis$_{IE}$ can aid the user to discover and select the K most relevant datasets for one or more entities. In particular, one can discover the K datasets that maximize the available information for a set of entities, i.e., the union of these K datasets contains the maximum number of triples for the given entities, comparing to any other combination of K datasets.

Use Case 4. Data Veracity. The user has the opportunity to explore the relationships between any pair of recognized entities (which are included in the text), i.e., whether there is a property (or edge) that connects these two entities. In this way, the user can see which facts that occur in the given text, can also be confirmed from one or more datasets (which are indexed from LODsyndesis).

5   Conclusion

In this paper, we presented the research prototype LODsyndesis$_{IE}$, which exploits existing *Entity Recognition* tools (i.e., *DBpedia Spotlight*, *Stanford CoreNLP* and *WAT*) for recognizing the entities of a given text, and offers *Entity Enrichment* through LODsyndesis. We introduced the steps of LODsyndesis$_{IE}$, and we showed several use cases where LODsyndesis$_{IE}$ could be useful, including *Data Enrichment, Annotation, Data Integration, Data Discovery* and *Data Veracity*. As a future work, we plan to extend LODsyndesis$_{IE}$ for covering more tasks of the *Information Extraction* process, e.g., to extract also the properties of a given text and link them to LODsyndesis. Finally, we plan to enrich the produced RDFa file by including more information (i.e., more triples for each entity).

Acknowledgements. The research work was supported by the Hellenic Foundation for Research and Innovation (HFRI) and the General Secretariat for Research and Technology (GSRT), under the HFRI PhD Fellowship grant (GA. No. 166).

References

1. Al-Moslmi, T., Ocaña, M.G., Opdahl, A.L., Veres, C.: Named entity extraction for knowledge graphs: a literature overview. IEEE Access **8**, 32862–32881 (2020)
2. Auer, S., Bizer, C., Kobilarov, G., Lehmann, J., Cyganiak, R., Ives, Z.: DBpedia: a nucleus for a web of open data. In: Aberer, K., et al. (eds.) ASWC/ISWC -2007. LNCS, vol. 4825, pp. 722–735. Springer, Heidelberg (2007). https://doi.org/10.1007/978-3-540-76298-0_52
3. Beek, W., Raad, J., Wielemaker, J., van Harmelen, F.: sameAs.cc: the closure of 500M `owl:sameAs` statements. In: Gangemi, A., et al. (eds.) ESWC 2018. LNCS, vol. 10843, pp. 65–80. Springer, Cham (2018). https://doi.org/10.1007/978-3-319-93417-4_5
4. Diefenbach, D., Singh, K., Maret, P.: WDAqua-core1: a question answering service for RDF knowledge bases. In: Companion Proceedings of the The Web Conference 2018, pp. 1087–1091 (2018)
5. Dimitrakis, E., Sgontzos, K., Mountantonakis, M., Tzitzikas, Y.: Enabling efficient question answering over hundreds of linked datasets. In: Flouris, G., Laurent, D., Plexousakis, D., Spyratos, N., Tanaka, Y. (eds.) ISIP 2019. CCIS, vol. 1197, pp. 3–17. Springer, Cham (2020). https://doi.org/10.1007/978-3-030-44900-1_1
6. Dimitrakis, E., Sgontzos, K., Tzitzikas, Y.: A survey on question answering systems over linked data and documents. J. Intell. Inf. Syst. **55**(2), 233–259 (2019). https://doi.org/10.1007/s10844-019-00584-7
7. Guha, R.V., Brickley, D., Macbeth, S.: Schema. org: evolution of structured data on the web. Commun. ACM **59**(2), 44–51 (2016)
8. Manning, C.D., Surdeanu, M. , Bauer, J., Finkel, J.R., Bethard, S., McClosky, D.: The stanford CoreNLP natural language processing toolkit. In: Proceedings of 52nd Annual Meeting of the Association for Computational Linguistics: System Demonstrations, pp. 55–60 (2014)
9. Mendes, P.N., Jakob, M., García-Silva, A., Bizer, C.: DBpedia spotlight: shedding light on the web of documents. In: SEMANTiCS, pp. 1–8. ACM (2011)
10. Mountantonakis, M., Tzitzikas, Y.: Large scale semantic integration of linked data: a survey. ACM Comput. Surv. (CSUR) **52**(5), 103 (2019)

11. Mountantonakis, M., Tzitzikas, Y.: Content-based union and complement metrics for dataset search over RDF knowledge graphs. J. Data Inf. Qual. (JDIQ) **12**(2), 1–31 (2020)
12. Piccinno, F., Ferragina, P.: From TagME to WAT: a new entity annotator. In: Proceedings of Workshop on Entity Recognition & Disambiguation, pp. 55–62 (2014)
13. Röder, M., Usbeck, R., Ngonga Ngomo, A.-C.: Gerbil-benchmarking named entity recognition and linking consistently. Semant. Web **9**(5), 605–625 (2018)

How Many Stars Do You See in This Constellation?

Fabrizio Orlandi[✉][iD], Damien Graux[✉][iD], and Declan O'Sullivan[iD]

ADAPT SFI Centre, Trinity College Dublin, Dublin, Ireland
{orlandif,grauxd,declan.osullivan}@tcd.ie

Abstract. With the increase of Knowledge Graphs available on the Web came the need of characterising them, adding for example provenance information. To facilitate adding statement-level metadata, an RDF syntax extension has recently been proposed to the Semantic Web community: RDF*. In this article, we examine the current coverage of RDF* by SPARQL engines. We identify a few issues arising even when performing simple operations such as counting the number of statements. We raise awareness on these issues and derive new research directions for the community.

1 Introduction

During the past decades, the number of linked datasets has rapidly increased, see for instance the current state of the Linked Open Data cloud[1]. These datasets are structured following the W3C standard Resource Description Framework (RDF) [8] and share knowledge on various domains, from the generalist ones such as DBpedia [1] or WikiData [12] to the most specialised ones, *e.g.* SemanGit [7].

The increasing number of these available sources of information, which can also be updated on a regular basis, implies that metadata characterising the datasets themselves is needed to help users find the correct pieces of information. For instance, provenance [10], versioning [3] and ownership of facts could be recorded on a statement-level and added to the datasets [2]. Hence, there is a need for expressing statements about statements, or statement-level metadata.

Technically, there exist several methods to express statements over a set of RDF triples. One might consider the various reification methods designed by experts in the community. However, these strategies lead, in practice, to an extensive amount of RDF triples generated [9], *e.g.* standard reification requires the use of four additional triples for each reified statement. In order to help users generating and maintaining their RDF statements of statements, Hartig et al. introduced the RDF* syntax [5,6]. This syntactical extension of the RDF

---

[1] As of March 2019, the LOD-cloud gathers more than 1 200 datasets sharing more than 16 000 links. https://lod-cloud.net/.

© Springer Nature Switzerland AG 2020
A. Harth et al. (Eds.): ESWC 2020 Satellite Events, LNCS 12124, pp. 175–180, 2020.
https://doi.org/10.1007/978-3-030-62327-2_30

standard has been received with enthusiasm by the Semantic Web community[2] and is now implemented by a few SPARQL engines.

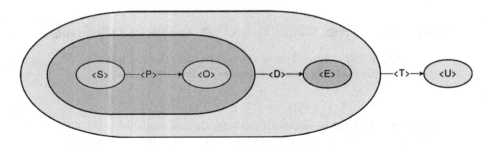

Fig. 1. A simple RDF* constellation of triples with nested "stars".

In this article, we explore the internal representations of RDF* data inside three SPARQL engines. Our simple test suite shows that the community should establish stricter guidelines and standardised methods to deal with RDF* datasets, as it appears that the considered engines are not treating this extension in a uniform way.

2   RDF*, Internal Representations and Star Counting

In 2014, Hartig & Thompson introduced the RDF* extension for RDF [6]. It allows data providers to shape statements about RDF graphs in an intuitive manner, while still being compliant with the RDF standard syntax. To do so, the RDF graph to be characterised should be encapsulated between double angular brackets and can act either as subject or object of another triple. In other words, RDF* graphs have the following generic structure: (Subj|<<Graph>>) Pred (Obj|<<Graph>>). Moreover, the RDF* syntax allows data providers to nest their characterisations. Simultaneously, Hartig & Thompson proposed to extend the accepted syntax of SPARQL (the RDF associated query language) to allow users to extract this additional data level at query time.

While, in general, RDF* and SPARQL* syntax and semantics are described in [5], SPARQL* syntax is based on Pérez et al.'s algebraic SPARQL syntax [11]. A more detailed formalization of SPARQL*, and extension of the full W3C specification of SPARQL 1.1 [4], is available in [6]. However, as the W3C has not yet standardised the RDF*/SPARQL* syntax and semantics, a certain degree of freedom is taken by the community that does not have very strict guidelines to adhere to. This freedom of choice is especially true regarding the techniques

---

[2] The *W3C Workshop on Web Standardization for Graph Data* (2019) has set a direction to bridge the Semantic Web and Property Graph communities together indicating RDF* as a viable option. https://www.w3.org/Data/events/data-ws-2019/index.html.

used by the RDF* stores to internally represent datasets. In this case, a relevant example is the one regarding "Redundancy in RDF* Graphs" (*cf.* Section 2.4 in [5]) where implementation techniques are explicitly left free to choose how to deal with redundancy in order to achieve performance gains.

In order to illustrate this variety of possible representations, let's consider the simplest RDF* dataset: `<< <s> <p> <o> >> <d> <e>;` and let's try to answer the following question: "once stored, what should `SELECT (count(*) as ?c) WHERE {?s ?p ?o}` return?". One possible solution is to consider the reification method where actually **six** triples are to be created. Another one is to use the singleton property method [9] which would lead to **four** triples created. Finally, a more naïve one could be to answer **two**, as there are two predicates (`<p>` and `<d>`) in the dataset. Moreover, as the extension allows "stars" to be nested in one another, we can also consider the graph depicted in Fig. 1, nesting two levels and corresponding to the following statement:

```
<< << <S> <P> <O> >> <D> <E> >> <T> <U> .
```

With this statement, we can as well ask the same simple question: "how many triples?". In the rest of our analysis, we are going to test such queries with SPARQL engines claiming to support RDF*/SPARQL*.

3   Comparing SPARQL* Engines' Results

Currently, only a few RDF management systems claim to cover the RDF* extension and natively support SPARQL* queries. Stardog[3] and Blazegraph[4] are among them. In addition, as a common basis of comparison, we use the tool provided by Hartig[5] which is built on top of Jena. In order to review their capabilities, we design the simple dataset which follows. It is composed of 4 statements: 1 classic RDF triple, 2 basic RDF* statements and 1 nested RDF* statement (as the one presented in Fig. 1).

```
<s1> <p1> <o1> .
<< <s2> <p2> <o2> >> <d2> <e2> .
<< << <s3> <p3> <o3> >> <d3> <e3> >> <t3> <u3> .
<< <s4> <p4> <o4> >> <d4> <e4> .
```

One Star – First, we only load in the systems the first two statements (Lines 1–2). Both Stardog and Blazegraph return that 3 entities were created during the loading phase. The `ExecuteSPARQLStar` tool can only query, on-the-fly, data stored in an RDF* file (*e.g.* using Turtle*). Then, we ran the following queries:
Q1: `Select * Where{?s ?p ?o}`.
Q2: `Select * Where{<<?s ?p ?o>> ?d ?e}`.

---

[3] **Stardog** version 7.1.2 https://www.stardog.com/.
[4] **Blazegraph** version 2.1.5 https://blazegraph.com/.
[5] **ExecuteSPARQLStar** version 0.0.1 https://github.com/RDFstar/RDFstarTools.

The obtained results, for both the engines and the Jena-based tool, were:
R_{Q1}: {`<s1>`,`<p1>`,`<o1>`}{`<s2>`,`<p2>`,`<o2>`}{`<< <s2><p2><o2> >>`,`<d2>`,`<e2>`}.
R_{Q2}: {`<s2>`,`<p2>`,`<o2>`,`<d2>`,`<e2>`}.
This implies that all systems consider the RDF-Graph of an RDF* statement as
a subject and, in case of *Q1*, counted **3** triples (which corresponds to the naïve
counting idea we had in the previous section).

Table 1. Behaviours with nested RDF* statements.

Select * Where ...	Stardog	Blazegraph	ExecuteSPARQLStar
{?s ?p ?o}	s1 p1 o1, s2 p2 o2, s3 p3 o3, s4 p4 o4, {s2 p2 o2} d2 e2, {s4 p4 o4} d4 e4, {s3 d3 e3} t3 u3, s3 d3 e3	s1 p1 o1, s2 p2 o2, s3 p3 o3, s4 p4 o4, {s2 p2 o2} d2 e2, {s4 p4 o4} d4 e4, {s3 p3 o3} d3 e3, {{s3 p3 o3} d3 e3} t3 u3	s1 p1 o1, s2 p2 o2, s3 p3 o3, s4 p4 o4, {s2 p2 o2} d2 e2, {s4 p4 o4} d4 e4, {s3 p3 o3} d3 e3, {{s3 p3 o3} d3 e3} t3 u3
{<<?s ?p ?o>> ?d ?e}	s2 p2 o2 d2 e2, s4 p4 o4 d4 e4, s3 d3 e3 t3 u3	s2 p2 o2 d2 e2, s4 p4 o4 d4 e4, s3 p3 o3 d3 e3, {s3 p3 o3} d3 e3 t3 u3	s2 p2 o2 d2 e2, s4 p4 o4 d4 e4, s3 p3 o3 d3 e3, {s3 p3 o3} d3 e3 t3 u3
{<<<<?s ?p ?o>> ?d ?e>> ?t ?u}	No results	s3 p3 o3 d3 e3 t3 u3	s3 p3 o3 d3 e3 t3 u3

Nested Star – For the second round of experimentation we loaded all the 4
statements presented above. We used again the same queries *Q1*, *Q2* and added
Q3: `Select * Where{<<<<?s ?p ?o>> ?d ?e>> ?t ?u}`.
The results are displayed in Table 1. We observe that both Blazegraph and the
Jena-based tool present the same behaviour as the one observed in the previous
test. Inversely, Stardog cannot deal correctly with nested RDF* statements. It
is visible that Stardog "flattens" one level of the encapsulation as *Q3* does not
offer any result and `s3 d3 e3` is present as a result of *Q1*, instead of the expected
{`s3 p3 o3`} `d3 e3`.

Findings – As explained prior, the goal of our study is **<u>not</u>** to analyse the engines'
performances, but rather to comparatively examine how they internally represent simple RDF* statements[6]. Despite the simplicity of the experiments, we
find multiple syntax anomalies: *(i)* Stardog needs its own syntax based on curly-
brackets (the RDF* angular-brackets often raise some exceptions); *(ii)* Blazegraph cannot deal with spaces at some places and raises errors when "Select *"
is used (all the variables need to be specifically listed); *(iii)* the ExecuteSPAR-
QLStar tool doesn't return the subject column[7] when there is an RDF* triple at
the subject place in the clauses. More importantly, in addition to the syntactical
errors, we discover that the three engines do not have the same internal representations. Further, it appears that Stardog's representation leads to errors, as
it is "flattening" the nested statements.

---

[6] More details are available from: https://github.com/dgraux/RDFStarObservatory.
[7] Similarly to Blazegraph, instead of using "Select *", users need to specify all the
variables in the Select clause.

4   Conclusions

Leveraging the simple example of counting the "stars" inside simple nested RDF* statements, we would like to alert the community on the current divergences that are appearing in the domain of RDF* storage and management. According to our observations, the tested versions of the engines diverge when dealing with nested statements. That is why we would not recommend to use nested RDF* statements in production systems yet, at least until a form of agreement in representing them has been reached. Indeed, as RDF* can drive the community forward and bridge the gap between the Semantic Web and Property Graph worlds, reaching an early agreement is of paramount importance as compatibility between engines would allow them to communicate and, in turn, enable features such as query federation. Our goal is to continue our systematic exploration of RDF* engines, paying attention to their behaviours and performances when dealing with more complex SPARQL* queries and with richer datasets.

Acknowledgment. This research was conducted with the financial support of the European Regional Development Fund and the European Unions Horizon 2020 research and innovation programme under the EDGE Marie Skłodowska-Curie grant agreement No. 713567 at the ADAPT SFI Research Centre at Trinity College Dublin. The ADAPT SFI Centre for Digital Media Technology is funded by Science Foundation Ireland through the SFI Research Centres Programme and is co-funded under the European Regional Development Fund (ERDF) Grant # 13/RC/2106.

References

1. Auer, S., Bizer, C., Kobilarov, G., Lehmann, J., Cyganiak, R., Ives, Z.: DBpedia: a nucleus for a web of open data. In: Aberer, K., et al. (eds.) ASWC/ISWC -2007. LNCS, vol. 4825, pp. 722–735. Springer, Heidelberg (2007). https://doi.org/10.1007/978-3-540-76298-0_52
2. Frey, J., Müller, K., Hellmann, S., Rahm, E., Vidal, M.E.: Evaluation of metadata representations in RDF stores. Semant. Web **10**(2), 205–229 (2019)
3. Frommhold, M., Piris, R.N., Arndt, N., Tramp, S., Petersen, N., Martin, M.: Towards versioning of arbitrary RDF data. In: Proceedings of the 12th International Conference on Semantic Systems, pp. 33–40 (2016)
4. Harris, S., Seaborne, A., Prud'hommeaux, E.: SPARQL 1.1 query language. W3C Recomm. **21**(10), 778 (2013)
5. Hartig, O.: Foundations of RDF* and SPARQL* (an alternative approach to statement-level metadata in RDF). In: 11th Alberto Mendelzon International Workshop on Foundations of Data Management (AMW) (2017)
6. Hartig, O., Thompson, B.: Foundations of an alternative approach to reification in RDF. arXiv preprint arXiv:1406.3399 (2014)
7. Kubitza, D.O., Böckmann, M., Graux, D.: SemanGit: a linked dataset from `git`. In: Ghidini, C., et al. (eds.) ISWC 2019. LNCS, vol. 11779, pp. 215–228. Springer, Cham (2019). https://doi.org/10.1007/978-3-030-30796-7_14
8. Manola, F., Miller, E., McBride, B., et al.: RDF primer. W3C Recomm. **10**(1–107), 6 (2004)

9. Nguyen, V., Bodenreider, O., Sheth, A.: Don't like RDF reification? Making statements about statements using singleton property. In: Proceedings of the 23rd International Conference on World Wide Web, pp. 759–770 (2014)
10. Orlandi, F., Passant, A.: Modelling provenance of DBpedia resources using Wikipedia contributions. J. Web Semant. **9**(2), 149–164 (2011)
11. Pérez, J., Arenas, M., Gutierrez, C.: Semantics and complexity of SPARQL. ACM Trans. Database Syst. (TODS) **34**(3), 1–45 (2009)
12. Vrandečić, D., Krötzsch, M.: Wikidata: a free collaborative knowledgebase. Commun. ACM **57**(10), 78–85 (2014)

A Study About the Use of OWL 2 Semantics in RDF-Based Knowledge Graphs

Pierre-Henri Paris[✉], Fayçal Hamdi, and Samira Si-said Cherfi

Conservatoire National des Arts et Métiers, Paris, France
pierre-henri.paris@upmc.fr, {faycal.hamdi,samira.cherfi}@cnam.fr

Abstract. RDF-based knowledge graphs have been attracting increasing attention since Google popularized the term in 2012. However, historically, knowledge graphs are based on Semantic Web technologies. Many years ago, several works pointed out the lack of semantics in some RDF graph. So the question is whether semantics is there somewhere. Hence, we conducted an up-to-date large-scale study of the current state of the Web of data regarding the OWL 2 semantics to confirm or deny older results. Moreover, we propose an ontology to capture which OWL 2 features are defined or used in a given RDF-based knowledge graph and the tools to instantiate such an ontology.

Keywords: Knowledge graph · Statistics · Semantics · OWL · Ontology

1 Introduction

One of the key points using RDF-based knowledge graphs (KGs) is the possibility to reason on data thanks to OWL 2 and description logic. For example, users can check the consistency of the KG or infer new data. Furthermore, many tools rely on semantics to perform at their best for a given task. However, when dealing with a KG, human or automated agents might deal with the lack of necessary OWL 2 features.

A decade ago, several works focused on the study of OWL semantics in KGs and found that data was often devoid of semantics. Hence, in this paper, we propose a large-scale study of the current state of the Web of data from the OWL 2 semantics perspective. Moreover, we built an ontology to express, for a given KG, which OWL 2 and RDFS features (e.g., functional properties or subclasses) are used and in what proportions. This ontology allows the necessary information to be brought directly to the data consumer to select the appropriate tool for the realization of his or her task. Besides, we provide applications to instantiate the ontology for a given KG thanks to its SPARQL endpoint. The objective is to enable data consumers to know precisely how and to what extent OWL 2 and RDFS are used in the KG.

© Springer Nature Switzerland AG 2020
A. Harth et al. (Eds.): ESWC 2020 Satellite Events, LNCS 12124, pp. 181–185, 2020.
https://doi.org/10.1007/978-3-030-62327-2_31

2   Related Work

In this section, we present some works that focus on the study of the use of semantics in knowledge graphs of Linked Open Data. In [3], the authors analyzed 25500 knowledge graphs in terms of expressivity. Although compelling, this study is old and deals with a tiny number of knowledge graphs. [8] denounces the lack of expressiveness of knowledge graphs, i.e., that many knowledge graphs do not use all the different features of OWL 2, far from it. In [6], the authors emphasize that some data publishers focus solely on publishing data (i.e., triples) without annotating them with shared ontologies. They conclude that, apart from the *owl:sameAs* property, the features of OWL 2 are little used. However, this study is more of an empirical finding than a systematic study. [7] covers 12.5 million triples and aims to raise the various issues facing the Semantic Web. However, the small sample size and the age of the study this study does not provide answers to our questions. Moreover, the study lacks relevant metrics on the use of semantics. In [5], the authors proposed the biggest and deepest evaluation of OWL 2 usage so far. They evaluated more than 2 billion triples and found a wide disparity in usage among the features of OWL 2. Our study covers more recent and more numerous data (more than 30 billion triples). [4] proposes to investigate the quality of some of the best-known knowledge graphs. The authors provide basic statistics on DBpedia, Freebase, OpenCyc, Wikidata, and YAGO. Although not a large-scale study of the use of semantics, some statistics are interesting (number of triples, number of classes, number of relations, etc.), but do not sufficiently address the semantics expressed by ontologies based on OWL 2. In [1], the authors proposed a study of the modeling style in Linked Open Data. Hence, they mostly focus on the hierarchies of the classes.

None of the cited works proposes a complete study on the use of OWL 2 semantics in RDF knowledge graphs with precise figures and at such a scale.

3   Current State of the LOD

In this paper, we only present some OWL 2 results, but RDFS and the rest of OWL 2 results are also available on our GitHub repository[1].

3.1   Data Sources

We chose *LOD Laundromat* [2] that gives access to about 650 thousand KGs in HDT format. Some of these graphs refer to different versions of the same dataset, e.g., DBpedia-en, DBpedia-fr, or DBpedia 3.8. Because our demonstrator works only with SPARQL endpoints, we used Jena Fuseki[2] to query those HDT files.

Thanks to *LOD Laundromat*, 647,858 KGs have been analyzed (an HDT file represents a graph). We consider an RDF KG as a serialization of a graph expressed using the RDF graph model, i.e., composed of subject-predicate-value triples. It contains data (A-Box) and ontology (T-Box).

---

[1] https://github.com/PHParis/sem_web_stats.
[2] http://www.rdfhdt.org/manual-of-hdt-integration-with-jena/.

3.2   Results

The first view of these results is presented in Fig. 1. Each of the three box plots describes a subset of knowledge graphs with their number of subjects, i.e., the graphs have been ranked by their number of subjects. It is the easiest way to expose the global shapes of KGs through their quartiles. The first box plot describes all 650K knowledge graphs. As we can see, there are a large number of very small graphs. The vast majority of the KGs contains barely 1000 subjects. However, several KGs are above the millions of subjects. Only a very small portion of the KGs (1.53%, ~10K KGs) uses at least one OWL 2 feature. This is really astonishing, since we were expecting a small portion, according to the previous studies, but not that small. The statistics of this small portion, i.e., KGs with semantics, can be read on the second box plot. As we can see, KGs with semantics are a little bit larger in terms of the number of subjects. Finally, the last box plot represents the 100 largest KGs in terms of the number of triples. Large KGs have almost all more than 1M of subjects. Surprisingly, only 34% of top 100 KGs use at least one OWL 2 feature. It is largely more than when considering all KGs, but it is still a very low percentage if we consider they are composed of millions of triples and subjects.

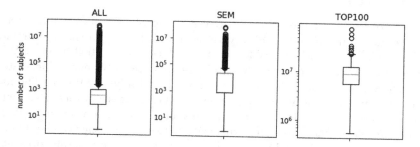

Fig. 1. Box plots of the number of subjects by selectors. ALL = all KGs, SEM = KGs with at least one OWL 2 feature, TOP100 = top 100 KGs w.r.t. their number of triples.

Table 1 concerns the types of properties (for example a property that would be defined as functional). The second column shows the number of graphs using a property of the considered type, and the third column their weighted average regarding the number of triples. The last two columns are similar, but for subjects and predicates. For example, inverse functional properties are found in 310 graphs. Among these 310 graphs, we can expect to find an average of 2.54 definitions of such properties that are used in 22.7 triples with 20.6 different subjects. As we can see, some predicates are used very little, such as the *owl:ReflexiveProperty* which is only used in 16 graphs. In these 16 graphs, very few reflexive properties are defined (1.28) and used.

Table 1. Analysis by type of property.

Type	# of graphs	Weighted mean of triples	Weighted mean of subjects	Weighted mean of predicates
FunctionalProperty	434	9	5.76	3.06
InverseFunctionalProperty	310	22.7	20.6	2.54
TransitiveProperty	396	2.84	2.63	2.4
SymmetricProperty	320	7	4.77	2.87
AsymmetricProperty	15	4.7	4.66	4.66
IrreflexiveProperty	21	1.66	1.65	1.65
ReflexiveProperty	16	1.32	1.32	1.32

Because of space limitation, we present many other results on our GitHub repository, e.g., an analyze by topics of graphs (life science, cross domain, etc.), or class restrictions and domain/range axiom statistics.

3.3 Discussion

The main objective of our study is to verify the old results on more recent and more important data. Our observations do not defer from those of previous work. Indeed, despite being a W3C recommendation since 2009, many OWL 2 features have not been adopted by ontologist or data publishers. The state of Linked Data is the same as it was for the last large study in 2012 [5]. The most surprising results are the very low number of KGs using semantics. Even when considering the largest KGs, a great number of them still do not use OWL 2 features. Moreover, there is a great disparity between the usage of the different features. While several are heavily used, most features are barely present in studied KGs. There is a need to understand why such inertia. Is OWL 2 too powerful regarding the needs of data modelers? Or too hard to be used? Even if more complex OWL 2 features were used in KGs, will users need them? Maybe a specification like SHACL [9] will encounter a greater success and could be considered as a viable alternative or a complement in some cases.

4 Ontology

We propose an ontology[3] to explicit the use of classes and properties defined with OWL 2 and RDFS features in a KG. For instance, an objective for a user could be to know the number of properties that are transitive and their number of uses in the graph. We extended the VoID[4] vocabulary with properties to explicit *(i)* how many properties and classes are defined with a given OWL 2

---

[3] http://cedric.cnam.fr/isid/ontologies/OntoSemStats.owl.

[4] https://www.w3.org/TR/void/.

feature, or *(ii)* the number of use of a given OWL 2 feature. The OWL 2 features are organized depending on their utility, e.g., *owl:sameAs* and *owl:differentFrom* have the same superclass because they both are related to identity.

To instantiate the ontology for a given SPARQL endpoint, we propose OntoSemStatsWeb[5], an open-source software (under the GPL open-source license) written in C# (using dotnetRDF[6]). The application has three different forms: *(i)* a Web page that is our live demonstrator, *(ii)* a Web API to operate seamlessly with an automated agent, and *(iii)* a command-line application. All the tools that we developed are available as Docker images (one for the command-line application and one for the Web application and the Web API), in order to promote ease of use and adoption.

5   Conclusion

In this paper, we conducted a large-scale study that provides an up-to-date overview of the semantic usages in the LOD. This study confirmed older papers results: only a small portion of KGs uses OWL 2 semantics, and those KGs use only some features of OWL 2 heavily. Moreover, we proposed an ontology to capture the present semantics in a KG. The ontology *(i)* facilitate knowledge discovery for users and *(ii)* may increase the visibility of data publishers' KG.

References

1. Asprino, L., Beek, W., Ciancarini, P., van Harmelen, F., Presutti, V.: Observing LOD using equivalent set graphs: it is mostly flat and sparsely linked. In: Ghidini, C., et al. (eds.) ISWC 2019. LNCS, vol. 11778, pp. 57–74. Springer, Cham (2019). https://doi.org/10.1007/978-3-030-30793-6_4
2. Beek, W., Rietveld, L., Bazoobandi, H.R., Wielemaker, J., Schlobach, S.: LOD laundromat: a uniform way of publishing other people's dirty data. In: Mika, P., et al. (eds.) ISWC 2014. LNCS, vol. 8796, pp. 213–228. Springer, Cham (2014). https://doi.org/10.1007/978-3-319-11964-9_14
3. d'Aquin, M., Baldassarre, C., Gridinoc, L., Angeletou, S., Sabou, M., Motta, E.: Characterizing knowledge on the semantic web with Watson (2007)
4. Färber, M., Bartscherer, F., Menne, C., Rettinger, A.: Linked data quality of DBpedia, Freebase, OpenCyc, Wikidata, and Yago. Semant. Web (Preprint) **9**, 1–53 (2016)
5. Glimm, B., Hogan, A., Krötzsch, M., Polleres, A.: OWL: yet to arrive on the web of data? In: LDOW. CEUR Workshop Proceedings, vol. 937. CEUR-WS.org (2012)
6. Hitzler, P., van Harmelen, F.: A reasonable semantic web. Semant. Web **1**, 39–44 (2010)
7. Hogan, A., Harth, A., Passant, A., Decker, S., Polleres, A.: Weaving the pedantic web. In: LDOW. CEUR Workshop Proceedings, vol. 628. CEUR-WS.org (2010)
8. Jain, P., Hitzler, P., Yeh, P.Z., Verma, K., Sheth, A.P.: Linked data is merely more data. In: AAAI Spring Symposium: Linked Data Meets Artificial Intelligence (2010)
9. Knublauch, H., Kontokostas, D.: Shapes constraint language (SHACL). W3C Candidate Recommendation **11**(8) (2017)

---

[5] https://github.com/PHParis/OntoSemStatsWeb.
[6] https://github.com/dotnetrdf/dotnetrdf.

Visual Analysis of Ontology Matching Results with the MELT Dashboard

Jan Portisch[1,2]([✉]) [iD], Sven Hertling[1] [iD], and Heiko Paulheim[1] [iD]

[1] Data and Web Science Group, University of Mannheim, Mannheim, Germany
{jan,sven,heiko}@informatik.uni-mannheim.de
[2] SAP SE Product Engineering Financial Services, Walldorf, Germany
jan.portisch@sap.com

Abstract. In this demo, we introduce *MELT Dashboard*, an interactive Web user interface for ontology alignment evaluation which is created with the existing *Matching EvaLuation Toolkit (MELT)*. Compared to existing, static evaluation interfaces in the ontology matching domain, our dashboard allows for interactive self-service analyses such as a drill down into the matcher performance for data type properties or into the performance of matchers within a certain confidence threshold. In addition, the dashboard offers detailed group evaluation capabilities that allow for the application in broad evaluation campaigns such as the *Ontology Alignment Evaluation Initiative (OAEI)*.

Keywords: Ontology alignment · Evaluation framework · OAEI · Matching evaluation

1 Introduction

The *Matching EvaLuation Toolkit (MELT)*[1] [6] is an open (MIT-licensed) Java framework for ontology matcher development, tuning, evaluation, and packaging, which integrates well into the existing ontology alignment evaluation infrastructure used by the community, i.e. *SEALS*[2] [3,11] and *HOBBIT*[3] [8]. While those frameworks offer programmatic tooling to evaluate ontology matching systems, advanced analyses have to be specifically implemented. Similarly, alignment results are typically presented in the form of static tables which do not allow to explore the actual data.

2 Related Work

The *Alignment API* [1] is the most well-known ontology matching framework. It allows to develop and evaluate ontology matchers and to render matching results,

---

[1] https://github.com/dwslab/melt.
[2] http://www.seals-project.eu.
[3] http://project-hobbit.eu.

J. Portisch and S. Hertling—Equal contribution.

© Springer Nature Switzerland AG 2020
A. Harth et al. (Eds.): ESWC 2020 Satellite Events, LNCS 12124, pp. 186–190, 2020.
https://doi.org/10.1007/978-3-030-62327-2_32

for example as a LATEX figure. The *Semantic Evaluation at Large Scale (SEALS)* framework allows to package matching systems and also provides an evaluation runtime which is capable of calculating precision, recall, and F_1. The more recent *Holistic Benchmarking of Big Linked Data (HOBBIT)* runtime works in a similar fashion. In terms of visualization, *Alignment Cubes* [7] allow for a fine grained, interactive visual exploration of alignments. Another framework for working with alignment files is *VOAR* [10] which is a Web-based system where users can upload ontologies and alignments which are then rendered.

Compared to existing work, *MELT Dashboard* is the first interactive Web UI for analyzing and comparing multiple matcher evaluation *results*. The dashboard is particularly helpful for exploring correct and wrong correspondences of matching systems and is, therefore, also suitable for matcher development and debugging.

3   Architecture

The dashboard can be used for matchers that were developed in *MELT* but also allows for the evaluation of external matchers that use the well-known alignment format of the *Alignment API*. It is implemented in Java and is included by default in the *MELT* 2.0 release which is available through the maven central repository[4]. The `DashboardBuilder` class is used to generate an HTML page. Without further parameters, a default page can be generated that allows for an in-depth analysis. Alternatively, the dashboard builder allows to completely customize a dashboard before generation – for instance by adding or deleting selection controls and display panes. After the generation, the self-contained Web page can be viewed locally in the Web browser or be hosted on a server. The page visualization is implemented with *dc.js*[5], a JavaScript charting library with *crossfilter*[6] support. Once generated, the dashboard can be used also by non-technical users to analyze and compare matcher results.

As matching tasks (and the resulting alignment files) can become very large, the dashboard was developed with a focus on performance. For the *OAEI 2019 KnowledgeGraph* track [4,5], for instance, more than 200,000 correspondences are rendered and results are recalculated on the fly when the user performs a drill-down selection.

4   Use Case and Demonstration

One use case for the framework are OAEI campaigns. The *Ontology Alignment Evaluation Initiative* is running evaluation campaigns [2] every year since 2005. Researchers submit generic matching systems for predefined tasks (so called *tracks*) and the track organizers post the results of the systems on each track.

---

[4] https://mvnrepository.com/artifact/de.uni-mannheim.informatik.dws.melt.
[5] https://dc-js.github.io/dc.js/.
[6] http://crossfilter.github.io/crossfilter/.

The results are typically communicated on the OAEI Web page in a static fashion through one or more tables.[7]

In order to demonstrate the capabilities of the dashboard, we generated pages for the following tracks: *Anatomy, Conference*, and *KnowledgeGraph*. We included the first two tracks in one dashboard[8] to show the multi-track capabilities of the toolkit. The *KnowledgeGraph* dashboard[9] was officially used in the OAEI 2019 campaign and shows that the dashboard can handle also combined schema and instance matching tasks at scale. The code to generate the dashboards is available in the **example** folder of the *MELT* project.[10] It can be seen that few lines of code are necessary to generate comprehensive evaluation pages.

An annotated screenshot of the controls for the *Anatomy/Conference* dashboard is depicted in Fig. 1. Each numbered element is clickable in order to allow for a sub-selection. For example, in element ②, the *Conference* track has been selected and all elements in the dashboard show the results for this subselection. The controls in the given sample dashboard are as follows: ① selection of the track, ② selection of the track/test case (the *Conference* track is selected with all test cases), ③ confidence interval of the matchers (an interval of $[0.59, 1.05]$ is selected), ④ relation (only equivalence for this track), ⑤ matching systems, ⑥ the share of true/false positives (TP/FP) and false negatives (FN), ⑦/⑧ the type of the left/right element in each correspondence (e.g., class, object property, datatype property), ⑨ the share of residual true positives (i.e., non-trivial correspondences generated by a configurable baseline matcher), ⑩ the total number of correspondences found per test case – the performance result of each match (TP/FP/FN) is color coded, and ⑪ the color-coded correspondences found per matcher.

Below the controls, the default dashboard shows the performance results per matcher, i.e. micro and macro averages of precision (P), recall (R), and F-score (F_1) in a table as well as concrete correspondences in a further table (both are not shown in Fig. 1). The data and all controls are updated automatically when a selection is performed. For example, if the *Anatomy* track is selected (control ②) for matcher *Wiktionary* [9] (control ⑤), and only false negative correspondences (control ⑥) are desired, the correspondence table will show examples of false negative matches for the *Wiktionary* matching system on the *Anatomy* track.

---

[7] For an example, see the *Anatomy Track* results page 2019: http://oaei.ontology matching.org/2019/results/anatomy/index.html.

[8] Demo link: https://dwslab.github.io/melt/anatomy_conference_dashboard.html.

[9] Demo link: http://oaei.ontologymatching.org/2019/results/knowledgegraph/knowl edge_graph_dashboard.html.

[10] https://github.com/dwslab/melt/tree/master/examples/meltDashboard.

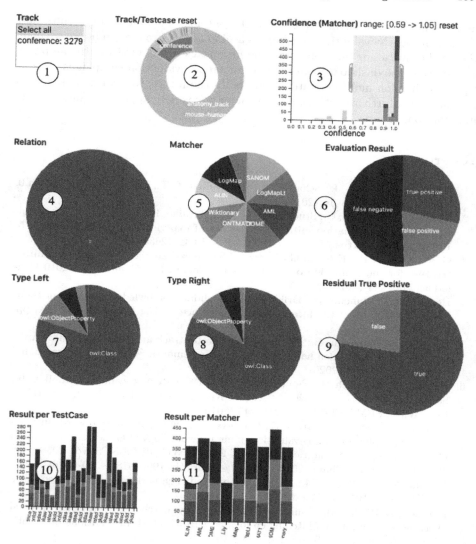

Fig. 1. Dashboard for the *OAEI Anatomy/Conference Tracks*. The numbered controls are clickable to drill down into the data. If clicked, all elements change automatically to reflect the current selection.

5   Conclusion and Future Work

In this paper, we presented the *MELT Dashboard*, an interactive Web user interface for ontology alignment evaluation. The tool allows to generate dashboards easily and to use them for a detailed evaluation in a drill-down fashion. With the new functionality, we hope to increase the transparency and the understanding of matching systems in the ontology alignment community and to make in-depth evaluation capabilities available to a broader audience without the need of installing any software. The first usage in the OAEI 2019 campaign showed that the dashboard can be used for broad evaluation campaigns of multiple matchers on multiple matching tasks. In the future, we plan to extend the interface with further controls, to make it more visually appealing, and to grow its adoption.

References

1. David, J., Euzenat, J., Scharffe, F., dos Santos, C.T.: The alignment API 4.0. Semant. Web **2**(1), 3–10 (2011)
2. Euzenat, J., Meilicke, C., Stuckenschmidt, H., Shvaiko, P., dos Santos, C.T.: Ontology alignment evaluation initiative: six years of experience. J. Data Semant. **15**, 158–192 (2011). https://doi.org/10.1007/978-3-642-22630-4_6
3. García-Castro, R., Esteban-Gutiérrez, M., Gómez-Pérez, A.: Towards an infrastructure for the evaluation of semantic technologies. In: eChallenges e-2010 Conference, pp. 1–7 (2010)
4. Hertling, S., Paulheim, H.: DBkWik: a consolidated knowledge graph from thousands of wikis. In: IEEE International Conference on Big Knowledge, ICBK, pp. 17–24 (2018)
5. Hertling, S., Paulheim, H.: The knowledge graph track at OAEI - gold standards, baselines, and the golden hammer bias. In: The Semantic Web - 17th International Conference, ESWC (2020)
6. Hertling, S., Portisch, J., Paulheim, H.: MELT - matching evaluation toolkit. In: Semantic Systems. The Power of AI and Knowledge Graphs - 15th International Conference, SEMANTiCS, pp. 231–245 (2019)
7. Ivanova, V., Bach, B., Pietriga, E., Lambrix, P.: Alignment cubes: towards interactive visual exploration and evaluation of multiple ontology alignments. In: d'Amato C. et al. (eds.) The Semantic Web-ISWC 2017. ISWC 2017. LNCS, vol. 10587, pp. 400–417. Springer, Cham (2017). https://doi.org/10.1007/978-3-319-68288-4_24
8. Ngomo, A.C.N., Röder, M.: HOBBIT: holistic benchmarking for big linked data. ERCIM News **105**, 46–67 (2016)
9. Portisch, J., Hladik, M., Paulheim, H.: Wiktionary matcher. In: 14th International Workshop on Ontology Matching co-located with the 18th International Semantic Web Conference (ISWC), pp. 181–188 (2019)
10. Severo, B., Trojahn, C., Vieira, R.: VOAR 3.0: a configurable environment for manipulating multiple ontology alignments. In: International Semantic Web Conference (Posters, Demos & Industry Tracks). CEUR Workshop Proceedings, vol. 1963 (2017)
11. Wrigley, S.N., García-Castro, R., Nixon, L.: Semantic evaluation at large scale (SEALS). In: 21st International Conference Companion on World Wide Web - WWW, pp. 299–302 (2012)

WarVictimSampo 1914–1922: A Semantic Portal and Linked Data Service for Digital Humanities Research on War History

Heikki Rantala[1]([✉]) [iD], Esko Ikkala[1] [iD], Ilkka Jokipii[2,3], Mikko Koho[1] [iD],
Jouni Tuominen[1,2] [iD], and Eero Hyvönen[1,2] [iD]

[1] Semantic Computing Research Group (SeCo), Aalto University, Espoo, Finland
{heikki.rantala,esko.ikkala,mikko.koho}@aalto.fi
https://seco.cs.aalto.fi
[2] Helsinki Centre for Digital Humanities (HELDIG), University of Helsinki,
Helsinki, Finland
{ilkka.jokipii,jouni.tuominen,eero.hyvonen}@helsinki.fi
https://heldig.fi
[3] The National Archives of Finland, Helsinki, Finland
https://arkisto.fi

Abstract. This paper presents the semantic portal and Linked Open Data (LOD) service WARVICTIMSAMPO 1914–22 about the war victims, battles, and prisoner camps in the Finnish Civil and other wars. The system is based on a database of the National Archives of Finland and related data compiled during the project. The system contains detailed information about some 40 000 deaths extracted from several data sources, and data about prisoner camps and over 1000 battles of the Civil War. A key novelty of WARVICTIMSAMPO 1914–22 is the integration of ready-to-use Digital Humanities tooling with the data service, which allows, e.g., studying information about wider prosopographical groups in addition to individual victims. We demonstrate how the tools of the portal, as well as the underlying SPARQL endpoint, can be used to explore and analyze war history in flexible and visual ways. WARVICTIM-SAMPO 1914–22 is a new member in the series of "Sampo" model based semantic portals. It was published in late 2019 and got 20 000 users in two weeks.

Keywords: Linked data · Semantic web · War history

1 Introduction

This paper presents the semantic portal and Linked Open Data (LOD) service WARVICTIMSAMPO 1914–22[1] about the war victims, battles, and prisoner

---

[1] WarVictimSampo 1914–1922 Semantic Portal: https://sotasurmat.narc.fi/en.

© Springer Nature Switzerland AG 2020
A. Harth et al. (Eds.): ESWC 2020 Satellite Events, LNCS 12124, pp. 191–196, 2020.
https://doi.org/10.1007/978-3-030-62327-2_33

camps in the Finnish Civil and other wars. The tools offered by the service help researchers and general public to better access the historical data. The main focus of the service is the Finnish War Victims 1914–1922 database that includes some 40 000 victims and is maintained by the National Archives of Finland. Most, over 90%, of the deaths recorded here are related to the Finnish Civil War in 1918, and the rest are related to the other wars of the period. Figure 1 depicts the distribution of death dates in the data during 1918 as shown by the service. The data includes people who have died in Finland and abroad.

In this paper we show how LOD and modern web technologies can be used to enhance and update an old data service. The paper also demonstrates how modern tools can be used with LOD to analyze the data for Digital Humanities research. The original War Victims data was recorded in 1999–2003 as a government project [11] and includes 39 931 deaths. The original data was converted into LOD form and updated with 1590 new previously unknown victims and some new information concerning the old records [9]. An important contribution of the new system is making the access to the data more versatile and easier.

The old database is not directly open for public access. There is an old web application[2] in use for exploring the data with simple search functionality and a homepage for each person. A person's homepage includes basic information about the victim, but many pieces of information are not shown, even though they would be available in the underlying database. The end users of the system have deemed the search interface fairly inflexible and with too few options to choose from. Also means of exporting the data from the database ware asked for.

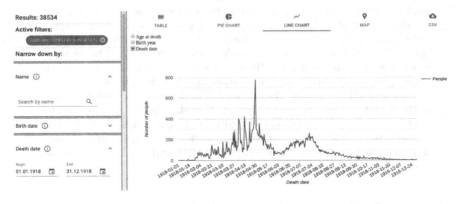

Fig. 1. Distribution of death dates in 1918 as shown in WARVICTIMSAMPO 1914–22

The death records contain basic information of the people (e.g., name, place of birth, date of birth, date of death), socioeconomic information (e.g., occupation, marital status), and war related information (e.g., military rank, military

---

[2] http://vesta.narc.fi/cgi-bin/db2www/sotasurmaetusivu/main?lang=en.

organization, time of imprisonment). During the conversion to LOD form the data was ontologized where appropriate, and mapped to some outside sources. This made it easy to, for example, create links to outside web pages relating to certain famous people in the data, and to get coordinates for the municipalities to use with map visualisations.

To publish the data we use the "Sampo" publishing model [4]. The data in LOD form is loaded into a triplestore hosted at the Linked Data Finland platform[3] [3], where it can be queried using SPARQL. The semantic portal makes queries to this publicly open endpoint, and a researcher can also query the endpoint for her own purpose.

2   WarVictimSampo 1914–22 Semantic Portal

A semantic portal was developed to allow different user groups to access the data easily. The user groups include researchers, students, and the wider public interested in either the Finnish Civil War in general or the fates of their relatives. Even though the data can be accessed by anyone with SPARQL queries this can be too technically demanding for many users. Also a researcher who is able to create her own SPARQL queries finds it useful to have an easy way to explore the data and to create simple visualizations quickly. The visualization tools provided by the portal are expected to be useful for both finding new data and for educating the public about history. These tools should not be expected to fully replace manual research and close reading. They are aimed to be used to spot interesting phenomena in the data that require more detailed analysis.

The user interface of the semantic portal is implemented as a full stack JavaScript web application, using the Sampo-UI framework[4] [6]. The user interface is built around the concept of faceted search [10]. With faceted search, the user can easily narrow the search step by step by making selections based on predetermined orthogonal hierarchies of property values called facets. Facets also show the number of available items with each possible selection. This allows the user to immediately see the number of solutions of each possible selection. Combined with selections on other facets like occupation, party, and age, the user may also draw interesting conclusions by observing the hit distributions on the facets. Faceted search can therefore be used to not only find individuals that fit certain criteria, such as relatives, but it can also be used to find information about the distributions of different kind of the casualties. The faceted search paradigm is an example of exploratory search [7].

The user interface currently includes two main perspectives for exploring the underlying knowledge graph: 1) The main perspective is based on searching and exploring the casualties. 2) There is also a perspective based on the battles of the Finnish Civil War, covering currently 1182 geo-coded battles. Other views may be added later in the same way as in other "Sampo" series semantic portals[5].

---

[3] http://www.ldf.fi/dataset/siso.

[4] https://github.com/SemanticComputing/sampo-ui.

[5] https://www.europenowjournal.org/2019/09/09/linked-data-in-use-sampo-portals-on-the-semantic-web.

For the both perspectives there are multiple tabs to view the data in different ways. Currently the data can be shown as a table or downloaded as a CSV file, and it can be visualized with pie charts, line charts, and maps. All the visualizations are dynamic, reflecting the selections made with the facets. This allows for visualizing different aspects of the data quickly and easily. For example, Fig. 2 shows how people in the data from the Vaasa province clearly have died mainly in the city of Tampere for some reason that can be explored further.

The table view can be considered the default view and can be used to browse the individual war victims in the data. This table shows the names of the people and their basic information. By clicking the name of the person, the user can navigate to that person's homepage in the application. The person's page shows all the information related to the person, including the sources of all the individual pieces of information.

Both the line chart and pie chart visualizations can be used for multiple different purposes. For example, the line chart can be used to visualize age distributions, birth years, or death dates as shown in Fig. 1. The line chart can be used, for example, by researchers to compare the age distributions of different groups of people within the data by using one or more facets to select the desired group of people. Line charts could also be used, for example, by school students to see the dates when people from their hometown died during the Finnish Civil War. The pie chart can be used to visualize distributions within one facet. For example, it could be used to visualize the relative amount of people with different occupations in the data.

The Battles perspective includes an animation view that can be used to visualize the battles of the Finnish Civil War. The animation advances by day and shows the battles that start that day as red dots that stay on the map, but turn dark when the time advances. The purpose of this view is mainly educational.

The WARVICTIMSAMPO 1914–22 semantic portal and data service were opened to public on 20 November, 2019, and has had tens of thousands of users. There is an English translation of the user interface available, but all the data are only in Finnish.

The plan is to continue developing the portal and updating the data service. For example, a perspective of the prison camps of the Finnish Civil War could be added to the portal. Because the data and the source code of the user interface of the semantic portal are open to all, new views and perspectives could be developed by anyone interested. The user interface of the portal could also be used as a model for creating user interfaces for some other data services.

3   Related Work

WARVICTIMSAMPO 1914–22 is a follow up project of WarSampo [5], which uses LD to present and publish information related to the Second World War in Finland, including death records. The novelty of WARVICTIMSAMPO 1914–22 lays in the idea of developing new data-analytic tooling for research in war

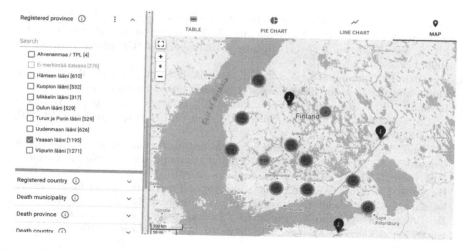

Fig. 2. A map visualization of death places of the people who were registered in Vaasa province and supported Whites in the Finnish Civil War.

history, as well as in creating, cleaning, extending, and publishing the former War Victims 1914–22 database for open use on the Semantic Web.

There have been several projects publishing linked data about the World War I on the Web, such as Europeana Collections 1914–1918[6], 1914–1918 Online[7], WW1 Discovery[8], Out of the Trenches[9], CENDARI[10], Muninn[11], and WW1LOD [8]. In addition to WarSampo, there are a few works that use the Linked Data approach to WW2, such as [1,2], Open Memory Project[12] on holocaust victims, and the Dutch project Network Orloogsbronnen[13].

Acknowledgements. Our research was funded by the Prime Minister's Office. Thanks to CSC – IT Center for Science, Finland, for computational resources.

References

1. de Boer, V., van Doornik, J., Buitinck, L., Marx, M., Veken, T.: Linking the kingdom: enriched access to a historiographical text. In: Proceedings of the 7th International Conference on Knowledge Capture (KCAP 2013), pp. 17–24. ACM (2013)

---

[6] http://www.europeana-collections-1914-1918.eu.
[7] http://www.1914-1918-online.net.
[8] http://ww1.discovery.ac.uk.
[9] http://www.canadiana.ca/en/pcdhn-lod/.
[10] http://www.cendari.eu/research/first-world-war-studies/.
[11] http://blog.muninn-project.org.
[12] http://www.bygle.net/wp-content/uploads/2015/04/Open-Memory-Project_3-1.pdf.
[13] https://www.oorlogsbronnen.nl.

2. Collins, T., Mulholland, P., Zdrahal, Z.: Semantic browsing of digital collections. In: Gil, Y., Motta, E., Benjamins, V.R., Musen, M.A. (eds.) ISWC 2005. LNCS, vol. 3729, pp. 127–141. Springer, Heidelberg (2005). https://doi.org/10.1007/11574620_12

3. Hyvönen, E., Tuominen, J., Alonen, M., Mäkelä, E.: Linked data Finland: a 7-star model and platform for publishing and re-using linked datasets. In: Presutti, V., Blomqvist, E., Troncy, R., Sack, H., Papadakis, I., Tordai, A. (eds.) ESWC 2014. LNCS, vol. 8798, pp. 226–230. Springer, Cham (2014). https://doi.org/10.1007/978-3-319-11955-7_24

4. Hyvönen, E.: "Sampo" model and semantic portals for digital humanities on the semantic web. In: Proceedings of the Digital Humanities in the Nordic Countries (DHN 2020). CEUR Workshop Proceedings (2020)

5. Hyvönen, E., et al.: WarSampo data service and semantic portal for publishing linked open data about the second world war history. In: Sack, H., Blomqvist, E., d'Aquin, M., Ghidini, C., Ponzetto, S.P., Lange, C. (eds.) ESWC 2016. LNCS, vol. 9678, pp. 758–773. Springer, Cham (2016). https://doi.org/10.1007/978-3-319-34129-3_46

6. Ikkala, E., Hyvönen, E., Rantala, H., Koho, M.: Sampo-UI: A full stack javascript framework for developing semantic portal user interfaces (2020). https://seco.cs.aalto.fi/publications/2020/ikkala-et-al-sampo-ui-2020.pdf

7. Marchionini, G.: Exploratory search: from finding to understanding. Commun. ACM **49**(4), 41–46 (2006)

8. Mäkelä, E., Törnroos, J., Lindquist, T., Hyvönen, E.: WW1LOD: an application of CIDOC-CRM to world war 1 linked data. Int. J. Digit. Librar. **18**(4), 333–343 (2017)

9. Rantala, H., Jokipii, I., Koho, M., Ikkala, E., Tuominen, J., Hyvönen, E.: Building a linked open data portal of war victims in Finland 1914–1922. In: Proceedings of Digital Humanities in Nordic Countries (DHN 2020). CEUR Workshop Proceedings (2020)

10. Tunkelang, D.: Faceted Search. Synthesis Lectures on Information Concepts, Retrieval, and Services. Morgan & Claypool, Palo Alto (2009)

11. Westerlund, L. (ed.): Sotaoloissa vuosina 1914–22 surmansa saaneet. Tilastoraportti. Valtioneuvoston kanslia, Helsinki, Finland (2004)

An HTTP/RDF-Based Agent Infrastructure for Manufacturing Using Stigmergy

Daniel Schraudner[(✉)] and Victor Charpenay

Chair of Technical Information Systems, Friedrich-Alexander-University,
Erlangen-Nürnberg, Germany
{daniel.schraudner,victor.charpenay}@fau.de

Abstract. We have built a demonstrator for the communication infrastructure of a multi-agent system controlling a simplified shop floor. We use the concept of stigmergy which does not allow inter-agent communication but only between agents and the environment. Furthermore we keep the agents as simple as possible by using only simple-reflex agents. The environment is modelled as a RDF Knowledge Graph and communication takes place using HTTP request. We carried out experiments regarding the agent scalability and identified open questions.

Keywords: Multi-agent system · Stigmergy · Knowledge graph

1 Introduction

Information systems in many businesses still are following a quite centralized approach – as opposed to the Web which has an inherently decentralized architecture. Many of those systems could profit from the properties and effects that come along with a decentralized system architecture such as more reliability and less complexity.

A common approach for tackling this problem are multi-agent systems which have been around for a long time in the research field of decentralized manufacturing [4]. Not that well established, however, is the concept of stigmergy which is capable of greatly reducing the complexity of a multi-agent system. It is a communication paradigm which does not allow agents to communicate directly with each other but only indirectly by using the environment. Using stigmergy has several advantages including no need for explicit synchronization between the agents and a clear separation of concerns [2].

In our approach we want to take this idea even further and try to shift as much complexity out of the agents into the environment. This idea is (like stigmergy) taken from biological systems in nature where it works quite well.

This work was funded by the German Federal Ministry of Education and Research through the MOSAIK project (grant no. 01IS18070A).

A. Harth et al. (Eds.): ESWC 2020 Satellite Events, LNCS 12124, pp. 197–202, 2020.
https://doi.org/10.1007/978-3-030-62327-2_34

An ant colony, e.g. comprises a very large number of quite simple agents (the ants) which do not communicate directly but only by using their environment (pheromones, etc.) but it is able to accomplish a lot of tasks (like food foraging) very efficiently.

This specific type of agent we want to use for our system is called simple-reflex agent [5] and its functionality can be seen in Fig. 1. It is the simplest form of an agent where the current state of the environment is read through sensors. The agent decides based on a set of simple condition-action rules, which action to take next and executes it using its actuators. No internal state of the agent or further reasoning are involved.

To allow agents to actually do things, one needs a robust communication infrastructure which lets the agents read their environment and change its state concurrently and asynchronously. We propose that the environment can be represented using a RDF-based Knowledge graph and that communication between agents and the environment should be carried out using HTTP requests.

For this demonstration we modelled a the scenario of a simple shop floor producing IoT boards which is described in Sect. 2. We built a working communication infrastructure for the agents. The architecture of this system is explained in Sect. 3. Furthermore we carried out some experiments regarding the scalability of agents in the system (Sect. 4) and identified some open questions that we want to address in the future (Sect. 5).

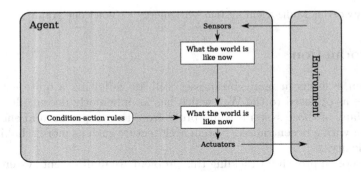

Fig. 1. Schema of a simple-reflex agent based on [5]

2   Scenario

The RDF model of our simplified shop floor scenario is available online[1]. It comprises five different kinds of products in an assembly tree which can be seen in Fig. 2. The manufacturing of an IoT board requires specific actions with specific products at different workstations.

---

[1] https://purl.org/mosaik/demo/arena.

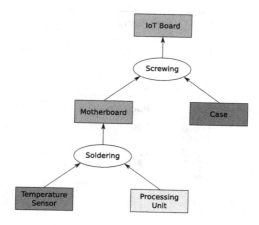

Fig. 2. Assembly tree of an IoT board

The shop floor has five different types of stations. At *Delivery* the base products (*Temperature Sensor*, *Processing Unit* and *Case*) enter the factory. At *Shipping* assembled *IoT Boards* leave the factory. *Soldering Stations* and *Screwing Stations* can carry out their respective assemble actions if the needed products are available at the station. Between the stations products are stored in the *Rack* which acts as a buffer. Products do not move by themselves but transport actions have to be carried out by *Forklifts* which can move between the different stations. The general structure of the shop floor can be seen in Fig. 3.

As each assemble station and forklift can only execute one action at a time, we scaled up the numbers a bit for our experiments (3 *Screwing Stations*, 3 *Soldering Stations*, 10 *Forklifts*).

3   Architecture

The architecture of our demonstrator can be seen in Fig. 4.

The client is able to run an arbitrary number of simple-reflex agents. We use Linked-Data-Fu [3] for carrying out the HTTP requests and applying the condition-action rules. The agents decide autonomously whether to carry out a specific action or not, using the rules which are stated in Notation 3 [1] (an extension of RDF with logical operations).

Agents are constantly and asynchronously querying the state of the Knowledge Graph and trying to match their rules. In order for the agents to make sensible decisions, they need a semantically rich representation of the current state of the shop floor which they get in response to their HTTP requests. If they can apply a rule, they send a HTTP POST request to change the Knowledge Graph. More specifically they are proposing an action which should be carried out (in this case either an assemble action for a station or a transfer action for a forklift).

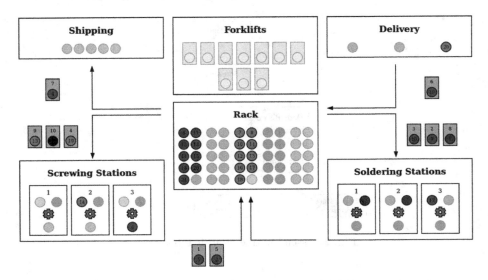

Fig. 3. Structure of the shop floor (screenshot of the GUI)

On the server side the state of the environment is maintained as a RDF Knowledge Graph. It comprises the current location of all the forklifts and products as well as the state of the workstations. Furthermore all possible, active and completed actions are contained. These entities and the relationships between them are represented using Schema.org[2] and, where this was not sufficient, our own vocabulary which is also available online[3].

Also on the server there runs a simulation part which mimics the behavior of the stations and forklifts on the shop floor (i.e. it executes the actions). This is done by constantly observing the Knowledge Graph for new proposed actions (*Action Observer*) and spawning a new *Action Runner* which – after a exponentially distributed time – changes the Knowledge Graph according to the action (e.g. moving the product).

However, as the agents are sending their request asynchronously, some kind of synchronization mechanism has to be implemented such that no conflicting actions are (trying to be) executed (e.g. one product being transported to two different stations at the same time). In our implementation every *Action Runner* checks before the start of the execution of its action, whether there exist conflicting action and, if this is the case, discards its action.

A graphical user interface is also available at the server-side to watch the current state of the shop floor. A screenshot of the GUI can be seen in Fig. 3. All elements that are numbered have an URI and are clickable links to their RDF representation in the Knowledge Graph.

---

[2] https://schema.org/.

[3] https://purl.org/mosaik/demo/vocab.

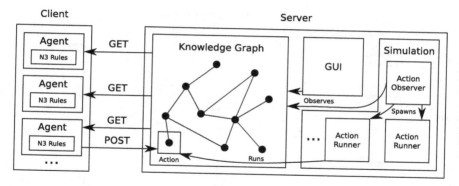

Fig. 4. Architecture of our demonstrator

4 Demo and Experiments

A running instance of our demonstrator is publicly available[4].

We also ran some experiments with a different number of agents and measured those actions that were successful (i.e. they were executed by an *Action Runner*) and those that were conflicting (i.e. they were discarded by an *Action Runner*).

The agents we used can be divided in two classes depending on whether they had a rule for proposing an assemble action or a transport action. The number of assemble and transfer agents always was equal (i.e. *4 Agents* means two assemble agents and two transfer agents.

For each number of agents we ran the experiment ten times and took the averages over those runs to reduce the effect of the random action duration. Figure 5 shows the number of successes over time for each experiment (which directly correlates to the number of assembled IoT boards). There seems to be a optimal number of agents around 24–28 (as to few agents are not producing enough action proposals and to much are producing a lot of conflicts which hinder the successful actions).

5 Conclusion and Future Work

From our experiment we can see that the communication architecture we proposed generally seems suited to tackle a problem like in our exemplary scenario. However, further investigation on the optimal number of agents to deploy needs further investigation.

Another interesting question is, whether the performance of the system could be improved if the assignment of agents to action is changed (one or multiple agents have rules for one type of stations or one kind of product instead of all assemble actions, etc.).

---

[4] https://purl.org/mosaik/demo.

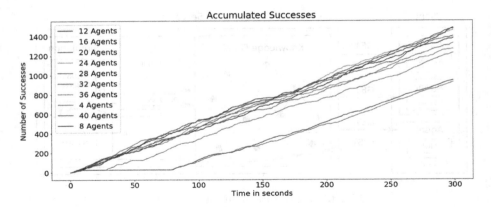

Fig. 5. Successful actions over time for different numbers of agents

Our synchronization technique (conflict detection) could be further improved or other methods could be applied (e. synchronizing the agents using tokens).

Furthermore it might be interesting to investigate how rules for agents can be written such that the number of occurring conflicts is reduced. It seems likely that a reduced number of conflicts will allow more successful actions and thus lead to a better overall performance.

References

1. Berners-Lee, T., Connolly, D.: Notation3 (N3): a readable RDF syntax (2011)
2. Hadeli, Valckenaers, P., Kollingbaum, M., Van Brussel, H.: Multi-agent coordination and control using stigmergy. Comput. Ind. **53**(1), 75–96 (2004). https://doi.org/10.1016/S0166-3615(03)00123-4
3. Harth, A., Käfer, T.: Linked data techniques for the web of things: tutorial. In: Proceedings of the 8th International Conference on the Internet of Things. IOT 2018. Association for Computing Machinery, New York (2018). https://doi.org/10.1145/3277593.3277641
4. Leitão, P.: Agent-based distributed manufacturing control: a state-of-the-art survey. Eng. Appl. Artif. Intell. **22**(7), 979–991 (Oct 2009). https://doi.org/10.1016/j.engappai.2008.09.005
5. Russell, S., Norvig, P.: Artificial Intelligence a Modern Approach Third Edition. Prentice Hall, Upper Saddle River (2010). https://doi.org/10.1017/S0269888900007724

Entity Typing Based on RDF2Vec Using Supervised and Unsupervised Methods

Radina Sofronova[1,2(✉)], Russa Biswas[1,2(✉)], Mehwish Alam[1,2], and Harald Sack[1,2]

[1] FIZ Karlsruhe – Leibniz Institute for Information Infrastructure, Eggenstein-Leopoldshafen, Germany
{russa.biswas,mehwish.alam,harald.sack}@fiz-karlsruhe.de
[2] Karlsruhe Institute of Technology, Institute AIFB, Karlsruhe, Germany
radina.sofronova@student.kit.edu

Abstract. Knowledge Graphs have been recognized as the foundation for diverse applications in the field of data mining, information retrieval, and natural language processing. So the completeness and the correctness of the KGs are of high importance. The type information of the entities in a KG, is one of the most vital facts. However, it has been observed that type information is often noisy or incomplete. In this work, the task of fine-grained entity typing is addressed by exploiting the pre-trained RDF2Vec vectors using supervised and unsupervised approaches.

1 Introduction

Entity typing is the process of assigning a type to an entity which is a fundamental task in Knowledge Graph (KG) construction and completion. Most of these KGs are created either via automated information extraction from Wikipedia infoboxes, information accumulation provided by the users, or by using heuristics. Therefore, one primary problem is that majority of the entities have coarse-grained type information. The classes in DBpedia have a hierarchical structure, in which the classes in the same branch of hierarchy share common characteristic features. A class retains the basic characteristics of the parent as well as has some unique features of its own. Fine-grained type prediction is the task of assigning a type or class to an entity. For example, in DBpedia, the actor *dbr: Tom_Hanks* is of type *dbo: Person*, whereas the most appropriate class, would be *dbo: Actor*, which is a subclass of *dbo: Person*. Table 1 depicts a brief statistics of the missing fine-grained types in DBpedia. For instance, class *dbo: SportsTeam* has 14 subclasses in DBpedia and 352006 entities, out of which only 8.9% are assigned to its subclasses. To deal with this challenge, a few approaches have already been proposed. The first approach is based on statistical heuristics [6] and the second approach uses a supervised hierarchical classification [4,5]. On the other hand, [2] considers the text as well as the structural information in KGs for entity typing. In [1], the authors use the abstracts from the Wikipedia pages to predict the Wikipedia infobox types using word embeddings. Since

© Springer Nature Switzerland AG 2020
A. Harth et al. (Eds.): ESWC 2020 Satellite Events, LNCS 12124, pp. 203–207, 2020.
https://doi.org/10.1007/978-3-030-62327-2_35

Table 1. Distribution of entities in some of the subclasses in DBpedia.

Class	#Entities	#Coarse-Grained Typed entities	%Fine-Grained Typed entities
SportsTeam	352006	320835	8.9%
Company	70208	55524	20.9%
Settlement	478906	246163	48.6%
Activity	19464	8824	54.7%
Event	76029	19418	74.5%

DBpedia type information is extracted from the Wikipedia infobox types, these models can be used for entity typing. However, none of these approaches have exploited KG embeddings to solve the problem of type prediction. This work focuses on evaluating the role of KG embeddings only in assigning fine-grained type information to entities in DBpedia that already have a coarse-grained type.

2   Supervised and Unsupervised Entity Typing

RDF2Vec. RDF2Vec [7] generates latent representations of entities in a KG into a lower dimensional feature space. The embedding space comprises of entities and properties, in which the semantically similar entities are closely spaced. In this work, the pre-trained DBpedia embeddings generated using RDF2Vec have been used. The original study uses graph walks and word2vec for generating the embeddings of DBpedia.

Unsupervised Approach - Vector Similarity. In order to assign fine-grained type to an entity with an already assigned coarse-grained type, class hierarchy in DBpedia has been exploited. Cosine similarity between the entity vector and all the class vectors of the classes in that branch of the class hierarchy in DBpedia were calculated. For example, in DBpedia, for the entity *dbr:Baker&McKenzie*, the `rdf:type` class is *dbo:LawFirm*. Next, class hierarchy of *dbo:LawFirm* is traversed to find the highest level parent class dbo:Organisation after *dbo:Agent*. Now, all the subclasses of dbo:Organisation in the hierarchy are extracted and the cosine similarity between all the subclasses and the entity *dbr:Baker&McKenzie* has been calculated.

The approach has been explored with two alternatives for the class vectors. The first uses the pre-trained RDF2Vec vectors of the classes for the cosine similarity. Since, a set is represented by its members, which exhibit the same properties. Similarly, the entities of the classes in DBpedia have the same or similar properties. Therefore, following this concept, the average of the entity vectors of a class is a representation of the class in DBpedia and is given by,

$$class\_vector = \frac{1}{n}(\mathbf{v_1} + \mathbf{v_2} + ... + \mathbf{v_n}), \tag{1}$$

Table 2. Accuracy of Vector Similarity and CNN for different datasets

Datasets	RDF2Vec				
	Vector similarity				CNN
	Original class vector		Class vector as avg. of entity vectors		
	Hits@3	Hits@1	Hits@3	Hits@1	
59 classes, 500 entities/class	68.91%	21.63%	**95.63%**	86.51%	81.78%
86 classes, 2k entities/class	34.74%	12.26%	**84.78%**	74.9%	53.67%
81 classes, 4k entities/class	32.51%	11.01%	**84.61%**	74.33%	53.49%

where n is the number of entities in a class and the $\mathbf{v_i}$, $i \in [1, n]$ are the RDF2Vec vectors of all entities of the class. This class vector is used for the vector similarity in the second approach.

Supervised Approach - 1D CNN. The entity typing problem is converted to a classification problem with the `rdf:type` as classes in which, a 1D CNN model [3] is built on top of RDF2Vec. The model consists of a convolutional layer which involves a feature detector followed by a global max pool layer. For regularization, a dropout on the output of the pooling layer is used which is then passed through a fully connected final layer.

3 Experiments and Results

Dataset. In order to have fine-grained type prediction of the entities which are already coarse-grained typed in DBpedia 2016-10[1], a dataset with 59 classes considering the type hierarchy was generated. Moreover, the selected classes are less popular i.e., 15 classes have less than 500 entities per class, 20 classes have entities between 500 and 1000, and the remaining 24 classes have more than 1000 entities. From each of the chosen classes, 500 entities were extracted. The other datasets contain 86 classes with 2000 entities per class and 81 classes with 4000 entities per class respectively. Therefore, this study provides a basic analysis of the quality of vectors for lesser known classes and entities and their performance in entity typing task. The uniform vectors in RDF2Vec model[2] with a dimension of 200, have been used.

Experiments

Unsupervised Approach. Hits@1 and Hits@3 have been computed on the values of vector similarity compared against the current entity types in DBpedia. The vector similarity values for a certain entity are ranked to determine if the

---

[1] https://wiki.dbpedia.org/downloads-2016-10.
[2] https://zenodo.org/record/1320211#.Xbnwf25FydI.

Table 3. Comparison with SDType model

Datasets	#Common Entities	Accuracy		
		SDType	RDF2Vec vector similarity	
			Hits@1	Hits@3
59 classes, 500 entities/class	7425	**82.35%**	73.24%	79.5%
86 classes, 2k entities/class	57467	80.43%	74.44%	**81.2%**
81 classes, 4k entities/class	109948	81.22%	75.12%	**82%**

Table 4. Accuracy of 1D CNN models.

CNN models	20 classes, 150 entities/class	59 classes, 500 entities/class
1 1D layer	59.83%	42.61%
2 1D layers	93.5%	81.78%

correct entity type is present in top 1 and 3 in the list of types. Table 2 shows that the experiments depict that RDF2Vec pre-trained class vectors do not reflect the characteristics of the entities of the class. This is due to the fact that RDF2Vec is path dependent and considers only the outgoing edges in the RDF graph. In contrast, the class vectors generated by the average of the entity vectors are able to reflect the characteristics of a class. It is observed that with this approach, the best results of entity typing is achieved with this method in Hits@3. The detailed results and plots are available online[3]. Moreover, the unsupervised model is compared with the statistical heuristic based entity typing approach [6] in Table 3. For this, the publicly available results of SDType method[4] have been used. However, only a small fraction of the entities are common between the available results and our datasets as depicted in the second column of Table 3. Therefore, a comparison with the whole dataset is not possible. The accuracy provided in this table is calculated based on the number of common entities. It is to be noted that KG embedding based vector similarity method works better than SDType for two of the datasets.

Supervised Approach. Two approaches have been followed here. The first model consists of two 1D CNN layers and was trained with 150 entities for 20 classes each with a 80-20 split of training and test set. Since the number of entities per class is small, the model is overfitting with two convolutional layers yielding 93.5% accuracy as shown in Table 4. The two basic ways of reducing overfitting in neural network models are training the network on more data or by changing the complexity of the network, have been examined. In the second experiment, 59 classes with 500 entities were taken which results in 81.78%

---

[3] https://github.com/ISE-FIZKarlsruhe/DBpedia-Entity-Typing-with-RDF2Vec.

[4] http://downloads.dbpedia.org/2016-10/core-i18n/en/instance_types_sdtyped_dbo_en.ttl.bz2.

accuracy. Also, the complexity of the model is reduced to only one convolutional layer which results in 42.61% accuracy for 59 classes. It can be concluded from the results that a CNN model on the top of the RDF2Vec works better for entity typing. Moreover, reducing the complexity of model works better for the smaller datasets. For the other two datasets, it has been observed that the accuracy does not affect much with the increase in the dataset size and reducing the number of classes. Overall, it is to be noted that unsupervised vector similarity approach with the averaged class vector works best for all the datasets.

4 Conclusion and Future Work

In this paper, different approaches for entity typing in a KG have been analyzed. The achieved results using the set theory concept when applied to generate the class vectors from the pre-trained entity vectors proved to be the best approach for the task with this embedding model. On the other hand, the pre-trained RDF2Vec vectors coupled with CNN work second best. The method can be adapted to any other KG with any pre-trained embedding model. In future work, the vectors from the graph kernel method of RDF2Vec for entity typing will be explored as well as more information from the KG. Moreover, contextual word embeddings will also be exploited on the abstract of the entities coupled with KG embeddings to improve the entity type prediction.

References

1. Biswas, R., Türker, R., Moghaddam, F.B., Koutraki, M., Sack, H.: Wikipedia infobox type prediction using embeddings. In: Proceedings of the 1st Workshop on Deep Learning for Knowledge Graphs and Semantic Technologies DL4KGS 2018. CEUR Workshop Proceedings (2018)
2. Jin, H., Hou, L., Li, J., Dong, T.: Attributed and predictive entity embedding for fine-grained entity typing in knowledge bases. In: Proceedings of the 27th International Conference on Computational Linguistics. Association for Computational Linguistics (2018)
3. Kim, Y.: Convolutional neural networks for sentence classification. In: Proceedings of the 2014 Conference on EMNLP. Association for Computational Linguistics (2014)
4. Kliegr, T., Zamazal, O.: LHD 2.0: a text mining approach to typing entities in knowledge graphs. J. Web Semant. **39**, 47–61 (2016)
5. Melo, A., Paulheim, H., Völker, J.: Type prediction in RDF knowledge bases using hierarchical multilabel classification. In: Proceedings of the 6th International Conference on WIMS 2016. Association for Computing Machinery (2016)
6. Paulheim, H., Bizer, C.: Type inference on noisy RDF data. In: Alani, H., et al. (eds.) ISWC 2013. LNCS, vol. 8218, pp. 510–525. Springer, Heidelberg (2013). https://doi.org/10.1007/978-3-642-41335-3_32
7. Ristoski, P., Paulheim, H.: RDF2Vec: RDF graph embeddings for data mining. In: Groth, P.P., et al. (eds.) ISWC 2016, Part I. LNCS, vol. 9981, pp. 498–514. Springer, Cham (2016). https://doi.org/10.1007/978-3-319-46523-4_30

Automatic Annotation Service APPI: Named Entity Linking in Legal Domain

Minna Tamper[1,2]($\boxtimes$) ⓘ, Arttu Oksanen[1,3] ⓘ, Jouni Tuominen[1,2] ⓘ,
Aki Hietanen[4], and Eero Hyvönen[1,2] ⓘ

[1] Semantic Computing Research Group (SeCo), Aalto University, Espoo, Finland
{minna.tamper,arttu.oksanen,jouni.tuominen,eero.hyvonen}@aalto.fi
[2] HELDIG – Helsinki Centre for Digital Humanities,
University of Helsinki, Helsinki, Finland
[3] Edita Publishing Ltd., Helsinki, Finland
[4] Ministry of Justice, Helsinki, Finland
aki.hietanen@om.fi
http://seco.cs.aalto.fi, http://heldig.fi, http://www.editapublishing.fi,
http://oikeusministerio.fi

Abstract. Texts referencing court decisions and statutes can be difficult to understand without context. It can be time consuming and expensive to find related statutes or to learn about context specific terminology. As a solution, we utilized a named entity linking tool for extracting information and tailored it into a service, APPI, that can automatically annotate legal documents to provide context to the readers. The service can identify and link named entities and references to legal texts to corresponding vocabularies and data sources by combining statistics- and rule-based named entity recognition with named entity linking. The results provide users with enhanced reading experience with contextual information and the possibility to access related materials, such as statutes and court decisions.

Keywords: Automatic annotation service · Legal texts · Named entity linking · Linked data

1 Introduction

The research hypothesis of this paper is that by annotating and linking legal texts to knowledge bases it is possible to assist readers to understand the text and context by offering information about legislation, context, and terminology. To understand and interpret legal texts correctly, it is often important to get acquainted with other related contextual material. The linking of texts through similarity or references can aid in finding information. To support end users in close reading and to enable linking of legal texts, we created a service called APPI[1]. It utilizes a named entity linking tool, NELLI [13], for identifying domain

---

[1] A demonstrator that is under development is available at http://nlp.ldf.fi/appi.

© Springer Nature Switzerland AG 2020
A. Harth et al. (Eds.): ESWC 2020 Satellite Events, LNCS 12124, pp. 208–213, 2020.
https://doi.org/10.1007/978-3-030-62327-2_36

specific information and to enable named entity linking of legal texts. As a result, the APPI service can identify and link named entities, terminology, and references to legal texts to corresponding vocabularies and data sources by combining statistics- and rule-based named entity recognition (NER) with named entity linking (NEL). The end results can be edited in the APPI service's web application and they can be downloaded in JSON format. In this paper, the APPI tool is piloted for Finnish court decisions and legislation.

2 Data

Semantic Finlex[2] [9] is a web service that hosts the Finnish legislation and case law as Linked Open Data. Currently, the data published in Semantic Finlex includes consolidated statutes with version history (approx. 2500 statutes), the original statutes as published in the official journal (approx. 50 000 statutes), Judgments of the Supreme court (5500), and Judgments of the Supreme administrative court (7500). In addition, the data contains keywords for the statutes, and keywords used by the Supreme Court and the Supreme Administrative Court to annotate the court judgments. The judgments are also linked to judges and personnel contributing to the case. The original statutes are also linked to EU legislation and Finnish government bills. The service includes the legal texts in text, HTML, and XML formats. The documents are written in Finnish and Swedish.

3 Method

In order to automatically annotate the legal texts of Semantic Finlex, the NELLI tool [13] was developed further. NELLI is a combination of NER (FiNER [4,11], LINFER [13]) and NEL (ARPA [5]) tools and it disambiguates entities using a scoring scheme where popularity of the interpretation of the named entity type, the string length, and successful linking are taken into account. Initially, NELLI was a command line tool that could be only used for annotating text documents. In order to annotate and provide context to legal texts, the tool was transformed into a restful API service. The support for input formats was extended to HTML, XML, and text formats, and the output format was changed to JSON that returns the annotated document in the original form and a list of recognized entities. Also, new tools were added in order to recognize more named entity types: FinBERT[3] [15], a regular expression-based named entity linker tool called Reksi[4], and Person Name Finder[5].

FinBERT is a Finnish version of the Google's BERT [1] deep transfer learning model. It was added to improve identification of named entities in text by adding

---

[2] http://data.finlex.fi.
[3] http://turkunlp.org/FinBERT/.
[4] http://nlp.ldf.fi/reksi.
[5] http://nlp.ldf.fi/name-finder.

a deep learning based method to complement the two rule based NER tools (FiNER, LINFER) to find more named entities that go unnoticed with the rule-based tools. Reksi is a NEL tool that uses numerous regular expressions to identify named entities, such as registry numbers, references to statutes, and case law from the text and links them to corresponding knowledge bases. It utilizes the regularity of the forms of the entities in texts and formats them to find the matching entities from the target ontologies. It was developed to enable better identification of named entities that appear in a form that is easy to identify using regular expressions. These entities are common in legal documents, such as court decisions, where, for example, references are made to earlier court decisions and statutes, and punishments (sentence times and fines) are given. The Person Name Finder service is a tool for identifying references to people by linking the names to the Finnish person name ontology HENKO[6] [14]. The tool was added to improve identification of person names that are mentioned in the texts. In addition, an existing tool, LINFER, was upgraded to identify more organizations from the texts. The service is currently only for the Finnish language documents but it is possible to configure NELLI for other languages.

4   Application

The APPI web application was built on top of the results of the NELLI service to visualize them and to provide context and recommendations to the legal texts by linking the given text to different ontologies and to other legal texts in the Semantic Finlex dataset. For this purpose, the application form for annotating consists of an input field, input format (e.g., text, XML) selection, toggles for selecting what tools to use in NELLI, and linking options. The linking options consist of a list of ARPA configurations for ontologies and vocabularies located in a drop-down menu. Based on the selected configuration, the ARPA tool can form n-grams from the given text and linguistically manipulate it (e.g., lemmatize) to match it to the given ontology. Currently, the linking options enable linking of mentions in the text to common Finnish place names (YSO places[7]), legal terminology (the consolidated vocabulary of Finnish legal terms (draft) [3], the Helsinki Term Bank for Arts and Sciences[8], DBpedia, and terms used by EU institutions (EuroVoc[9]) in addition to Semantic Finlex keywords, statutes, and case law. The user can retrieve textually similar court decisions by selecting the option to enable fetching of recommendations from the Semantic Finlex case law finder [12].

The APPI tool can be used as follows. Firstly, the application is given an input, e.g., an abstract of a Finnish court decision in text format. Next, the application is configured to identify and link named entities, e.g., using Fin-BERT, Reksi, and ARPA. The ARPA tool can be used by selecting a linking

---

[6] http://light.onki.fi/henko/en/.

[7] https://finto.fi/yso-paikat/en/.

[8] https://tieteentermipankki.fi/wiki/Termipankki:Etusivu/en.

[9] http://eurovoc.europa.eu.

option, e.g., a configuration for domain information such as legal terminology. Lastly, the user can enable the fetching of recommendations using the case law finder. After configuring the application, the user can click the "Annotate" button, and APPI annotates the given input and retrieves recommendations. The results are presented as shown in Fig. 1.

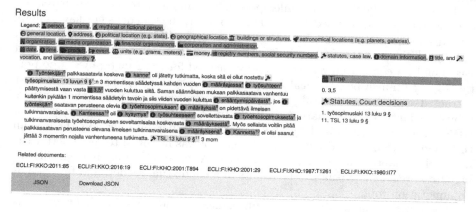

Fig. 1. Results of annotating an abstract of a court decision.

The results are presented under the configuration interface accompanied by a legend that shows available named entity types and how they are shown in text. Below the legend is the annotated text and on its right side a list of entities found in the text (by type). The recognized entities are shown in text with links, and by clicking them a popup appears and shows the description of the given entity. Occasionally, when there is more than one option for an entity, all of them are shown in the popup and the user can select the correct one. In case the application has not found a matching entity, the user can use an autocompletion search field in the popup to query for suitable entities and link the entity manually. Below the text, there is also a list of similar documents that have been retrieved for the input text. At the bottom of the page, the results are presented in JSON form that can be viewed or downloaded by clicking the tab.

In this example (Fig. 1), APPI has identified a reference to time, statutes, and references to different contextual terms in an abstract of a court decision. The linking options were set to link legal terminology (i.e., domain information) to the consolidated vocabulary of Finnish legal terms and to the Helsinki Term Bank for Arts and Sciences. The Reksi tool links statutes and case law to Semantic Finlex. However, currently the endpoint doesn't contain all the alternative names for the statutes and the linking fails for missing names. Below the text, the application has retrieved six related court decisions. The user can click the links to read the related documents in Semantic Finlex.

5   Related Work and Discussion

The APPI service provides easy access to related legal texts and helps to understand the terminology. The inspiration for the application has been the contextual reader application CORE [6] that was created to link text into ontologies in real-time to provide related materials and context. This application was initially utilized in the Semantic Finlex portal [9], configured to use content-related ontologies to provide context for the user. However, the tool does not have a powerful disambiguation system like other named entity linking tools, e.g., DBpedia Spotlight[10] [8] and Gate Cloud[11] [7]. For this purpose, NELLI was created, and based on it, a contextual reader was implemented for the BiographySampo portal [13] for Finnish biographical texts. In BiographySampo, the entities are not extracted with NELLI in real time but in a preprocessing phase that ensures robust semantic disambiguation similarly to [2,10]. The results are recorded in RDF format and visualized by the contextual reader by querying them from the BiographySampo endpoint. The NELLI tool was modified to serve better the needs of Semantic Finlex and used to build APPI application that can disambiguate in real time, visualize the results in a contextual reader, and function as an annotation tool.

The initial demo application, APPI, manages to identify, highlight, and link named entities from a text. The annotation accuracy using NELLI was approximately 80% [13] for people and places in biographical texts. The service has been upgraded and the results are promising but it still needs a formal evaluation, which will be carried out in the future. The recommendations and legal text references can be identified with varying accuracy partially due to lack of document metadata. The current version is still under development and more work needs to be done so that it can be utilized to extract all references to legislative texts such as EU statutes and link them to the CELLAR system[12]. The APPI demo presents how by annotating documents it is possible to cater information and related documents to provide context to the reader automatically.

Acknowledgments. This work is part of the ANOPPI project (https://seco.cs.aalto.fi/projects/anoppi/en/) funded by the Ministry of Justice in Finland. CSC – IT Center for Science, Finland, provided us with computational resources.

References

1. Devlin, J., Chang, M.W., Lee, K., Toutanova, K.: BERT: pre-training of deep bidirectional transformers for language understanding. arXiv preprint arXiv:1810.04805 (2018)

---

[10] https://www.dbpedia-spotlight.org/demo/.
[11] https://cloud.gate.ac.uk.
[12] https://data.europa.eu/euodp/data/dataset/sparql-cellar-of-the-publications-office.

2. Ferragina, P., Scaiella, U.: TAGME: on-the-fly annotation of short text fragments (by Wikipedia entities). In: Proceedings of the 19th ACM International Conference on Information and Knowledge Management, pp. 1625–1628. ACM (2010)
3. Frosterus, M., Tuominen, J., Hyvönen, E.: Facilitating re-use of legal data in applications–Finnish law as a linked open data service. In: Proceedings of the 27th International Conference on Legal Knowledge and Information Systems (JURIX 2014), pp. 115–124. IOS Press (2014)
4. Kettunen, K., Mäkelä, E., Ruokolainen, T., Kuokkala, J., Löfberg, L.: Old content and modern tools-searching named entities in a Finnish OCRed historical newspaper collection 1771–1910. arXiv preprint arXiv:1611.02839 (2016)
5. Mäkelä, E.: Combining a REST lexical analysis web service with SPARQL for mashup semantic annotation from text. In: Presutti, V., Blomqvist, E., Troncy, R., Sack, H., Papadakis, I., Tordai, A. (eds.) ESWC 2014. LNCS, vol. 8798, pp. 424–428. Springer, Cham (2014). https://doi.org/10.1007/978-3-319-11955-7_60
6. Mäkelä, E., Lindquist, T., Hyvönen, E.: CORE - a contextual reader based on linked data. In: Proceedings of Digital Humanities 2016, Krakow, Poland (Long Papers), pp. 267–269 (2016)
7. Maynard, D., Roberts, I., Greenwood, M.A., Rout, D., Bontcheva, K.: A framework for real-time semantic social media analysis. J. Web Semant. **44**, 75–88 (2017)
8. Mendes, P.N., Jakob, M., García-Silva, A., Bizer, C.: DBpedia Spotlight: shedding light on the web of documents. In: Proceedings of the 7th International Conference on Semantic Systems, pp. 1–8. ACM (2011)
9. Oksanen, A., Tuominen, J., Mäkelä, E., Tamper, M., Hietanen, A., Hyvönen, E.: Semantic Finlex: transforming, publishing, and using Finnish legislation and case law as linked open data on the web. In: Peruginelli, G., Faro, S. (eds.) Knowledge of the Law in the Big Data Age, Frontiers in Artificial Intelligence and Applications, vol. 317, pp. 212–228. IOS Press (2019)
10. Piccinno, F., Ferragina, P.: From TagME to WAT: a new entity annotator. In: Proceedings of the First International Workshop on Entity Recognition & Disambiguation, pp. 55–62. ACM (2014)
11. Ruokolainen, T., Kauppinen, P., Silfverberg, M., Lindén, K.: A Finnish news corpus for named entity recognition. Lang. Resour. Eval. **54**(1), 247–272 (2019). https://doi.org/10.1007/s10579-019-09471-7
12. Sarsa, S., Hyvönen, E.: Searching case law judgements by using other judgements as a query. In: Proceedings of the 9th Conference Artificial Intelligence and Natural Language. AINL 2020, Helsinki, Finland, 7–9 October 2020. Springer-Verlag (2020)
13. Tamper, M., Hyvönen, E., Leskinen, P.: Visualizing and analyzing networks of named entities in biographical dictionaries for digital humanities research. In: Proceedings of the 20th International Conference on Computational Linguistics and Intelligent Text Processing (CICling 2019). Springer (2019, forthcoming)
14. Tamper, M., Leskinen, P., Tuominen, J., Hyvönen, E.: Modeling and publishing Finnish person names as a linked open data ontology. In: 3rd Workshop on Humanities in the Semantic Web (WHiSe). CEUR Workshop Proceedings (2020)
15. Virtanen, A., et al.: Multilingual is not enough: BERT for Finnish (2019). arXiv preprint arXiv:1912.07076

PhD Symposium Papers

Towards Transforming Tabular Datasets into Knowledge Graphs

Nora Abdelmageed[1,2]([✉]) [ID]

[1] Heinz Nixdorf Chair for Distributed Information Systems,
Computer Vision Group, Michael Stifel Center Jena, Jena, Germany
`nora.abdelmageed@uni-jena.de`
[2] Friedrich Schiller University Jena, Jena, Germany

Abstract. Many applications rely on the existence of reusable data. The FAIR principles identify rich descriptions of data and metadata as the key ingredients for achieving reusability. However, creating descriptive data requires massive manual effort. One way to ensure that data is reusable is by integrating it into a Knowledge Graph (KG). The semantic foundation of these graphs provides the necessary description for reuse. In this paper, we focus on tabular data and how that can be integrated into a KG. Besides the tabular data itself, we leverage existing metadata and publications describing the datasets for the KG construction. To tackle this task, we introduce a machine-learning based framework. Our framework consists of three core modules. The first module predicts the concepts of the KG from various data sources. In the second module, we extract possible relations among these concepts. Afterwards, we will integrate the two modules to build the final KG. As an example domain to develop and evaluate our approach, we focus on Biodiversity research. This is a data-rich domain with a particularly high need for data reuse. We present preliminary results in the context of building a KG schema given table headers. We cluster these headers using two types of representations, word embeddings, and syntactic representation. Our results show that embeddings can catch high-level semantics of headers; thus, they are better descriptors.

Keywords: Knowledge Graph construction · Table understanding · Named Entity Recognition (NER) · Relation Extraction (RE)

1 Introduction

Recently, Knowledge Graphs (KGs) have become popular as a means to represent a domain knowledge. Auer et al. [2] propose them as a way to bring scholarly communication to the 21st century. In the Open Research KG, they propose to model artifacts of scientific endeavors, including publications and their key messages. Datasets supporting these publications are important carriers of scientific

N. Abdelmageed—Early Stage PhD.

knowledge and should thus be included in KGs. An important side effect of this inclusion is that it supports FAIRness of data [23]. The FAIR principles identify rich descriptions as the major prerequisite for reusabilty. Since KGs make the semantics of the data explicit, they provide these rich descriptions. It is not trivial, however, to add datasets to KGs by manual transformation is prohibitively expensive. In our work, we aim to enable (semi-)automatic integration of information from tabular datasets into KGs. We will exploit the datasets themselves, but also auxiliary information like existing metadata and the associated publications. To address this problem, we will combine semantic web technologies and machine learning techniques. In this way, we can extend and enrich existing KGs. We will develop and test the proposed approach using datasets from Biodiversity research. This is an area of science of particular societal importance and a field with a strong need for data reuse, e.g., by KGs.

As a basis for our work, we held several meetings with Biodiversity scientists. We found that Biodiversity synthesis work is done today as follows: the research team searches for all datasets relevant to their research question. This happens via searches in data repositories, literature search and personal connections. The publications found are then read to find essential references. Metadata about datasets is extracted from them and, in the case of data repositories, the information uploaded. All of this information is then manually collated. This serves as a basis to decide on which data is usable for the study at hand, which conversions and error corrections are necessary and how the data can be integrated. This process can take several months. Providing well described data in a KG would drastically reduce the required effort.

Various solutions aim at domain-specific KG construction exist. Page [18] shows guidelines for the construction of a Biodiversity KG. However, the resultant KG is coarse-grained. For example, the author proposes linking a whole dataset to a publication and an author. A more fine-grained solution, a rule-based framework [4] constructs a Biodiversity KG from publication text. It covers both named entity recognition and relation extraction tasks. The authors use different types of taggers to capture a wide range of information inside the document. A similar approach is taken in [14] with a broader goal of information extraction from textual scientific data in general. At this point, there is a broad interest in building scientific KGs evidenced by the existing approaches. However, none of them deal efficiently with tabular datasets yet.

The rest of the paper is organized as follows: Sect. 2 covers the main categories of the related work. The problem statement, research questions and contributions are mentioned in Sect. 3. Section 4 discusses the research strategy. Section 5 presents the evaluation strategies. Preliminary experiments and results are outlined in Sect. 6. Finally, we conclude and discuss future work in Sect. 7.

2   State of the Art

In this section, we cover the essential related work needed for our proposed framework in the following subsections: i) Understanding tabular data, and ii)

Understanding textual data. Both focus on obtaining entities of interest and their relations from tables and publication text respectively.

2.1   Understanding Tabular Data

Two classes of approaches address the tabular dataset understanding. The first category aims at matching the values of table cells, columns and column-column to KG entities, classes and properties. The second category, learning semantic table properties, allows to predict a general column's class that might not exist in knowledge base (KB).

Table Cells and Columns to KG Matching. In this category, the current works aim at creating ontology mappings for the table on various levels, like cells, columns, and column-column relations. For example, a cell has a value *Germany* will be linked to *dbr:Germany*, while a column contains a list of countries will be mapped to *dbo:Country*. Both annotations are DBpedia [1] entity and class. There are two possibilities to achieve this task. First, there are semi-automatic approaches, which involve human intervention. Karma [10], for instance, provides recommendations for ontology mappings or lets users define a new mapping. These methods are very time-consuming. Second, there are fully-automatic techniques, which do not require any manual effort. The Sem-Tab challenge[1], which took place for the first time at ISWC 2019, presents three different tasks for the automatic approaches: i) Cell Entity Assignment (CEA) matches a cell of the table to a KG entity. ii) Column Type Assignment (CTA) assigns a KB class to a column. iii) Column Property Assignment (CPA) selects relations between two different columns. All the presented works use the solution of the CEA as a core part of solving the others. So for our discussion, we will focus on the CEA task.

MTab [16] relies on the brute force lookup of all table signals, then applies majority voting as a selection criterion. This technique achieves the best results, but it is computationally expensive and does not suite real-world systems. Another approach introduced is Tabularisi [21]. It also looks up the KB services, but it converts the results into a feature space using TF-IDF[2]. Then, the final decision is the top-1 value. Finally, DAGOBAH [5] searches the entities in the vector space model of the KB. Then, it applies the K-means clustering algorithm on the embeddings. Finally, it selects the cluster with the highest score to assign the entity type. However, the performance of these works presented will decrease when there are missing or inaccurate mappings in the KBs. We define such a problem as a knowledge gap. In other words, a problem appears when the dataset and the target KB are not derived from the same distribution, from e.g. DBpedia. In our scope, which targets Biodiversity datasets, we need a way to

---

[1] http://www.cs.ox.ac.uk/isg/challenges/sem-tab/.
[2] Term Frequency-Inverse Document Frequency, a well known information retrieval metric, capturing importance of a term for a document.

infer types and discover new entities and relationships that co-occurred in real data and might be missing in the KB.

Table Semantic Properties Learning. These approaches capture the semantic structure of the table. They heavily depend on machine learning. An exciting work, TabNet [17], classifies the Genuine web tables[3] into one of several predefined categories. TabNet relies on a hybrid neural network to learn both the inter-cell and high-level semantics of the whole table. We consider using TabNet in our work as a preprocessing step, such that, it can filter the input tables. A further exciting work [6] introduces ColNet for learning the semantic type of a table column. In the prediction part, they combine the pure prediction by the network with the majority voting by the lookup services. They achieve the best results using an ensemble strategy. By this means, ColNet proposes a solution for the knowledge gap which exists in the DBpedia KB. In our context, we plan to start from this architecture for column type prediction and extend it to our domain.

2.2   Understanding Textual Data

As we will combine data from publications, we discuss both Named Entity Recognition (NER) and Relation Extraction (RE) as the most important techniques for natural language processing. According to [12], NER involves the extraction of mentioned entities in natural language text and their classification in predefined categories. The authors also present a framework of a typical NER system. They divide the approaches to NER into two main categories. 1) Traditional approaches, including rule-based, unsupervised, and feature-based supervised approaches. For all of these techniques, selecting meaningful features remains a crucial problem. 2) Deep learning techniques can solve the mentioned problem by automatically selecting features by using, for example, a Recurrent Neural Network (RNN). An interesting domain-specific NER is Bio-NER [24]. Mainly, it leverages the input representation using word vectors by automatically learning them from unlabeled biomedical text. In this way, it solves the problem of feature engineering. Another exciting work leverages semantics from external resources [9]. The authors explore Wikipedia[4] as an external source of knowledge to improve the performance of NER. They extract the first part of the corresponding Wikipedia entry and the category labels from it. For better input representation, these category labels are added to the engineered features.

Relation Extraction techniques aim at semantic relations extraction between entity mentions and classification of them inside natural language text [3]. This classical survey covers both supervised and semi-supervised techniques for this task. However, it shows many limitations, like the overhead of the manual annotations and the criteria for selecting a good training seed. Moreover, such

---

[3] Tables that contain semantic triples, i.e., subject-predicate-object.

[4] https://www.wikipedia.org/.

approaches are hard to extend and require new training data to detect new relations. However, [20] solves these problems by introducing the distant supervision technique. The authors also address the relation extraction as a supervised learning method but, without paying the cost of labeling the dataset. They leverage the KB as an external source of the existing relations. This technique has various challenges. It helps extend an existing KB but it is not useful to construct one from scratch.

3 Problem Statement and Contribution

We discuss in this section our main research problem and questions we aim to address, and our contributions.

3.1 Problem Statement and Research Questions

Our core research problem is how to enable the reusability of tabular data by adopting and extending machine learning techniques. For successful data reuse, a good, ideal machine-readable description of the data is essential. The desired descriptions are represented as a KG. However, today, creating such descriptions requires considerable manual effort. We believe that building such a KG automatically will only be possible by leveraging auxiliary information besides the dataset itself. The crucial sources of additional information are in our case metadata and publications. Our evaluations comparing the addition of these various data sources will show the correctness of this assumption.

Our research focuses on how to automate transformation of tabular datasets into a KG using various machine learning techniques. Since there is a massive amount of Biodiversity data available, we choose it as our first domain of interest. We divide this general research problem into three fine-grained research questions:

- **RQ1** - How can we use tabular datasets for KG construction?
- **RQ2** - How can we leverage the existing metadata in understanding the original dataset?
- **RQ3** - How can we benefit from the information in the associated publications to enrich the constructed KG?

3.2 Contributions

Our overall contribution will be to enable the automatic integration of tabular datasets into KGs thereby considerably increasing FAIRness, in particular reusability. This aim will be reached by several contributions:

- We will develop methods that take a tabular dataset as input and automatically create a KG out of it. These methods will determine the meaning of individual columns and their data type as well as relationships across columns. Such tools are useful to increase tabular data understanding even without the subsequent transformation in a KG.

- We will extend these tools to leverage potentially available auxiliary information, in particular metadata and publications describing the dataset.
- We will implement these methods into a framework.
- We will evaluate the individual methods as well as the overall system.

4   Research Methodology and Approach

In this section, we discuss research methodology pipeline and our proposed framework's conceptual model overview.

4.1   Research Methodology

Figure 1 shows our research methodology. In the first step of our pipeline, we conducted several meetings with domain experts from the Biodiversity field for requirement gathering as described in Sect. 1. Based on their requirements, we came up with three main stages for our project: Firstly, we will aim to build a KG from the tabular dataset itself as a standalone data source. Secondly, we will add information gained from metadata or any auxiliary semi-structured data. Finally, we do further extensions to the resultant KG using the related publications, either by the use of abstracts or the full texts. For each of these stages, we will perform a complete development cycle from an analysis of the state of the art and concept development to implementation, evaluation and publication. At this phase in the project, the evaluation will focus on performance metrics (see below). Once the complete system has been implemented, a final overall evaluation including a user study will be undertaken.

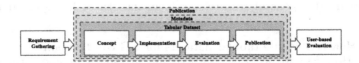

Fig. 1. Research methodology pipeline

4.2   Conceptual Model View

Figure 2 illustrates the architecture of our proposed framework in the first stage. It receives a tabular dataset in an Excel sheet or a CSV file as input. The framework transforms this tabular dataset into a full KG, such that the resultant KG has schema and instances inferred from the tabular dataset. In the country-city example, object entities[5], e.g., "Country", contribute graph nodes. However, non-object entities, e.g., "Area", contribute the relations. Our framework consists of three core modules: i) Concept Prediction; it predicts the

---

[5] Object entities: are entities that can be a page on Wikipedia.

KG schema class of a given column in the table. It also encapsulates various approaches like NER, lookup services, taggers, and classifiers (i.e., neural networks). ii) Relations Detection, on the one hand, finds a possible relation between two object columns by using a relation extraction technique (i.e., distant supervision). On the other hand, it looks up the domain knowledge for a relation between a concept and a non-object entity (e.g., "Country", "Area"). We will filter both concepts and relations candidates on specific criteria. iii) KG Construction builds the final full graph given the filtered concepts and relations with the original dataset. In Stage 2 and 3 of the project, we will leverage information about the dataset in other resources that are not existing in the tabular dataset itself. For example, a metadata file or a publication could have the unit of "Area" in km². By this means, we enrich the constructed KG from tabular data by the secondary information that exists in the other sources. This extension will require adaptations to all three core modules.

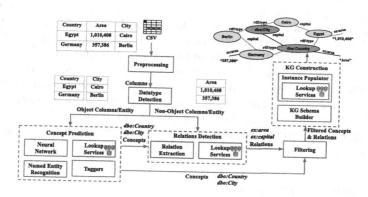

Fig. 2. System architecture of the proposed framework with a simple Country-City example in tabular dataset.

5   Evaluation Plan

We will need two types of evaluation for this work: Firstly, we will evaluate the performance of the framework and the effect of using additional information in Stages 2 and 3 using standard evaluation metrics. Secondly, we will evaluate the quality of the resulting KG with a user-based evaluation.

5.1   Performance Evaluation of the Framework

At the end of each stage, we will evaluate the performance of the framework and of individual modules using evaluation metrics like the standard Precision (Pr), Recall (R), and F-score. Besides these metrics, we can adopt others like Macro and Micro versions of them, especially when we have an unbalanced dataset or when implementing the natural language processing modules. These modules are multi-class classification tasks. Thus, we are interested in measuring the robustness of the system per each class. At first, this strategy gives an impression of the system performance after each step. Secondly, it enables agile development by dividing and focusing on each separate module as a standalone project. Additionally, for testing the first phase, we will use benchmark datasets: T2Dv2 [11], Limayae [13] and SemTab2019 Data Sets [8].

5.2   User-Based Evaluation

We claim that transforming tabular datasets into a KG enhances their reusability. A user study is needed to examine whether that is indeed true. This user study will be performed at the end of Stage 3. We consider two possible options for this evaluation: First we will conduct an end-to-end assessment. It differs from the previous evaluation strategy. This assessment concerns the information encapsulated inside the KG itself. We can achieve this kind of evaluation by preparing a list of predefined questions and issuing them in the form of queries against the SPARQL endpoint of the constructed KG. Thus, the retrieved answers can be used as a metric. We will held this type of evaluation on the final KG using the tabular dataset and after including the metadata and finally after including the related publications. A second option would be to design a synthesis task and ask users to perform this task in the traditional way (see Sect. 1) and using the KG. In this setting, we could measure the required time, result quality and user satisfaction.

6   Preliminary Results

In this part, we conduct a preliminary experiment for table understanding using column headers. Here, we describe our hypothesis and the dataset we use. Then, we explain the experimental pipeline and discuss our initial results.

6.1   Hypothesis

We aim at understanding tabular datasets by inferring the schema of a corresponding KG using column headers. Our two experiments rely on this hypothesis: Interesting concepts in column headers could be captured using a clustering technique, such that cluster names nominate graph concepts while members show the related objects. For example, a cluster named *Author* has a member set {*Name, Email*}. This yields into two triples: *(Author, name, "Name")* and *(Author, email, "Email")*. However, manual user intervention is required to refine the resultant clusters. In fact, we cannot fully automate the conversion process from a CSV file into a KG [7,22].

6.2   Dataset

We used a dataset [19] used in the compilation of data for the sWorm in our two experiments. This dataset presents information about earthworms in different geographical sites during a range of years. Additionally, it provides information on site level, species level, and metadata about the dataset itself. Our experiments shown here directly use the the column headers with at least one meaningful word. For example, *bio10_1* and *bio10_4* are excluded.

6.3   Experimental Pipeline

Figure 3 explains the pipeline of our experiments. The basic idea here is to apply a cosine distance-based clustering technique on the table headers represented in meaningful vectors. In fact, sWorm dataset has no unified convention of the headers; some are camel others are snake cases. So, the first block contains a parser which receives a list of headers, and it aims at getting a set of words inside the human-made header. The second component converts a header into a vector representation. We support two choices of vectors, either an ASCII code for the letters inside the header (syntactic representation) or using the word embeddings [15] (semantic representation). In this way, we can compute distances to determine the similarity among headers. After that, a distance-based clustering technique populates the initial clusters. Distance threshold would vary based on the type of vectors used. Then, the user has a facility to merge the clusters or to move some members from one cluster to another. The next component can suggest a cluster name based on the commonality among its members. If no common word found, *Unknown* would be the nominated name. Lastly, the user can rename the suggested names manually and export the schema in RDF/XML format.

6.4   Experimental Results and Discussion

Figure 4 illustrates the cosine distances among words' representation. Such that Eq. 1 shows cosine distance between two vectors A, B. While Eq. 2 gives the distance. We choose cosine similarity because it is independent on vector size, two vectors might be far apart by other metrics due to their sizes. As shown, the ASCII representation of the headers (Syntactic representation), is not a good discriminator among header names. Due to sharing a large amount of the same characters as in Fig. 4a. Thus, it yields into a few but large (coarse-grained) clusters. However, the use of the pre-trained word embeddings (Semantic representation) discriminates among the headers very well, as in Fig. 4b. We can conclude that the semantic representation is better than the syntactic representation in terms of the misplaced members (number of mistakes). But, it requires long vectors, such that a 300D vector represents each word. Although, the longest header consists of 4 words, so the final vector length for each header is a 1200D. Unlike the syntactic representation, which efficiently represents the header. Table 1 summarizes the results. We calculate the number of mistakes by comparing the initial clusters result against a manually created graph schema for the sWorm dataset. Thus, the more mistakes we have, the more user input we will need. In summary, this method would work well if we have relatively descriptive column headers that contain meaningful words. But, due to its constraints, this approach demonstrates the idea and requires additional information from table cells.

Table 1. Summary of experimental results

Representation	Granularity	No. init. clusters	Mistakes	Distance threshold	Vector dim.
Syntactic	Coarse-grained	4	14	0.15	82
Semantic	Fine-grained	11	6	0.6	1200

$$similarity = cos(\theta) = \frac{A.B}{||A||||B||} = \frac{\sum_{i=1}^{n} A_i B_i}{\sqrt{\sum_{i=1}^{n} A_i^2} \sqrt{\sum_{i=1}^{n} B_i^2}} \qquad (1)$$

$$distance = 1 - similarity \qquad (2)$$

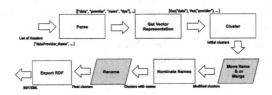

Fig. 3. Table header processing pipeline

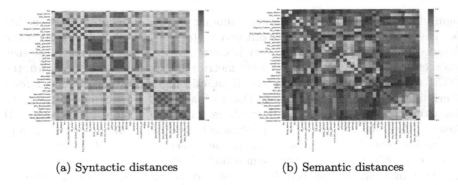

(a) Syntactic distances   (b) Semantic distances

Fig. 4. Distances using two different representations of the column headers, blue cells mean two words are close, red ones indicate large distance. (Color figure online)

7   Conclusions

In this paper, we presented a KG construction framework. It processes various data sources initially from the Biodiversity domain. Mainly the tabular dataset itself, metadata, and the related publication. Our framework consists of three core modules: i) Concept Prediction, ii) Relation Detection, and iii) KG Construction which integrates the other two modules. Besides, we have discussed preliminary experiments[6] concerning table understanding using the column headers. Our results showed that the use of semantic embeddings as a column header representation is better than the syntactic one. Meanwhile, we will extend our existing methods to overcome the current limitations by considering column cells with headers. Moreover, we plan to make our proposed framework publicly available.

Acknowledgment. The authors thank the Carl Zeiss Foundation for the financial support of the project "A Virtual Werkstatt for Digitization in the Sciences (P5)" within the scope of the program line "Breakthroughs: Exploring Intelligent Systems" for "Digitization - explore the basics, use applications". I thank Birgitta König-Ries, Joachim Denzler, and Sheeba Samuel for their guidance and feedback.

References

1. Auer, S., Bizer, C., Kobilarov, G., Lehmann, J., Cyganiak, R., Ives, Z.: DBpedia: a nucleus for a web of open data. In: Aberer, K., et al. (eds.) ASWC/ISWC -2007. LNCS, vol. 4825, pp. 722–735. Springer, Heidelberg (2007). https://doi.org/10.1007/978-3-540-76298-0_52
2. Auer, S., Kovtun, V., Prinz, M., Kasprzik, A., Stocker, M., Vidal, M.E.: Towards a knowledge graph for science. In: Proceedings of the 8th International Conference on Web Intelligence, Mining and Semantics, pp. 1–6 (2018). https://doi.org/10.1145/3227609.3227689
3. Bach, N., Badaskar, S.: A review of relation extraction. Literature review for Language and Statistics **II**(2), 1–15 (2007)
4. Batista-Navarro, R., Zerva, C., Ananiadou, S.: Construction of a biodiversity knowledge repository using a text mining-based framework. In: SIMBig, pp. 22–25 (2016)
5. Chabot, Y., Labbe, T., Liu, J., Troncy, R.: DAGOBAH: an end-to-end context-free tabular data semantic annotation system. In: CEUR Workshop Proceedings, vol. 2553, pp. 41–48 (2019). CEUR-WS.org
6. Chen, J., Jiménez-Ruiz, E., Horrocks, I., Sutton, C.: ColNet: embedding the semantics of web tables for column type prediction. In: Proceedings of the AAAI Conference on Artificial Intelligence, vol. 33, pp. 29–36 (2019). https://doi.org/10.1609/aaai.v33i01.330129
7. Ermilov, I., Auer, S., Stadler, C.: User-driven semantic mapping of tabular data. In: Proceedings of the 9th International Conference on Semantic Systems, pp. 105–112. ACM (2013). https://doi.org/10.1145/2506182.2506196

---

[6] Code and the manually created KG are publicly available: https://github.com/fusion-jena/ClusteringTableHeaders.

8. Hassanzadeh, O., Efthymiou, V., Chen, J., Jiménez-Ruiz, E., Srinivas, K.: SemTab2019: Semantic Web Challenge on Tabular Data to Knowledge Graph Matching - 2019 Data Sets, October 2019. https://doi.org/10.5281/zenodo.3518539

9. Kazama, J., Torisawa, K.: Exploiting wikipedia as external knowledge for named entity recognition. In: Proceedings of the 2007 Joint Conference on Empirical Methods in Natural Language Processing and Computational Natural Language Learning (EMNLP-CoNLL), pp. 698–707 (2007)

10. Knoblock, C.A., et al.: Interactively mapping data sources into the semantic web. In: Proceedings of the First International Conference on Linked Science, vol. 783, pp. 13–24 (2011). CEUR-WS.org

11. Lehmberg, O., Ritze, D., Meusel, R., Bizer, C.: A large public corpus of web tables containing time and context metadata. In: Proceedings of the 25th International Conference Companion on World Wide Web, International World Wide Web Conferences Steering Committee (2016), pp. 75–76. https://doi.org/10.1145/2872518.2889386

12. Li, J., Sun, A., Han, J., Li, C.: A survey on deep learning for named entity recognition. arXiv preprint arXiv:1812.09449 (2018)

13. Limaye, G., Sarawagi, S., Chakrabarti, S.: Annotating and searching web tables using entities, types and relationships. Proc. VLDB Endow. **3**(1–2), 1338–1347 (2010). https://doi.org/10.14778/1920841.1921005

14. Luan, Y., He, L., Ostendorf, M., Hajishirzi, H.: Multi-task identification of entities, relations, and coreference for scientific knowledge graph construction. arXiv preprint arXiv:1808.09602 (2018)

15. Mikolov, T., Chen, K., Corrado, G., Dean, J.: Efficient estimation of word representations in vector space. arXiv preprint arXiv:1301.3781 (2013)

16. Nguyen, P., Kertkeidkachorn, N., Ichise, R., Takeda, H.: MTab: matching tabular data to knowledge graph using probability models. In: CEUR Workshop Proceedings, vol. 2553, pp. 7–14 (2019). CEUR-WS.org

17. Nishida, K., Sadamitsu, K., Higashinaka, R., Matsuo, Y.: Understanding the semantic structures of tables with a hybrid deep neural network architecture. In: Thirty-First AAAI Conference on Artificial Intelligence (2017)

18. Page, R.: Towards a biodiversity knowledge graph. Res. Ideas Outcomes **2** (2016). https://doi.org/10.3897/rio.2.e8767

19. Phillips, H.R., et al.: Global distribution of earthworm diversity. Science **366**(6464), 480–485 (2019). https://doi.org/10.1101/587394

20. Smirnova, A., Cudré-Mauroux, P.: Relation extraction using distant supervision: a survey. ACM Comput. Surv. (CSUR) **51**(5), 106 (2018). https://doi.org/10.1145/3241741

21. Thawani, A., et al.: Entity linking to knowledge graphs to infer column types and properties. In: CEUR Workshop Proceedings, vol. 2553, pp. 25–32 (2019). CEUR-WS.org

22. Vander Sande, M., De Vocht, L., Van Deursen, D., Mannens, E., Van de Walle, R.: Lightweight transformation of tabular open data to RDF. In: I-SEMANTICS (Posters & Demos), pp. 38–42. Citeseer (2012)

23. Wilkinson, M.D., et al.: The fair guiding principles for scientific data management and stewardship. Sci. Data **3** (2016). https://doi.org/10.1038/sdata.2016.18

24. Yao, L., Liu, H., Liu, Y., Li, X., Anwar, M.W.: Biomedical named entity recognition based on deep neutral network. Int. J. Hybrid Inf. Technol. **8**(8), 279–288 (2015). https://doi.org/10.14257/ijhit.2015.8.8.29

Enabling Web-Scale Knowledge Graphs Querying

Amr Azzam[✉]

Vienna University of Economics and Business, Vienna, Austria
aazzam@wu.ac.at

Abstract. Knowledge Graphs (KGs) have become an asset for integrating and consuming data from heterogeneous sources. KGs have an influence on several domains such as health-care, manufacturing, transportation and energy. Over the years, the Web of Data has grown significantly. Today, answering complex queries on open KGs is practically impossible due to the SPARQL endpoints availability problem caused by well-known scalability and load balancing issues when hosting Web-size data for concurrent clients. To maintain reliable and responsive open Knowledge Graph query services, several solutions have been proposed: while SPARQL endpoints enforce restrictions on server usage such as imposing limited query execution time or providing partial query results, alternative solutions such as Triple Pattern Fragments (TPF) attempts to tackle the problem of availability by pushing query processing workload to the client-side but suffer from the unnecessary transfer of irrelevant data on complex queries as a result of the large intermediate results. The aim of our research is to develop a new generation of smart clients and servers to balance the load between servers and clients, with the best possible query execution performance, and at the same time reducing data transfer volume, by combining SPARQL endpoints, TPF and shipping compressed KG partitions. The proposed solution shall, on the server-side, offer a suitable query execution service according to the current status of the server workload. On the client-side, we plan research on novel client-side caching mechanisms on the basis of compressed and queryable KG partitions that can be distributed in a modular fashion. In addition, we plan to leverage query logs to optimize the number and the distribution of partitions as well as distributing the query load across a network of collaborative clients.

Keywords: Knowledge Graphs · Availability · Query performance

1   Introduction

Knowledge Graphs (KGs) have emerged as a rising data management and knowledge representation framework to provide scalable knowledge models that can capture facts about entities as well as relations among these entities. Several implementations of Knowledge Graphs have been introduced in diverse areas

© Springer Nature Switzerland AG 2020
A. Harth et al. (Eds.): ESWC 2020 Satellite Events, LNCS 12124, pp. 229–239, 2020.
https://doi.org/10.1007/978-3-030-62327-2_38

such as the pharmaceutical industry [27], IT services, telecommunication, and government [23,25]. The proliferation of the KG concept offers the potential for building creative products and services that introduce a wide range of commercial applications. For instance, Google's Knowledge Graph[1], Knowledge Vault [10], Microsoft Satori[2] and Facebook's Entities Graph[3].

In addition to these commercial Knowledge Graphs, currently existing open interlinked KGs include DBpedia [4], Yago [19], Wikidata [29] and NELL [9]. These open KGs are typically published following the Linked Data principles [7], using a semi-structured RDF data model and support querying through SPARQL query language. However, there are several open challenges in order to maintain public SPARQL services on the Web, serving multiple concurrent clients.

That is, providing reliable public access to KGs through SPARQL querying is still an open issue due to the unpredictable number of clients executing arbitrary SPARQL queries. To mitigate these availability problems, data providers who expose SPARQL endpoints typically add several constraints on the queries such as limiting the query execution time on the server or limiting the number of retrieved results. Another solution, Triple Pattern Fragments (TPF) [28] provides a more balanced query processing between the client and the server but with the cost of high network traffic. Finally, SaGe [21] introduces a Web preemption mechanism that prevents the long-running queries from consuming the server resources. However, SaGe lacks the ability to handle the potential load of several concurrent complex queries at a time.

The proposed doctoral thesis aims to address the open research questions related to the trade-off between the availability and performance in Web Knowledge Graph interfaces. The main challenge is to provide a Knowledge Graph querying interface that maintains high availability alongside high query execution performance, besides minimizing the data transfer.

2   State of the Art

Overall four orthogonal approaches have been proposed in the literature that enable hosting and querying open Knowledge Graphs that we will describe in the following:

2.1   SPARQL Endpoints

SPARQL endpoints offer SPARQL query interface over Knowledge Graphs. First, The submitted queries are executed on top of a triple store such as Jena TDB [24], Stardog[4] and Virtuoso [11]. Then, the SPARQL query results are shipped via HTTP to the requesting clients [12].

---

[1] https://developers.google.com/knowledge-graph.

[2] https://www.microsoft.com/en-us/research/project/knowledge-mining-api/.

[3] https://developers.facebook.com/docs/graph-api/.

[4] https://www.stardog.com/.

Although current SPARQL endpoints provide a high performance query processing, it requires to run under low query workloads due to the excessive consumption of the long-running queries to the server CPU and memory. Knowledge Graphs (KGs) that are exposed via SPARQL endpoints suffer from well-known problems of low availability and recurrent downtime [3,28].

In order to tackle these challenges to provide live queryable Knowledge Graphs, SPARQL endpoints with high demands generally introduce a set of usage restrictions to ensure fair utilization of the server resources. For instance, Data providers impose a time quota restriction [3] as DBpedia administrators set a running time quantum of 120 s on the server for each submitted query, limit results sizes to 10K results, refuse the complex queries and limit the number of parallel requests per IP.[5]

2.2 Linked Data Fragments

Linked Data Fragments framework (LDF) [28] laid the basis to define Triple Pattern Fragments (TPF) a simple interface that attempts to tackle the problem of availability through providing intelligent TPF clients which shift complex query processing to the client-side, but with the cost of the increased network overhead due to potentially unnecessary transfer of large intermediate results. This can lead to longer query execution time that lowers the overall performance.

To address the drawbacks of TPF, Bindings-Restricted Triple Pattern Fragments [18] (brTPF) is proposed as an extended interface of TPF that gives a slight boost to the performance of the query execution through attaching intermediate results to triple pattern requests together with distributing the join between the client and the server using the bind join strategy [14]. In this manner, brTPF [18] reduces the number of HTTP requests in addition to minimizing the amount of data transferred compared to the "vanilla" TPF. However, brTPF still would require a potentially high number of HTTP requests. In addition to the shortcoming of the ability to scale with large datasets.

2.3 SaGe

SaGe [21] is a Web preemption based SPARQL query interface designed to avoid the starvation of the simple queries waiting for the complex ones that consume the server resources. SaGe utilized a Round-Robin algorithm to maintain a fair allocation of server resources between queries. To this end, SaGe formalizes a model that enables to suspend and proceed queries with the mechanism to save the state of the query execution to the client for later resumption. Additionally, SaGe has implemented some client-side operators such as ORDER BY, OPTIONAL as well as aggregation functions to execute parts of the query on the client-side.

Experiments show that SaGe enhances the average completion time per client in addition to reducing the average network traffic per client. However, SaGe still

---

[5] https://wiki.dbpedia.org/public-sparql-endpoint.

extensively consumes the server resources. Besides, the performance of SaGe is degrading with the increasing sizes of the Knowledge Graphs, plus the execution time of concurrent complex queries is potentially increasing significantly.

2.4 Data Dumps

Last, Data Dumps provide a possibility to access Knowledge Graphs through granting access to download KG data thereafter the clients can execute SPARQL queries on their local machines. This approach, however, somewhat defeats the vision of live Knowledge Graph querying which is to offer live querying Web data. Furthermore, even if bandwidth to download full data dumps is not considered, their sheer size may be prohibitive in terms of local query processing for clients with limited resources.

3   Problem Statement and Contributions

To maintain querying interfaces on Knowledge Graphs on the Web, state-of-the-art SPARQL query processing techniques can be categorized into three main strategies that are explained in the following:

S1 Query Shipping: Knowledge Graphs are exposed for public querying through a full SPARQL endpoint with high query performance but with low server availability. The endpoints are responsible for executing the full SPARQL queries and only retrieve the query results.

S2 Data Shipping: To alleviate the low availability problem of **S1**, several client-side solutions such as Squin [16,17] which perform query execution on the Web through KG traversal. These approaches try to retrieve RDF data that can be processed locally. Unfortunately, the evaluation of complex queries is impractical due to the non-deferenceable URIs besides many non-trivial queries require the full KG dump to be shipped to the client. Hence, These approaches increase the availability of the server yet require strong client machines.

S3 Hybrid Shipping: Hybrid shipping approaches attempt to overcome the weaknesses of S1 and S2 through a more balanced client/server distribution such as the aforementioned approaches TPF [28] and SaGe [21]. However, these approaches have several potential issues which were discussed in Sect. 2.

In this dissertation, we plan to design, build and evaluate a KG interface that distributes the load of query evaluation between clients and servers *by fruitfully combining* data shipping, query shipping and extending the space of hybrid shipping methods, recombining them in novel ways, under the following hypothesis:

Hypothesis: Our hypothesis is that each of the three discussed shipping strategies to KG query services has its pros and cons for different scenarios, query workloads, and concurrency parameters. Therefore, we aim at developing hybrid approaches that combine all three strategies in the most efficient manner, depending on server load, client resources, and potential collaboration among clients.

The main contribution of this dissertation shall, therefore, be to propose an efficient approach to execute SPARQL queries on remote Knowledge Graphs while balancing the trade-off between the high availability of the Knowledge Graph server and the efficient query execution. Generally, we expect to reduce the overall server cost as we enhance the usage of CPU, caching and concurrency.

According to the problem statement, the hypothesis and the proposed contribution, we have derived the following more concrete research questions:

RQ1. How can we achieve significant speedups to the decentralized querying of Knowledge Graphs by developing a novel client/server distribution?
This research question can be further divided into three sub-questions, corresponding to the smart client and server-side respectively:

RQ1.1. Can compressed partitions shipping reduce the load on servers as a novel intermediate solution in between TPF and downloading full dumps?

RQ1.2. How can a (distributed) caching mechanism in smart clients further enhance KG availability?

RQ1.3. How can log analysis help to find trending queries and improve the graph partitioning?

RQ2. How can we build a framework of hybrid server interfaces that dynamically select the appropriate interface based on the given query, client capabilities, and the current server load?

RQ2.1. Which further novel optimization of joins and other operators in a hybrid setting can yield further performance improvements?

RQ2.2. Client collaboration: How can clients - sharing their processing and caching resources - collaboratively improve query processing?

RQ3. How can we build efficient update strategies for the server data (i.e.g.raph partitions) and the smart client metadata (i.e. discoverability metadata)?

4 Research Methodology and Approach

We divide the research process into the set following tasks, to be carried out for each of the aforementioned RQ's:

T1. Investigation of the state-of-the-art research that is relevant to the identified problem. This includes the study of literature about Web Knowledge Graphs query interfaces, RDF data partitioning, peer to peer query processing, caching mechanisms, join optimization and indexing in the areas of Semantic Web and Databases.

T2. Definition of solutions to the currently existing limitations requires the identification of novel contributions. In addition to providing a concrete prototype implementation for the proposed contributions.

T3. Extensive experimental evaluation for the proposed contributions will be conducted in comparison to state-of-the-art approaches. In addition, the experimental setup will be designed according to the studied research questions based on (new)existing benchmarks and the evaluation criteria.

This research approach has been followed in the contribution related to RQ1, smart-KG, which we first presented in [5], we have already gone through these steps. We identified a gap in terms of processing full dumps on the client-side vs. only shipping part(ition)s of the KG to the client. We have already implemented a prototype for this proposed solution[6] and performed an extensive experimental evaluation following the plan described in Sect. 5 to compare smart-KG to other state-of-the-art approaches. Am analysis of intermediate results is presented in Sect. 6 below.

5   Evaluation Plan

In this section, we describe the details of our evaluation plan to compare our proposed approach with state-of-the-art approaches. This particularly includes the choice of suitable baselines, benchmark datasets, query workloads, and evaluation metrics. The goal of the experimental evaluation is to assess the performance of the implemented solutions to the challenges associated with the formulated research questions by conducting a series of experiments and analyzing the insights. The evaluation plan is explained in the following:

Knowledge Graphs and Query Benchmarks
For the experimental evaluation, we will use synthetic as well as real-world RDF Knowledge Graph datasets of variable sizes.

We use three synthetic datasets from Waterloo SPARQL Diversity Benchmark (WatDiv) [2] which is a recent benchmark that provides a wide spectrum of queries with varying structural characteristics and selectivity classes with sizes of 10M, 100M, and 1B triples. In addition, we will employ the synthetic LUBM data generator to create a dataset of 1.36 billion triples. Moreover, we will use Berlin SPARQL Benchmark V3.1 (BSBM) [8] with three datasets from one up to three million products which will generate three different dataset sizes 350, 700 and 1050 million RDF triples.

Additionally, we use real-world datasets. We will use SPARQL queries from FEASIBLE [26] for RQ1.2 in order to test the optimization with respect to query logs. FEASIBLE is a set of queries that have been generated by real users of DBpedia [20] dataset (v.2015A). Furthermore, we plan to use YAGO2 [19] which is a real dataset extracted from Wikipedia, WordNet, and GeoNames. Finally, Bio2RDF [6] is a life science RDF Knowledge Graph that connects a set of different biological datasets with 4.64 billion. Both YAGO2 and Bio2RDF do not provide benchmark queries, therefore we have reused a set of representative test queries that were created to test the performance of distributed SPARQL query engines [15].

---

[6] https://ai.wu.ac.at/smartkg.

Evaluation Metrics. We plan to consider evaluation metrics that provide an insight into the trade-off between server availability, query execution performance, and client resources consumption. Our evaluation considers the following metrics:

- **Number of timeouts:** Number of queries that time out. We set a timeout of 5 min for WatDiv and 30 min for DBpedia queries.
- **Average workload completion time per client:** Elapsed time spent by a client executing a workload of queries, measured with the `time` command of Linux.
- **Server/Client Resource Consumption:** We report on CPU usage per core, RAM usage, and network traffic.
- **Average time for the first tuple:** The time for first results (TFFT) for a query is the time between the query starting and the production of the first query results.
- **Average number of requests and data transfer:** the number of requests that the smart client sent to the server to get complete results for a query. In addition, the total transferred data when executing a SPARQL query.
- **The Diefficiency metrics dief@t and dief@k:** Two experiment metrics that are able to capture and evaluate systems that produce incremental results [1].
  dief@t measures the diefficiency of a query engine during the first t time units of query execution. It computes the area under the curve of the answer distribution function until t time unit. In our experiments, we will consider the dief@5 and dief@10 in seconds as a time unit.
  dief@k measures the diefficiency of an engine while producing the first k answers when executing a query. We compare the performance of the different systems at different answer completeness $k = 25\%, k = 50\%, k = 75\%, k = 100\%$.

6   Intermediate Results

smart-KG is a novel approach that introduces a new paradigm to distribute the query processing between the client and the server through combining shipping compressed Knowledge Graph partitions influenced by characteristic sets [13,22] with intermediate results shipped using TPF. The experimental evaluation demonstrated that smart-KG outperforms existing approaches in server resource usage in addition to the average workload execution time as well as fewer timeout queries under highly concurrent query workloads. On the other hand, SPARQL endpoints and SaGe have a better performance than smart-KG with less number of clients and small-scale Knowledge Graphs. That is, although smart-KG has better average workload execution time, TPF and SaGe outperform smart-KG in certain types of queries.

In our recent research [5], which we briefly described above, we have investigated RQ1 and especially the question RQ1.1. In this research, we introduced a novel paradigm, smart-KG, to balance the load of evaluating SPARQL queries on Web Knowledge Graphs by leveraging shipping compressed KG partitions. We presented a KG partitioning technique named *Family-Based Partitioning* which is, based on *characteristic sets* [13,22] as an initial partition heuristics, designed to combine the set of predicates are shared between subjects of the same type. Family-Based Partitioning allowed us to have descent KG partitions to be shipped over the Web.

Our empirical evaluation showed that smart-KG has significantly outperformed the state-of-the-art server- and client-side Knowledge Graphs query engines. In our study [5], we reported the performance of smart-KG in comparison to the currently existing approaches SPARQL endpoints represented by Virtuoso, Triple Pattern Fragments (TPF) and SaGe on three sizes of the synthetic dataset Watdiv on a benchmark query workload [18]; plus, we tested the performance of the systems on the real-world DBpedia [20] dataset (v.2015A).

As shown in Figs. 1 and 2, smart-KG outperformed query performance of the compared systems at increasing number of clients and variant dataset sizes. smart-KG has no timeout queries in WatDiv-100M workload at different numbers of concurrent clients (1, 10, 20, 40 and 80). Moreover, smart-KG showed a superior average workload execution time per client compared to the other systems specifically with more than 20 concurrent clients. We should emphasize that in our experiments so far, going up to 80 clients, as Fig. 1 shows, we did not yet manage to stress smart-KG: on the server-side, where it more or less still showed almost constant effort by client. It could be expected that this behavior degrades at even higher client numbers, which we plan to investigate in the future.

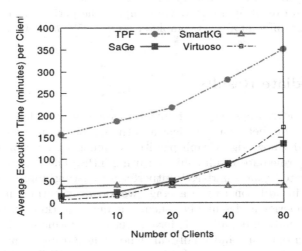

Fig. 1. Average execution time on Watdiv-100M, from [5]

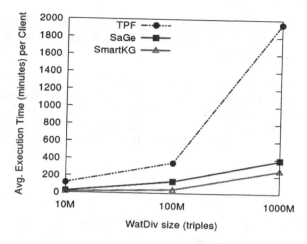

Fig. 2. Performance on the workloads (80 clients) at increasing KG sizes, from [5]

We also plan to re-assess our results from [5] wrt. the proposed metrics in Sect. 5 in more setups and analyze which types of queries, datasets and setups favor smart-KG with respect to other approaches.

7   Conclusions and Lessons Learned

In this doctoral work, we aim to tackle the lack of reliable live public querying to Knowledge Graphs on the Web. We have formulated 3 main research questions that aim to democratize the access to Knowledge Graphs by enabling Web-scale SPARQL querying. Our intermediate results on RQ1 provide an insight into how shipping compressed graph partitions that can be locally queried could balance the load between servers and clients. Our empirical results demonstrate significant improvements in server availability with enhanced query performance.

Our current work addressing RQ1 will investigate further other partitioning strategies that could provide a reasonable trade-off of shipping sizes. In addition, we plan to explore the space of query-driven partitions through analyzing the Knowledge Graphs query logs so that we could achieve the promised balancing between efficient query execution and the availability of the public services.

Thereafter, we intend to determine suitable heuristics for a cost model in RQ2.1 in order to explore the space of feasible query plans so that the proposed framework could find the best query execution plan based on the server and the client available resources.

Lastly, we plan to address RQ2.2. We will explore building a peer-to-peer collaborative smart clients network in order to enhance the server availability through sharing the shipped graph partitions rather than downloading it from the KG server. This will lead us to a decentralized architecture for KG querying.

As for RQ3, we intend to explore novel update strategies to the compressed graph partitions in order to avoid the overhead of the partitions regeneration in case of evolving Knowledge Graphs.

Acknowledgments. This work has been supported by the European Union Horizon 2020 research and innovation programme under grant 731601 (SPECIAL) and by the Austrian Research Promotion Agency (FFG) grant no. 861213 (CitySPIN). I thank my doctoral supervisor Prof. Dr. Axel Polleres and my co-authors Dr. Javier D. Fernández and Dr. Maribel Acosta and Martin Beno for their helpful discussions, comments and feedback.

References

1. Acosta, M., Vidal, M.-E., Sure-Vetter, Y.: Diefficiency metrics: measuring the continuous efficiency of query processing approaches. In: d'Amato, C., et al. (eds.) ISWC 2017. LNCS, vol. 10588, pp. 3–19. Springer, Cham (2017). https://doi.org/10.1007/978-3-319-68204-4_1
2. Aluç, G., Hartig, O., Özsu, M.T., Daudjee, K.: Diversified stress testing of RDF data management systems. In: Mika, P., et al. (eds.) ISWC 2014. LNCS, vol. 8796, pp. 197–212. Springer, Cham (2014). https://doi.org/10.1007/978-3-319-11964-9_13
3. Buil-Aranda, C., Hogan, A., Umbrich, J., Vandenbussche, P.-Y.: SPARQL web-querying infrastructure: ready for action? In: Alani, H., et al. (eds.) ISWC 2013. LNCS, vol. 8219, pp. 277–293. Springer, Heidelberg (2013). https://doi.org/10.1007/978-3-642-41338-4_18
4. Auer, S., Bizer, C., Kobilarov, G., Lehmann, J., Cyganiak, R., Ives, Z.: DBpedia: a nucleus for a web of open data. In: Aberer, K., et al. (eds.) ASWC/ISWC -2007. LNCS, vol. 4825, pp. 722–735. Springer, Heidelberg (2007). https://doi.org/10.1007/978-3-540-76298-0_52
5. Azzam, A., Fernández, J.D., Acosta, M., Beno, M., Polleres, A.: SMART-KG: hybrid shipping for SPARQL querying on the web. In: Proceedings of The Web Conference 2020, WWW 2020, pp. 984–994. Association for Computing Machinery, New York (2020)
6. Belleau, F., Nolin, M.A., Tourigny, N., Rigault, P., Morissette, J.: Bio2RDF: towards a mashup to build bioinformatics knowledge system. J. Biomed. Inform. **41**, 706–716 (2008)
7. Bizer, C., Heath, T., Berners-Lee, T.: Linked data - the story so far. Int. J. Semantic Web Inf. Syst. **5**(3), 1–22 (2009)
8. Bizer, C., Schultz, A.: The Berlin SPARQL benchmark. Int. J. Semant. Web Inf. Syst. **5**, 1–24 (2009)
9. Carlson, A., Betteridge, J., Kisiel, B., Settles, B., Hruschka Jr., E.R., Mitchell, T.M.: Toward an architecture for never-ending language learning. In: AAAI (2010)
10. Dong, X.L., et al.: Knowledge vault: a web-scale approach to probabilistic knowledge fusion. In: The 20th ACM SIGKDD International Conference on Knowledge Discovery and Data Mining, KDD 2014, New York, NY, USA, 24–27 August 2014, pp. 601–610 (2014). Evgeniy Gabrilovich Wilko Horn Ni Lao Kevin Murphy Thomas Strohmann Shaohua Sun Wei Zhang Geremy Heitz

11. Erling, O., Mikhailov, I.: RDF support in the Virtuoso DBMS. In: Pellegrini, T., Auer, S., Tochtermann, K., Schaffert, S. (eds.) Networked Knowledge - Networked Media, pp. 7–24. Springer, Heidelberg (2009). https://doi.org/10.1007/978-3-642-02184-8_2
12. Feigenbaum, L. , Williams, G.T., Clark, K.G., Torres., E.: SPARQL 1.1 protocol. Recommendation, W3C, March 2013
13. Gubichev, A., Neumann, T.: Exploiting the query structure for efficient join ordering in SPARQL queries. In: EDBT, vol. 14, pp. 439–450 (2014)
14. Haas, L.M., Kossmann, D.E., Wimmers, L., Yang, J.: Optimizing queries across diverse data sources. In: VLDB (1997)
15. Harbi, R., Abdelaziz, I., Kalnis, P., Mamoulis, N., Ebrahim, Y., Sahli, M.: Accelerating SPARQL queries by exploiting hash-based locality and adaptive partitioning. VLDB J. 25(3), 355–380 (2016)
16. Harti, O.: SQUIN: a traversal based query execution system for the web of linked data. In: Proceedings of SIGMOD, pp. 1081–1084. ACM (2013)
17. Hartig, O., Bizer, C., Freytag, J.C.: Executing SPARQL queries over the web of linked data. In: Proceedings of ISWC, pp. 293–309 (2009)
18. Hartig, O., Buil-Aranda, C.: Bindings-restricted triple pattern fragments. In: Debruyne, C., et al. (eds.) OTM 2016. LNCS, vol. 10033, pp. 762–779. Springer, Cham (2016). https://doi.org/10.1007/978-3-319-48472-3_48
19. Hoffart, J., Suchanek, F.M., Berberich, K., Weikum, G.: YAGO2: a spatially and temporally enhanced knowledge base from Wikipedia. Artif. Intel. 194, 28–61 (2013). Artificial Intelligence, Wikipedia and Semi-Structured Resources
20. Lehmann, J., et al.: DBpedia - a large-scale, multilingual knowledge base extracted from Wikipedia. Semant. Web 6(2), 167–195 (2015)
21. Minier, T., Skaf-Molli, H., Molli, P.: SaGe: web preemption for public SPARQL query services. In: The Web Conference, pp. 1268–1278. ACM (2019)
22. Neumann, T., Moerkotte, G.: Characteristic sets: accurate cardinality estimation for RDF queries with multiple joins. In: Proceedings of ICDE, pp. 984–994. IEEE (2011)
23. Noy, N., Gao, Y., Jain, A., Narayanan, A., Patterson, A., Taylor, J.: Industry-scale knowledge graphs: lessons and challenges. Commun. ACM 62(8), 36–43 (2019)
24. Owens, A., Seaborne, A., Gibbins, N., Schraefel, M.C.: Clustered TDB: a clustered triple store for Jena. Project report (2008)
25. Ronzhin, S., et al.: Kadaster knowledge graph: beyond the fifth star of open data. Information 10, 310 (2019)
26. Saleem, M., Mehmood, Q., Ngonga Ngomo, A.-C.: Feasible: a feature-based SPARQL benchmark generation framework. In: International Semantic Web Conference (ISWC) (2015)
27. Shen, F., Lee, Y.: Knowledge discovery from biomedical ontologies in cross domains. PLoS ONE 11, e0160005 (2016)
28. Verborgh, R., et al.: Triple pattern fragments: a low-cost knowledge graph interface for the Web. J. Web Semant. 37–388, 184–206 (2016)
29. Vrandečić, D., Krötzsch, M.: Wikidata: a free collaborative knowledgebase. Commun. ACM 57, 78–85 (2014)

Semantic Parsing of Textual Requirements

Ole Magnus Holter[(✉)]

Department of Informatics, University of Oslo, Oslo, Norway
olemholt@ifi.uio.no

Abstract. Requirements are critical components in the industry, describing qualities that a product or a service needs to have. Most requirements are only available as natural language text embedded in a document. Working with textual requirements is getting increasingly difficult due to the growing number of requirements, and having the requirements available as structured data would be beneficial. However, the work required for the translation of natural language requirements into structured data is daunting. Thus, we need tools to aid in this process. In this Ph.D. project, we propose to use state-of-the-art knowledge extraction techniques and develop novel methods to identify the terms and relationships in a requirement and align them with an existing domain-ontology. To achieve this goal, we must overcome the difficulties in working with both domain-specific technical corpora and ontologies. Furthermore, existing tools and NLP models must be adapted to the domain.

Keywords: Semantic parsing · NLP · RDF · Requirements

1 Introduction

Requirements describe the features and qualities that a product or a service needs to have, including legal regulations. Being essential to most industries today, the requirements usually form part of the legal agreements between parties. Requirements are also used to direct work processes, ensure worker safety, and to reduce environmental impact. In most cases, the requirements are available only within textual documents (e.g., PDF, Word). In large companies, this does not scale well. Moreover, natural language is inherently ambiguous and imprecise; consequently, misunderstandings are common. Besides, the use of natural language documents makes it hard to organize the requirements in a way that avoids requirements to be repeated. Thus, the situation today is that many requirements are hard to find and duplicated or conflicting requirements are not uncommon.

Current solutions for digital management of requirements (e.g., Polarion [22]) focus on better organization of existing natural language requirements. By ensuring that every requirement has a unique identifier across all documents, and by

© Springer Nature Switzerland AG 2020
A. Harth et al. (Eds.): ESWC 2020 Satellite Events, LNCS 12124, pp. 240–249, 2020.
https://doi.org/10.1007/978-3-030-62327-2_39

adding metadata, such as about the author of a requirement and comments, single requirements can be uniquely identified in the entire workflow, and changes can be managed for each requirement. Although the decoupling with the document is an important step, it does not solve the industry's challenges with managing requirements.

An attempt to improve the quality of natural language requirements is to define clear guidelines for writing requirements, for example, the guides for writing requirements by the International Council on Systems Engineering (INCOSE) [11].

The READI project [23] creates standards for requirement modeling and for expressing requirements as structured data. This is a top-down approach to requirement modeling where existing requirements are currently ignored, and the aim is to develop new approaches for describing and modeling. As part of READI, research on how to effectively model requirements in OWL 2 is also being done [14].

Having the requirements described as structured data can open up for novel ways to organize, process, and think about requirements. It could potentially transform how the industry works with requirements. However, even if requirements are not completely modeled, annotation and categorization can prove a useful step towards better requirement management and adherence. By exploiting the hierarchies in taxonomies and by the use of automatic reasoning, identification and maintenance of the requirements will be more manageable, and the identification of duplicate and conflicting requirements can be enabled. In the future, documentation can be automatically generated and sent to the stakeholders. It might even be possible to build applications that automatically retrieve requirements relevant for a project and check automatically whether the requirements are fulfilled.

We cannot, however, ignore the existing textual requirements. The industry is committed to following the existing corpus of textual requirements, and the textual requirements will continue to play an essential role in communication between parties. The existing situation could be improved by having existing requirements translated into a structural representation. However, the cost of manually translating requirements is daunting. Consequently, there is a need for (semi-)automatic tools that can aid the task. Knowledge extraction from general text is hard. Our task, however, is not to understand general text but rather text from the domain of technical requirements, in which we expect the authors to have some degree of adherence to guidelines and aim to be clear and concise.

Further, we expect that existing tools, being trained on general corpus text, are insufficient for this purpose. We also expect the documents to contain non-textual elements (e.g., graphs and tables, which can only be understood in the current context). While these elements are central to the understanding of the requirements, we choose to ignore them and focus only on the text to limit the scope of this project.

The ideal solution to address the industry's challenges with requirements would be a fully automatic system that translates from natural language representation into high-quality structural representation (i.e., an RDF graph).

Such a system may not be realistic due to the nature of natural language text being both inherently ambiguous and complex. Even human experts will not agree on how to perform certain translations. We expect, however, that the work towards the vision of a fully automated system will provide several subtasks with a lower level of complexity that could equally benefit requirements management and adherence to requirements in the industry such as the identification of single requirements in the text, the categorization of requirements, and the identification of domain-specific terminology.

The rest of this paper is organized as follows. Section 2 summarizes related work, and Sect. 3 describes the task in detail. Sections 4 and 5 describe the research methodology and plan for evaluation, respectively, and some preliminary results are presented in Sect. 6 before the conclusions are presented in Sect. 7.

2   State of the Art

This Ph.D. project is related to NLP work on industry requirements. Most of the work in this area, however, is related to the field of software development. Winkler and Vogelsang used word vectors and Convolutional Neural Networks (CNN) to identify requirements in a document [26], while Abualhaija et al. propose to use various parsing strategies together with a random forest classifier for the same task [1]. In [24], Sultanov and Hayes propose to use reinforcement learning for requirement traceability. Other works aim at helping authors to express requirements with higher quality [21,25] and to identify non-functional requirements [3].

While the research in the software industry is relevant to other domains, we cannot assume it to be directly transferable. The challenges in industries such as, for instance, oil and gas, can be quite different from the challenges in the software industry. For example, a major challenge in the software industry is problems of understanding due to limited domain knowledge of software developers and the limited knowledge about software development by the stakeholders [4]. We expect this challenge to be less pronounced in other industries as requirements are often written by professionals in that particular domain.

The Ph.D. project is also related to knowledge extraction in general, machine-reading, and open information extraction. Extracting knowledge from text is traditionally realized as a pipeline where one first extracts named entities before extracting the relations using either handcrafted rules or via supervised learning. The entities and relations are disambiguated and made available in a machine-understandable form. Typically, these tasks require large corpora of manually labeled sentences. Etzioni et al. argue that it is "time for the AI community to set its sights on Machine Reading" [7]. Central to Machine Reading is Open Information Extraction (OpenIE), a paradigm that has a focus on domain independence and unsupervised understanding of text [2].

An important step in the knowledge extraction pipeline is named entity recognition [10]. NER is commonly seen as a sequence labeling task. Rule-based approaches, probabilistic models (e.g., Markov models), and more advanced neural network algorithms are used for this task [15].

Works on entity disambiguation and the detection of emerging entities are also relevant for the Ph.D. project, but are out of the scope of this paper.

Identification of domain-specific terms in domain-specific documents, or automatic terminology acquisition (ATA), is an essential step in many NLP tasks dealing with domain-specific documents and has been studied extensively. Some examples are [6,12,13,19]. TermoStat [6] uses a general domain corpus and identifies (simple and complex) domain-specific terms in an input document by comparing the frequency of the terms between the general domain corpus and the input document. More recent approaches to domain-specific term extraction also use supervised and unsupervised machine learning approaches [13].

Gangemi et al., in the work on FRED [8], propose that natural language can be automatically translated to linked data using classical NLP techniques together with Discourse Representation Theory by first using Semantic Role Labeling (SRL) and NER. The text is then transformed into Discourse Representation Structures (DRTs), which are translated into RDF and OWL 2 statements.

Besides the work on NLP, there is also related work on modeling requirements. The work by Klüwer et al. [14] suggests a model where a requirement is an individual of the class `requirement`. A requirement has a relationship `positedBy` to an individual and a `hasSCDclause` relationship to a clause with the following three properties: *(i)* `hasScope` which is the scope of the requirement (e.g., a *Shell boiler*), *(ii)* `hasCondition` which is an optional condition (e.g., *with a diameter of 1400 mm or greater*), and *(iii)* `hasDemand` what is required (e.g., a *Manhole*) . This representation of requirements uses the punning feature of OWL 2 (i.e., it treats classes as individuals).

3 Problem Statement

Our goal is to automatically translate industry requirements into high-quality machine-understandable structured data. For this specific task, quality must be measured both in terms of completeness and correctness. We also want to make the translation conform to a domain-specific ontology. The identification of requirements sentences in the document is in itself a task that is important to the Ph.D. project but is not discussed further in this paper. Assuming that we have correctly identified an individual requirement in a document, we break down the goal into four sub-tasks with increasing complexity. First, we need to identify its main components, namely the scope, the condition (if any), and the demand. The second task is to link these fragments with the relevant classes and properties from a knowledge base. At this point, the approach may also suggest new classes and properties be added to the ontology. The third task is to formalize the relationship as an RDF graph.

Consider the requirement 1.1.5 from DNV GL's "Rules for classification Ships, part 4 – Systems and components, Chap. 7 – Pressure equipment" [5]:

1.1.5 Shell boilers with a shell diameter of 1400mm or greater shall be designed to permit entry of a person and shall be provided with a manhole for this purpose.

Using the ontology proposed by Klüwer et al. [14], this requirement can be translated into the following RDF graph (in Turtle syntax):

```
ex:1.1.5 a ex:Requirement ;
    ex:hasSCDclause ex:scd1 ;

ex:scd1 a ex:SCDclause ;
    ex:hasScope ex:ShellBoiler ;
    ex:hasCondition ex:cond1 ;
    ex:demandStatement "permit entry of a person" .

ex:cond1 a ex:Condition ;
    ex:subject ex:ShellDiameter ;
    ex:predicate xsd:minInclusive ;
    ex:object 1400 ;
    ex:unit "mm" .

ex:1.1.5b a ex:Requirement ;
    ex:hasSCDclause ex:scd2 .

ex:scd2 a ex:SCDclause ;
    ex:hasScope ex:ShellBoiler ;
    ex:hasCondition ex:cond1 ;
    ex:hasDemand ex:Manhole .
```

Having all the information parsed and resolved against classes and properties is ideal. However, complex statements can be hard to parse and align with an ontology. If we are not able to resolve natural language strings with relevant concepts from the ontology, but instead only label parts of a sentence as scope, condition and demand, then that would already be helpful for the organization of requirements and the retrieval of relevant requirements for a given project, especially in a semi-automatic process with a human in the loop.

From the outlined goal, we formulate the following four research questions for the Ph.D. project.

RQ 1: *To what extent can we automatically translate textual requirements into high-quality machine-understandable structured data?*

We will look at approaches on how to automatically generate RDF graphs from given requirements.

RQ 2: *To what extent can we make the automatic translation conform to a given domain-specific ontology?*

A translation from a textual requirement to structured data is not very helpful if it cannot be used together with existing systems and knowledge bases. By creating a graph that conforms to a domain ontology, however, we can integrate the requirements with other existing requirements and can make effective use of them.

RQ 3: *To what extent can a domain ontology help in processing natural language by providing more accurate parses of textual requirements into a structured representation?*

As domain ontologies describe concepts and relations between concepts in a given domain, they contain useful information that could improve parsing. We will investigate to what extent domain ontologies can help in this step of the process as well.

RQ 4: *Does an automatic translation from textual requirements to a preliminary structured representation, followed by manual improvements, reduce the total time required to produce high-quality structured representations?*

With this question, we want to find out if we can, by using the automatically translated textual requirements, reduce the effort over a manual translation, including potential manual corrections.

Proposed Methods

The translation of the requirements into an RDF graph can be considered a pipeline of smaller tasks. There are many strategies we can use that can give us valuable features that might help to classify and extract knowledge from the documents. These strategies include *(i)* automatic extraction of domain-specific terms. *(ii)* sentence tokenizing and word tokenizing, *(iii)* normalizing words (e.g., lemmatization, case normalizing), *(iv)* POS-tagging, *(v)* chunking (NP chunking), *(vi)* constituency parsing, *(vii)* dependency parsing, *(viii)* Semantic Role Labeling, *(ix)* class recognition (in contrast to NER where individuals are recognized), *(x)* identification of patterns in text, *(xi)* relation extraction, and *(xii)* linking classes and relations to a domain ontology.

Currently, most state-of-the-art systems for these types of processing are using end-to-end neural modeling [27,28]. One key difficulty for this project, however, is the limited amount of data existing for the domain, making the use of neural modeling challenging. We need to evaluate if such systems, together with weak supervision [18] and transfer learning methods such as in [16], can be used effectively for this task. We may also need to approach the problem using declarative strategies or hybrid strategies.

In requirement texts, we do not expect to find named entities, but more abstract domain-specific terms (T-box terms). Tagging concepts with domain-specific terminology using a few general classes can prove to be a useful feature for the retrieval of knowledge. From the example in Sect. 3, we would consider

`Shell boiler` to be a class (i.e., it does not refer to a specific instantiation of the concept) that is a subclass of `boiler`, which is again a subclass of `container`. This, we believe, can be done, for example, as shown in [17] or by terminology lookup, as proposed in [20].

Relation extraction can also be done using either neural, declarative or hybrid methods. Once some relationships are found, these can be used to find even more concepts and relationships.

The identification of the three elements scope, condition, and demand in a sentence can be thought of as a sequence labeling task. This task is, however, specific to the work on textual requirements, so any training data would have to be created from scratch.

4   Research Methodology

Finding and reading relevant literature is essential as this Ph.D. project requires competence and in-depth knowledge of the state-of-the-art in several domains.

For **RQ 1**, we will test several approaches for the extraction of knowledge from requirements documents and evaluate which approaches are effective for real industry requirements. Further, we will extend existing approaches and devise a new method for knowledge extraction from industry requirements.

We have to develop a quality criteria in order to determine if a translation is of high quality. To evaluate the quality of our method, we have the opportunity to work together with experts both in technical domains and in the general domain of requirements.

For **RQ 2** and **RQ 3**, we will test approaches taken by other methods that deal with linking and annotating textual data and elaborate on these. We have access to technical experts in several domains. However, we have yet to decide on a specific domain where a (possibly incomplete) ontology already exists. We can also make use of industry taxonomies and other available ontologies.

For **RQ 4**, we would need to divide domain experts randomly into two teams where one team does the manual translation of the requirements, and the other team uses the method that we aim to develop during the Ph.D. project. We measure the time and the quality of the translations. We also plan to let the first group do the translations with the system afterward and do qualitative interviews with the domain experts to evaluate the experiences.

5   Evaluation Plan

We will evaluate the method on real industry requirements with the help of domain experts. We intend to manually annotate a set of requirements and let domain experts create translations into structured representations before we agree upon a gold standard. We will also consider the differences between translations and determine a human standard deviation. The gold standard will be shared with the community.

We will evaluate the method in a stacked approach. First, we can evaluate the scope, condition, demand labeling approach, then the linking of the concepts to classes and properties before we evaluate the actual translation into an RDF graph. For each step, we evaluate how suitable existing tools are to solve the problems and then how much our novel approach can improve on the existing tools.

We plan to evaluate the different stages using standard metrics such as accuracy, precision, and recall. We need to define completeness and accuracy of the translation and expected human performance must be defined. Structural differences that are functionally equivalent should be considered equal. Another measure of quality for the actual translation is how good we can translate the individual requirements. (i.e., To what extent are we dealing with natural language, and to what extent do we have classes in the resulting RDF graph).

6 Preliminary Results

As an initial experiment, we investigate what can be expected by existing systems on typical textual requirements from the oil and gas industry.

TermoStat [6] identifies more than 1000 domain-specific terms from the DNV GL's requirements for ship classification [5].

AllenNLP [9] is a deep learning library for NLP that includes pretrained models for several common NLP tasks. It comes with an online demo-version that was used to generate the Figs. 1 and 2, showing quite promising results for the example.

We have also manually annotated requirements from the DNV GL Ship classification document[1] [5]. What we find is that, in most cases, manually identifying the overall scope and demand parts of a single requirement is not difficult. It is, however, challenging to distinguish between a condition and a refinement of the scope (e.g., if it is a subclass of the scope or a condition on the requirement). Some times, the scope is implicit from the structure of the document. We also find that some requirements contain multiple scopes or multiple demands. When identified, some scopes, conditions, and demands are very complex and will not align easily with a taxonomy.

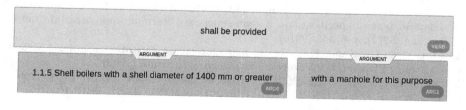

Fig. 1. Open information extraction (AllenNLP)

---

[1] The annotation is available at https://gitlab.com/oholter/scd-annotations.

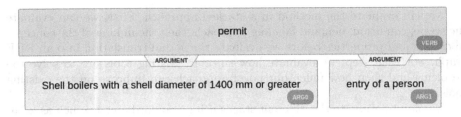

Fig. 2. Semantic role labeling (AllenNLP)

7 Conclusions

This Ph.D. project proposes to translate natural language industry requirements to structured data automatically, by the use state-of-the-art knowledge extraction techniques This is, however, not trivial as the techniques mostly depend on large amount of training data, and because natural language is complex and ambiguous.

The translation can be done with different levels of complexity, all of which could be of interest to the industry. First, identify the three main components of a single requirement from the text, namely scope, condition, and demand. Second, to link these fragments to relevant classes and properties from a knowledge base. Third, to formalize the relationship as an RDF graph.

Acknowledgements. The Ph.D. project is supervised by Basil Ell, Martin Giese, and Lilja Øvrelid and is funded by the SIRIUS centre (http://sirius-labs.no): Norwegian Research Council project number 237898. It is co-funded by partner companies, including DNV GL and Equinor.

References

1. Abualhaija, S., Arora, C., et al.: A Machine learning-based approach for demarcating requirements in textual specifications, pp. 51–62. In: RE (2019)
2. Betteridge, J., Carlson, A., et al.: Toward never ending language learning. In: AAAI Spring Symposium: Learning by Reading and Learning to Read, pp. 1–2 (2009)
3. Casamayor, A., Godoy, D., Campo, M.: Identification of non-functional requirements in textual specifications: a semi-supervised learning approach. Inf. Softw. Technol. **52**(4), 436–445 (2010)
4. Christel, M.G., Kang, K.C.: Issues in requirements elicitation. Carnegie-Mellon University Pittsburgh PA Software Engineering Institute (1992)
5. DNV GL: DNV-RU-SHIP-Pt4-Ch7: Rules for classification - Ships. https://rules.dnvgl.com/docs/pdf/DNVGL/RU-SHIP/2018-01/DNVGL-RU-SHIP-Pt4Ch7.pdf. Accessed 07 Feb 2020
6. Drouin, P.: Term extraction using non-technical corpora as a point of leverage. Terminology **9**(1), 99–115 (2003)
7. Etzioni, O., Banko, M., Cafarella, M.J.: Machine reading. In: AAAI, vol. 6, pp. 1517–1519 (2006)

8. Gangemi, A., Presutti, V., Recupero, R., et al.: Semantic web machine reading with FRED. Semant. Web **8**(6), 873–893 (2017)
9. Gardner, M., Grus, J., et al.: AllenNLP: a deep semantic natural language processing platform. arXiv:1803.07640 (2018)
10. Grishman, R., Sundheim, B.: Message understanding conference-6: a brief history, p. 6. In: COLING (1996)
11. International Council on Systems Engineering: INCOSE. https://www.incose.org/. Accessed 21 Jan 2020
12. Jacquemin, C., Bourigault, D.: Term Extraction and Automatic Indexing, vol. 1. Oxford University Press, Oxford (2012)
13. Judea, A., Schutze, H., Bruegmann, S.: Unsupervised training set generation for automatic acquisition of technical terminology in patents, p. 11. In: COLING (2014)
14. Klüwer, J.W., Waaler, A.: Reified requirements ontology (2019). https://w3id.org/requirement-ontology/ontology/core/A01A. Accessed 30 Jan 2020
15. Lample, G., Ballesteros, M., Subramanian, S., Kawakami, K., Dyer, C.: Neural architectures for named entity recognition. arXiv:1603.01360 (2016)
16. Lee, J.Y., Dernoncourt, F., et al.: Transfer learning for named-entity recognition with neural networks. arXiv:1705.06273 (2017)
17. Nooralahzadeh, F., Lønning, J.T., Øvrelid, L.: Reinforcement-based denoising of distantly supervised NER with partial annotation, pp. 225–233. In: DeepLo (2019)
18. Ratner, A., De Sa, C., Wu, S., Selsam, D., Ré, C.: Data programming: creating large training sets, quickly. In: NeurIPS (2016)
19. Rigouts Terryn, A., Drouin, P., Hoste, V., Lefever, E.: Analysing the impact of supervised machine learning on automatic term extraction: HAMLET vs Termo-Stat, pp. 1012–1021. In: RANLP (2019)
20. Savova, G.K., Masanz, J.J., et al.: Mayo clinical Text Analysis and Knowledge Extraction System (cTAKES): architecture, component evaluation and applications. J. Am. Med. Inform. Assoc. **17**, 507–513 (2010)
21. Seresht, S.M., Ormandjieva, O., Sabra, S.: Automatic conceptual analysis of user requirements with the requirements engineering assistance diagnostic (READ) tool, pp. 133–142. In: SERA (2008)
22. Siemens AG: Polarion ALM. https://polarion.plm.automation.siemens.com. Accessed 07 Jan 2020
23. SIRIUS: DREAM and READI: Cooperation to Manage Digital Requirements. https://sirius-labs.no/dream-and-readi-cooperation-to-manage-digital-requirements/. Accessed 15 Nov 2019
24. Sultanov, H., Hayes, J.H.: Application of reinforcement learning to requirements engineering: requirements tracing, pp. 52–61. In: RE (2013)
25. Wang, Y.: Automatic semantic analysis of software requirements through machine learning and ontology approach. J. Shanghai Jiaotong Univ. (Sci.) **21**(6), 692–701 (2016). https://doi.org/10.1007/s12204-016-1783-3
26. Winkler, J., Vogelsang, A.: Automatic classification of requirements based on convolutional neural networks. pp. 39–45. In: REW (2016)
27. Wu, S., He, Y.: Enriching pre-trained language model with entity information for relation classification. eprint arXiv:1905.08284 (2019)
28. Zhao, Y., Wan, H., Gao, J., Lin, Y.: Improving relation classification by entity pair graph. In: Asian Conference on Machine Learning, pp. 1156–1171 (2019)

Domain-Specific Knowledge Graph Construction for Semantic Analysis

Nitisha Jain[✉]

Hasso-Plattner-Institut, University of Potsdam, Potsdam, Germany
nitisha.jain@hpi.de

Abstract. Knowledge graphs are widely used for systematic representation of real-world data. Large-scale, general purpose knowledge graphs, having millions of facts, have been constructed through automated techniques from publicly available datasets such as Wikipedia. However, these knowledge graphs are typically incomplete and often fail to correctly capture the semantics of the data. This holds true particularly for domain-specific data, where the generic techniques for automated knowledge graph creation often fail due to several challenges, such as lack of training data, semantic ambiguities and absence of representative ontologies. The focus of this thesis is on automated knowledge graph construction for the cultural heritage domain. The goal is to tackle the research challenges encountered during the creation of an ontology and a knowledge graph from digitized collections of cultural heritage data. This paper identifies the specific research problems for these tasks and presents a methodology and approach for a solution, along with preliminary results.

Keywords: Knowledge graphs · Ontology learning · Cultural heritage

1 Introduction

Knowledge graphs (KG) have become fairly common as structured, machine readable repositories of data. Several large KGs have been developed by industry and academia that are in widespread use for supporting downstream applications such as search and question answering. Knowledge graphs rely on an underlying schema or *ontology* that consists of the concepts (that define the *type* of the entities) and the possible relations between them. The ontology holds the key to the semantic meaning of the facts in a KG and dictates the logical rules as well as restrictions for populating the KG. There have been several efforts at automatic construction of general purpose knowledge graphs by extracting information from the Web [2,19]. However, the resulting KGs are rarely fully correct and never complete in their coverage [10]. This problem is further exacerbated in domain-specific use cases. General purpose KGs constructed from Web sources cover a wide range of domains and therefore they cannot be expected to be comprehensive and semantically aligned to any single domain in particular.

© Springer Nature Switzerland AG 2020
A. Harth et al. (Eds.): ESWC 2020 Satellite Events, LNCS 12124, pp. 250–260, 2020.
https://doi.org/10.1007/978-3-030-62327-2_40

In order for KGs to be useful for a specific domain, it is essential to have a semantically-rich and comprehensive representation of the domain in the KG. For instance, the most important concepts and relations differ from one domain to the other, such as Bank and Loans for the financial domain and names of Proteins and Genes for the biomedical domain. Due to this, the underlying ontologies in general KGs are insufficient for semantic representation of specific domains. Gold standard annotated datasets required for the training as well as evaluation of automated techniques are also largely absent for domain-specific tasks. As a result, knowledge graphs end up having specific tailor-made construction pipelines for different domains, while the domain ontologies are largely manually designed with the help of expensive human expertise.

In order to motivate and explore these research problems, we consider cultural heritage as a representative domain. We are working in collaboration with the Wildenstein Plattner Institute[1] that was founded to promote scholarly research on cultural heritage collection. A wealth of information is buried in large collections of recently digitized art resources. In these resources, cultural objects such as artworks, auctions, art collections, artistic movements etc. are often mentioned within semi-structured or unstructured texts. Identification of the mentions of these cultural objects as named entities and establishing their relations can facilitate search and browsing in digital resources, help art historians to track the provenance of artworks and enable wider semantic text exploration for digital cultural resources. However, extraction of this information to construct a representative *art* knowledge graph is a non-trivial task.

In this thesis, we identify the challenges of designing a framework for constructing a domain-specific KG in an automated manner. In particular, we examine how to automate the process of design of an ontology for a new domain as well as populate a KG based on this ontology with domain relevant facts via automated techniques. We explore the role of modern deep learning techniques for the different tasks of KG construction, including named entity recognition (NER), linking and relation extraction. Our goal is to devise methods and techniques for knowledge representation that perform well for the cultural heritage domain, while also being sufficiently robust and generic to be applicable to other domains.

1.1   Domain-Specific Challenges

Cultural heritage data is vastly heterogeneous and comprises of multiple topics, multiple languages as well numerous different text formats ranging from structured tabular data to long passages of unstructured text descriptions. Data obtained from historical archives also poses significant linguistic challenges in terms of outdated vocabularies and phrases, such that the modern natural language processing tools are unable to perform well for these texts [9]. In the absence of large annotation datasets, the adaptation of existing solutions faces many challenges, some of them being unique to this domain. As an example,

---

[1] https://wpi.art/.

if we consider the task of NER, existing state-of-the-art tools fail to recognize important entities of the cultural heritage domain, such as artworks. Due to the ambiguities that are inherent in artwork titles, the identification of their mentions from texts is a challenging task and requires significant domain expertise to tackle. Consider the painting with the title '*Head of a woman*'—such phrases can be hard to get distinguished as named entities from the surrounding text due to their generality. Even the presence of typical formatting cues such as capitalization, quotes, italics or boldface fonts cannot be assumed or guaranteed, especially in digitized texts obtained from scans of art historical archives. The issue of noisy data due to OCR limitations further exacerbates the challenges for automated text analysis for the cultural heritage domain [18].

Fig. 1. Dataset samples

1.2 Dataset

A large collection of digitized art historical documents has been provided by our project partners as a representative cultural heritage dataset. The dataset consists of texts in many different languages including English, French, German, Italian, Dutch, Spanish, Swedish and Danish among others. The collection comprises of different types of documents: auction catalogues, art books related to particular artists or art genres, catalogues of art exhibitions and other documents. The auction and exhibition catalogues contain semi-structured and unstructured texts that describe artworks on display, mainly paintings and sculptures. Art books may contain more unstructured text about the origins of artworks and their creators. For reference, a few sample documents from a similar collection of digitized exhibition catalogues[2] and historical art journals[3] are shown in Fig. 1.

---

[2] https://digi.ub.uni-heidelberg.de/diglit/koepplin1974bd1/0084,0095.

[3] https://digi.ub.uni-heidelberg.de/diglit/studio1894/0019.

2   Related Work

This work builds upon research in several domains. The relevant previous works and their limitations are briefly discussed here.

Semantic Web and Cultural Heritage. With the principles of linked open data[4] gaining momentum in the cultural heritage domain [21], there has been a recent surge in the availability of digitized cultural data. Initiatives such as OpenGLAM[5] and flagship digital library projects such as Europeana[6] and Digital Public Library of America[7] aim to enrich open knowledge graphs with cultural heritage data by improving the coverage of the topics related to the cultural domain. Several efforts have been made to digitize historical archives and collections [8]. This is especially true for the art domain where a large collection of raw texts are yet to be explored that could benefit greatly from a systematic representation of the information in the form of a KG. Although there is previous work on creating ontologies and knowledge repositories for several specific use cases [6,12], yet a comprehensive method for automatically constructing an *art* knowledge graph has thus far eluded this domain. This thesis aims to identify and overcome the unique challenges of the cultural heritage domain in order to automate the ontology and KG creation.

Ontology Learning. Ontology learning or ontology inference has been a subject of active research. Towards this goal, previous works have focused on automatic taxonomy induction from structured and unstructured texts [23]. However, these approaches suffer from low coverage and do not scale well to domains with noisy datasets, thus requiring manual cleanup efforts. A number of tools for building ontologies from large datasets have also been developed [4,17]. Inspite of existing frameworks, ontology construction for specialized domains still requires extensive collaboration between ontology engineers and domain experts for enabling accurate reasoning and knowledge inferencing. Automated methods for inferencing and extending domain ontologies is one of the research questions that will be addressed in this thesis.

Knowledge Graph Construction. Due to the popularity of knowledge graphs, automated KG construction has garnered a lot of attention from the research community. Large multi-lingual KGs such as Yago [16] and DBpedia [14] have been generated by leveraging Wikipedia for data and schema derivation. There have been several efforts towards automatic construction of general purpose KGs from the Web based on machine learning techniques [2,19]. However, automated KG construction techniques suffer from a number of shortcomings in terms of their coverage and scalability. Generic techniques fail to achieve comparable per-

---

[4] Linked Open Data: http://www.w3.org/DesignIssues/LinkedData.
[5] OpenGLAM: http://openglam.org.
[6] Europeana: http://europeana.eu.
[7] DPLA: https://dp.la/.

formance for domain-specific datasets, particularly for cultural heritage collections. Though there have been some efforts in this direction [3], previous work on automated KG construction for the cultural heritage domain is relatively sparse and therefore, the main focus of this thesis.

3   Problem Statement

The main goal of this thesis is to *enable automated construction of a domain-specific, semantically-rich knowledge graph from cultural heritage datasets.*

The construction of a knowledge graph from any data source involves ontology design as well as several information extraction tasks including named entity recognition (NER), entity linking and relation extraction. While these tasks are already subject to active research, the construction of an *art* knowledge graph faces domain-specific challenges and needs customized solutions for several research problems. We identify the following research questions as the focus of this thesis:

How can a domain-specific ontology be learnt automatically from data? Ontology design and construction is one of the first and most important steps for KG construction, yet it has largely remained a manual task, particularly for new domains. In order to create a KG from domain-specific data, experts are sought out to manually build a suitable representative ontology. General purpose ontologies, such as those that are included in DBpedia and Yago, may already contain a few concepts that are relevant for the domain and thus could be borrowed. However, to encompass all aspects of the domain, especially with reference to a specific dataset, the extension of the existing ontologies becomes essential. There are several ontologies that are have been designed for the semantic representation of specific cultural heritage datasets. For example, the OpenART ontology [1] describes a research dataset about London's art world. The CIDOC-CRM [5] is a well-known ontology that provides a description of heterogeneous cultural heritage information. However, these ontologies have been largely designed and derived from underlying datasets via manual efforts that could be laborious and expensive. Our problem statement is to enable automated ontology learning with the help of domain-specific datasets and existing ontologies in the context of the cultural heritage domain.

How can we extract artwork titles from cultural heritage data collections through named entity recognition? Titles of artworks, such as paintings and sculptures, are one of the most important entities in cultural heritage. It is common to have generic artwork titles such as '*Girl before a mirror*' (by Pablo Picasso) and abstract titles such as '*untitled*', making it hard to identify such titles as named entities. Most existing NER efforts are restricted to only a few common categories of named entities, i.e., *person, organization, location,* and *date*. Fine-grained NER or FiNER aims to classify the entities into several more entity types [15] which is essential for domain-specific NER. However, previous works on FiNER are not specifically catered to the cultural heritage domain and therefore, do not explicitly identify artwork titles as a named entity type. For the construction of an *art* KG, we want to identify the mentions of artworks, as important named entities, from cultural heritage collections.

How can cultural heritage entities be connected by meaningful relations? Understanding the relations between the various entities of a domain is essential for semantic analysis. A comprehensive *art* knowledge graph will not only consist of artwork and artist entities, but also include cultural institutions (such as museums and galleries), art styles and movements, auction and exhibition events related entities such as auction houses, exhibition venues, artwork owners etc., along with specific attributes and relations. A domain ontology can act as a guide for automated relation discovery by restricting the possible types of relations between two entities. E.g., an artwork can be connected with a museum through *exhibited* or *acquired* relation but not with *created* relation. Existing KGs (such as Wikidata that contains almost 15,000 artwork entities) can be leveraged to obtain an initial set of relations to train machine learning models for further inference. However, due to their skewed and incomplete representation of the domain (limited to instances of only a few popular entities such as artworks and artists), an accurate and comprehensive representation of domain-specific datasets is not possible by merely re-using the existing KGs, but requires the construction of a domain-specific KG. In order to make such a KG useful for semantic exploration by the domain experts, further enrichment is desirable, which leads to the next research question.

How can enrichment of an art knowledge graph enable efficient semantic exploration? The augmentation of the cultural heritage entities and relations with additional attributes can prove useful for exploration by art experts. Artwork entities can be enriched with provenance information to facilitate the tracking of their history and origins, whereas relations between artists can be enhanced with data about their influence on each other's work. Taking advantage of the multilingual texts present in cultural heritage collections, the KG can be enriched with multilingual labels for different entities, especially artworks. Further, clustering techniques can be used for inference tasks such as identification of art styles for artists, this insight can be added back to the KG for discovery and analysis by art historians. We focus on the enrichment and refinement of the KG to alleviate its usefulness for semantic exploration of cultural heritage.

4 Research Methodology and Approach

The overall methodology adopted for addressing the research problems in this thesis consists of the following steps:

1. Identification and exploration of the research space, including work on the same task from other domains.
2. Investigation of the limitations of any existing solutions and formulation of the challenges specific to cultural heritage domain.
3. Formalization and implementation of the possible solutions.

4. Evaluation of performance as compared to state-of-the-art techniques.
5. Iterative improvement in performance and usability based on feedback from our project collaborators as well as art historians.

We discuss more on the planned approach for the ongoing research tasks in this section, i.e. automated ontology learning and NER for artwork titles.

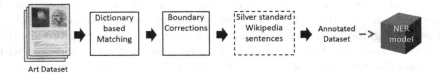

Fig. 2. First approach for NER for artwork titles

Automated Ontology Learning for Domain-Specific Datasets. In spite of several previous efforts, automated ontology construction is still considered to be an open problem. We propose to build an ontology for cultural heritage domain with the help of *knowledge graph embeddings*. KG embedding models based on general purpose KGs, such as Yago and DBpedia, have gained significant attention in the past decade [22]. They have been shown to successfully improve KGs by performing link prediction, entity typing and resolution. However, most KG embeddings only model entity triples and ignore the rich semantic information which comes from the ontological triples that are already present in many modern KGs. The addition of ontological information to KG embedding models can improve their performance for KG completion as well as extend their utility towards completion of the underlying ontological structure [7,11]. We propose that general KG embeddings enriched with domain-specific ontological information can be used for predicting incomplete ontological triples, thereby helping in ontology learning. We envision to leverage the existing ontological information pertaining to cultural heritage that is present in frameworks such as CIDOC-CRM (or even Yago and DBpedia) and extend these ontologies to comprehensively describe previously unseen datasets.

Named Entity Recognition for Artwork Titles. Towards building an *art* KG, we have started with the task of identifying mentions of artworks as named entities from digitized art archives. Recognizing the lack of annotated training datasets as one of the major bottlenecks, we are designing a framework for generating a large annotated corpus for training an NER model (Fig. 2). Firstly, existing art resources, that are integrated in popular knowledge bases, such as Wikidata[8] were leveraged to create a large entity dictionary or *gazetteer* of around 15,000 artwork titles. By matching the titles in the entity dictionary with the text, we obtained precise annotations of named entity type *artwork* from

---

[8] https://www.wikidata.org.

the underlying dataset, from which the NER model was able to learn useful features. Annotation errors due to partial matching of named entities were handled by heuristics-based boundary corrections to obtain higher recall of annotations. Further, to enable an NER model to learn from the textual patterns present in the dataset for identification of artworks, we plan to further augment the training dataset with clean and well-structured silver standard annotations that can be derived from Wikipedia articles [20]. Through this process, we aim to generate a large corpus of annotated data via automated approaches from any art corpus for retraining existing NER tools and identify mentions of artwork titles from art collections.

5   Evaluation Plan

The evaluation of the quality of a knowledge repository geared towards the cultural heritage domain must be determined by its usefulness for the domain experts. As such, we hope to enlist the assistance of our project partners to provide the necessary feedback as well as critical comments at different stages of knowledge graph construction. This is particularly important for ontology creation, where the quality of an inferred ontology can best be judged by domain experts. In order to perform an empirical evaluation of our proposed method to learn ontologies using knowledge graph embeddings, gold standard test data can be created by deleting some concepts from an existing ontology and inferring these concepts to test the effectiveness of the method.

For judging the quality of the overall KG from an information extraction point of view, we plan to consider two aspects - *completeness* in terms of the coverage of the facts, and *correctness* in terms of number of erroneous facts. The precision, recall and F1 scores will be used for quantifying the completeness whereas the accuracy measure can be used for correctness. Although a deterministic measurement of the completeness of the KG is difficult due to the open world assumption, we plan to make estimations based on the coverage of facts that can be extracted from pre-identified texts (such as Wikipedia articles). For performing these intrinsic evaluations, we plan to manually create a gold standard dataset against which the scores will be calculated. We also plan to perform the extrinsic evaluation for the KG in the context of domain-specific use cases to determine whether the KG can support certain desirable downstream tasks such as search and retrieval of artwork entities and other semantic tasks including named entity disambiguation, semantic similarity and pattern mining.

6   Preliminary Results

In this section, we present the first results from our research efforts on NER for artworks that have been peer-reviewed [13]. As discussed in Sect. 1.2, the dataset for this work consisted of a sizeable collection of digitized art historical documents. After initial pre-processing the dataset consisted of 19,310,429 sentences, which was then transformed into annotated NER data with the first two steps of the approach as described in Sect. 4 (Fig. 2). The number of annotations and unique entities in the training dataset were respectively - 413,932 and 24,966. In order to measure the impact of the quality of the training data on NER performance, we trained the baseline NER model for the new entity type *artwork* on the annotated training dataset and evaluated the trained model with the help of a manually created test dataset. The performance of the re-trained NER model in terms of precision, recall and F1 scores was evaluated with strict[9] as well as relaxed[10] metrics (based on exact and partial boundary matches).

Table 1. Performance of NER models trained on different datasets

NER model	Strict				Relaxed			
	P	R	F1	Acc	P	R	F1	Acc
Baseline	.14	.06	.08	.24	.22	.08	.12	.37
Re-trained	.23	.22	.23	.61	.39	.41	.40	.68

The preliminary results as shown in Table 1 have demonstrated notable improvement in performance for the NER models that were trained with annotated data as compared to the baseline performance. Though the improvements are encouraging, the absolute numbers are still low for the NER model to be useful in practice. Thus, we are exploring further improvement in performance by the addition of contextual features to the training dataset, such as annotations for artist names and art styles.

7   Conclusion

The main goal of this thesis is the automated construction of domain-specific knowledge graphs and ontologies. To this end, we consider the cultural heritage domain and adapt information retrieval tasks to overcome specific domain challenges. So far, we have studied related work and defined a methodology that will guide our research efforts throughout this work. We have partially addressed the problem of named entity recognition for artworks in a cultural heritage collection and obtained promising preliminary results that highlight the potential for the practical applications of this work.

Acknowledgement. I am thankful to my advisor Ralf Krestel for his feedback and Felix Naumann and Fabian Suchanek for their valuable comments. I would also like to thank Elena Demidova for guidance and suggestions during revisions.

---

[9] https://www.clips.uantwerpen.be/conll2003/ner/.
[10] https://www-nlpir.nist.gov/related_projects/muc/proceedings/muc_7_proceedings/ overview.html.

References

1. Allinson, J.: OpenART: Open Metadata for Art Research at the Tate. Bull. Am. Soc. Inf. Sci. Technol. **38**(3), 43–48 (2012)
2. Carlson, A., Betteridge, J., Kisiel, B., Settles, B., Hruschka, E.R., Mitchell, T.M.: Toward an Architecture for Never-Ending Language Learning. In: Proceedings of the 24th AAAI Conference on Artificial Intelligence, pp. 1306–1313 (2010)
3. Carriero, Valentina Anita., et al.: ArCo: The Italian cultural heritage knowledge graph. In: Ghidini, C., et al. (eds.) ISWC 2019. LNCS, vol. 11779, pp. 36–52. Springer, Cham (2019). https://doi.org/10.1007/978-3-030-30796-7_3
4. Cimiano, Philipp, Völker, Johanna: Text2Onto. In: Montoyo, Andrés, Muñoz, Rafael, Métais, Elisabeth (eds.) NLDB 2005. LNCS, vol. 3513, pp. 227–238. Springer, Heidelberg (2005). https://doi.org/10.1007/11428817_21
5. Crofts, N., Doerr, M., Gill, T., Stead, S., Stiff, M.: Definition of the CIDOC conceptual reference model. ICOM/CIDOC Documentation Standards Group. CIDOC CRM Special Interest Group 5 (2008)
6. van Dalen-Oskam, K., et al.: Named entity recognition and resolution for literary studies. Comput. Linguist. Netherlands J. **4**, 121–136 (2014)
7. Diaz, G.I., Fokoue, A., Sadoghi, M.: EmbedS: Scalable, ontology-aware graph embeddings. In: Proceedings of the EDBT Conference, pp. 433–436 (2018)
8. Dijkshoorn, C., et al.: The Rijksmuseum collection as linked data. Semant. Web **9**(2), 221–230 (2018)
9. Ehrmann, M., Colavizza, G., Rochat, Y., Kaplan, F.: Diachronic evaluation of NER systems on old newspapers. In: Proceedings of the 13th Conference on Natural Language Processing (KONVENS 2016), pp. 97–107 (2016)
10. Galárraga, L., Razniewski, S., Amarilli, A., Suchanek, F.M.: Predicting Completeness in Knowledge Bases. In: Proceedings of the 10th ACM International Conference on Web Search and Data Mining, pp. 375–383 (2017)
11. Hao, J., Chen, M., Yu, W., Sun, Y., Wang, W.: Universal representation learning of knowledge bases by jointly embedding instances and ontological concepts. In: Proceedings of the 25th ACM SIGKDD International Conference on Knowledge Discovery & Data Mining, pp. 1709–1719 (2019)
12. Hellmund, T., et al.: Introducing the HERACLES ontology-semantics for cultural heritage management. Heritage **1**(2), 377–391 (2018)
13. Jain, N., Krestel, R.: Who is Mona L.? Identifying mentions of artworks in historical archives. In: Doucet, Antoine, Isaac, Antoine, Golub, Koraljka, Aalberg, Trond, Jatowt, Adam (eds.) TPDL 2019. LNCS, vol. 11799, pp. 115–122. Springer, Cham (2019). https://doi.org/10.1007/978-3-030-30760-8_10
14. Lehmann, J., et al.: DBpedia- A large-scale, multilingual knowledge base extracted from Wikipedia. Semant. Web **6**(2), 167–195 (2015)
15. Ling, X., Weld, D.S.: Fine-grained entity recognition. In: Proceedings of the 26th AAAI Conference on Artificial Intelligence, pp. 94–100 (2012)
16. Mahdisoltani, F., Biega, J., Suchanek, F.: YAGO3: a knowledge base from multilingual Wikipedias. In: 7th Biennial Conference on Innovative Data Systems Research. CIDR Conference (2014)
17. Navigli, R., Velardi, P.: Learning domain ontologies from document warehouses and dedicated web sites. Comput. Linguist. **30**(2), 151–179 (2004)
18. Rodriquez, K.J., Bryant, M., Blanke, T., Luszczynska, M.: Comparison of named entity recognition tools for raw OCR text. In: Konvens, pp. 410–414 (2012)

19. Shin, J., Wu, S., Wang, F., De Sa, C., Zhang, C., Ré, C.: Incremental knowledge base construction using DeepDive. In: Proceedings of the VLDB Endowment International Conference on Very Large Data Bases, vol. 8, p. 1310 (2015)

20. Tsai, C.T., Mayhew, S., Roth, D.: Cross-lingual named entity recognition via Wikification. In: Proceedings of the 20th SIGNLL Conference on Computational Natural Language Learning, pp. 219–228 (2016)

21. Van Hooland, S., Verborgh, R.: Linked Data for Libraries, Archives and Museums: How to Clean, Link and Publish Your Metadata. Facet Publishing, London (2014)

22. Wang, Q., Mao, Z., Wang, B., Guo, L.: Knowledge graph embedding: a survey of approaches and applications. IEEE Trans. Knowl. Data Eng. **29**(12), 2724–2743 (2017)

23. Yang, H., Callan, J.: A metric-based framework for automatic taxonomy induction. In: Proceedings of the Joint Conference of the 47th Annual Meeting of the ACL and the 4th International Joint Conference on Natural Language Processing of the AFNLP, pp. 271–279. Association for Computational Linguistics (2009)

Explicable Question Answering

Endri Kacupaj[✉]

Smart Data Analytics, University of Bonn, Bonn, Germany
kacupaj@iai.uni-bonn.de

Abstract. Question answering over Knowledge Graphs has emerged as an intuitive way of querying structured data sources and has witnessed significant progress over the years. However, there is still plenty of space for improvement and there exist specific challenges that are still far from being effectively solved. In this research project, we aim to address some of these challenges and provide innovative solutions in the field. Our research will mainly focus on deep learning approaches such as sequence to sequence models and ranking methods. We plan to contribute to the challenges of explicability and complex queries by further researching the areas and providing resources together with more robust models by using probabilistic methods and meta-learning approaches.

Keywords: Question answering · Knowledge graphs · Semantic web · Machine learning

1 Introduction

Nowadays Question Answering (QA) systems over Knowledge Graphs (KG) have revolutionized the way of providing on-demand and accurate information. Most of the business sectors are moving towards and trying to adopt this type of systems - referred to also as chatbots - for providing more reliable services. The research area has already achieved significant contributions, by developing more and more robust methods by using different machine learning techniques.

2 State of the Art

The KGQA task involves answering a natural language question by using the information stored in a KG. The input question is first translated into a formal query language e.g., lambda calculus, lambda DCS, SPARQL. After, this formal query is executed over the KG to retrieve the answer. The task of converting a natural question into a formal KG query is called semantic parsing. The prediction models commonly used in semantic parsing can be categorized into - 1) classification, 2) ranking and 3) translation based models.

Classification models [18,20] are commonly used for simple queries. Simple queries comprise one subject entity, one relation, and one object entity. For these

© Springer Nature Switzerland AG 2020
A. Harth et al. (Eds.): ESWC 2020 Satellite Events, LNCS 12124, pp. 261–269, 2020.
https://doi.org/10.1007/978-3-030-62327-2_41

models it is assumed that formal queries follow a fixed structure. Therefore classification models do not preform well on complex queries. On the other hand, ranking models [2,3,8,17] that operate on a two-step procedure are considered better candidates for complex queries. The first step here is to find the top few probable query candidates, so that afterwards a neural network-based ranking model can be used to find the best candidate.

Finally, translation based models [5,7,13,15] treat semantic parsing as a translation problem. Usually, sequence to sequence models are used to translate an input natural language question to the corresponding logical form. The encoder is used to encode the input sequence and create context-dependent representations while the decoder generates the output sequence one token at a time, conditioning on the previously generated tokens and the input sequence. Different neural architectures are used for translation-based models such as RNN, CNN, and transformers.

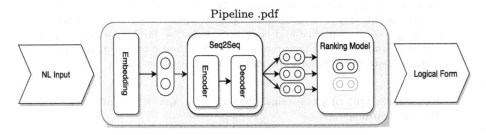

Fig. 1. A typical KGQA system, using a sequence to sequence and ranking model.

Figure 1 illustrates a typical way of implementing a KGQA system using sequence to sequence translation model alongside with a ranking model. The input to the system is a natural language question and the output is the best generated logical form. Initially, the system transforms the input question into embeddings and forwards it through an encoder-decoder model. There, by using approaches such as beam search, the model outputs multiple logical form candidates that might represent the correct interpretation of the question. After this step a ranking model is used for better matching the input with the respective logical form. The result is the final output of the system. This architecture serves as the core of our research and our work intends to improve the design and performance of such systems. We believe that there is optimization potential in at least two phases of this system. The first is the sequence to sequence model and the outputs it produces, and the second one is the ranking model.

3   Problem Statement and Contributions

Despite their current success, Question Answering over Knowledge Graphs (KGQA) systems still have many challenges to overcome. One of the biggest challenges is the question/query complexity [4,14]. Even though researchers have already done work in this field, today's systems are still suffering from handling multi-hop questions. Another challenge is the interoperability between different KGs [4]. Most of KGQA systems are built on top of one particular knowledge graph (e.g. DBpedia, Wikidata, Freebase). It will be ideal if can have systems that can operate on different knowledge graphs simultaneously. This intends to make the system more robust and provide more concrete results. Furthermore, a huge challenge is multilinguality in those systems [4]. The ideal QA system should be able to accept inputs in different languages and still be able to provide a correct answer. This area is quite unexplored for KGQA and the main reason is the lack of resources. Currently, the available datasets [16] are quite small and not sufficient for deep learning approaches.

Another relevant challenge is the explicability of KGQA systems [14]. Currently, all QA systems are responsible for providing only the answer from the knowledge graph. But no hint is given of how the systems interpreted the input question and how it accomplished the way to the answer. Explicability in those systems intends to provide further details on what the answers means. Finally, another challenge is the robustness of KGQA systems [4]. While researchers advance the field regularly by providing new architectures that always push the state-of-the-art, we argue that not all the systems are appropriate for productive deployment. The robustness of those systems is something that definitely needs more attention.

The two important challenges that we aim to address are the **explicability**, and **question/query complexity**. Our goal is to use - mainly - machine learning techniques. Specifically, we intend to use deep learning approaches such as encoder-decoder and ranking models.

3.1   Explicability

In the context of explicability, we plan to focus on enhancing the interaction of the user with the QA system by providing additional information that helps to understand how the question was interpreted and the answer was retrieved.

In an attempt to enable the users to verify the answer provided by a QA system, researchers employ various techniques such as (i) revealing the generated formal query [11], (ii) graphical visualizations of the formal query [24] and (iii) verbalizing the formal query [6,10,19].

We take a different approach to addressing the problem of validating the answers given by the QA system. We aim to verbalize the answer in a way that it conveys not only the information requested by the user but also includes additional characteristics that are indicative of how the answer was determined. In order to do this we have built a dataset and experiment with different models that can perform reasoning. The dataset aims to cover the verbalizations of answers in a KGQA task. The goal here is to further support the answers of a QA system by providing a sentence verbalization that better captures the semantic content of the questions combined with the answer. This allows the users to better understand how the system interpreted their question and to better understand the meaning of the presented answer. Considering the question "Which Nobel has Marie Curie won?", a normal system would provide the answers [Nobel Prize in Chemistry, Nobel Prize in Physics]. It would be more informative if we can provide a verbalized answer stating "Marie Curie has been awarded Nobel prize both in Chemistry and Physics".

Alongside with the dataset, we intend to build models for handling this task. Initially, we plan to build models that can easily extend different existing QA systems for supporting the verbalization of answer. Our optimal goal here is to build an end-to-end QA system that performs both query construction and verbalization at once and, if possible, in one model. Most of the research here will be facilitating translations based systems.

3.2   Question/Query Complexity

Building QA systems for handling questions with high complexity is currently an active research field. By complex queries (also referred to as multi-hop questions), we consider questions with multiple entities and/or multiple relations that might require aggregations, filtering or ranking. These types of questions are quite difficult for the state-of-the-art systems. An example can be "Which awards do Marie Curie and Pierre Curie have in common?". The question here is still a simple example but is considered as a multi-hop question, since it requires 2 entities and one property to retrieve the answer.

Our work on question complexity is based on developing frameworks including grammars, deep semantic parsers, and models that will be able to capture the entire information of the input.

Considering the two KGQA challenges we believe that we can make new contribution by using probabilistic methods and meta-learning approaches. Probabilistic methods will help us handle the uncertainty in machine learning models and therefore will be a great basis for advancing the explicability of a KGQA system.

Moreover, meta-learning has been proposed as a framework to address the challenging few-shot learning setting. The key idea is to leverage a large number of similar few-shot tasks in order to learn how to adapt a base-learner to a new task, for which only a few labeled samples are available. Currently most meta-learning approaches (related to QA) refer to semantic parsing [1,12,22] and not directly to KGQA. We aim to research meta-learning approaches so that we can use them for developing more robust KGQA systems.

3.3   Research Questions

In order to investigate these two challenges, we aim to address the following main research question, which represents the philosophy behind the project:

– How can we enhance Knowledge Graph Question Answering systems to support explicability and complex queries?

In order to restrict and specify the scope of our research work, we plan to investigate the following sub-questions:

- How can translation and ranking models be incorporated in order to develop explicable KGQA systems?
- How we leverage probabilistic methods for improving translation based KGQA models to support a more expressive query language and answer verbalization?
- How can meta-learning be used for KGQA models regarding the explicability and complex queries?

Considering the research sub-questions, we aim to make the following contributions. We will develop systems using sequence to sequence and ranking methods for handling the explicability of a KGQA system and generate verbalizations that will surpass the state-of-the-art. We will research probabilistic methods in order to advance both sequence to sequence and ranking models for generating better verbalizations and handling complex queries. Finally, we will adopt meta-learning approaches to KGQA models, in particular, to target the explicability of the system and complex queries.

4   Research Methodology

During our research, we aim to focus on ranking and translation based models in order to address the challenges we mentioned. Translation models can be considered appropriate for generating the most probable candidates, while ranking models will be used to select the top candidate. We intend to contribute to both models using probabilistic and meta-learning approaches.

stages.pdf

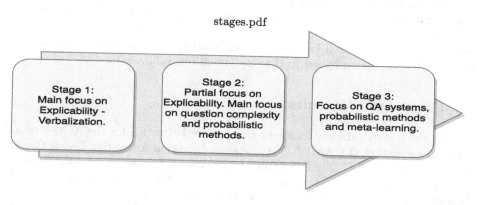

Fig. 2. Research project stages.

For addressing the first research question we plan to investigate approaches for generating multiple candidates using translations models (e.g. with beam search) and aim to further improve them alongside the ranking models. For the second question, we will further research probabilistic methods for generating more suitable candidates and also advancing the ranking models. Finally, we are interested in meta-learning techniques and will examine how to involve them for the KGQA task. The idea here is to create models that can be trained for one task using meta-learning approaches and allow them to be used more efficiently for other domains or tasks.

Figure 2 illustrates the stages of our research work. Initially we plan to focus on the explicability and partially on question complexity. In the second stage we plan to continue working on explicability but our main focus will turn to QA systems and to handling complex queries by using probabilistic methods. Finally, for the last stage, we aim to incorporate meta-learning approaches.

5   Evaluation Plan

Our evaluation plan focuses on the two KGQA challenges - explicability and complex queries. At the moment we do not intend to perform any specific evaluation for the probabilistic methods and meta-learning approaches. Our results will be evaluated by adopting commonly used metrics and will be compared to other state-of-the-art approaches for the respective tasks.

For the explicability, we have created a dataset named VQuAnDa with KGQA answer verbalizations. The dataset will aim to support both explicability and question answering task. Our goal will be to develop various models that can provide better verbalizations. The models will be evaluated using metrics such as the BLEU score or accuracy.

For evaluating the KGQA models, which we plan to develop for handling complex queries, we intend to use different available datasets such as LC-QuAD 1, 2 [9,23] and CSQA [21]. The whole evaluation process will be automated and no manual effort will be required. Our models are expected to surpass the state-of-the-art when applied to the upon mentioned datasets.

6   Preliminary Results

During the last months, we focused on answer verbalization for the KGQA task. The dataset called VQuAnDa[1] (Verbalization Question Answering Dataset) was built on top of the LC-QuAD dataset and intends to further support the answer verbalization of the respective questions. Currently the dataset contains natural language questions, with their respective SPARQL query and the verbalized answer. Both questions and answers are only in English language. To generate the dataset we followed a semi-automated approach. Initially, we retrieved the answers to all questions by using the DBpedia endpoint. Next, we generated the

---

[1] http://vquanda.sda.tech/.

templates for the verbalized answers and we filled them with entities, properties, and query results. The last 2 steps had to be done manually in order to ensure the correctness of the verbalizations. First, we corrected and, if necessary, rephrased all answers to sound more natural and fluent. Finally, to ensure the grammatical correctness of the dataset, we peer-reviewed all the generated results. We plan to focus on this dataset and develop models that will be able to provide better and more accurate verbalizations. We also aim to extend the dataset with multiple verbalizations for each question. The work-related to the VQUAnDa dataset aims to cover the explicability part of our research.

At the same time, we have worked on creating a QA framework for supporting complex queries on a scientific knowledge graph. The framework consists of different steps and models, which analyze the input natural language question and construct the respective query representation. Our framework is still in an early stage of development and we plan to further focus our work on it. Currently, the framework will be considered only for domain specific knowledge graphs but we plan to find ways and expand it in order to address open domain. For evaluating the system we built a dataset with complex queries that can be answered by the scientific knowledge graph.

Currently, we are working on releasing the first version of VQuAnDa dataset together with some sequence to sequence baseline models. We are already working on new models that can outperform the baselines and we expect to publish them later this year.

7   Conclusions

Our research focuses on Knowledge Graph Questions Answering systems. In particular, we emphasize on 2 main challenges related to the task. In the first one – explicability, we focus on how to provide better and more explicable results to the users. We handle explicability by focusing on answer verbalizations. The second challenge, which has become quite popular nowadays, is the one on complex queries. We intend to produce models and frameworks that can handle questions with high complexity (multi-hop with many entities and/or properties). At the same time, we aim to enhance current models by using probabilistic methods and meta-learning approaches.

References

1. Agarwal, R., Liang, C., Schuurmans, D., Norouzi, M.: Learning to generalize from sparse and underspecified rewards. arXiv e-prints (2019)
2. Bordes, A., Chopra, S., Weston, J.: Question answering with subgraph embeddings. In: Proceedings of the 2014 Conference on Empirical Methods in Natural Language Processing (EMNLP), Doha, Qatar. Association for Computational Linguistics (2014)
3. Bordes, A., Usunier, N., Chopra, S., Weston, J.: Large-scale simple question answering with memory networks. arXiv e-prints (2015)

4. Chakraborty, N., Lukovnikov, D., Maheshwari, G., Trivedi, P., Lehmann, J., Fischer, A.: Introduction to neural network based approaches for question answering over knowledge graphs. arXiv e-prints (2019)
5. Cheng, J., Lapata, M.: Weakly-supervised neural semantic parsing with a generative ranker. arXiv e-prints (2018)
6. Diefenbach, D., Dridi, Y., Singh, K., Maret, P.: SPARQLtoUser: did the question answering system understand me? In: ISWC 2017 (2017)
7. Dong, L., Lapata, M.: Coarse-to-fine decoding for neural semantic parsing. arXiv e-prints (2018)
8. Dong, L., Wei, F., Zhou, M., Xu, K.: Question answering over Freebase with multi-column convolutional neural networks. In: Proceedings of the 53rd Annual Meeting of the Association for Computational Linguistics and the 7th International Joint Conference on Natural Language Processing (Volume 1: Long Papers), Beijing, China. Association for Computational Linguistics (2015)
9. Dubey, M., Banerjee, D., Abdelkawi, A., Lehmann, J.: LC-QuAD 2.0: a large dataset for complex question answering over Wikidata and DBpedia. In: Ghidini, C., et al. (eds.) ISWC 2019. LNCS, vol. 11779, pp. 69–78. Springer, Cham (2019). https://doi.org/10.1007/978-3-030-30796-7_5
10. Ell, B., Harth, A., Simperl, E.: SPARQL query verbalization for explaining semantic search engine queries. In: Presutti, V., d'Amato, C., Gandon, F., d'Aquin, M., Staab, S., Tordai, A. (eds.) ESWC 2014. LNCS, vol. 8465, pp. 426–441. Springer, Cham (2014). https://doi.org/10.1007/978-3-319-07443-6_29
11. Ferré, S.: SPARKLIS: an expressive query builder for SPARQL endpoints with guidance in natural language. Semant. Web **8**, 405–418 (2017)
12. Guo, D., Tang, D., Duan, N., Zhou, M., Yin, J.: Coupling retrieval and meta-learning for context-dependent semantic parsing. arXiv e-prints (2019)
13. He, X., Golub, D.: Character-level question answering with attention. In: Proceedings of the 2016 Conference on Empirical Methods in Natural Language Processing, Austin, Texas. Association for Computational Linguistics (2016)
14. Kacupaj, E., Zafar, H., Lehmann, J., Maleshkova, M.: VQuAnDa: Verbalization QUestion ANswering DAtaset. e-prints (2019)
15. Liang, C., Berant, J., Le, Q., Forbus, K.D., Lao, N.: Neural symbolic machines: learning semantic parsers on freebase with weak supervision. arXiv e-prints (2016)
16. Lopez, V., Unger, C., Cimiano, P., Motta, E.: Evaluating question answering over linked data. Web Semant. Sci. Serv. Agents World Wide Web (2013). https://doi.org/10.1016/j.websem.2013.05.006
17. Lukovnikov, D., Fischer, A., Lehmann, J., Auer, S.: Neural network-based question answering over knowledge graphs on word and character level. In: Proceedings of the 26th International Conference on World Wide Web. International World Wide Web Conferences Steering Committee, Republic and Canton of Geneva, CHE (2017)
18. Mohammed, S., Shi, P., Lin, J.: Strong baselines for simple question answering over knowledge graphs with and without neural networks. In: Proceedings of the 2018 Conference of the North American Chapter of the Association for Computational Linguistics: Human Language Technologies, Volume 2 (Short Papers), New Orleans, Louisiana. Association for Computational Linguistics (2018)
19. Ngonga Ngomo, A.C., Bühmann, L., Unger, C., Lehmann, J., Gerber, D.: SPARQL2NL: verbalizing SPARQL queries. In: Proceedings of the 22nd International Conference on World Wide Web (2013)

20. Petrochuk, M., Zettlemoyer, L.: SimpleQuestions nearly solved: A new upperbound and baseline approach. In: Proceedings of the 2018 Conference on Empirical Methods in Natural Language Processing, Brussels, Belgium. Association for Computational Linguistics (2018)
21. Saha, A., Pahuja, V., Khapra, M.M., Sankaranarayanan, K., Chandar, S.: Complex sequential question answering: towards learning to converse over linked question answer pairs with a knowledge graph. arXiv e-prints (2018)
22. Sun, Y., Tang, D., Duan, N., Gong, Y., Feng, X., Qin, B., Jiang, D.: Neural semantic parsing in low-resource settings with back-translation and meta-learning. arXiv e-prints (2019)
23. Trivedi, P., Maheshwari, G., Dubey, M., Lehmann, J.: LC-QuAD: a corpus for complex question answering over knowledge graphs. In: d'Amato, C., et al. (eds.) ISWC 2017. LNCS, vol. 10588, pp. 210–218. Springer, Cham (2017). https://doi.org/10.1007/978-3-319-68204-4_22
24. Zheng, W., Cheng, H., Zou, L., Yu, J.X., Zhao, K.: Natural language question/answering: Let users talk with the knowledge graph. In: Proceedings of the 2017 ACM on Conference on Information and Knowledge Management (2017)

Towards Matching of Domain-Specific Schemas Using General-Purpose External Background Knowledge

Jan Philipp Portisch[1,2]([✉]) [ID]

[1] Data and Web Science Group, University of Mannheim, Mannheim, Germany
jan@informatik.uni-mannheim.de
[2] SAP SE Product Engineering Financial Services, Walldorf, Germany
jan.portisch@sap.com

Abstract. Schema matching is an important and time consuming part within the data integration process. Yet, it is rarely automatized – particularly in the business world. In recent years, the amount of freely available structured knowledge has grown exponentially. Large knowledge graphs such as BabelNet, DBnary (Wiktionary in RDF format), DBpedia, or Wikidata are available. However, these knowledge bases are hardly exploited for automated matching. One exception is the biomedical domain: Here domain-specific background knowledge is broadly available and heavily used with a focus on reusing existing alignments and on exploiting larger, domain-specific mediation ontologies. Nonetheless, outside the life sciences domain such specialized structured resources are rare. In terms of general knowledge, few background knowledge sources are exploited except for WordNet. In this paper, we present our research idea towards further exploiting general-purpose background knowledge within the schema matching process. An overview of the state of the art is given and we outline how our proposed research approach fits in. Potentials and limitations are discussed and we summarize our intermediate findings.

Keywords: Data integration · Schema matching · Ontology matching · Background knowledge · Knowledge graphs · Financial services industry

1 Introduction

1.1 Motivation

Data integration describes the effort to allow for a unified access across multiple autonomous and heterogeneous sources of data [5]. Up to date, the data integration process is manual and requires technical experts as well as domain specialists for most systems. As a consequence, data integration is slow and

Category: Early Stage Ph.D.

© Springer Nature Switzerland AG 2020
A. Harth et al. (Eds.): ESWC 2020 Satellite Events, LNCS 12124, pp. 270–279, 2020.
https://doi.org/10.1007/978-3-030-62327-2_42

expensive. Within the data integration process for two given schemas (depicted in Fig. 1), schema matching is the first step and, therefore, of main interest for this research project. It is typically very complex and not automatized. One reason is that schemas are often defined with deep background knowledge that is not itself present within the schemas [7]. Schema matching is a problem for Open Data (e.g. matching publicly available domain ontologies or interlinking concepts in the linked open data cloud) as well as for private companies which need to integrate disparate data stores. The overall research goal is to improve the data integration process by exploiting general-purpose knowledge graphs for schema matching. In terms of a business scenario, a favorable outcome would be the reduction of time that needs to be invested by human domain experts in order to accelerate data integration projects. Even though usability studies are not the main research interest of this project, an improvement can likely be achieved by providing users with a matching proposal that can be reviewed or used for human refinement. The focus of this work will be fully automatized schema matching but findings are also relevant for semi-automatic schema matching.

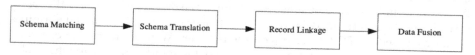

Fig. 1. Process for integrating two schemas, compiled from [34].

1.2 Industry Use Case: Matching Data Models from the Financial Services Industry

The software landscape of enterprises often resembles a heterogeneous patchwork of various systems by different vendors. Sometimes there are even multiple systems for the same task (e.g. after an acquisition). Different software components use their own data models with a large amount of overlapping parts. For a holistic understanding of the company, data has to be federated into one view. This problem is particularly pronounced in the financial services sector: Here, an understanding of a company's financial standing as well as its risk exposure is crucial for sustainable business decisions. Hence, there is an endogenous motivation to federate data. Additionally, regulators emerge to be an exogenous driver for this process by obligating financial institutions to report risk KPIs in a timely manner and even by regulating the IT infrastructure (like BCBS 239 [2]). The costs caused by regulation in the banking sector are considerable [11]. To handle the need of data federation and reporting, all individual data models of different software components have to be reconciled into one holistic view. The large size of corporate data models further complicates this process. SAP SE is developing such a data model for the financial services industry. Many applications and data stores need to be mapped into the defined data model. The company recognizes the stated problem of schema matching and is, therefore, sponsoring this PhD project.

2   State of the Art

2.1   Background Knowledge in Ontology Matching

Schema matching can be interpreted as ontology matching task because techniques for ontology matching can also be applied to other schema matching tasks such as database schema matching [7]. In addition, approaches exist to transform other data schemas, such as entity relationship (ER) models, into ontologies [8]. Ontology and schema matching systems are evaluated by the *Ontology Alignment Evaluation Initiative (OAEI)* every year since 2005 [6]. In terms of background knowledge, many systems[1] use *WordNet* as a general language resource. Besides the latter one, few other general-purpose resources are exploited: Lin and Krizhanovsky [20] employ *Wiktionary* for translation look-ups within a larger matching system [21]. The *WikiMatch* [14] system exploits the *Wikipedia* search API by determining concept similarity through the overlap of returned *Wikipedia* articles for a search term. *WeSeE Match* [24] queries search APIs and determines similarity based on TF-IDF scores on the returned Web site titles and excerpts. Background knowledge sources are also used for multilingual matching tasks. Here, translation APIs are typically called, for example *Microsoft Bing Translator* by *KEPLER* [18] or *Google Translator* by *LogMap* [17].

In the biomedical and life science domain, specialized external background knowledge is broadly available and heavily exploited for ontology matching. Chen et al. [3] extend the LogMap matching system to use *BioPortal*, a portal containing multiple ontologies, alignments, and synonyms, by (i) applying an overlap based approach as well as by (ii) selecting a suitable ontology automatically and using it as mediating ontology. As mappings between biomedical ontologies are available, those are used as well: Groß et al. [12] exploit existing mappings to third ontologies, so called *intermediate ontologies*, to derive mappings. This approach is extended by Annane et al. [1] who use the BioPortal by exploiting existing alignments between the ontologies found there for matching through a path-based approach: By linking source and target concepts into the global mapping graph, the paths that connect the concepts in that graph are used to derive new mappings. In the same domain, research has also been conducted on background knowledge selection. Faria et al. [9] propose the usage of a metric, called *Mapping Gain (MG)*, which is based on the number of additional alignments found given a baseline alignment. Quinx et al. [31] use a keyword-based vector similarity approach to identify suitable background knowledge sources. Similarly, Hartung et al. [13] introduce a metric, called *effectiveness*, that is based on the mapping overlap between the ontologies to be matched. While in the biomedical

---

[1] In 2013, Euzenat and Shvaiko [7] counted more than 80 schema matching systems that exploit *WordNet*.

domain, many specialized resources are available and data schemas are heavily interlinked, this is not the case for other domains. As a consequence, such methods cannot be easily translated and applied.

In terms of the exploitation strategies, i.e. methods to use background knowledge to derive mappings, that are applied, it is notable that embedding-based approaches, such as *RESCAL* [23] or *RDF2Vec* [32], are largely underexplored.

2.2 Tooling

In order to evaluate and compare existing as well as new matching approaches, sufficient tooling is required. The Alignment API [4] defines an interface for matchers as well as alignments. It has been gradually extended and also contains evaluation capabilities. The API is used by the main evaluation platforms presented below and defines the alignment output format that is in use by the OAEI today. Two well-known evaluation platforms are employed in the ontology matching community: The *Semantic Evaluation at Large Scale (SEALS)* and the more recent *Holistic Benchmarking of Big Linked Data (HOBBIT)*. Both platforms define a matcher interface as well as a packaging pattern. Packaged matchers can be run on the platforms on evaluation data sets and evaluation scores such as *precision, recall,* and F_1 can be calculated. Both platforms are used in OAEI campaigns.

3   Problem Statement and Contributions

3.1   Research Questions

Up to date, publicly available knowledge graphs and resources are rarely exploited outside the biomedical domain despite their continuous growth. In particular when it comes to general background knowledge, few other resources than WordNet are used. Therefore, we see a great potential for general external knowledge sources within the matching process in the public and also in the private domain. By now, even general knowledge sources such as Wikidata contain many tail-entities and facts that might be valuable for domain specific matching tasks. While the exploitation of domain-specific knowledge sources may be more desirable, this is very often not feasible due to missing availability of such resources. We strive to explore and answer the following research questions:

RQ 1: How can general-purpose background knowledge be integrated into the schema matching process to provide value?
RQ 2: Which general-purpose external resources are valuable for data integration and what are determining factors?
RQ 3: Which background-knowledge-focused exploitation strategies are valuable in the schema matching process and are applicable to general-purpose resources?
RQ 4: Which combination of background knowledge source and exploitation strategy is most helpful in schema matching?

3.2 Further Contributions

As the stated research problem is very relevant for businesses, in particular in the financial services sector, a further contribution of this PhD will be the evaluation and application of findings in concrete business applications. Thereby, Semantic Web technologies may also be integrated into SAP standard products.

4 Research Methodology and Approach

The schema matching problem is interpreted as ontology matching problem. This allows implementing matchers against a predefined API and reduces the technical heterogeneity problem that occurs with different data schemas. In addition, existing alignments and matching tasks of the ontology matching community can be easily reused due to the same technical setting.

Naturally, schemas are not always available as ontologies – particularly in the enterprise sector. However, due to the versatility of ontologies, schemas (and their semantic definitions such as ER models) can be translated into ontologies without any loss of information. Here, the OWL format is exploited as mediating technical format.[2] After the transformation process, the ontologies can be fed into a matching system. Here, we intend to develop a unitized system that allows using different sources of background knowledge as well as different matching strategies. Unlike many other matching systems, the focus of the system here is not limited to only 1:1 correspondences but also to 1:N ones which makes it more applicable for matching relational database schemas. The resulting alignments are then parsed by an evaluation platform that allows comparing different matching systems (see Sect. 5). This approach has been piloted for five SAP integration scenarios and proven as technically feasible [26]. An overview of the approach is depicted in Fig. 2.

5 Evaluation Plan

In terms of comparison and evaluation metrics, the most common approach is to compare the *precision, recall*, and F_1 scores of different approaches. We also plan to consider runtime performance aspects whereas memory consumption is regarded of lower importance given that matching itself does not have to be performed on a consumer PC. An additional suitable evaluation metric is mapping gain (although introduced in a different context). Lastly, statistical significance testing can also be applied: Recently, McNemar's test has been used to determine whether matching results are significantly different in a statistical sense [22]. We plan to benchmark different background knowledge sources combined with

---

[2] Note that the semantic expressiveness or quality of the generated technical ontologies is only as good as the inputs for the transformation and influences the results of automated matching methods. However, the outlined approach is also used for semantically richer models such as conceptual data models that are frequently used in the financial services industry, for instance.

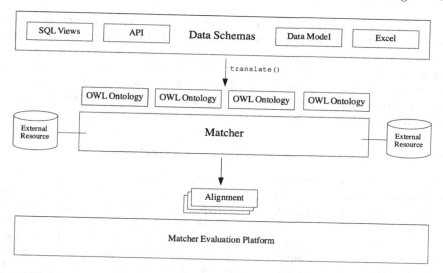

Fig. 2. High-level approach to evaluate matchers with different sources of background knowledge and strategies on existing ontologies as well as proprietary industry data models.

different knowledge exploitation strategies on publicly available (OAEI) data sets as well as on industry specific data sets provided by SAP SE. First preliminary results are outlined in Subsect. 6.4. We further plan to explore and include novel exploitation approaches, i.e. embedding-based ones, into our evaluation.

6   Preliminary or Intermediate Results

6.1   Evaluation Runtime

In order to evaluate and compare matching systems, the *Matching EvaLuation Toolkit (MELT)* [16] has been developed. MELT allows to develop, package, and evaluate various matching systems and is integrated with the existing tooling that is used within the ontology matching community, i.e., it is compatible with SEALS and HOBBIT. Compared to existing evaluation frameworks, MELT is superior in terms of the granularity of the evaluation that can be performed and the provided functionality to evaluate multiple matchers on multiple tasks. MELT is also capable of generating an interactive dashboard which alows consume matcher results through a Web interface [25].

6.2   Creation and Evaluation of Data Model Mappings from the Financial Services Domain

In order to evaluate the matcher performance on real-world data models, five preliminary SAP data model alignments that have been created by domain experts have been translated into ontologies using a set of predefined translation rules. The translations were inspired by the ones suggested in [8] and have been extended. The existing mappings were translated into the alignment format as defined by the Alignment API. After all data was translated into publicly known data formats, current OAEI ontology matchers have been run on the data. First results [26] indicated that even top-notch OAEI matchers performed comparatively bad on real-world financial services data models.

6.3   Training of Embedded Background Knowledge

So far, embedding strategies have rarely been exploited when it comes to external knowledge in schema matching. First experiments have been conducted with the *WebIsALOD* [15] data set, a large hypernymy knowledge graph extracted from the Web, and showed positive results [29,30] for schema matching. For a deeper exploration of these strategies in schema matching, knowledge graph embeddings have been trained on four large knowledge graphs: *DBpedia* [19], *WebIsALOD* [15], *Wiktionary* [33], and *WordNet* [10]. In order to obtain the concept vectors from the knowledge graph, the *RDF2Vec* approach has been applied. The embedding models as well as the code have been published together with Web APIs[3] [28]. The models have been evaluated on three semantic similarity gold standards. First results indicate that the embeddings rather represent relatedness than similarity. As a consequence, they are likely capable of generating mappings that cannot be found by other methods but are less precise. In their current form, they could be used to improve current matching methods but perform badly when used as the only similarity function (see Subsect. 6.4). In the evaluation, it could furthermore be shown that combining different graph models can outperform the single best model.

6.4   A Comparison of Sources of General Knowledge: Strategy vs. Data Source

In a larger study, three different exploitation strategies (synonymy-based, hypernymy-based, embedding-based) have been evaluated on four different knowledge graphs (DBpedia, WebIsALOD, DBnary, WordNet) with the objective to determine whether the strategy or the choice of the knowledge graph is a more dominant factor for ontology matcher performance. The results showed that – given the evaluation setting – the synonymy-based strategy performs best on all knowledge graphs. In addition, no superior general-purpose knowledge graph could be identified. This study is yet to be published.

6.5   Further Findings

Two OAEI matchers have been submitted to the OAEI: (i) The *Alod2Vec Matcher* [29] showed that it is possible to train embeddings for a background

---

[3] http://kgvec2go.org/.

knowledge set and to exploit them, albeit the contribution of the background data set was low in this case. (ii) The *Wiktionary Matcher* [27] exploits multiple recent Wiktionary graphs in different language versions. It could be shown that Wiktionary can be used as background source with reasonable matching and run time performance. An additional finding was that the publicly built knowledge source is capable of handling multilingual matching tasks.

7 Conclusions and Lessons Learned

The presented approach has potential because it explores further sources of general background knowledge that can easily be integrated in any matcher and at the same time is compatible with existing exploitation strategies on domain-specific data sets. In addition, a specific business use case for the financial services domain is explored that may push the usage of Semantic Web technologies in the business world. Lastly, new exploitation methods are explored and compared which may give guidance to practitioners.

The inclusion of real-world data schemas introduces additional complications such as many-to-one correspondences that are not well represented in most existing matching systems and still need to be addressed. One risk is that the proposed background knowledge sources are insufficient for domain specific matching tasks and do not contribute at all to solving the problem. However, first results indicate that there is a positive effect in introducing larger general knowledge graphs to domain-specific problems.

Preliminary findings showed that it is possible to translate existing schemas into ontologies. It could also be shown that existing matching systems perform comparatively bad on real-world financial services data schemas. In the current (preliminary) evaluation, it was found that embedding based strategies on background knowledge do not yet outperform explicit strategies. Additionally, it could be shown that collaboratively built, non-expert reviewed background data sets such as *BabelNet* or *Wiktionary* achieve similar or better results for the task of ontology matching compared to *WordNet*.

Acknowledgements. I would like to thank my supervisor, Prof. Heiko Paulheim, for his valuable feedback, guidance, and support in the realization of this work.

References

1. Annane, A., Bellahsene, Z., Azouaou, F., Jonquet, C.: Selection and combination of heterogeneous mappings to enhance biomedical ontology matching. In: Blomqvist, E., Ciancarini, P., Poggi, F., Vitali, F. (eds.) EKAW 2016. LNCS (LNAI), vol. 10024, pp. 19–33. Springer, Cham (2016). https://doi.org/10.1007/978-3-319-49004-5_2
2. Basel Committee on Banking Supervision: Principles for Effective Risk Data Aggregation and Risk Reporting. Bank for International Settlements, Basel (2013)

3. Chen, X., Xia, W., Jiménez-Ruiz, E., Cross, V.V.: Extending an ontology alignment system with bioportal: a preliminary analysis. In: Proceedings of the ISWC 2014 Posters & Demonstrations Track a track within the 13th International Semantic Web Conference, ISWC 2014, Riva del Garda, Italy, October 21, 2014. CEUR Workshop Proceedings, vol. 1272, pp. 313–316. CEUR-WS.org (2014)

4. David, J., Euzenat, J., Scharffe, F., dos Santos, C.T.: The alignment API 4.0. Semant. Web **2**(1), 3–10 (2011)

5. Doan, A., Halevy, A., Ives, Z.: Principles of Data Integration, Chap. 1, p. 6. Morgan Kaufmann, Burlington (2012)

6. Euzenat, J., Meilicke, C., Stuckenschmidt, H., Shvaiko, P., dos Santos, C.T.: Ontology alignment evaluation initiative: six years of experience. J. Data Semant. **15**, 158–192 (2011)

7. Euzenat, J., Shvaiko, P.: Ontology Matching, Chap. 13, 2nd edn. Springer, New York (2013). https://doi.org/10.1007/978-3-642-38721-0

8. Fahad, M.: ER2OWL: generating OWL ontology from ER diagram. In: Shi, Z., Mercier-Laurent, E., Leake, D. (eds.) IIP 2008. ITIFIP, vol. 288, pp. 28–37. Springer, Boston (2008). https://doi.org/10.1007/978-0-387-87685-6_6

9. Faria, D., Pesquita, C., Santos, E., Cruz, I.F., Couto, F.M.: Automatic background knowledge selection for matching biomedical ontologies. PLoS ONE **9**(11), e111226 (2014)

10. Fellbaum, C. (ed.): WordNet: An Electronic Lexical Database. Language, Speech, and Communication. MIT Press, Cambridge (1998)

11. Groenfeldt, T.: Taming the high costs of compliance with tech (2018). https://www.forbes.com/sites/tomgroenfeldt/2018/03/22/taming-the-high-costs-of-compliance-with-tech/

12. Groß, A., Hartung, M., Kirsten, T., Rahm, E.: Mapping composition for matching large life science ontologies. In: Proceedings of the 2nd International Conference on Biomedical Ontology, Buffalo, NY, USA, 26–30 July, 2011. CEUR Workshop Proceedings, vol. 833. CEUR-WS.org (2011)

13. Hartung, M., Gross, A., Kirsten, T., Rahm, E.: Effective composition of mappings for matching biomedical ontologies. In: Simperl, E., et al. (eds.) ESWC 2012. LNCS, vol. 7540, pp. 176–190. Springer, Heidelberg (2015). https://doi.org/10.1007/978-3-662-46641-4_13

14. Hertling, S., Paulheim, H.: WikiMatch - using wikipedia for ontology matching. In: Shvaiko, P., Euzenat, J., Kementsietsidis, A., Mao, M., Noy, N., Stuckenschmidt, H. (eds.) OM-2012: Proceedings of the ISWC Workshop, vol. 946, pp. 37–48 (2012)

15. Hertling, S., Paulheim, H.: WebIsALOD: providing hypernymy relations extracted from the web as linked open data. In: d'Amato, C., et al. (eds.) ISWC 2017, Part II. LNCS, vol. 10588, pp. 111–119. Springer, Cham (2017). https://doi.org/10.1007/978-3-319-68204-4_11

16. Hertling, S., Portisch, J., Paulheim, H.: MELT - matching evaluation toolkit. In: Proceedings of the Semantic Systems. The Power of AI and Knowledge Graphs - 15th International Conference, SEMANTiCS 2019, Karlsruhe, Germany, 9–12 September 2019 , pp. 231–245 (2019)

17. Jiménez-Ruiz, E., Cuenca Grau, B.: LogMap: logic-based and scalable ontology matching. In: Aroyo, L., et al. (eds.) ISWC 2011, Part I. LNCS, vol. 7031, pp. 273–288. Springer, Heidelberg (2011). https://doi.org/10.1007/978-3-642-25073-6_18

18. Kachroudi, M., Diallo, G., Yahia, S.B.: KEPLER at OAEI 2018. In: Proceedings of the 13th International Workshop on Ontology Matching co-located with the 17th International Semantic Web Conference. CEUR Workshop Proceedings, vol. 2288, pp. 173–178. CEUR-WS.org (2018)
19. Lehmann, J., et al.: Dbpedia - a large-scale, multilingual knowledge base extracted from Wikipedia. Semant. Web **6**(2), 167–195 (2015)
20. Lin, F., Krizhanovsky, A.: Multilingual ontology matching based on Wiktionary data accessible via SPARQL endpoint. CoRR abs/1109.0732 (2011)
21. Lin, F., Sandkuhl, K., Xu, S.: Context-based ontology matching: concept and application cases. J. UCS **18**(9), 1093–1111 (2012)
22. Mohammadi, M., Atashin, A.A., Hofman, W., Tan, Y.: Comparison of ontology alignment systems across single matching task via the McNemar's test. TKDD **12**(4), 51:1–51:18 (2018)
23. Nickel, M., Tresp, V., Kriegel, H.: A three-way model for collective learning on multi-relational data. In: Proceedings of the 28th International Conference on Machine Learning, ICML 2011, Bellevue, Washington, USA, 28 June–2 July 2011, pp. 809–816. Omnipress (2011)
24. Paulheim, H.: Wesee-match results for OEAI 2012. In: Proceedings of the 7th International Workshop on Ontology Matching, Boston, MA, USA, 11 November 2012. CEUR Workshop Proceedings, vol. 946. CEUR-WS.org (2012)
25. Portisch, J., Hertling, S., Paulheim, H.: Visual analysis of ontology matching results with the MELT dashboard. In: The Semantic Web: ESWC 2020 Satellite Events (2020, to appear)
26. Portisch, J., Hladik, M., Paulheim, H.: Evaluating ontology matchers on real-world financial services data models. In: Proceedings of the Posters and Demo Track of the 15th International Conference on Semantic Systems (SEMANTiCS 2019), Karlsruhe, Germany, September 9–12 2019. CEUR Workshop Proceedings, vol. 2451. CEUR-WS.org (2019)
27. Portisch, J., Hladik, M., Paulheim, H.: Wiktionary matcher. In: Proceedings of the 14th International Workshop on Ontology Matching co-located with the 18th International Semantic Web Conference (ISWC 2019), Auckland, New Zealand, 26 October 2019. CEUR Workshop Proceedings, vol. 2536, pp. 181–188. CEUR-WS.org (2019)
28. Portisch, J., Hladik, M., Paulheim, H.: KGvec2go - knowledge graph embeddings as a service. In: Proceedings of the International Conference on Language Resources and Evaluation (LREC), Marseille, France (2020, to appear)
29. Portisch, J., Paulheim, H.: ALOD2Vec matcher. In: Proceedings of the 13th International Workshop on Ontology Matching Co-located with the 17th International Semantic Web Conference, pp. 132–137 (2018)
30. Portisch, J.P.: Automatic schema matching utilizing hypernymy relations extracted from the web (2018). https://madoc.bib.uni-mannheim.de/52029/
31. Quix, C., Roy, P., Kensche, D.: Automatic selection of background knowledge for ontology matching. In: Proceedings of the International Workshop on Semantic Web Information Management, SWIM 2011, Athens, Greece, 12 June 2011, p. 5. ACM (2011)
32. Ristoski, P., Rosati, J., Noia, T.D., Leone, R.D., Paulheim, H.: Rdf2vec: RDF graph embeddings and their applications. Semant. Web **10**(4), 721–752 (2019)
33. Sérasset, G.: DBnary: Wiktionary as a lemon-based multilingual lexical resource in RDF. Semant. Web **6**(4), 355–361 (2015)
34. Wang, X., Haas, L.M., Meliou, A.: Explaining data integration. IEEE Data Eng. Bull. **41**(2), 47–58 (2018)

Evolving Meaning for Supervised Learning in Complex Biomedical Domains Using Knowledge Graphs

Rita T. Sousa[✉][iD]

LASIGE, Faculdade de Ciências, Universidade de Lisboa, Lisbon, Portugal
risousa@ciencias.ulisboa.pt

Abstract. Knowledge graphs represent an unparalleled opportunity for machine learning, given their ability to provide meaningful context to data through semantic representations. Knowledge graphs provide multiple perspectives over an entity, describing it using different properties or multiple portions of the graph. State-of-the-art semantic representations are static and take into consideration all semantic aspects, ignoring that some may be irrelevant to the downstream learning task. The goal of this Ph.D. project is to discover suitable semantic representations of knowledge graph entities that are adapted to specific supervised learning tasks. I will use Genetic Programming to evolve tailored semantic representations, and develop novel approaches that integrate them with different supervised learning techniques. These novel approaches will be anchored by a framework that integrates different semantic representation approaches and two representative learning approaches, Support Vector Machine and Graph Convolutional Neural Networks, and allows a comparative evaluation using benchmarks. The developed approaches will be applied to two bioinformatics tasks, prediction of protein interactions and gene-disease associations, where the impact of data size and complexity will be investigated.

Keywords: Knowledge graph · Ontology · Semantic similarity · Graph embedding · Graph kernel · Machine learning · Genetic Programming · Protein-protein interaction prediction · Gene-disease association prediction

1 Introduction

Semantic information is recognized as a valuable knowledge resource in supporting data mining tasks, since it associates meaning and context to raw data in a structured way. Although many data mining approaches are limited to what can be extracted directly from the data, understanding the meaning of data increases the performance of these approaches for knowledge discovery [20].

There are three main sources of meaning used to build semantic representations: (i) text corpora that can be used to produce vectorial representations based

© Springer Nature Switzerland AG 2020
A. Harth et al. (Eds.): ESWC 2020 Satellite Events, LNCS 12124, pp. 280–290, 2020.
https://doi.org/10.1007/978-3-030-62327-2_43

on distributional semantics [6,15,16]; (ii) handcrafted rules, generally designed using expert knowledge or learning from real data [14]; (iii) knowledge graphs (KGs) (typically built by integrating ontologies and linked data) which provide a conceptualization of a domain based on a formal definition of its entities and their relations. In recent years, the explosion in complexity and heterogeneity of biomedical data has motivated a new paradigma, where millions of semantically-described biological entities are available as linked data, building a biomedical Semantic Web [20]. Given their ability to provide meaningful context to the data, KGs represent an unparalleled opportunity for machine learning [20]. A cornerstone challenge to this is how to represent or encode the semantic information contained in the graph structure so that it can be easily exploited by machine learning models (i.e., producing semantic representations). KG-based representations, such as graph kernels [13] and graph embeddings [4], are a solution to bridge the gap between KGs and the typical vector-based representations of entities used by most machine learning techniques. A less well-known alternative is to employ semantic similarity as a representation [24]. Different machine learning algorithms can then process these representations for a wide variety of downstream learning tasks.

A severe limitation of several approaches for machine learning using KGs is that the construction of semantic representations often ignores the learning task. Consider the prediction of protein-protein interactions. It is well established that semantic similarity kernels over protein KGs can support the prediction task. However, the prediction is more accurate if just a portion of the KG is used (in this case, the one concerning biological processes) rather than the whole KG [1]. Therefore, adjusting the semantic representation to the machine learning task can improve its performance, but achieving it in an automated fashion is an open challenge.

The research focus of the Ph.D. is addressing this issue by using Genetic Programming (GP) to learn suitable semantic representations of data objects extracted from KGs to support supervised learning tasks. Thus, the plan of this thesis proposal includes the development of GP-based methods for evolving semantic representations (graph kernels, graph embeddings, and semantic similarity). Also, the plan comprises the adaptation of existing machine learning algorithms to explore semantic representations. The developed approaches will be evaluated in bioinformatics applications, particularly the prediction of protein interaction and disease-associated genes.

2   State of the Art

The research associated with this Ph.D. thesis proposal builds on the state of the art and related work from two domains: KG-based semantic representations and machine learning algorithms.

2.1   KG-Based Semantic Representations

State-of-the-art KG-based semantic representations include graph kernels and graph embeddings. Semantic similarity kernels can also be used as a semantic representation by comparing entities based on the properties they share and their taxonomic relationships.

Graph Kernels. In the past years, many graph kernels [13] have been proposed and widely-used for solving classification tasks in graphs. Graph kernels are functions that measure the similarity between graphs. Most of the graph kernels are instances of convolution kernels. The main idea is to decompose structured objects into their sub-structures and define valid local kernels among them. The three major graph kernel families considered in this proposal are (i) graph kernels based on the distribution of limited-size subgraphs; (ii) graph kernels based on subtree pattern; (iii) graph kernels based on walks and paths.

Graph Embeddings. An embedding maps each node to a lower-dimensional space in which its graph position and the structure of its local graph neighborhood is preserved as much as possible. There are a variety of methods for building KG embeddings [4]. While some focus on exploring solely the KG facts (like translational distance models or semantic matching models), others also include additional information, such as entity types, relation paths, axioms, and rules or textual information. More recently, path-based approaches have been proposed by transforming the KG into node sequences [19]. After representing a graph as a set of random walk paths sampled from it, natural language methods are then applied to the sampled paths for graph embedding.

Semantic Similarity. Semantic similarity kernels [10] compare entities (ontology classes or KG entities) based on the taxonomic relations within the ontology graph. The majority of semantic similarity measures explore the properties of each class involved, typically relying on the information content of a class, a measure of how specific and informative a class is. In instance-based semantic similarity, each instance is annotated with a set of classes which are then processed using one of two approaches: pairwise, where pairwise comparisons between all classes annotating each instance are considered; groupwise, where set, vector, or graph-based measures are employed, avoiding the need for pairwise comparisons [17].

2.2   Machine Learning

In the context of this Ph.D., machine learning is used both to learn a suitable representation for a specific classification task and to train the classification models based on the representation. While GP is employed in the first task, the second task is more flexible and can, in principle, employ any machine learning algorithm able to handle vector or graph-based inputs. SVM and GCNNs were selected as representative approaches of these types of algorithms, but during the course of research, others may be investigated as well.

Genetic Programming. GP is inspired by Darwinian evolution and Mendelian genetics and is a population-based search procedure that can evolve solutions to complex problems of different domains [18]. One of the major strengths of GP is its ability to explore large search spaces with a diverse population of free-form individuals and produce potentially readable white-box models, without compromising predictive ability. GP can be easily applied to supervised learning problems, with regression and classification being the most common types [8].

Support Vector Machine. SVM is a kernel method that performs classification tasks by constructing hyperplanes in a multidimensional space that separate cases belonging to different classes. In the last decade, some approaches combining SVM with graph kernels have been proposed, which can be adapted to be used with KGs [20]. More recently, attention has shifted to approaches that use graph embeddings to learn vectorial representations that are then used with SVM [19].

Graph Convolutional Neural Networks. GCNNs are powerful deep neural networks for graph structured data [9]. The "graph convolution" operation applies the same linear transformation to all the neighbors of a node, followed by mean pooling and nonlinearity. By stacking multiple graph convolution layers, GCNNs can learn node representations by using information from distant neighbors [3,5,7,12]. Very recently, relational GCNNs [22] were proposed as a generalization of GCNNs developed for dealing with highly multi-relational data, such as KGs, and were applied to link prediction and entity classification.

3   Problem Statement and Contributions

KGs are a recognized valuable source for background information in many data mining tasks, encoding semantics that describes entities in terms of several semantic aspects (Definition 1) [20].

Many of the existing KG-based approaches use KGs for generating semantic representations (Definition 2) which are used as features in various data mining tasks. These can be considered static semantic representations (Definition 3), since they take equally in consideration all semantic aspects, blind to the fact that some may be irrelevant to the downstream machine learning task, potentially introducing noise. In some applications, such as link prediction, the classification target is encoded in the KG, so this aspect is mitigated. But in applications where the classification target is not encoded in the KG, this is inevitable, since embeddings cannot be trained on the targets. Furthermore, in complex domains, KGs can be quite large and using the whole graph can be time-consuming and cumbersome and employing irrelevant features can negatively impact the performance of machine learning algorithms.

Definition 1. *A **semantic aspect** represents a perspective of the representation of KG entities. It can correspond to a given set of property types or portions of the graph.*

Definition 2. *A semantic representation is a set of features describing a KG entity and obtained by processing the KG.*

Definition 3. *A static semantic representation is a set of features describing a KG entity that are obtained by processing the full KG without additional external input or tailoring to a specific task.*

The guiding hypothesis of this Ph.D. proposal is that GP can learn suitable semantic representations of data objects extracted from KGs optimized towards a specific supervised learning task and without needing to have the target encoded in the KG. Although an analysis of the related work showed that there are no known approaches that use GP to improve semantic representations, preliminary results for semantic similarity kernels [23] encourage this direction of investigation.

The developed approaches will be used to support classification tasks, taking as input a KG and a set of KG entity pairs. The models are trained using external information (not encoded in the KG) about the classification targets for each pair. Many important biomedical tasks can benefit from this work. The detection of biomedical relations between pairs of biological entities has received growing attention recently, with numerous biological and clinical applications including prediction of protein interactions, drug interactions, and gene-disease relationships. High quality predictions in these areas can help target biomedical research into more promising areas. For these reasons, this domain is the main evaluation target for the proposed approaches.

This proposal is organized around three research questions (RQ):

RQ1 Which are the static semantic representations that are more suitable to support supervised learning over KGs?

RQ2 How can GP be applied to adapt semantic representations, improving on the best solutions achieved by domain experts?

RQ3 Are the improved semantic representations useful to bioinformatics applications?

Therefore, the expected contributions (C) of this research are:

C1 A novel GP-based approach to learn suitable semantic representations for KG-based classification tasks;

C2 A novel integration of semantic representations with GCNNs;

C3 An evaluation framework to support the comparative evaluation of expert and machine learning-based semantic representations focusing on bioinformatics classification tasks;

C4 Open source release of all produced software.

4   Research Methodology and Approach

The core of the research will be supported by a framework that integrates semantic representations and machine learning approaches, allowing the comparative evaluation of existing semantic representation approaches for machine learning, as well as the development and evaluation of novel approaches to learn improved semantic representations using GP. The methodology adopted is organized around three tasks that articulate themselves to answer the RQs: construction of static semantic representation (T1), evolving semantic representations (T2), application of evolved semantic representations (T3).

T1: Construction of Static Semantic Representations. This task focuses on two goals: (1) building the framework; and (2) the comparative evaluation of existing approaches for semantic representation. The framework will be composed of two modules: the semantic representation module and the machine learning module. The semantic representation module will comprise three different approaches for semantic representation: graph embeddings, graph kernels, and semantic similarity. The machine learning module will encompass the two targeted supervised learning approaches: SVMs and GCNNs. A comparative evaluation of the three semantic representation approaches combined with the two machine learning algorithms will be conducted using a state-of-the-art benchmark suite of KGs for supervised learning tasks [21].

T2: Evolving Semantic Representations. The main goal of this task is to address RQ2. To do so, it will focus on developing novel approaches based on GP that are able to learn which properties or portions of the graph are more relevant and how to combine them to produce adaptive semantic representations to address a given machine learning task. These novel approaches will focus on two targets: (1) evolving a combination of properties, from which a partial graph can be extracted to support semantic representation methods; (2) evolving a combination of subgraphs that can be employed by semantic representation methods. GP can be seen as a wrapper method, where the fitness function that guides evolution is based on the success of a given combination of semantic representation and machine learning algorithm in a specific task.

The notion behind using both SVMs and GCCNs as the machine learning approaches is to support a comparison between a more classical approach and a deep learning-based one, investigating the impact of dataset size and complexity, as well as the potential contributions of adaptive semantic representations versus static ones. Furthermore, it will also allow a comparison to employing directly GCCNs to learn the semantic representations.

T3: Application of Evolved Semantic Representations. In this task, the novel approaches will be integrated into the framework developed in T2, evaluated using the benchmark datasets, and applied to bioinformatics challenges.

5   Evaluation Plan

The proposed methodology will be evaluated in general-purpose benchmarks and the tasks of protein-protein interaction (PPI) prediction and gene-disease association prediction. Both tasks address RQ3.

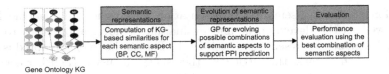

Fig. 1. evoKGsim methodology

Evaluation in General-Purpose Benchmarks. The reference datasets that will be used are presented in [21]. This benchmark suite is comprised of 22 datasets that cover multiple domains (e.g., automotive, geology, common knowledge), range in size from 100 to 4.6 million instances, and support both classification and regression tasks.

Application to Protein-Protein Interaction Prediction. A major challenge in systems biology is the accurate mapping of the interactome, i.e., the set of all PPI within a cell [1]. The developed approaches will be applied to the prediction of PPI, employing the Gene Ontology (GO), the most popular biomedical ontology, and several benchmark datasets [23].

Application to Gene-Disease Association Prediction. The identification of genes responsible for human hereditary diseases can contribute to the improvement of medical care and the understanding of disease mechanisms [11]. In this task, the approaches developed and implemented will be used to predict disease-associated genes using datasets extracted from human disease databases, and KGs covering protein function, biomolecules, and metabolic pathways.

6   Preliminary Results

This PhD project is still in an early stage. So far, investigations have focused on similarity-based semantic representations using GP directly as a classifier. This novel approach, evoKGsim, uses GP to learn suitable combinations of semantic similarity aspects to support the classification of instances modeled as pairs of KG individuals. We evaluate its performance in PPI prediction using the GO as the KG, with its three semantic aspects, molecular function (MF), biological process (BP) and cellular component (CC), and a set of nine benchmark datasets[1]. evoKGsim currently supports two different approaches based on different semantic representations: taxonomic semantic similarity (evoKGsim-SS) calculated using $ResnikMax_{Seco}$ [17] and graph embedding similarity (evoKGsim-ES) calculated as cosine similarity over RDF2Vec embeddings [19]. The models returned by GP are the combinations of the similarity scores of the three GO aspects, evolved to support PPI prediction. An overview of the evoKGsim methodology for PPI prediction is shown in Fig. 1.

We have used five static representations as baselines: the BP, CC and MF single aspects, and the average (Avg) and maximum (Max) of the single aspect

---

[1] These results have been partially published in [23].

scores. The static representations are employed as a simple similarity threshold-based classifier, where a semantic similarity score for a protein pair exceeding a certain threshold predicts a positive interaction. To select the threshold, we applied stratified 10-fold cross-validation, where the training set is used to select the best classification threshold, which is then applied to the test set. This emulates the best choice that a human expert could theoretically select.

Table 1. Median of WAFs with static representations and with evoKGsim using embeddings similarity (evoKGsim-ES) and semantic similarity (evoKGsim-SS). In bold, the best result for each dataset. The median WAF for each baseline is underlined when evoKGsim significantly outperforms the baseline (p-value < 0.01).

Dataset (# interactions)		Static semantic representations					evoKGsim
		BP	CC	MF	Avg	Max	
STRING-EC	ES	0.729	0.806	0.716	0.815	0.813	**0.824**
(2245)	SS	0.667	0.821	0.644	0.815	0.827	**0.861**
STRING-DM	ES	0.809	0.871	0.761	0.872	0.882	**0.891**
(550)	SS	0.908	0.883	0.745	0.910	**0.945**	0.936
BIND-SC	ES	0.760	0.768	0.733	0.801	0.764	**0.803**
(1366)	SS	0.876	0.852	0.779	0.905	0.894	**0.919**
DIP/MIPS-SC	ES	0.787	0.761	0.723	0.801	0.773	**0.811**
(13807)	SS	0.841	0.793	0.701	0.832	0.834	**0.847**
STRING-SC	ES	0.778	0.758	0.695	0.796	0.768	**0.806**
(30384)	SS	0.826	0.788	0.677	0.830	0.824	**0.844**
DIP-HS	ES	0.698	0.577	0.632	0.643	0.659	**0.705**
(2739)	SS	0.877	0.818	0.755	0.876	0.859	**0.894**
STRING-HS	ES	0.766	0.712	0.679	0.756	0.743	**0.782**
(6912)	SS	0.853	0.763	0.722	0.851	0.814	**0.873**
GRID/HPRD-unbal-HS	ES	0.607	0.560	0.567	0.601	0.594	**0.613**
(31320)	SS	0.715	0.677	0.662	0.731	0.706	**0.738**
GRID/HPRD-bal-HS	ES	0.639	0.617	0.599	**0.663**	0.641	**0.663**
(31349)	SS	0.653	0.602	0.598	0.654	0.641	**0.658**
Average on all datasets	ES	0.730	0.714	0.678	0.750	0.737	0.766
	SS	0.802	0.777	0.698	0.823	0.816	0.841

Table 1 presents the results obtained when using the graph embeddings similarity representation (evoKGsim-ES) and the semantic similarity representation (evoKGsim-SS). For evaluating the quality of a predicted classification, we use the weighted average of F-measures (WAF) for stratified 10-fold cross-validation. Statistical significance of the results was determined using pairwise non-parametric Kruskal-Wallis tests [2] at $p < 0.01$. The results indicate that the performance of evoKGsim is always better than the static baselines, except against SS Max for STRING-DM (and against ES Avg for GRID/HPRD-bal-HS, with equal performance). These results are especially relevant when we recall that the baselines were built to emulate a domain expert using an optimal threshold selection. When comparing evolved semantic representations, evoKGsim-SS achieves a better performance than evoKGsim-ES in all datasets except GRID/HPRD-bal-HS. Since the SS representation is limited to the taxonomic relations within the ontology, whereas ES takes into account all types of relations, the ES representations could, in principle, be more informative. However, they do not take into account the specificity of annotations, which can hinder their ability to estimate similarity more accurately.

These results are a first step towards answering our research questions and may be used as a starting point for extending to other semantic representations and classification problems.

7   Conclusions and Lessons Learned

This Ph.D. project aims to develop novel GP-based approaches that can learn suitable semantic representations based on KGs to support supervised learning. Until now, I have developed a methodology that employs GP to evolve similarity-based semantic representations for KGs. The work to follow includes integrating machine learning algorithms and extending the approach to other semantic representations. To do so, some challenges will need to be overcome. First, machine learning algorithms such as SVM and CNNs, are usually suitable for problems with a significant number of features. This needs to be considered to ensure a fair comparison between feature-rich representations such as embeddings and the simpler similarity-based representations. Second, for semantic representations like graph embeddings, the embeddings themselves can be evolved. This may prove challenging since existing GP implementations are unable to handle vectors as a single data item.

Acknowledgements. I would like to thank my Ph.D. supervisors, Prof. Catia Pesquita and Prof. Sara Silva, for their valuable feedback and support in the realization of this work. This research has been supported by the Fundação para a Ciência e a Tecnologia through the LASIGE Research Unit, UIDB/00408/2020 and UIDP/00408/ 2020, the PhD grant SFRH/BD/145377/2019, and the projects DSAIPA/DS/0022/ 2018, PTDC/CCI-CIF/29877/2017, PTDC/CCI-INF/29168/ 2017, PTDC/EEI-ESS/ 4633/2014.

References

1. Bandyopadhyay, S., Mallick, K.: A new feature vector based on gene ontology terms for protein-protein interaction prediction. IEEE/ACM Trans. Comput. Biol. Bioinform. **14**(4), 762–770 (2017)
2. Breslow, N.: A generalized Kruskal-Wallis test for comparing K samples subject to unequal patterns of censorship. Biometrika **57**(3), 579–594 (1970)

3. Bruna Estrach, J., Zaremba, W., Szlam, A., LeCun, Y.: Spectral networks and deep locally connected networks on graphs. In: 2nd International Conference on Learning Representations (2014)

4. Cai, H., Zheng, V.W., Chang, K.C.: A comprehensive survey of graph embedding: problems, techniques, and applications. IEEE Trans. Knowl. Data Eng. **30**(9), 1616–1637 (2018)

5. Defferrard, M., Bresson, X., Vandergheynst, P.: Convolutional neural networks on graphs with fast localized spectral filtering. In: Proceedings of the 30th International Conference on Neural Information Processing Systems, p. 3844–3852 (2016)

6. Dumais, S.T.: Latent semantic analysis. Annu. Rev. Inf. Sci. Technol. **38**(1), 188–230 (2004)

7. Duvenaud, D., et al.: Convolutional networks on graphs for learning molecular fingerprints. In: Proceedings of the 28th International Conference on Neural Information Processing Systems, pp. 2224–2232 (2015)

8. Gandomi, A.H., Alavi, A.H., Ryan, C. (eds.): Handbook of Genetic Programming Applications, 1st edn. Springer, Cham (2015). https://doi.org/10.1007/978-3-319-20883-1

9. Gu, J., et al.: Recent advances in convolutional neural networks. Pattern Recogn. **77**(C), 354–377 (2018)

10. Harispe, S., Ranwez, S., Janaqi, S., Montmain, J.: Semantic Similarity from Natural Language and Ontology Analysis. Morgan & Claypool Publishers, San Rafael (2015)

11. Jimenez-Sanchez, G., Childs, B., Valle, D.: Human disease genes. Nature **409**(6822), 853–855 (2001)

12. Kipf, T.N., Welling, M.: Semi-supervised classification with graph convolutional networks. CoRR abs/1609.02907 (2016)

13. Kriege, N.M., Johansson, F.D., Morris, C.: A survey on graph kernels. Appl. Netw. Sci. **5**(1), 1–42 (2019). https://doi.org/10.1007/s41109-019-0195-3

14. Liu, H., Gegov, A., Cocea, M.: Rule-based systems: a granular computing perspective. Granul. Comput. **1**(4), 259–274 (2016). https://doi.org/10.1007/s41066-016-0021-6

15. Mikolov, T., Chen, K., Corrado, G., Dean, J.: Efficient estimation of word representations in vector space. arXiv preprint arXiv:1301.3781 (2013)

16. Pennington, J., Socher, R., Manning, C.: Glove: global vectors for word representation. In: Proceedings of the 2014 Conference on Empirical Methods in Natural Language Processing, pp. 1532–1543 (2014)

17. Pesquita, C., Faria, D., Falcao, A.O., Lord, P., Couto, F.M.: Semantic similarity in biomedical ontologies. PLoS Comput. Biol. **5**(7), e1000443 (2009)

18. Poli, R., Langdon, W.B., McPhee, N.F., Koza, J.R.: A field guide to genetic programming (2008). Published via http://lulu.com and freely available at http://www.gp-field-guide.org.uk

19. Ristoski, P., Paulheim, H.: RDF2Vec: RDF graph embeddings for data mining. In: Groth, P., et al. (eds.) ISWC 2016. LNCS, vol. 9981, pp. 498–514. Springer, Cham (2016). https://doi.org/10.1007/978-3-319-46523-4_30

20. Ristoski, P., Paulheim, H.: Semantic web in data mining and knowledge discovery. Web Semant. **36**(C), 1–22 (2016)

21. Ristoski, P., de Vries, G.K.D., Paulheim, H.: A collection of benchmark datasets for systematic evaluations of machine learning on the semantic web. In: Groth, P., et al. (eds.) ISWC 2016. LNCS, vol. 9982, pp. 186–194. Springer, Cham (2016). https://doi.org/10.1007/978-3-319-46547-0_20

22. Schlichtkrull, M., Kipf, T.N., Bloem, P., van den Berg, R., Titov, I., Welling, M.: Modeling relational data with graph convolutional networks. In: Gangemi, A., et al. (eds.) ESWC 2018. LNCS, vol. 10843, pp. 593–607. Springer, Cham (2018). https://doi.org/10.1007/978-3-319-93417-4_38
23. Sousa, R.T., Silva, S., Pesquita, C.: Evolving knowledge graph similarity for supervised learning in complex biomedical domains. BMC Bioinform. 21(1), 6 (2020)
24. Zhu, G., Iglesias, C.A.: Computing semantic similarity of concepts in knowledge graphs. IEEE Trans. Knowl. Data Eng. 29(1), 72–85 (2017)

Industry Track Papers

Knowledge Graph-Based Legal Search over German Court Cases

Ademar Crotti Junior[1]([⊠]) [ID], Fabrizio Orlandi[1] [ID], Damien Graux[1] [ID],
Murhaf Hossari[1], Declan O'Sullivan[1] [ID], Christian Hartz[2],
and Christian Dirschl[2]

[1] ADAPT SFI Research Centre, Dublin, Ireland
{ademar.crotti,fabrizio.orlandi,damien.graux,
murhaf.hossari,declan.osullivan}@adaptcentre.ie
[2] Wolters Kluwer Deutschland GmbH, Cologne, Munich, Germany
{christian.hartz,christian.dirschl}@wolterskluwer.com

Abstract. The information contained in legal information systems are often accessed through simple keyword interfaces and presented as a simple list of hits. In order to improve search accuracy one may avail of knowledge graphs, where the semantics of the data can be made explicit. This article reports on challenges encountered and achievements made during the development of a knowledge graph-based search engine designed for German court case data at Wolters Kluwer Germany.

1 Introduction

The body of law to which citizens and businesses have to adhere is constantly increasing in volume and complexity [1]. Such information is usually provided by unstructured text within legal documents, for which various solutions have been developed to enable search (based *e.g.* on natural language processing [10] or on structure extraction [8]) and browsing capabilities (using solutions from question-answering systems [3] to multi-facet exploration tool [9]) on large legal corpora. Nonetheless, existing systems usually provide limited keyword-based search interfaces displaying results as a simple list of hits [6]. This makes the process of information retrieval time consuming and inefficient, especially when dealing with large amounts of information [11]. Moreover, the usefulness of such information varies widely and depends on its structure and its representation (see [2] for a classification of 23 legal ontologies). Even though the information is available, users and legal professionals may find the exploration of legal information problematic when interested in specific circumstances or investigating a particular case.

In this context, ADAPT[1] and Wolters Kluwer Germany[2] (WKD) joined forces. Through the years, WKD built a very large dataset containing about a million German language XML-based legal documents. A detailed taxonomy, which

---

[1] A leading centre developing Linked Data solutions. https://www.adaptcentre.ie/.
[2] A leading knowledge provider in the legal domain. https://wolterskluwer.com/.

© Springer Nature Switzerland AG 2020
A. Harth et al. (Eds.): ESWC 2020 Satellite Events, LNCS 12124, pp. 293–297, 2020.
https://doi.org/10.1007/978-3-030-62327-2_44

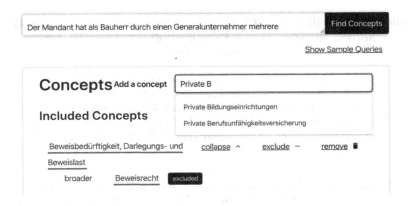

Fig. 1. Search engine user interface.

is associated with their court case dataset, has also been developed by WKD to structure these XML files. The XML format, however, restricts data analysis capabilities by keeping implicit the relationships between concepts and text fragments within legal documents. From these documents, the two partners built together a German-based legal knowledge graph (KG) [4] focusing their efforts on improving the search accuracy and the enrichment opportunities that interlinking features underpinning the Semantic Web approach brings. This paper reports on the search system that was developed leveraging this new KG approach.

2   Enabling Semantic Search over German Court Cases

The starting point of this project was a dataset of about one million documents, in German, containing information about legal court cases in Germany that has been built by WKD over the past decades. A taxonomy covering legal concepts was also developed by WKD's experts to provide structure to the information contained in their dataset. The Simple Knowledge Organization System (SKOS)[3] vocabulary is used to describe legal concepts and their relations in this taxonomy. In WKD's taxonomy, each legal concept is represented as an instance of `skos:Concept`, with their relationships being expressed through the properties `skos:narrower` and `skos:broader`.

---

[3] SKOS is a W3C Recommendation designed for representation of thesauri, classification schemes, taxonomies, subject-heading systems, or any other type of structured controlled vocabulary. https://www.w3.org/TR/skos-reference/.

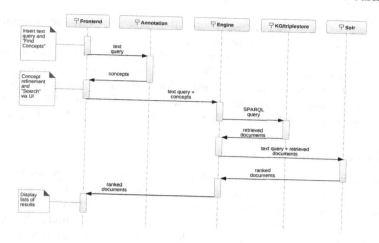

Fig. 2. Sequence diagram for the proposed search engine.

2.1   Challenges

The first challenge has been to annotate and take into account the preexisting structure of such a large, domain-specific, corpus of legal text, in order to build the knowledge graph. Secondly, extensive effort has been invested into capturing the requirements that needed to be featured in the developed engine, working in close collaboration with legal experts. Finally, close collaboration with German end-users has been undertaken in order to evaluate the accuracy of the results achieved and the value created for the business. Keeping in mind that the new search system was bound not to revolutionise the preexisting search experience of the legal experts, typically based on traditional keyword based search.

2.2   Data Processing Pipeline

The main input of our data pipeline, and the search engine itself, is the WKD legal text corpus. The legal documents were originally stored as XML files with complex schema. The first step of our data pipeline aimed at segmenting these legal documents into smaller and logically coherent fragments, following a specifically developed ontology. Further, an automatic annotation tool was developed to leverage WKD's taxonomy of legal concepts, and applied to the generated fragments. The annotation of taxonomy concepts expresses the connection between legal documents and textual pieces of supporting evidence - the fragments - within and across different documents. These documents are then used to generate two artefacts: the knowledge graph, which is later stored into an RDF triple store; and a Solr[4] index which is later used to support the ranking of documents to be retrieved by the search engine (see Sect. 2.3). RML [5] mappings were used for the semantic uplift phase. We chose to use mapping languages for allowing

---

[4] https://lucene.apache.org/solr/.

mapping definitions to be expressed separately from the implementations that execute them. The use of declarative mappings facilitate the reuse and maintenance of mappings, where changes in the semantic model or in the input data only require mapping definitions to be updated accordingly, without the need for adjustments in the engine responsible for the generation of the KG. The semantic model used to represent the legal documents from WKD's dataset, as well as the semantic uplift process, have been described in details in [4].

2.3 Search Engine

Once the knowledge graph is generated, the search engine operates by transforming a query written in legal German (typically describing court case facts) into taxonomy concepts, before matching them against the structured annotated documents in the KG. A user interface (Fig. 1) renders the automatically matched concepts and allows users to manually add, or remove, relevant concepts to the query. The UI supports users in navigating the hierarchy of the legal taxonomy concepts and refining their search query. The identified concepts are then used to query the KG, directly using SPARQL [7]. The SPARQL query matches annotated documents and fragments in the KG with the query concepts. It also ranks the retrieved documents by assigning more weight to those annotated with more specific concepts (*i.e.* narrower concepts in the taxonomy). In order to improve the ranking of the documents, the documents retrieved using SPARQL are then re-ranked using Solr. Figure 2 illustrates a sequence diagram for the KG based search engine, while the UI is in Fig. 1. As a result, the Semantic Web powered architecture allows experts to explore further a legal knowledge base, offering an interactive and transparent concept-based search as an alternative to the conventional "black-box" approach which relies on pure text-search engines.

3 Conclusions

This paper presents ongoing efforts towards the development of a knowledge graph-based search system for the legal domain. Despite the challenges, mainly due to the complexity of the domain, this novel design provides WKD's end-users with a transparent search experience occurring at the legal concept level. Moreover, the Semantic Web standards and technologies unlock new possibilities for future developments, allowing cutting edge features such as data interlinking and logical inferring of knowledge. Furthermore, the engine could benefit from the latest findings in the area of statistical relational learning, paving the way for new applications. Finally, we believe our approach, not only could save end-users' time, but above all offers their companies new ranges of information and ways of exploration.

Acknowledgments. This paper was supported by Wolters Kluwer Germany, Science Foundation Ireland (Grant 13/RC/2106) and EDGE Marie Skłodowska-Curie grant agreement No. 713567, as part of the ADAPT Centre for Digital Content Technology (http://www.adaptcentre.ie/) at Trinity College Dublin.

References

1. Boella, G., Caro, L.D., Humphreys, L., Robaldo, L., Rossi, P., van der Torre, L.: Eunomos, a legal document and knowledge management system for the web to provide relevant, reliable and up-to-date information on the law. Artif. Intell. Law **24**(3), 245–283 (2016)

2. Breuker, J., Casanovas, P., Klein, M.C., Francesconi, E.: The flood, the channels, and the dykes: managing legal information a globalized and digital world. Law, ontologies and the semantic web channeling the legal informational flood, pp. 0199–220 (2009)

3. Collarana, D., et al.: A question answering system on regulatory documents. In: JURIX, pp. 41–50 (2018)

4. Crotti Junior, A., Orlandi, F., O'Sullivan, D., Dirschl, C., Reul, Q.: Using mapping languages for building legal knowledge graphs from XML files. In: Workshop on Contextualized Knowledge Graphs Co-located with the 18th International Semantic Web Conference (ISWC) (2019)

5. Dimou, A., Vander Sande, M., Colpaert, P., Verborgh, R., Mannens, E., Van de Walle, R.: RML: a generic language for integrated RDF mappings of heterogeneous data. In: Proceedings of the 7th LDoW Workshop at WWW (2014)

6. Filtz, E.: Building and processing a knowledge-graph for legal data. In: Blomqvist, E., Maynard, D., Gangemi, A., Hoekstra, R., Hitzler, P., Hartig, O. (eds.) ESWC 2017. LNCS, vol. 10250, pp. 184–194. Springer, Cham (2017). https://doi.org/10.1007/978-3-319-58451-5_13

7. Harris, S., Seaborne, A., Prud'hommeaux, E.: SPARQL 1.1 query language. W3C Recomm. **21**(10) (2013)

8. Koniaris, M., Papastefanatos, G., Vassiliou, Y.: Towards automatic structuring and semantic indexing of legal documents. In: Proceedings of the 20th Pan-Hellenic Conference on Informatics, pp. 1–6 (2016)

9. Lee, S., Kim, P., Seo, D., Kim, J., Lee, J., Jung, H., Dirschl, C.: Multi-faceted navigation of legal documents. In: 2011 International Conference on Internet of Things and 4th International Conference on Cyber, Physical and Social Computing, pp. 537–540. IEEE (2011)

10. Nejad, N.M., Jabat, P., Nedelchev, R., Scerri, S., Graux, D.: Establishing a strong baseline for privacy policy classification. In: IFIP International Conference on ICT Systems Security and Privacy Protection (2020)

11. Schweighofer, E.: Semantic indexing of legal documents. In: Francesconi, E., Montemagni, S., Peters, W., Tiscornia, D. (eds.) Semantic Processing of Legal Texts. LNCS (LNAI), vol. 6036, pp. 157–169. Springer, Heidelberg (2010). https://doi.org/10.1007/978-3-642-12837-0_9

Enabling Digital Business Transformation Through an Enterprise Knowledge Graph

Christian Dirschl[1(✉)], Jessica Kent[2(✉)], Jamie Schram[2(✉)], and Quentin Reul[2(✉)]

[1] Wolters Kluwer Deutschland GmbH, Cologne, Germany
Christian.Dirschl@wolterskluwer.com
[2] Wolters Kluwer R&D U.S. LP, Riverwoods, USA
{Jessica.Kent,Jamie.Schram,Quentin.Reul}@wolterskluwer.com

1 Overview

Wolters Kluwer (WK) is a global provider of information, software and services for legal, tax, accounting, health, and risk and compliance professionals. WK's strategy [1] involves continuous innovation and expansion of expert solutions, including extensive use of domain knowledge, increasingly represented in the WK Knowledge Graph (KG).

KGs are a flexible knowledge representation paradigm intended to facilitate the processing of knowledge for both humans and machines. They are based on standard Semantic Web technologies and are widely regarded as a key enabler for several increasingly popular use cases, including Web search, question answering, personal assistants and enabling other AI-based applications across most industry sectors, including the legal market.

KGs are quite often generic, fragmented and incomplete, which limits their usage and coverage potential. In an industrial environment, knowledge models like KGs, controlled vocabularies and thesauri need to be combined from heterogeneous sources, mainly via mapping mechanisms. Creating an enterprise KG requires a lot of intellectual and manual knowledge work in order to end up with a scalable and sustainable result.

2 Challenges

An informed KG supports and acts as a central hub for the following four legal industry use cases (as well as many others). First, easy access to legal information across countries and languages to enhance international business efforts, e.g. in global sectors like energy, pharma or for all companies working in jurisdictions that are influenced/dominated by several jurisdictions like in the EU.

Second, better integration with standard-based legal information tools and services (e.g. EUR-LEX [2]) to accelerate LegalTech coverage, which brings added value to both companies and citizens.

Third, open (legal) data integration to enhance legal business with governmental agencies, many of which already use open data standards like EUROVOC [3].

And finally, extending legal information services to other business-oriented applications and services. For example, by adding geo information via geonames [4] to courts,

© Springer Nature Switzerland AG 2020
A. Harth et al. (Eds.): ESWC 2020 Satellite Events, LNCS 12124, pp. 298–302, 2020.
https://doi.org/10.1007/978-3-030-62327-2_45

one could start socioeconomic analysis of coverage of legal advice with respect to demographics, economics and political federal structures. As per linked data principles, this could enable insights for administrations as well as for business that would otherwise not be possible.

Addressing these use cases supports WK's strategic goal to heavily expand expert solutions, like WK Germany's CaseWorx application [5], as a core means for digital business transformation [6].

The main advantages of KGs, which are their flexibility and their ability to easily aggregate large chunks of data, are also one of their main unsolved problem areas when it comes to the scalability of data. This means that it is difficult to have the information available in an easy, secure, reliable and fast way. The major challenges here are:

- Easy selection of data required in a specific project setting, e.g. better handling of multi-graph environments.
- Specific implementation of and access to universal entities that are useful in most usage contexts.
- Fast and reliable access to de-centralized KGs, both run by external as well as internal knowledge teams.
- Efficient way to query triples beyond standard SPARQL interfaces, e.g. by normalized JSON-LD usage for JSON parsers.

Flexibility also leads to the situation where the KG lacks sustainability, because a growing KG has the strong tendency to add complexity, knowledge gaps, contradictions and semantic drift over time. The major challenges here are:

- Effective data curation, including incremental updates from external sources, in order to keep the resulting KG up to date and consistent over time.
- Visualization of KG assets, so that its benefits can be made transparent to IT and business professionals. This helps to increase the usage of the KG in the end and therefore also its sustainability as part of the company's knowledge backbone.
- Creation and availability of specific domain schemas, acting as quasi-industry standards (e.g. for the construction domain within CaseWorx).
- Tools for disambiguation, e.g. company names. This requires both recognition of duplicates as well as an easy and transparent resolution.

All these challenges can and should be supported by (semi-) automated processes with high levels of insight and explanatory power, so that business-critical tasks can be leveraged by these technologies in an efficient manner.

3 Approach

The creation of a unified enterprise KG requires several components. First, unified KGs rely heavily on the adoption of a common terminology/ontology to represent the nodes and their relationships in the graph. This is, for WK, a natural use of the already existing enterprise ontology, which is both WK-specific and makes use of widely adopted external ontologies (such as SKOS, Dublin Core, FOAF, etc.). This enables easy mapping and technology usage: for example, only minor extensions were necessary for CaseWorx (e.g. adding domain-specific properties such as "hasDefect" which models specific facts relevant to the construction domain).

Second, there need to be requirements for sources that will be used, whether they are fragmented KGs or other structured or unstructured data. The requirements that were determined to be the most important in evaluating data sources were inspired by ISO 25012 [7] and research papers on data standards (for example, "Quality Assessment for Linked Data" [8] and "Data Quality Assessment" [9]). A sample of the evaluation criteria is as follows:

- Accuracy/Reliability
  - Clear ownership – the author/website is well regarded
  - The data is commonly used
  - Data does not seem to be incorrect or inconsistent

- Relevance
  - Data or a subset of the data is specifically for the area of interest (for WK, the data is for legal, tax and accounting, or medical)
  - The data is universally useful (e.g. ISO 3166, ISO 639)

- Currency
  - Clear dates of creation/update
  - The data is updated regularly
  - The data was updated within the last 3 years (the more recent the better)

- Licensing
  - License/copyright information is easily accessible
  - License allows for commercial use
  - License is not a "share alike" license

There are several more points of evaluation WK employs which aid in our ability to quickly, accurately, and consistently determine whether to use a source. Because there is a wide variety of data in a wide variety of states, WK's evaluation criteria makes use of the MoSCoW Method [10].

Third, technology with which to build and maintain the KG must be determined. WK uses a triple store, knowledge management software, and creates programmatic transformations which support the whole Linked Data lifecycle [11]:

- Knowledge Management: Cogito Studio Express [12], PoolParty [13], VocBench [14]
- KG storage: AllegroGraph [15]
- Programmatic Transformations (proprietary and easily added to project pipelines): Conversion Services (including a program to convert Excel); Data Clean-up (removal/integration of duplicate entries, creation of persistent URIs, etc.), etc.

WK jump-started populating the KG by first adding shared controlled vocabularies/taxonomies/thesauri that are already consistently used throughout WK products. Then, outside sources (fragmented KGs, linked data, etc.), such as government websites, shared standard vocabularies like ISO, NAICS, medical codes, and generic knowledge graphs, e.g. Wikidata, were mapped to WK's enterprise ontology and added to the KG.

Once the original mapping is completed, the process of populating the KG from a specific source can be automated and replicated, keeping the KG current and relevant.

Finally, the ability to allow for semi-open contribution in a standardized process is necessary for sustainability.

When these pieces are in place, the enterprise KG will be scalable and sustainable. WK is experienced in using Semantic Web assets and was therefore able to make use of available standards, technology, and the ongoing advocacy of contribution to/use of Semantic Web technologies already implemented in operational WK processes [16].

4 Evaluation and Lessons Learned

The approach taken is working so far. Easy inclusion of multiple sources and languages as well as acceptance and usage within the company is encouraging. However, challenges still lie in the implementation of an efficient and sustainable maintenance process. Another challenge is addressing flaws within parts of the technology used. Semantic Web Technology has made a lot of progress; however, the contextualization and usage of data are still major challenges. For example, the contextualization of CaseWorx requires disambiguation (e.g. company names) and semantic integration (e.g. each mandate is represented as a subgraph within CaseWorx; building different views on top of KGs). Both aspects are aided by the enterprise KG, but there is still work that needs to be done. Similarly, data usage is a major concern for CaseWorx as public ontologies are still very generic and may have licensing or governance issues and need to comply with customer privacy needs (e.g. each customer only sees his own data). Licensing is very important, since many open sources are only available under a ShareAlike copyright [17], which prevents real business usage. Dual licensing models would be highly appreciated.

We recommend adhering to the following basic rules: a) use either stable vocabularies or mature vocabularies with associated governance and documented maintenance processes; b) establish clear rules for KG integration beyond being mapped to the ontology; c) use Named Graphs to make maintenance easier.

5 Conclusion and Future Work

KGs have the potential to support and enable WK's strategic goals. Already existing fragments are available for general usage (e.g. within CaseWorx), and first extensions have been made. Use case and business impact analysis is on its way. We are currently adding new sub-graphs and are working towards sustainable mapping mechanisms with stable and scalable maintenance and development processes in the existing WK ecosystem. Further collaboration with the scientific community is needed.

References

1. Wolters Kluwer Homepage. https://wolterskluwer.com/company/about-us/strategy.html. Accessed 04 Mar 2020
2. EUR-LEX Homepage. https://eur-lex.europa.eu/. Accessed 30 Apr 2020
3. EUROVOC Homepage. https://eur-lex.europa.eu/browse/eurovoc.html. Accessed 30 Apr 2020
4. CaseWorx Homepage. https://www.caseworx-baurecht.de/. Accessed 30 Apr 2020
5. Geonames Homepage. https://www.geonames.org/. Accessed 30 Apr 2020
6. Pellegrini, T., Dirschl, C., Eck, K.: Linked data business cube: a systematic approach to semantic web business models. In: AcademicMindTrek '14 Proceedings of the 18th International Academic MindTrek Conference: Media Business, Management, Content & Services, pp 132–141. ACM (2014)
7. ISO/IEC 25012:2008 page. https://www.iso.org/standard/35736.html. Accessed 30 Apr 2020
8. Zaveri, A., Rula, A., Maurino, A., Pietrobon, R., Lehmann, J., Auer, S.: Quality assessment for linked data: a survey. Semant. Web 7(1), 63–93 (2015). https://doi.org/10.3233/sw-150175
9. Pipino, L.L., Lee, Y.W., Wang, R.Y.: Data quality assessment. Commun. ACM 45, 211–218 (2002)
10. Wikipedia page: "Moscow Method". https://en.wikipedia.org/wiki/MoSCoW_method. Accessed 30 Apr 2020
11. Auer, S., et al.: Managing the life-cycle of linked data with the LOD2 stack. In: Cudré-Mauroux, P., et al. (eds.) ISWC 2012. LNCS, vol. 7650, pp. 1–16. Springer, Heidelberg (2012). https://doi.org/10.1007/978-3-642-35173-0_1
12. Cogito Studio Homepage, https://expertsystem.com/products/cogito-studio/. Accessed 30 Apr 2020
13. PoolParty Semantic Suite Homepage. https://www.poolparty.biz/. Accessed 30 Apr 2020
14. VocBench Homepage. http://vocbench.uniroma2.it/. Accessed 30 Apr 2020
15. Allegrograph Homepage. https://franz.com/agraph/allegrograph/. Accessed 30 Apr 2020
16. Hondros, C.: http://linkeddatadeveloper.com/Projects/Linking-Enterprise-Data/Manuscript/led-hondros.html. Accessed 30 Apr 2020
17. Creative Commons Homepage. https://creativecommons.org/licenses/by-sa/2.5/. Accessed 30 Apr 2020

Enabling FAIR Clinical Data Standards with Linked Data

Javier D. Fernández[✉], Nelia Lasierra, Didier Clement, Huw Mason,
and Ivan Robinson

Medical Data and Information Solutions, F. Hoffmann-La Roche, Basel, Switzerland
{javier_d.fernandez,nelia.lasierra,didier.clement,huw.mason,
ivan.robinson}@roche.com

Abstract. This article reports on our efforts to support FAIR Clinical Data Standards with Semantic Web technologies, including the challenge of bridging the gap for non-technical users.

1 Introduction

The biopharmaceutical industry is traditionally led by strict (clinical) standards to regulate how clinical trial data are collected, tabulated, analyzed, and finally submitted to regulatory authorities. However, with the advent of the data deluge era, adherence to data standards not only ensures data will meet regulatory expectations, but it can also spark and fuel scientific insights when mastering well-curated, integrated, and complex data.

In this context, the novel concepts of FAIR data [3], and the corresponding FAIRification processes play a crucial role. FAIR provides guidelines to improve the findability, accessibility, interoperability, and reuse of digital assets. FAIR emphasises machine-actionability and data-driven processes to deal with the current increase in volume, complexity, and creation speed of data. The biopharmaceutical industry and academia have rapidly embraced these principles to improve its efficiency [4]. Proof of that is the collaboration emerging within the non-profit Pistoia Alliance[1], that pursuits these efforts.

The Roche Global Data Standards Repository (GDSR) is a system that stores and retrieves selected data for different information domains in the Roche product development system landscape. Although GDSR does not restrict the domain of the data, the main source of information has traditionally been Clinical Global Data Standards (GDS), aligned with CDISC[2] standards.

In the following, we show how GDSR adheres to FAIR principles thanks to the underlying Linked Data technology, and how these concepts are brought to non-technical users.

---

[1] http://www.pistoiaalliance.org.
[2] https://www.cdisc.org/.

A. Harth et al. (Eds.): ESWC 2020 Satellite Events, LNCS 12124, pp. 303–306, 2020.
https://doi.org/10.1007/978-3-030-62327-2_46

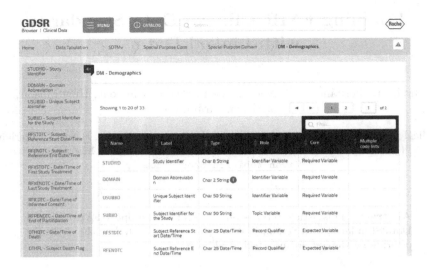

Fig. 1. The GDSR UI to browse Linked Data by non-technical users.

2 Enabling FAIR Clinical Data Standards

GDSR includes all the required standards (and extensions) to ensure consistency across our clinical trials. These standards are kept in GDSR in semantic graphs: clinical data standards are modeled as OWL/RDF ontologies and vocabularies, conforming a knowledge graph for (meta) data assets, which ensure common understanding and facilitates integration and sharing. In the following, we describe how GDSR supports FAIR principles.

2.1 Findable

Following Linked Data, each concept in GDSR is identified and can be referenced using URIs, e.g. http://gdsr.roche.com/instrument-lab#Analyte.ADIPOCYTE. The semantic data are indexed in a triplestore to support searching capabilities via a human-friendly GDSR browser for non-technical users (see Fig. 1), or through pre-defined SPARQL queries. In turn, metadata about the standards is provided by a summary catalog (see Fig. 2a), together with diverse predefined human-readable reports. We also make intensive use of RDF versioning, so URIs can be found across any of the GDSR archives where it is present. To do so, we implement a independent copy approach [1], maintaining the full copy of the data in different time snapshots, called publications. In each publication cycle, the new, updated, and retired data standards are made available to users and the previous publication is moved to an accessible archive (see Fig. 2b).

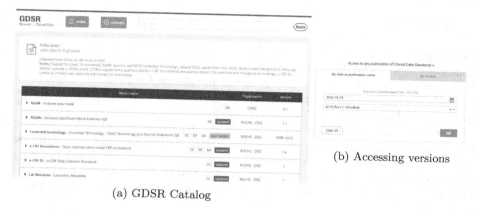

(a) GDSR Catalog

(b) Accessing versions

Fig. 2. GDSR catalog and access to different (graph) versions in the GDSR UI.

2.2 Accessible

Besides the aforementioned GDSR browser, GDSR leverages Linked Data to make content available through a public REST API, which is also bundled in an R package, called rGDSR, to access the information programmatically. This allows non-semantic web experts to still access the full data standard catalog programmatically and to create automated processes. In particular, rGDSR is used to maximize the use of data standards and terminologies in clinical studies during study design, as well as to detect potential deviation to standards in the study. It is worth noting that, due to the aforementioned gap, only technical users have direct access to the internal SPARQL endpoint while results of pre-defined SPARQL queries are served to all users.

2.3 Interoperable

Using Linked Data, GDSR supports the sharing and use of metadata with other semantic technologies and systems across Roche, such as the Roche Terminology System (RTS) [2]. In addition, GDSR links to external datasets such as CDISC ontologies, enabling the exploration of connected vocabularies. In fact, our ongoing work focuses on leveraging federated SPARQL queries to access and combine data available in multiple and disparate semantic systems at Roche, enabling seamless access across that ecosystem.

2.4 Reusable

Clinical data standards stored in the GDSR as Linked Data are accessible and valid globally and across molecules, study phases and therapeutic areas. We make use of the PROV-O ontology for managing changes in the Knowledge Graph from one publication to another, including the change description, owner and responsible entities. This information is also presented in a human-friendly version and via the aforementioned REST API to bridge the gap for non-technical users.

3   Conclusions

The biopharmaceutical industry, and Roche in particular, is embracing the FAIR principles to improve data-driven efficiency, leading to novel findings and faster filings, which means faster access to novel medicines for patients. This work shows how FAIR principles are translated to clinical data standard management in practice, thanks to Linked Data technologies.

Our ongoing work regards the challenge of authoring and managing existing clinical data standards, in the form of Linked Data, by non-semantic web experts. Thus, we are working on a visual editor to facilitate this task while still assuring the expected quality and conformance of the standards. To do so, we plan to leverage the SHACL W3C standard to represent and enforce key quality aspects of the data.

Acknowledgment. This work was been possible thanks to the support of the DAAV Information Architects, the GDSR dev team and the RGITSC Custom Apps team.

References

1. Fernández, J.D., Umbrich, J., Polleres, A., Knuth, M.: Evaluating query and storage strategies for RDF archives. Semant. Web **10**(2), 247–291 (2019)
2. Thalhammer, A., Romacker, M., Rupp, J.: Semantic terminology management for applications: contextualized SKOS-XL. In: Proceedings of the International Semantic Web Conference (ISWC) Posters, Demos & Industry Tracks (2017). http://ceur-ws.org/Vol-1963/paper477.pdf
3. Wilkinson, M.D., et al.: The FAIR guiding principles for scientific data management and stewardship. Sci. Data **3**, 1–9 (2016)
4. Wise, J., et al.: Implementation and relevance of FAIR data principles in biopharmaceutical R&D. Drug Discov. Today **24**(4), 933–938 (2019)

Semantic Data Integration for the SMT Manufacturing Process Using SANSA Stack

Mohamed Nadjib Mami[1]($^{(\boxtimes)}$) , Irlán Grangel-González[2] , Damien Graux[1,3] , Enkeleda Elezi[1], and Felix Lösch[2]

[1] IAIS, Fraunhofer Gesellschaft, Munich, Germany
{mami,s6enelez}@cs.uni-bonn.de
[2] Bosch Corporate Research, Renningen, Germany
{irlan.grangelgonzalez,felix.loesch}@de.bosch.com
[3] ADAPT Centre, Trinity College Dublin, Dublin, Ireland
damien.graux@adaptcentre.ie

Abstract. In this article, we report on our successful integration of Semantic Web techniques in a large Industry 4.0 context. We deploy the SANSA Stack to enable the uniform access to Surface-Mount Technology (SMT) data. An ergonomic visual user interface is proposed to help non-technical users coping with the various concepts underlying the process and conveniently interacting with the data.

1 Introduction

Semantic Data Integration is one of the prominent applications of Semantic technologies whose value has been showcased in a lot of use cases in Industry 4.0 [2,4]. Schemata of the data are mapped to high-level ontologies using so-called mapping languages. This allows to build a general schema against which queries can be posed uniformly using SPARQL query language [3]. Using this schema, semantic conflicts are resolved and data can be queried on-the-fly without requiring the conversion of the full data to RDF: a data model representing the world in triples (subject, property, objects) *e.g.*, (:*machine153, msmt:smdMachineName,* "*ABD3*"), where *msmt* is the ontology in which *smdMachineName* is defined. This project is an application of these techniques in an industrial application for accessing Surface Mount Technology (SMT) data.

Technically, SMT is a process for mounting electronic components, *e.g.*, microchips, resistors, or capacitors on printed-circuit boards. Several subprocesses are involved in producing these boards and are executed by specialized machines. In particular, we focus this effort on the Surface Mount Devices (SMD) and the Automatic Optical Inspection (AOI). The SMD places the electronic components on top of the printed-circuit boards, and the AOI inspects the boards for any error that could have occurred, *e.g.*, misplaced or bad solder components (see [9] for an example of error detection method). In SMT, both SMD and AOI are subprocesses generating large amounts of data. These data

© Springer Nature Switzerland AG 2020
A. Harth et al. (Eds.): ESWC 2020 Satellite Events, LNCS 12124, pp. 307–311, 2020.
https://doi.org/10.1007/978-3-030-62327-2_47

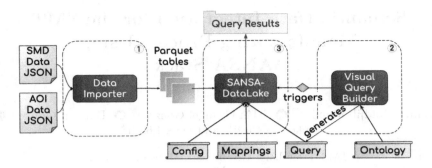

Fig. 1. General architecture of the proposed solution.

comprise semantic interoperability conflicts, *e.g.*, same objects in real life that are named differently in SMD and AOI. To properly explore this data, these conflicts demand to be resolved. To that end, we propose a solution that is composed of several components that extract SMT data, transfer it to an efficient format, and query it in a scalable manner. The solution also includes a user-friendly graphical interface that supports non-experts to construct queries and trigger their execution.

2   A SANSA-Based Solution to Access SMT Data

To enable and facilitate exploring the SMT data (SMD and AOI in particular), we propose a solution that consists of three main components (cf. Fig. 1).

2.1   Data Importer

Data generated by the SMT process is stored in JSON format. Since JSON format is not optimal for large-scale processing, we used a more efficient format called Parquet[1]. Parquet is a columnar file format that is well-suited for analytical queries, a prevalent class of queries in industrial applications. The Data Importer is created to convert SMD data to Parquet tables. Being columnar by nature, data in Parquet is stored by columns instead of rows. This means that if a query requests three columns, only those columns are accessed instead of the entire row. This also makes Parquet compression-friendly, since data of the same column are homogeneous, in contrast to data of the same row. Data Importer is built to create Parquet tables starting from parsing JSON files. Several tables are created, capturing any encountered foreign-primary key relations.

2.2   SANSA DataLake

SANSA-DL [6,7] is an extensible software solution that allows to query heterogeneous and large data sources using SPARQL. It is part of the SANSA Stack[2] [5],

---

[1] https://parquet.apache.org/.
[2] Scalable Semantic Analytics Stack http://sansa-stack.net/.

```
1   <#MachineMap>
2   rml:logicalSource [
3     rml:source: "../machine.parquet" ;
4     nosql:store nosql:parquet ] ;
5   rr:subjectMap [
6     rr:template "http://uri/../{MID}" ;
7     rr:class msmt:SMDMachine ] ;
8   rr:predicateObjectMap [
9     rr:predicate msmt:smdMachineName ;
10    rr:objectMap [rml:reference "Name"]]
```

Fig. 2. Mapping an entity using RML.

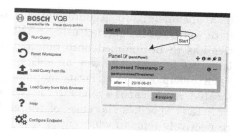

Fig. 3. Visual query builder.

a distributed framework for large scale RDF querying, inference and machine learning. SANSA-DL decomposes SPARQL queries into sub-queries, each one extracting an entity from the data. Relevant entities are detected based on a set of user-defined mappings in a language called RML [1]. Relevant entities are loaded into Spark's *in-memory* tabular structures [11], which can be filtered, joined, grouped or sorted following the input query. Data (entities) are internally stored following a partitioning scheme similar to the Property Tables [10]. A table is created for each group of triple patterns sharing the same subject in the SPARQL query. The table attributes correspond to the properties of the triple group. These tabular data structures are not materialized, but only used during query execution and then cleared. Practically, SANSA-DL is built on the OBDA [8] principles, including ontology, a unique query language and mappings.

Ontology. In order to develop a virtual general schema on top of the data sources, SANSA-DL needs to describe data schemata using ontology classes and properties. For example, *Machine* and *Failure* are classes and *hasPanel* and *smdMachineName* are properties of the class *Machine*. The links between data schemata and ontology classes and properties are defined in form of *mappings* using RML language. This virtual general schema abstracts away schemata difference, and thus, resolves semantic conflicts found across the data sources.

SPARQL Query. The main purpose of using a unique query language in SANSA-DL is to bring together (join) various data sources and, thus, derive cross-data knowledge and insights. SPARQL is the *de facto* query language for RDF data. A SPARQL query extracts data by matching its triple templates against the stored RDF data, e.g., (*?m fsmt:hasPanel "ABD3"*) matches all the triples where the property *fsmt:hasPanel* is equal to the object *"ABD3"*. The SPARQL query uses ontology properties and classes.

Mappings. In SANSA-DL, data is described (metadata) in terms of entities, *i.e.*, collections of data sharing the same structure and schema, *e.g.*, a table in a relational database or CSV file, a collection in a document database, *etc.* An entity has one or more attributes, *e.g.*, a column in a table or CSV, a field in a document, *etc.* A data source has one to many entities. In order for a data source to be queried using SANSA-DL, the schema of its containing entities has to be mapped onto ontology terms. For this matter, RML mapping language is used. The way an entity is mapped using RML is shown in Fig. 2. `MachineMap` denotes an entity mapping, `rml:source` refers to where the source is located, `nosql:store` refers to the type of data source where the entity is stored, `rr:class` specifies the class of the entity, `rml:reference` and `rr:predicate` respectively refer to what entity attribute to map to what ontology property.

2.3   Visual Query Builder (VQB)

VQB is a Web application (see Fig. 3) that is built[3] to lower the complexity of querying RDF data by stakeholders who are not familiar with Semantic technologies. SPARQL queries are visualized in a UML-like model, where classes are implemented as boxes and their properties inside of them as sub-boxes and relations between classes as arrows. We further developed VQB by improving the query graph construction and adding a feature to connect it to SANSA-DL. The connection is ensured using Apache Livy[4] and an intermediate Web service. Given a VQB-built query, the Web service uses Livy to remotely trigger SANSA-DL execution of the query using Spark. It then returns the response to VQB for it to display in a grid-like manner with pagination.

3   Conclusion

The solution operated internally over the SMT data (approx. 60 GB). Data Importer generated Parquet tables that are approximately 13% more compact than the original data size. The VQB used the underlying SMT ontology to generate the use case queries and trigger their execution by SANSA-DL. The queries were run and finished between 0.27 and 130 s depending on their complexity. As lessons learned, the incorporation of Semantic technologies has proven their effectiveness at bridging Industrial disparate data sources together. Further, the use case domain was complex, so only with the help of an interactive visual query builder that data can be conveniently exploited by non-SPARQL experts. SANSA-DL allowed to mediate over and query disparate data sources uniformly using SPARQL even if the supported fragment did not cover all the use case queries. Thanks to its resiliency and scalability, the current solution can be deployed in a much larger environment, and thus pave the way for future large-scale semantic adoptions in the Industry 4.0.

Acknowledgments. This work was supported by the EU H2020 projects BETTER (GA 776280) and QualiChain (GA 822404), and by the ADAPT Centre for Digital Content Technology (http://www.adaptcentre.ie/) funded under the SFI Research Centres Programme (Grant 13/RC/2106) and co-funded under the European Regional Development Fund.

---

[3] Initially implemented by Lukas Leipert https://github.com/leipert/vsb.

[4] https://livy.incubator.apache.org.

References

1. Dimou, A., Vander Sande, M., Colpaert, P., Verborgh, R., Mannens, E., Van de Walle, R.: RML: a generic language for integrated RDF mappings of heterogeneous data. In: LDOW (2014). https://rml.io
2. Grangel-González, I.: A knowledge graph based integration approach for industry 4.0. Ph.D. thesis, Universitäts-und Landesbibliothek Bonn (2019)
3. Harris, S., Seaborne, A., Prud'hommeaux, E.: SPARQL 1.1 query language. W3C Recomm. **21**(10) (2013)
4. Kharlamov, E., et al.: Capturing industrial information models with ontologies and constraints. In: Groth, P., et al. (eds.) ISWC 2016. LNCS, vol. 9982, pp. 325–343. Springer, Cham (2016). https://doi.org/10.1007/978-3-319-46547-0_30
5. Lehmann, J., et al.: Distributed semantic analytics using the SANSA stack. In: d'Amato, C., et al. (eds.) ISWC 2017. LNCS, vol. 10588, pp. 147–155. Springer, Cham (2017). https://doi.org/10.1007/978-3-319-68204-4_15
6. Mami, M.N., Graux, D., Scerri, S., Jabeen, H., Auer, S., Lehmann, J.: Squerall: virtual ontology-based access to heterogeneous and large data sources. In: Ghidini, C., et al. (eds.) ISWC 2019. LNCS, vol. 11779, pp. 229–245. Springer, Cham (2019). https://doi.org/10.1007/978-3-030-30796-7_15
7. Mami, M.N., Graux, D., Scerri, S., Jabeen, H., Auer, S., Lehmann, J.: Uniform access to multiform data lakes using semantic technologies. In: Proceedings of the 21st International Conference on Information Integration and Web-based Applications & Services (iiWAS), Munich, Germany, 2–4 December (2019)
8. Poggi, A., Lembo, D., Calvanese, D., De Giacomo, G., Lenzerini, M., Rosati, R.: Linking data to ontologies. In: Spaccapietra, S. (ed.) Journal on Data Semantics X. LNCS, vol. 4900, pp. 133–173. Springer, Heidelberg (2008). https://doi.org/10.1007/978-3-540-77688-8_5
9. Tavakolizadeh, F., Soto, J., Gyulai, D., Beecks, C.: Industry 4.0: mining physical defects in production of surface-mount devices. In: 17th Industrial Conference on Data Mining (2017)
10. Wilkinson, K.: Jena property table implementation. SSWS (2006)
11. Zaharia, M., et al.: Apache spark: a unified engine for big data processing. Commun. ACM **59**(11), 56–65 (2016)

Correction to: ABECTO: An ABox Evaluation and Comparison Tool for Ontologies

Jan Martin Keil

Correction to:
Chapter "ABECTO: An ABox Evaluation and Comparison Tool for Ontologies" in: A. Harth et al. (Eds.): *The Semantic Web: ESWC 2020 Satellite Events***, LNCS 12124,**
https://doi.org/10.1007/978-3-030-62327-2_24

Chapter, ["ABECTO: An ABox Evaluation and Comparison Tool for Ontologies"] was previously published non-open access. It has now been changed to open access under a CC BY 4.0 license and the copyright holder updated to 'The Author(s)'. The book has also been updated with this change.

The updated original version of this chapter can be found at
https://doi.org/10.1007/978-3-030-62327-2_24

© The Author(s) 2023
A. Harth et al. (Eds.): ESWC 2020 Satellite Events, LNCS 12124, p. C1, 2023.
https://doi.org/10.1007/978-3-030-62327-2_48

Author Index

Printed in the United States
by Baker & Taylor Publisher Services